I0160642

Ten Keys to the Bible

Dr. Charles R. Vogan Jr.

ISBN 978-1935969259

Ravenbrook Publishers

A subsidiary of
Shenandoah Bible Ministries

———— ∽ ————

www.shenbible.org
www.Ravenbrook.org

1 2

Contents

Introduction

The Bible is an inexhaustible mine of treasure, a limitless source of wisdom and power that God graciously gave his Church. Without the Bible we would be lost in this dark world and none of us would have a hope of making it to Heaven. But with the Scriptures in our hands (and in our hearts!) nothing can stand in our way. There is more power here than any of us can imagine.

The key to getting this awesome power out of the Bible is through studying it. I am assuming that you *want* to study the Bible. There are many people who aren't interested in Bible study, and at the mention of the word "study" they close the book and find something else easier to do. Do you think, however, that God would lay out his treasures on the surface where just anybody could pick them up and play with them? Hasn't he hidden diamonds and gold deep under the surface of the earth where only the most determined and persistent workers can get to them? Doesn't science have to work long and hard to win valuable discoveries out of Creation? He has done the same thing with his Truth! Lazy people won't find anything here, nor can they expect to benefit from the treasure in the Scriptures. The Lord has "hidden these things from the wise and learned" (Matthew 11:25) who wouldn't lift a finger to find out what the Bible has to say, and he has revealed them instead to his children who spend long hours searching out and meditating on God's special wisdom. It is a "workman" who will not be ashamed. (2 Timothy 2:15)

You may not know yet what to expect from the Bible, especially if you haven't been able to make much sense out of it till now. But with a little guidance from the Spirit and some dogged determination to stay with it, you *will* learn to unlock the secret halls of the mysteries of God in this book. With the right tools, the Bible is suddenly going to fall open to you and pour out more wisdom and insight and exciting things than you thought possible — and it will never stop. Once you start seeing what is going on in this book there will always be plenty of things to study and search for and try.

What we want to do now is look at some of the problems that may be in your way — the reasons that Bible study comes so hard for you — and why you *must* keep on working at it in spite of the problems. Your attitude must be that of determination and hard work, humbly waiting on God to show you what you can't see. Then, armed with this necessary attitude, we will discuss the keys that will unlock the hidden treasures of the Word. With this attitude, and the keys in your hand, you are finally going to start understanding the Bible.

Problems

Let me start by saying that, of all times in history, *we* ought to know the Bible better than any other generation that has ever lived. Our society is filled with the Bible! Everyone in our country has at least one Bible, I imagine, or has had opportunity to get one. All one has to do is go to the nearest bookstore and pick one up for little of nothing. The Bible is the number one best seller on the national book lists and has been for many years. Bible societies give millions of them away every year, and churches generally make sure everyone who attends has access to a Bible if they don't already have one.

The media is swamped with Bible programs; it is difficult to scan the radio and not find some station that isn't broadcasting sermons or Bible lessons. Christians hear the Word preached at least once every week and usually more. Christian bookstores sell millions of Bible study books and how-to materials for learning something about the Bible. Many church members are involved in Bible studies every week. New Christians are taught basic Bible truths. The Bible is the first book that steps ashore on the mission field as the Church spreads out to tell the world about the truth in the Gospel of Christ's kingdom.

Our culture rests on the Bible, whether people know it or not. Our legal system was patterned after Biblical principles. Our founding fathers worked and fought to preserve religious liberty for their posterity — us — and they valued a culture in which the Church and the Bible played a large and controlling part. Modern treatment of women, children and minority groups, for example, all grew out of Biblical principles put into practice.

I just mention all these various forms of getting out the Word because we probably live in the most Bible-saturated age in all of history. Even other countries in the world aren't so surrounded by the Bible as we are. Because of the press, and the media, and modern technology, and our ability to travel quickly and communicate effectively, the Bible has never had such a free opportunity to speak to its audience as it has now.

But it seems that there is still something wrong. I'm not at all impressed with published figures of how many Bibles are distributed, or whether more people go to Bible studies. Though these things are good (and may God continue the spread of his Word in these ways) I'm very concerned that people *understand* what this book is saying. From watching some alarming trends in our day, I get the feeling that as the amount of Bible material is increasing, our understanding of it is decreasing.

I know that's a serious charge to make, and it doesn't make much sense that we would be getting *less good* out of *more resources*. Here are some questions, though, that I want you to consider that may convince you that there is something wrong:

> **First**, if it's true that we are all studying the Bible as we claim, why are we coming up with conflicting theories? Why is there so much argument over what the Bible is saying? Why can't God's people agree on even the simplest things in the Word? Is God the author of confusion? Did he really put things in the Bible that none of us would agree on? It seems to me that if he wants us to be saved, and please him with how we live, then he would have made things *very plain to understand* (since our very futures are at stake!) so that even the simplest of us could see it and do it. But as long as everyone argues about what it says, or what they think it says, we can safely assume at least one thing — we aren't getting the point. Isn't this the reason for the

multitudes of churches, divisions and splits that characterize us?

Second, why is there so much spiritual failure in our lives? Many of us certainly know something about what the Bible teaches, but doing it is another matter entirely! We know its promises of joy but we often live in despair; we hear the message of salvation from our sin but we keep struggling under the bondage of those sins; we see that the Lord *can* defeat the enemy, but really the enemy keeps defeating us and pushing us to the wall instead. I can understand why the children of the world fail — they believe the lies of the devil and they are being destroyed because of it. We Christians, however, ought to be climbing out of our problems; spiritually, things ought to be looking up for us now! We claim that we have these great things in Christ, but how long will we play the game of religion before we admit that we aren't getting as far as we ought to be? For all that the Bible promises to give us, we are getting very little benefit from it.

Third, if it is true that the Bible fills our lives in many ways, why are so many Christians still ignorant about what it says? For example, too many Christians don't know the first thing about the Old Testament except for a few Sunday School stories, though it makes up three-fourths of our Bibles. In fact, teachers and preachers are often guilty of telling people that it isn't important for them to study the Old Testament! This just isn't true; no less an authority than Christ himself taught that "these are the Scriptures that testify about me." (John 5:39) Without the Old Testament, none of the New Testament would make sense or even be possible. This is the reason so much of modern Bible teaching lacks depth — it doesn't stand on a good understanding of the Old Testament. God wrote the Old, *then* the New! He intended it that way. It's no wonder that people can come away from sermons and lessons having gotten little light on the things of God. This is only one example of how little we know about the great themes that crisscross the Scriptures, even though we have so many Bibles at hand.

If these three questions uncover some serious problems among us then we have much work to do. Evidently, if we are honest with ourselves, we don't understand God's Word as well as we thought we did, or we would be better off spiritually than we are. The Bible is a record of what happens when God lives among his people: it records what he did in the past so that we know what he will *always* do for whoever will believe in him.

Of course you have to know who he is and what he does before you can believe in him, and that comes from studying his Word, which he gave us so that we might reach out to the God that it describes. *He* is not unfaithful; he doesn't change "like shifting shadows." (James 1:17) He always does what he says. So if things aren't working out as they should, it is we who aren't getting a hold on the Truth.

Obstacles to Bible Study

We have to admit that Bible study isn't easy. Not just anybody can sit down with it and get stupendous answers to life. Often we struggle against real problems — both in our hearts and with the book itself — that seem to put the Scriptures beyond our reach. Even seasoned veterans can spend years studying certain passages before some critical pieces start falling into place for them!

We may as well know what we are up against. At least if we know what the problems are, we can start looking around for something that will overcome these obstacles and help us get deeper into the Word in spite of these problems. Following are some of the things that get in our way or make it difficult for us when we try to study the Bible:

- *Its culture and language.* This is a strange book from a strange land about strange people! I don't know if you knew this or not, but the reason there are so many translations of the Bible is that the Old Testament was written first in Hebrew and the New Testament in Greek, both ancient languages and difficult to put into smooth English. No translation can do a perfect job of conveying the exact meaning of the original books; don't let anybody tell you differently. The fact that we have such good translations is a mercy of God and a testimony to the skill of Bible translators nowadays. Add to this problem of language the fact that all the thousands of manuscripts from those old days were hand-copied (and therefore prone to errors — no two of them agree perfectly!) and you can easily see that we have a big problem on our hands.

The culture, too, is a problem for us. Mercifully the Lord has spared us from much of that ancient culture and the Bible doesn't tell us much about it. But what do we do with stories like the Israelites killing off all the Canaanites before moving into the Promised Land? Why was it important (and the reason for his salvation!) that Lot welcomed the angels into his home? Why did Israel have such a problem with worshipping foreign gods? Very little of this makes sense to modern students who live in an age of police and courts and insurance claims, where everyone is guaranteed his rights, and there are no idols and plenty of motels.

• ***Our physical viewpoint.*** We understand this world that we live in very well. Our five senses are specially made to pick up on what is going on around us and enable us to take full advantage of what we can get out of the world. Because of schooling and books, experience and working with others, we are very good at understanding this world and surviving in it. But that's not true of God's world! It is spiritual, and we are physical; there is nothing there that our senses can relate to. Spiritual things don't appear to have any practical value — including the Bible itself. So when the Bible talks about the things of Heaven we have to take it on faith that such things do exist — there's just no way we could prove them otherwise! We are also going to find that we aren't very interested in these spiritual realities that we can't see or touch.

• *__Our sin.__* It would be difficult enough for us to understand God's world, spiritual as it is, if we didn't have this sin hanging around our necks getting in the way. Our sin is as close to us as our hearts: it keeps us from being interested in God, it perverts the truth when we hear it, and it interferes when we want to try out God's ways. It's for good reason that the writer of Hebrews talked about sin like this: "Let us throw off everything that hinders and the sin that so easily entangles." (Hebrews 12:1)

When we read the Bible our sin interferes with us and keeps us from understanding what it is saying. God wants to talk to us about certain important matters, and our sinful hearts won't let us hear it; we change the subject, turn the page, and look for something we are more interested in. Christ offers us spiritual weapons to fight his battles and we don't believe that they are as effective as the world's ways of doing things, nor are we interested in what he calls on us to fight for. The Spirit urges us on, through the Truth, to live in the presence of God continually, and we put our minds on things in this world instead. There is a constant battle between our sins and the Spirit, even during our Bible reading (perhaps *especially* then, because the devil is very interested in keeping us away from the truth!). It's a sobering thought that, after a fruitless session of trying to do Bible study and getting nothing out of it, our sins might be the reason for the failure.

• *__God's mystery.__* We are going to explore the mystery of the Bible and why the Lord's mercy in giving us a chance to understand it is so staggering an event. But that "built-in" mystery also explains why we don't understand it. These are things that we would not have known on our own; we will understand the Word of God only because God explains it to us and makes it plain to us.

We aren't dealing with just complex issues of science or history here! Universities specialize in difficult subjects that tax the most brilliant minds; the history of man has been full of deep thinkers in many areas of life who are still trying to figure out what our world is like. That's the point, however: eventually they see, they understand, and they can start using what they know to make our lives more productive or more comfortable. *This will never happen with the things of God.* The mysteries of God are forever beyond the wildest imaginations of the greatest geniuses of the world. The Bible says that even the "foolishness of God is wiser than man's wisdom." (1 Corinthians 1:25) "As the heavens are higher than the earth, so are my ways higher than your ways and my thoughts than your thoughts." (Isaiah 55:9) There is no way we can understand the truth about God, or even about his hand in his creation, unless he tells us. Look at all the theories about who God is that have sprung up in all of history, in all the civilizations of man! They were groping in the dark, coming up with wild stories of gods and powers that don't have any basis in reality. Man wishes he *did* know something about the true God; but unless God specifically tells him what to believe, he is going to get it all wrong.

•   *A huge book.* The Bible is actually a small library, a collection of books that, for the most part, are so different from each other that few people can see anything that connects them all. There are huge sections of history, chapters and chapters of Hebrew poetry, whole books full of civil and ceremonial Law, Hebrew prophets and their writings, apocalyptic literature, and a handful of letters dealing with complex theological issues. There have been entire studies done on just the different kinds of literature in the Bible! And of course the subjects discussed in the Bible number in the thousands, providing students with enough material for thousands of years of research and debate, and still there is much left that hasn't been developed or explored. A book like this had to have come from God; the mind of man isn't capable of putting together such a magnificent masterpiece like the Bible in all its fullness and variety. But its complexity also makes it difficult to grasp: we just can't seem to put our arms around this thing. It's bigger than we are.

• ___Many themes___. In an ordinary book the author has a point that he/she is driving at. You may not know what the theme is until you get to the end of the book, but eventually you will be told. The Bible, however, isn't like an ordinary book. Although some would disagree with me, I think that it has *one single theme* or overall point — and that theme is a web of several major sub-themes and hundreds, perhaps thousands, of other themes. This complexity makes Bible study very frustrating to us who like a scientific, one-point-at-a-time approach to things. Often what we will do, when we despair of getting a hold on the entire Bible, is focus on one favorite point as if *that* were the central theme of the Bible. Right away we get off-balance when we do this, because there are many other points that are just as important and we must somehow keep them *all* in mind when we study any part of the Bible. Besides, Jesus and the Apostles tell us what the main theme is: it's the Father/Son theme that runs from Genesis to Revelation. The Bible is bigger than any of us, and we ought to admit that right away and come to it in humility, ready to learn something new every time we read it.

• ___People don't like to read.___ It's a fact that *most* people don't like to read. Even among college graduates, as one statistic recently disclosed, more than half will never read another book again for the rest of their lives. Now there's nothing sinful about not reading, but I can tell you that you will get little or nothing from the Bible if you aren't willing to read it! Anybody who wants to learn God's Word must read the Word, or at least have someone else read it to them. You may not have to read anything else if you don't want to, but don't expect to be an expert (or even a responsible Christian!) in the things of God if you don't spend some quality time reading through the Bible. You will find that the useful Christians in the Church are the ones who spend much time reading and studying the Word; those who don't are generally useless to the Church.

It would take an entire book to explore and solve all the problems that come up during Bible study — and it probably ought to be written! I just mentioned these few points because, when you think about it, it's a miracle that we get *any* spiritual and lasting good from the Bible considering what we are up against. Consciously or unconsciously, it's a difficult spiritual battle to get profit from God's Word: people shouldn't be so surprised when it usually doesn't work for them. We should certainly give all the credit to the Lord when we actually understand something from his Word.

We must master this book!

I'm afraid that Bible study isn't the fashion nowadays. Many Christians, at the most, will go to a "Bible study" and listen to what someone else has found from their study, but they spend little or no time digging around in the Bible for themselves. The difficulties prove to be too much for them.

That's very unfortunate! God's Word is so rich, so pregnant with possibilities, that we ought to be eager to dig into it ourselves. We don't pay someone else to eat for us! If we knew what lay just below the surface of the pages of Scripture, we wouldn't put it off another minute — no matter what pains it might take to get at it.

May I entice you with a description of the menu that God has served up in his Word? The Bible is —

• ***A faithful witness.*** "Wounds from a friend can be trusted, but an enemy multiplies kisses." (Proverbs 27:6) The world will tell us what we want to hear, but they are all lies from the enemy. He certainly isn't going to tell us whether we are headed toward life or death, toward success or failure. He has our ruin in mind, and it is easy for him to ruin us by sweet-talking us into a false sense of security and contentment with the pleasures of life.

The Lord, however, is going to tell us what will really do our souls good. It may sound harsh, it may feel like rough treatment at times, but the truth of Scripture is designed to open up your problems and solve them, not gloss them over in silence. A doctor, if he is a good one, is going to cut open the cancer and get it all out so that you can live. The Lord is determined to do the same thing through his Word.

> For the word of God is living and active. Sharper than any double-edged sword, it penetrates even to dividing soul and spirit, joints and marrow; it judges the thoughts and attitudes of the heart. Nothing in all creation is hidden from God's sight. Everything is uncovered and laid bare before the eyes of him to whom we must give account. (Hebrews 4:12-13)

Now some people don't want to know the truth; they want to live for the here-and-now and take whatever comes as it comes. The less they know, the less their consciences have to deal with. But others appreciate somebody telling them *ahead of time* what is expected of them, what they can expect in the future, and where they need improvement. They want to know *all* that is necessary (no surprises, please!) so that they can work on important things and not waste their time on what won't be important. Isn't it nice to have somebody who will tell you when you have bad breath? Somebody who has your good at heart, and isn't trying to hurt you? God is going to be faithful and truthful with you in his Word.

• *__An explanation of what is really going on.__* People love to get the inside story, the real scoop on what is happening. It gives them an advantage that others, who don't know the truth, don't have. For example, if someone got an advertisement for a secret formula that is guaranteed to make them look younger and feel stronger, they wouldn't hesitate to fork over the money to get that formula. There is something in us that craves inside information.

That's all that the Bible is. While others labor in the dark needlessly about the real meaning of life, and what will bring them happiness and fulfillment, we *know* — because we believe what the Creator says about these things. We have an advantage that they don't have. Or I should say that they don't want it! Strange as it may sound, many people actually *turn down* the secret formulas available in the Bible and try the world's answers instead. They are dying as a result; they aren't getting what they are after. We, however, who search the Scriptures and are eager to try out what it says, are going to experience spectacular results: "Though outwardly we are wasting away, yet inwardly we are being renewed day by day. For our light and momentary troubles are achieving for us an eternal glory that far outweighs them all." (2 Corinthians 4:16-17)

While others are fooled by appearances, we know what will lead to life and what leads to death. We know what is important to work on; others waste their time working on what won't last and what won't do anybody any real good. When they lie down to die, all that they have lived for will be gone and they will wonder why they lived. We, however, know our calling and will be certain that our works will follow us to Heaven to testify that we were faithful servants who obviously don't need to be ashamed. All this will be true of us because we have the book of answers, the Bible, guiding us.

• ***From someone who cares.*** You mustn't think that the Bible is like other books — just a volume of pages filled with cold print, and it's up to you to make something out of it. This is a love letter to you from a God who cares deeply about you. He isn't satisfied with simply reciting cold words to you, but has put spiritual power behind those words so that you will live when you read them.

Many people heard the words of Christ when he lived on earth, but only a few felt those words in their hearts. "Were not our hearts burning within us while he talked with us on the road and opened the Scriptures to us?" (Luke 24:32) Just the words of the Bible will never help you, as you can see by all the people of the world who hear the words and don't benefit from them at all. But when the Spirit of God (sent by the Father) penetrates our hearts with those same words, working faith in us and bringing life to our souls through them, we know that God is feeding us like a baby lamb whom he loves. *We* are going to understand and live while others will get nothing from it. The doors in life will open up before us because our Father gives us the authority and wisdom to open them.

• *Hope*. Hope is a strange and wonderful quality that God has built into each of our hearts. It is the ability to put aside our fears, to ignore what the past has done to us and expect better things from tomorrow. Without hope we would never get up in the morning.

As someone once said, "Hope springs eternal in the heart of man." Everyone hopes; even a bum hopes that people will leave him alone and he will find the money he needs for the next drink! A person who is truly without hope will soon die, if he doesn't actually take his own life; he is a pitiful creature because he doesn't have the motivation to keep living and trying.

What do we hope for? We are hoping for justice, that someday all the wrongs will be made right and people will get what they deserve. We are hoping for good times, because the bad times have hurt us and we have had enough of them. We are hoping for meaning to life; it would be a shame to come to the end of life and find out that we have wasted our entire lives, were useless to others, and didn't accomplish anything with all of our hard work. We are hoping that there will be someone at the end waiting for us. We are hoping, when you get right down to it, that there is a God like the Bible describes.

So instead of keeping us in the dark our entire lives, the Lord has graciously written extensively on these subjects in his Word to give us a hope that we desperately need to keep on going. If you lose hope in these fundamental areas, you will head off into your own directions and try to find meaning and pleasure in the world's way. You won't find it there, though, and you are going to die in the end, hopeless and helpless. But if you sit down with the Bible and meditate on its promises and prophecies and doctrines, you are going to have hope again that things are going to work out after all. Then life will be much easier to live and you will have the reason to persevere, in spite of problems, until that day of fulfillment comes.

• *__A safeguard.__* If a ship doesn't drop its anchor at night, the tide is going to either drag it out to sea or throw it up on the shore and wreck it. If a plant's root doesn't reach way down to where the water is, a dry spell is going to kill it. In the same way, you must learn important Biblical principles so that you can remain steady on the Truth even when everyone else is swayed by the latest fads and fashions.

Unless you get a good grip on the important things that the Bible wants you to know about God, anybody who wants to will be able to persuade you over to his opinion on things, even if he is dead wrong about it — and you won't know how wrong you are! The Lord doesn't want you to get in such a predicament. He has provided his Word, and teachers to guide you in understanding it,

> ... until we all reach unity in the faith and in the knowledge of the Son of God and become mature, attaining to the whole measure of the fullness of Christ. Then we will no longer be infants, tossed back and forth by the waves, and blown here and there by every wind of teaching and by the cunning and craftiness of men in their deceitful scheming. Instead, speaking the truth in love, we will in all things grow up into him who is the Head, that is, Christ. (Ephesians 4:13-15)

Do you know where the cults are getting their millions of members? From established mainline denominations like the Baptists and Methodists and Presbyterians and Episcopalians! Somewhere along the line the churches failed to teach these people the basics of the faith, and now they are streaming over to the cults who teach false gods. It was inevitable.

Learn the Bible well, however, and you will be able to smell a rat in their game right away. You will know what precious doctrines they are trying to destroy, and you will put your hope in the truths that truly save the soul instead of secondary issues. You will, in fact, know far more about the truth than the average churchgoer does, and you will be able to avoid the pitfalls that so many people fall into.

There is an even deeper need that every human being has, one that was given to us at Creation and we can't escape: *to know God*. The Bible is the only book on earth that will fulfill that need in us. To know God is to live, just as to breathe oxygen is to live. When we eat food the cells in our body process that food and we find the strength we need to move. When we feed on the living Word, the revelation of God, our souls process that truth and we find spiritual strength to please him and obey him.

Most of the world lies in darkness about who God really is, and they are dying because of it. All the way from the idol worship of primitive cultures to American scientific unbelief, man has struggled to know that one thing that will let him live forever and has fallen short of finding it. There is nothing in this world that will help us live forever, nor is there anything worth fearing so much that we should change our way of living because of it, except God. Yet nobody knows that without the Bible, so they continue to try false gods in their search for a life they will never find.

There is a difference between knowing *about* God and actually knowing him. You can teach anybody a list of facts about God, and they can recite them back to you and talk intelligently about them with you. But that isn't knowing him. A believer has met this living God and came away changed forever from the experience; he doesn't go on hearsay anymore.

The believer ought to *keep on* knowing God, because the beginning isn't the end! He should have learned from that initial experience that to touch God in any way at all is to get a new surge of life: it helps him to achieve deeper wisdom, to humble himself more profoundly before the God of infinite possibilities. God is so huge, there is so much about him, that every time we come to him we will be changed. Since we are such needy creatures we are always needing something, and the world is hard put to keep up with our needs. In fact it *can't* satisfy us completely — today we eat and tomorrow we are hungry again. But now God — here is someone who can fill up the seemingly insatiable caverns in our hearts with stuff made in Heaven.

The Bible is the doorway to that limitless knowledge of God. Of course we will spend all of eternity enjoying God and being filled with him in ways that we can't presently conceive. For now, though, we see into a mirror with difficulty, because the world is in our way, and we can't see God fully. But anything is better than ignoring him! So open the book of life and listen as God speaks to you, watch as he shows you his world, and follow him as he makes his ways plain to you.

Keys to the Bible

There is hope, however. In spite of the many problems, we can start getting rich treasures from the Scriptures — with some special **keys** that God has graciously made available to us. With a Bible key, a passage that used to be a hopeless mystery suddenly opens up like a treasure chest, full of useful and precious things. These aren't things "never before revealed to men" — Christians who have seriously studied the Bible in past ages have always seen them, though they didn't necessarily call them *keys* — but they may be new to you if you aren't well acquainted with the deeper things of God.

We certainly can't solve all your problems here concerning Bible study; some of them you will have to lay out before the Lord and wait on him to help you. But some of your problems may disappear when you are experienced at using the following keys to the Bible. Like opening a locked box, these principles will open up the meaning that is inside a passage that, before now, you had no idea was hidden there.

But just because you know what the keys are, that doesn't mean that you will know how to use them! A key can be a tricky thing; how does one use it? What locks will it open? Does it take a half twist or a full twist? A Bible key is much more complicated than this, of course, because we are dealing with spiritual matters that are deeper than the human mind can grasp on its own. The Spirit of God has to help us understand what we are reading, and he also has to train us in how to use the keys to the Scriptures. The whole thing is only successful if he helps us along every step.

We can use science as an example here. Back a couple of hundred years ago, scientists had little idea of the mysteries of creation because they didn't have the right tools to unlock its secrets. Only in our century have they developed and used tools like electron microscopes, quantum mechanics, an understanding of DNA, and many other powerful concepts. Suddenly they are discovering so much about the world, because of these powerful tools, that they can't keep up with the new information! Our century has seen an unbelievable growth in knowledge and products that make our lives more efficient and safer because some powerful new tools in the scientist's tool kit make it all possible. They unlock the mystery of creation.

The following keys to the Bible will unlock God's Truth in the same way. But just as scientific tools take some getting used to (could you work an electron microscope if nobody showed you how?) these keys to the Bible will also take some getting used to. Here are some suggestions for learning about and using Bible keys:

• ***Get used to them***. First you have to study the key itself and believe that it's true! You have to be convinced that the Bible really does teach this, that it's an important idea to learn and use.

A Bible key is a simple yet profound idea that explains many other things in the Scriptures. But it is simple only because you master it, because you understand it so completely that you can easily apply it in any context. To be master of the key, you must do these things: **first**, find its best definition in the Bible and study it thoroughly. Somewhere there is a passage (or several) that best describes the meaning of the key. Make outlines, do word studies, find parallel passages — go through all the steps of good Bible study in order to plumb the depths of what this key is all about. Studying the keys first is time well spent: Bible study will go so much better for you in the long run if you start here first.

Second, dwell on the key and meditate on it. To meditate on something means to go over and over it, looking at it from every angle, looking for any application of it that you can find. Believe me, the more you dwell on it and think about it, the more you will see in it; not everything comes to light during the first five minutes of reading a Bible passage! This is especially true when working with Bible keys, which are themselves critical ideas that unlock the meaning of the rest of the Bible. When you train for your life's work in school it could take years before you reach mastery of the subject. You can hardly expect less work when it comes to the divine mysteries of the Gospel and applying them to the intricacies of the human heart!

Third, don't quit working on the key until you are overwhelmed with how important it is. A Bible key isn't just an interesting way of looking at Scripture; it is essential that you use this key during Bible study or *you will not understand what you are reading*. Your salvation depends on it; God's honor is at stake; the devil and all the rest of our enemies are hoping that you *don't* see it! Thank God when it starts to dawn on you how important and powerful a principle this key is, because then the Lord is handing you the key to life and you have finally matured in your spiritual walk so that you can do something useful and honoring to God.

Fourth, understand it so well that you can tell someone else what the key is. This is more difficult than you think! They say that you are ready to teach something only when you understand at least *ten times* more about it than you intend to tell your students. That's a lot of studying! That requires a profound and deep understanding. This makes sense, of course, because it means that the teacher not only understands what the idea *means* but also knows how to *apply* it and *use* it. Have you ever had trouble finding the right words when you try to explain a difficult idea to someone else? You know what it means, but for some reason you can't seem to explain it to him. This shows that you don't understand it well enough yet. More study, more thought, more application, and eventually you will be able to explain it to anybody in clear and simple terms so that they can use the key themselves.

• *__Look for the key.__* Whenever you are reading or studying a particular passage in the Bible, keep a lookout for the key in that passage. It's there. Most people never see it, of course, because they aren't trained to see it and they don't realize the importance of the key. But Bible keys are the pillars of the Scriptures: all parts of the Word depend on them for meaning and direction.

When God wrote the Bible he used these principles as the concrete foundation and the steel girders that the rest of the building depends on. The casual observer doesn't see all that, naturally, because it is hidden by the outside "skin" that makes a first impression. But an architect knows that those foundations are there: a building can't stand without them. The trained Bible student can see evidence of the keys in every passage, giving it strength and connecting it to the rest of the Bible. In fact, nothing makes sense without the keys!

To use another analogy, a piece of furniture makes different impressions on different people. To the average buyer it is something pretty made out of wood, and it will do the job well enough. But to another craftsman it shows the skill of its maker: the joints, the square cuts, the type of finish, all show to the trained eye whether the person who made it knew what he was doing. To the average Bible reader, the Scriptures are just a collection of proof texts, verses that one can pull out of one's hat when in need that will give a pat answer to some particular problem. But to the trained student the Bible is more than that. It is a profound explanation of life, and its ideas are skillfully joined in such a way that we know that the Maker of man wrote this to instruct man in the way he should go if he wants to find life. The spiritual craftsmanship is impressive, and you don't want to miss it.

So start looking for the keys when you are reading a passage. Every passage contains at least one of the keys and probably more; unless you find them you aren't understanding the text as you ought.

• ***Tie the Old and New Testaments together.*** The Bible is like a large house: there are different rooms in the house, in which you do different activities; but everything is under one roof. There is not a wall between the Old and New Testaments that separates them and keeps them apart. This is one book, with common themes running all through it, though some principles may be applied in different ways in each side.

The keys are those common themes between the two sides of the Bible. You will be surprised at how well the keys explain the mysteries of both testaments. Once you understand them you will see the same ideas in the stories of early Israel as in the Church where Paul ministered. Look at it this way: the Old Testament lays out basic arguments, foundation subjects, that we need to start thinking about. It talks about God the Creator, what he had in mind with his new world, the duties of man, man's sin and how it ruins everything. And then it starts describing God's solution to man's sin so that he can get creation back on track and have something that will glorify him. The New Testament picks up on those same themes and shows the solution finally at work! It gives us the hope that this solution will result in a "new Heaven and a new earth" in the end, and God will demonstrate that he knew what he was doing all along.

The entire Bible reflects the entire kingdom of God, which after all is one single house. The statement "Moses was faithful in all God's house" (Hebrews 3:2) comes first, then it is followed with — "Christ is faithful as a son over God's house. And we are that house ..." (Hebrews 3:6) The point is that it is one house, with one builder of the house, and one family who lives in it. You can expect, therefore, that the foundation of the house (the keys) is the same for whatever room you wish to inspect.

Knowing this, you will better appreciate the Old Testament when you go back and find the same keys there that the New Testament depends on. This leads us to believe that God really intended the *same things* for those people that he has for us — though it certainly *looked* different back then! This agrees with what Scripture has to say about it: "God had planned something better for us so that *only together with us* would they be made perfect." (Hebrews 11:40)

• **_Go back to familiar passages with it._** It's amazing how these keys will open up whole new dimensions of meaning in passages that you thought you understood already. We may think that we understand a particular verse because we have memorized it and used it so much; but perhaps our understanding is still superficial, still only skin deep. The Bible is a never-ending spring of revelation, of new ideas and perspectives. Digging a hole in one spot is like digging a hole in the earth: there are thousands of miles of dirt and ore under our little hole that we have yet to explore!

The Bible keys unlock the familiar passages just as they do other passages. Every text stands on these pillars of the truth, and we don't truly understand a passage until we see its foundations and how it fits in with the rest of the Bible. We will miss out on the real depth of a familiar verse if we think that we have it mastered already and we don't need to insert a key into it as well. We may be surprised at what we will find there!

• **_Don't let anything contradict it._** The Bible is so big, it deals with so many ideas, that it wouldn't be hard to find one passage that seemingly contradicts another passage. But the contradiction is only skin deep, so to speak: a little more study (and sometimes a lot more study!) will show that there is a solution to the problem.

Once you are convinced of the truth of the keys, don't let go of them. Even if you find another passage that seems to teach the opposite, don't let go of them. These keys are the *truth*, and you must see that for yourself before you can go on and understand anything else in the Bible. Sometimes it is better to let problem texts alone if you aren't ready to jump into them. You need the foundations first, the basics of the faith, before you can go on to more difficult doctrines. So if another verse causes trouble for you, you will have to wait until you get more light before you can say that you really understand it.

The Bible doesn't contradict itself, in spite of what its detractors may say about it. This book is the wisdom of God, so I'm not surprised when man has trouble understanding it. It is divine wisdom, knowledge from Heaven, God's explanations of spiritual mysteries — of course we are going to struggle through it and think that one truth seems to say the opposite of what another truth says. God is so huge, he is so far beyond man's comprehension, that we will never be able to see the *full* picture of God's nature and his ways in the way that he himself sees them. We will often have to be content with a one-sided view of things, and live with mysteries that we will never comprehend completely.

When you have problems reconciling one text with another, therefore, go with what you *know* is true and let the rest sit for a while. At least be willing to admit that you don't have infinite wisdom and you may not see all that is involved in a difficult passage! You should spend some quality time understanding the *essentials* that God expects you to master; these keys are a good place to begin.

• ***Don't get lost with secondary issues***. The importance of the keys is to nail down what the main points of the Bible are. *These* are the things you need to be learning more about; these are what the Bible is teaching primarily. It would be a mistake, and a waste of time on your part, to be tied up with secondary issues in the text when the Bible is obviously trying to teach you about these primary issues.

For example, let's take the story about Abraham sending his servant back to Haran to find a wife for his son Isaac. Most people use this story as a lesson on finding a godly partner. Although that point is there in the story (Abraham refused to let his son marry any of the local Canaanite girls, since they were pagans) that's not the primary point of the story. Once you get familiar with the keys you will see several of them at work here: first, this is a story of **miracle** from beginning to end! It teaches the **ways** of the Lord, people living by **faith** in what they don't see but know is true, it brings **glory** to God who alone could have guided such a series of events, and it was part of the fulfillment of the **covenant to Abraham**. Limiting your study to how to go about getting married is ignoring the best parts of the story!

You should especially be careful to stick to the issues of first importance when you are starting to learn how to study the Bible. Secondary issues are just too tempting to follow, like turning aside on rabbit trails, and they don't do you nearly as much good as the primary doctrines. The human heart really is "deceitful and desperately wicked," and you will be tempted to ignore what you ought to be working on and become caught up in what will not save you. For example, I knew someone who picked up a book on the end times. She had no love for God, would never admit being a sinner, hated the things of Christ, loved the world and its ways, yet she was fascinated with the different theories on how the world is going to end! It will be little consolation for her when, at Judgment Day, she knows all about eschatology and yet loses her soul.

These are some suggestions on how to use Bible keys. Get completely familiar with them, get skilled in their use, start seeing them everywhere in the Bible, and you will find that the Word of God will become precious to you. You are going to start understanding this book that used to cause you so much confusion. You will finally become a "workman who does not need to be ashamed and who correctly handles the Word of Truth." (2 Timothy 2:15) Knowledge is power, they say, and God's knowledge is the spiritual power that builds God's kingdom. Know it well and you are going to become a powerful Christian.

Discussion Questions For Introduction

- Is it necessary for everyone to know more about the Bible than just a few favorite verses here and there? What is at stake?

- Why is it that people can know what the Bible says and yet can't live what it promises?

- What should be the Church's approach to Bible study?

- Is the Bible our only source of spiritual knowledge?

- How do we know that we are studying it correctly?

- How much of the Bible does the Christian worker need?

- Why would God have put his truth in such a way that it requires keys to unlock it?

Key One: Revelation

Key One: Revelation

The Bible is about God. If you stop reading here, and from now on keep this fact before you whenever you read the Bible, you cannot go far wrong. It's true that it talks about many other things (including man) but its main purpose is to tell us *who God is* and *what he does.*

The truth about God is the most important thing that we can possibly learn. If we get this right, we will understand the truth about everything else in creation; if we don't find out who God is, then we won't get anything else right either. So many people *waste their time* studying the things of this world if they haven't first studied the Maker of this world, the one who gives it all purpose and meaning. There are basic spiritual principles about God that we must learn *first* before moving on to understand the world he made and what he expects of us. Unless we do, it's like putting together a complex jigsaw puzzle without having any idea of what the whole picture is supposed to be.

Thank God that we *can* learn the truth about God! Where would we be if he had maintained radio silence and never shown himself to us? We would all be in a panic, trying to get as much out of life as possible before we died, and we would all be caught spiritually naked and dead on Judgment Day, having done nothing at all to prepare for the next life. Although that doesn't seem to bother most people, some of us can't tolerate the thought. So the Bible becomes our most precious resource in life.

When we say that the Bible is *revelation*, we mean this: in it, God tells us the truth about himself. It is a window into God's world, which was once hidden, and we can look in and see him there in action. Artists often keep their works of art hidden until they are finished, and then schedule an unveiling when the veil is taken off and the public can then see it and enjoy it. In the same way, the Bible takes the veil away from God's world and we can see him in his true glory. The word "reveal" means just that: to uncover, to show what was hidden, to allow everyone to see.

Its primary purpose

The point that we want to keep in mind, however, is that the Bible is mainly interested in revealing *God* to us. We will learn the truth about many other things here as well, but it all starts with God.

Our problem is that we aren't so interested in God. We tend to use the Bible for other reasons: usually we pick it up when we need some consolation, for example, and we look for what will give us some hope and make us feel better in the middle of trying circumstances. Things will get better, we hope it will say. And when we *want* to see something in the Bible, we usually will — it is such a huge book and it is easy to twist its words to suit our purposes. So we end up with our favorite list of passages on consolation that we constantly turn to, while still knowing very little about what the Bible says about God.

The Bible is not about us primarily. We of course figure largely in the story of the Bible; God is always dealing with man in some way or another. But to focus on man alone while reading it is a great mistake and you will open yourself to all kinds of errors. For example, we have a bad habit of turning everything we read in the Bible into moralisms: little character lessons on how we should live. Be good, live by faith, keep on keeping on, don't give up, love your enemy, be holy — the lessons are endless, and we can find them everywhere in the Bible if we look at it simply from our viewpoint and cut God out of the picture. The trouble with this approach is that there is no salvation in it. No amount of moralisms will solve the basic problems of sin and death or get us into God's Heaven. It's true that unless we *take* medicine (man's action) when we are sick then we won't get well; but it's the *medicine* (God himself) that cures us, not the taking.

The Bible is not primarily a philosophy book, though there is philosophy in it. It is not a textbook on science or psychology or economics, though students of these disciplines would do well to study the Bible *first* before getting into their special interests — it will definitely keep them from going off into wrong directions.

No, the Bible is primarily about God. You need to keep this in mind whenever you pick it up to read it. The first question that ought to be on your lips when you read *any* passage is this: what does this tell me about God? Look and look until you find it; it is always there. You will never understand that passage correctly until you find out what it teaches you about God. Until you do, you will either get nothing out of the text or you will get the wrong point.

Let's put it like this: *the most important thing that you must do in life is to learn the truth about God.* Your job, your education, your family, your friends, your possessions are all second in importance; you could easily lose all of that and still find eternal life. Yet if you shove aside the knowledge of God and pursue "more important" things, you will find that you have made the greatest mistake of your life. "What good will it be for a man if he gains the whole world, yet forfeits his soul? Or what can a man give in exchange for his soul?" (Matthew 6:26) The Bible is handing you a golden opportunity to take care of this most important responsibility you have as a creature in God's world. The consequences of your success or failure are greater than you can imagine. The knowledge of God is literally your doorway to eternal life, and ignorance of him will doom you forever to utter darkness, where there is "weeping and gnashing of teeth." (Matthew 13:41-42)

So, you need this information desperately. Think of the Bible as the cure from the doctor for your terminal illness. If you ignore it you will die; if you open it and start learning about God, you will live — because *he is your life*. You will also find that as you learn about him, you will get answers for your problems. He is the beginning and ending of all things, and he is what this world needs, whether we know it or not. We see the rest of the world in its true colors when we shine the pure light of God on it.

What it is not

It is so important to see that the Bible is about God that we have to keep emphasizing it over and over from different angles. We all make a serious mistake with the Bible when we only see what we *want* to see in it instead of what it is trying to show us. It's amazing how much we can know about the Bible and at the same time how little we actually know about the God it speaks of!

These are some of the things that people find in the Bible, and what they *ought* to be finding in the Bible:

• **History** — The Bible is stuffed with history. It gives us the history of the beginning of the world, the history of the descendants of Adam, the history of the patriarchs, the history of the nation of Israel, the history of Jesus, the history of the Church — even a peek at the future "history" of the world before it happens. Most of the Bible is history.

And we all know what to do with history: memorize events, dates, and important people; back up and see the bigger sweep of events as one thing leads to the next thing; sift through the events and look for the important things that we can use in our own times — which is called "interpreting" history.

Although it is true that the Bible is history, and we must certainly study it as a historical account and learn from it, we miss the point of the Bible if we close our eyes to the most important element of its history: the fact that it is teaching us about God *through* this history. Biblical history isn't like other histories; we can't approach it in the same way we do European or American history because we will miss the truth entirely if we do.

God's history lessons are like this: *first,* he tells us only what is important for us to know. Modern students of history want to know every event, every incident, every person involved so that they can have a better chance of putting together the correct story, the way it really happened. God doesn't feel that way about his history. In any particular story in the Bible, there are certain details that he wants us to know — these particular things will do us spiritual good — and no other details will help us. These details direct our attention to *him*, not to other "interesting" things in the story. So it's useless to try to guess about details that the story doesn't tell us, and it won't do us any good anyway. What is written will save us, no more and no less.

Second, he glorifies himself in the story. He is always the main actor; all the details point to him and whatever we need to learn about him. Can we say, with all reverence, that he is "showing himself off" to the world in the Bible? He wants everyone who reads the histories to be amazed at his wisdom, his strength, and his skill. He wants people to put their trust in him who did these amazing things. So yes, the stories are slanted — they were specially written with that in mind: to draw our attention to him, not to others who were involved.

Third, he tells us what to believe about this historical event. We are not allowed to think whatever we like about it. God will interpret this story for us. Perhaps this is the biggest reason that there is little or no other historical evidence in the world for the events recorded in the Bible — the Lord doesn't want someone else's version of what happened to confuse us. When we read his account, we are told to believe, or fear, or hope, or fight, or many other things based on what we read. Reading about Caesar's wars won't change my life at all; but reading God's histories is supposed to change my life *drastically.*

• **Religion** — One would think that the Bible is certainly *the* textbook on religion. By the word "religion" I mean our awareness of God, our duties toward him, our ways of worshiping him, and so on. And I don't mean to say that this isn't an important part of the Bible — it is. But if we are only interested in what *we ourselves do* as religious creatures, then the Bible has some startling news for us. It's not what *we* do that is important — it is what God does. This is God's kingdom, not ours.

What I mean is this. Too often we read the Bible to find out what we must do to please God. Unbelievers think that this will get them into God's good graces and eventually pave the way into Heaven. Christians, however, know that God doesn't forgive their sins because of any good that they do; it is all founded on the work of Christ. But then they live as if Christ's work is of no further importance to them. They want to know what *they* have to do to please God — all their duties and responsibilities for Christian living — but they know very little about what Christ has already done for them, which means that they aren't depending on it much. As if to say that the work of Christ on the cross was the last time that Jesus ever did anything for us! Our religion has become man-centered because man is the principle actor now, the one who is making everything work. Isn't it true that we continually seek God's will so that we can do it? Isn't the church full of busy workers all doing *their* part in the work of the kingdom? Where is God in the meantime? Is he just looking on with approval as man does all the work?

If this is what we think about God, we have it all wrong. The Bible teaches us that God has always been, and will always be, the principal worker in his kingdom. We need to quit focusing on what we do and start asking God to do his work among us. The Scriptures keep turning our attention to the "works of the Lord" (Deuteronomy 3:24; Psalms 46:8; 92:5; 103:22; 107:24; 111:2 and others), and for good reason: God works miracles, he saves, he gives life, he has the answers. What *he* does is important to the kingdom; our works are only worth anything if they are solidly based on his works. The Bible isn't so much a manual of how *we* must do things, but a description of what God does on our behalf. If God will hear our prayers and come among us in power, our "religion" will turn into Heaven on earth, where God rules and miracles happen everywhere. Instead of empty ceremony, we will feel the hand of God *changing* us; the world will know that God is among us — how else will they explain what is going on?

We can tell if we are aware of the importance of God's works in the way that we pray. If we ask God for general blessings that aren't really any different than the way life normally runs ("Lord, please help me today in my work") then we have prayed, we have done our religious duty, and we may feel good about that — but God isn't in it. Prayer should be a time of excitement, of anticipation of the treasures of Heaven. We are coming before God! Subjects of kings, when allowed an audience (which rarely happened) with the king, never made the same mistake that we make with God. This was a once-in-a-lifetime opportunity! They asked for what only a king could give, because they would never have this chance again. He was giving them hope that he would grant their request by letting them in to see him. How much more could God give us than an earthly king!

The point here, I hope you see, is that our religion — what *we* do — isn't the point; it isn't what we really need. We need a God who works in our lives as he did in the times of the Bible. If God would do those same things now that he did then, our world wouldn't be in such a mess. We would get real solutions to life's problems. We don't want the traditions of our fathers, we want the God of our fathers. If we have him, those traditions will be filled with power from on high; without him they are no help at all.

• **Literature** — Again, the Bible is certainly a fascinating collection of Hebrew literature. It uses various ways of getting truth into our heads; through literature the Lord teaches us truth in a more effective way than a dry, scientific analysis of doctrine could do.

There are ways that people deal with the Bible's literature — *first*, they prefer a certain translation over others; in fact many people are ready to fight about what version to use! *Second*, they analyze the text grammatically to get the precise meaning and structure of each book. *Third* (and the scholars do this for the most part), they compare the literature of the Bible with the literature of other cultures, especially those of the Ancient Near East, to see how the Israelites learned to express their religious ideas over time. Most people, however, miss the fact that there are different styles of literature in the Bible and therefore miss the richness that is there.

There is a fundamental reason that the Bible was written in various styles of literature, however. *These literary styles are ways to reveal God.* Different styles slide the truth into our heads from different directions, so to speak. The histories record what God did for people in the past, so that we might trust him for *the same things that happened then*. The psalms were written to *move our hearts* to fear him and love him. They are the whole range of human emotions reaching out to God; they teach us how to feel about God and how he feels about us. The wisdom passages teach us how to *live successfully* in God's world — since he made it to run a certain way. The apocalyptic sections (Daniel and Revelation, for example) *motivate* us to get ready for that last day by showing what God has in store for the world.

The Bible is like a large house with many windows in it. In this case the Lord encourages us to be "peeping Toms" and look in the windows! What we will discover, however, is that we get a different view of God depending on which window we look through. That's what the different styles of literature do for us: they show us God in different ways, and we respond to what we see according to how the text presents him to us.

If you study more about theology and Bible doctrines and what scholars have done in the past, you will discover that they were most concerned with the *way* the Bible tells us about God, not with God himself. To them the literature is the most important aspect of the Bible, because they don't think there is much truth to it. They say that it is filled with myths and traditions. They accuse the prophets of writing about past events as if they were yet in the future — for the sake of effect. They accuse the apostles (especially Paul) of adding to the Gospel of Christ to make it fit better with the growing needs of the Church. Yet they still claim to be Christians! This was the biggest stumbling block of, for example, the Bible "experts" of the beginning of the twentieth century, especially beginning in Germany. Instead of simply sitting at God's feet and listening to God teach them in the Bible, believing what they heard like little children, they took a much more "mature" approach and analyzed the literature of the Bible to death. What happened was that they killed the Bible — or should we say they killed themselves. They weren't able to hear and believe its message any more. Take a warning from their example and let the Bible move you and teach you about God in its own way. This is the truth, no matter what form it takes.

• **Morals** — Morals have to do with how we should live — the Ten Commandments are an example. The Bible obviously has a lot to say about how we should live, so people are ready to jump right in and form a whole system of morals to live by.

The problem with this is, again, that they miss the God of the Bible when they focus only on morals. The unbeliever thinks that there is no God; and if that's true, there is no point to morality. Why worry about what is right or wrong when there is no reward for doing right and no punishment for doing wrong? But, the Christian says, there *is* a God and therefore morals are important. That is true, but practically speaking even Christians act as if there is no God when they put together systems of morality, carefully gleaned here and there from various passages, that have no real connection to the God of the Bible. In other words, take God out of the picture and the morals still stand. The problem with this is, of course, that many other religions teach these same morals without believing in the God of the Bible — so why do we call our standards "Christian"?

If you approach the Bible just to find out what the rights and wrongs are to life, you are missing the most important thing that the Bible teaches. It says, first and foremost, that there is a God — *and you must fear him.* That's the beginning point of morals. Starting with morals is starting at the wrong end: it's easy to make a list, add a few rights and wrongs of your own, and cut a few out that you don't like. But once you meet God, you realize that you must *listen* to him. You come away not with a list of morals but a healthy fear of God that makes you realize that you *can't* do what he commands. That leads to the second step, which is to find out how you are going to make him pleased with you — and the solution is, again, not your own doing. "For it is God who works in you to will and to act according to his good purpose." (Philippians 2:13)

When you focus on rights and wrongs in themselves, you are going to end up with a religion in which *you* are the principle actor and God has little or no part of your life. After all, if your religion is just obeying a list of rules, all you have to do is obey those rules and you will feel that you are acceptable to God. Yet there is *no life* in keeping the Commandments only! The rich young man told Jesus that he had kept all the commandments from his youth; Jesus answered that he still lacked what it takes to reach eternal life — to simply follow Christ. (Matthew 19:16-22) The man's mistake was to start with the rights and wrongs in the Bible, instead of starting with God who makes us holy.

Whatever system of morality that *man* puts together from the Bible is bound to go wrong somewhere. Man loves to rule over others, and one man's standards will usually go hard on his neighbor and easy on himself. What is unfortunate, however, is when he creates his standards from Biblical "rules" and burdens men's consciences with them. God is the only Lord, and we must obey him alone. It's no sin if we don't obey someone's misguided opinion on what the Bible teaches; it is definitely sin if we don't throw ourselves on God who saves the ungodly. The book of Proverbs put it all in a nutshell: "The fear of the LORD is the beginning of knowledge." (Proverbs 1:7)

The only revelation of God

The Bible is the only revelation of God that there is.* There is no other source of information about what he is like besides the book that he wrote to tell us. The other religions of the world are wrong: they do *not* have the truth, and man will only know the truth about God if he gets it from the Bible.

You may ask about Christian literature — doesn't this reveal God to us too? Yes, but only if the writer gets his material from the Bible. A teacher or preacher must be careful to stick to things that are plainly and solidly taught in the Word of God, or he will be judged as adding to or taking away from the Scriptures — and that is absolutely forbidden! (Revelation 22:18-19) There is life only in God's truth, and everyone who helps others in God's Name must use only God's truth or there will be death as a result.

---

* In theology we actually speak of two kinds of revelation: *natural* and *special*. *Natural* revelation is what Paul speaks about in Romans 1:19-20, when he says that Creation teaches us about God. The problem, however, is that our sin prevents us from seeing it (as Paul argues further on) and it is too easy to interpret our world without God, as modern science is determined to do. So we have to fall back on something else that spells it out in black and white, so to speak — the Bible. I can't *prove* to you anything about God by using Creation; but I can easily show you what the *Bible* says about him and you are obligated to believe it without further proof. *Special* revelation, then, is the Scriptures.

There is a simple yet profound reason for having such faith in the Bible's claim of being the only truth: **God said this.** It is not the work of men. He spoke, and now we have his words. That's a simple idea, but not very many people like the sound of it. If that's true then there are several things that we must believe about it: *first*, it's the only truth that there is. God knows the truth in such a way that no man can know. We have all sorts of opinions on everything in life, but God is the final authority and expects us to put away all our opinions and believe what he says. He has the perspective of the Creator, the Redeemer, the Judge, the Holy One. How can we possibly believe that our limited outlook on the world could compare to his vast, limitless view — especially when all the world and everything that happens in it is his own making? *Second*, this is what he wants us to know. When we are ignorant, when we are helpless in our problems, when we are breaking all the rules, he steps in and grabs our attention and tells us what we need to hear. He isn't letting man go on in his sin and death; he forces us to hear the truth that will both condemn and save us. Until God spoke his Word, the world lay in abysmal darkness without knowing what was wrong. Now he has spoken, and he expects us to hear and obey him.

It's obvious that God had a hand in the making of the Bible, and that makes sense when you think about it. Why entrust such an important step in the process of salvation to sinful men? To make sure that the Bible would get into the hands of his children, and do them good when they read it, the Lord himself supervised the making and distribution and preserving of the Bible for the last 4000 years. It is a long and fascinating story that we don't have time to get into here; but to the discerning eye it is obvious that the Lord is the author of this book, not man.

The most powerful description of the Bible is that it is the *Word of God.* God spoke this; it is the only existing record we have now of actual words from Heaven, from God's lips. People give thousands of dollars all the time for autographed copies of books by famous authors; yet we don't realize the precious wealth we have in the Bible — truth from another world! This is the way God sees things; these are truths from his viewpoint as Creator and Redeemer. He spoke them to us in a way that we can understand the mind of God; these are usable truths that we can put into practice and profit from. The divine, contrary to all reason, has taken on flesh and "lived for a while among us" (John 1:14) so that we can live in his presence and he can do his work among us. This is the dynamic of the Christian Church: that we are one with him, that we live with him and he with us, that we can talk to God and he to us. This is what makes all the impossible stories of the Bible so possible.

Remember who spoke this Word — God the Creator did! When he speaks, all Creation must listen and learn. He has all authority in himself and he will be heard! He doesn't tolerate other opinions or beliefs that contradict what he says. He not only reveals the truth but he also expects us to accept it *just the way it is.* When a child tells his brother that he mustn't do something wrong, he may listen or he may not; but when Dad comes in the room and says the same thing, he had *better* listen and do something about it! When God speaks, get your pencils and paper out and start paying attention; he expects you to listen to the Truth and act upon it.

Probably the strongest argument behind the Bible being the only revelation of God is this: strange things keep happening when the Bible is involved. For example, when people read the Bible they are convicted of their sins. Now this is *not* something that you would expect to happen from reading a book! Getting our sin exposed like this is shameful; it makes us want to hide from everyone so that they don't see our wickedness. But we can't help it: in the Bible we meet God, who is determined to uncover our sin and get it out in the open where he can deal with it. During the preaching and teaching of the Word, people repent and come to God for forgiveness — revivals happen. They change their lives overnight, and start doing what God wants instead of what they want. They fear the God they meet here and start living to please him instead of themselves.

The Spirit of God works in conjunction with the Word of God to cause results like these. Jesus said that "God is Spirit, and his worshipers must worship in Spirit and in truth." (John 4:24) The Spirit's work consists in revealing the things of God to us so that we see them plainly, spiritually, and can respond to what we see in a spiritual way. "God has revealed it to us by his Spirit ... We have not received the spirit of the world but the Spirit who is from God, that we may understand what God has freely given us." (1 Corinthians 2:10,12)

The Bible is unique in this: here we meet God face to face, as he is, and the encounter changes our souls so that we live in him and can understand who he is.

When people start taking God seriously you can be sure that the Bible is behind it. If miracles are happening, it is because someone read about the God of miracles in the Bible and believed in him for the same things: "LORD, I have heard of your fame; I stand in awe of your deeds, O LORD. Renew them in our day, in our time make them known; in wrath remember mercy." (Habakkuk 3:2) They heard of his fame from the Bible, the only record of the works of God. Then they went to God in his Word and found what they had hoped for.

Why we need revelation

God is determined to reveal himself in the Bible. Through many different ways he paints a true picture of who he is and the kinds of things he does. He gives even the most ignorant reader or hearer of the Word a clear view of himself that they can grasp and use. Why does he do this for us? Why do we have the Bible, and why does it spend so much time and effort on the subject of God? There are at least three reasons that we need this revelation of God in the Bible:

> *First,* there is a massive hole in our explanation of things. We were born without certain crucial information that we need. For example, without *God the Creator*, nothing makes sense. If this is God's world then it follows his laws, it depends on him to keep going, and it serves his purposes. We will never understand or be able to use creation successfully until we admit that he is the Creator and that all that we see and know in this world belongs to him.

> Without an understanding of *God the king*, we will never be able to get along with each other. Governments try to pass laws to control wickedness and provide a stable situation in which we can live and work successfully, but they don't get anywhere as long as people themselves do not know God. If they don't fear

God, they have no fear of men, and the laws end up doing no good.

Without the knowledge of *God the Savior*, we are going to be very confused about righteousness and sin and salvation. We will use ourselves as the standard of what is right, and end up with "every man doing what is right in his own eyes." Sin will be whatever we don't like in others, our salvation will come from doing good (what *we* think is good) for others, and the truth will be whatever strikes our fancy from day to day. It is a hopeless mess, this business of religion, if we don't find the true God and see what *he* says about all this.

Second, without the Bible we would never see him. Revelation is to uncover what is otherwise hidden; in this case, God does the uncovering. In other words, you cannot know these things about God unless he specifically shows you.

We think that we are capable of knowing many things, and we hate to appear ignorant or weak in front of others. So even if we don't know what we are talking about, we have ways of covering up our ignorance and appearing as if we know all about it. Or we will just brush it aside and say it isn't important enough to know, just to save face.

So it is humbling to admit that we really don't know the truth about God. We must, however, humble ourselves in this case and admit that we don't know him, and come to the Bible to learn about him. There are several things about us that have kept us in the dark about God and will continue to keep us from him if we don't get something done about it: for one thing, *our sin.* Our hearts are steeped in sin, we always have been sinners since the day we were born, and we don't want to come close to God. We want to live our own way! "Let us break their chains and throw off their fetters." (Psalm 2:3) Deep in the heart of every one of us is this rebellion against the true God; this is the worst problem we have and the biggest barrier to knowing God.

Another thing that keeps us from knowing God is that he is spiritual and we are *physical*. It is easy to learn about *this* world, since we live here and our senses are designed to take advantage of it. It is difficult to know a God who isn't anything like the world and our senses can't confirm. Add to that the fact that we are dead spiritually — in other words, our souls (which ordinarily would have the kind of spiritual senses to feel and know God) are incapable of knowing God from birth — and we have a real problem here from the start.

One more problem we have in knowing God is the kind of world we live in. There is the world, and then there is the *world system* — it is this system that is dead set against God and all his ways. The enemies of God run the world system and they force everyone to stay away from the true God, to believe the lies of the devil and live according to the traditions of men. They started steering people away from God in the beginning, in the Garden of Eden. (Genesis 3) You can read about the world system in passages like Ephesians 2:1-3 and 1 John 2:15-17. If this is the world you love, you will never know God.

Third, we need revelation so that we can prepare for the next life. Do you know anything about what Heaven is like? Do you know what those treasures are that Jesus spoke about in Matthew 6:19-21? Did you know that if you don't have the right clothes on when you step before God's judgment seat he will throw you out on your ear? (Matthew 22:11-14) These are just a few of the surprising things we learn from the Bible, ahead of time, getting us ready for the great unknown beyond the grave.

Now some people aren't worried about what is beyond the grave. They live for the "here and now" and they value only what is in this world. That is just stupid. We live in this world for only a few years; we will be in the next one forever. Here we are protected from the sight of God by the physical world and our needs are taken care of by physical means. There, on the other side of the grave, there will be nothing between us and God, and either we will feel the full power of his fury against us (who can imagine such a thing!) or the full glory of his sustaining grace. It's *that* world we should be concerned about, not this one. The wise know about this.

The Bible reveals that world to us and warns us ahead of time what it will take to survive there. If it weren't for this warning we would never know anything about it and every one of us would drop into eternity with no preparation and no hope of surviving. Thank God he has revealed the truth about the most important step in our lives — the step into eternity.

Purpose of revelation

The Bible is trying to do something with you. If you read it for the right purpose — in other words, to learn about God — then certain important results are going to start happening in you and God will successfully achieve his goal in your Bible reading. You may have thought that *you* were doing something *for God* when you read the Bible! Actually it is the other way around: he is doing something for you.

Remember when the Greeks in Jerusalem told the disciples that they wanted to see Jesus? (John 12:20-21) This should be your attitude too, when you open your Bible. If you want to see God — the Father, Son and Holy Spirit — then God will honor your request and reveal himself to you. As you read about him, expect the following things to start happening to you:

- ***He will turn your mind toward Heaven***. Heaven is where God lives among his people. Heaven is where no created thing will stand between us and God — we will feel full, pure, eternal joy in the very presence of our God. Heaven is our hope while we struggle through this world of sin and death; only God will be able to straighten out what thousands of years of devastation have done to the human race.

The Bible shows us what God can do for those who believe in him — both in this world and in the next one. While still in this life we can have a foretaste of what Heaven will be like, as he comforts us during times of trouble and cleanses our hearts from their sins. We experience a little bit of the wisdom of God and understand a little of what he is doing now in our world. We feel his power in small ways as he defeats our enemies and gives us the wings of eagles to fly above this world's cares. All this tasting is to whet our appetites for the full life to come in Heaven where we will really get down to business and live with him. In other words, by means of the Bible he gets us to start thinking about more important things than our lives here.

• ***He will make you skillful in his ways***. The Bible is a textbook on God and his ways. Just knowing texts from the Bible doesn't make you an expert on God; a child can spout off verses from memory without understanding what they mean. But you show your profound understanding of God's Word when you can see his hand working in your life and you correctly identify what he is doing. Not many people can do that.

When you spend much time with someone you begin to understand how they think, and why they go about things the way they do. You can predict, because you know them well enough, what they will do or say in any given situation. Believe it or not, that is God's goal for you in reading the Bible: to know him so well that you can "keep in step with the Spirit" (Galatians 5:25) as he moves this way and that. He wants you to respond in faith when others can't believe; he wants you to hope when others despair of hope; he wants you to submit to his authority when others rebel against the circumstances. This kind of life takes a great deal of study and thought and prayer, at God's feet, learning his ways and thinking his thoughts.

• ***He will re-make you into his image.*** Spend time in the light and you will be changed by the light. This is a powerful principle of change in God's world and it always works. The reason that unbelievers avoid the Bible (and I've seen many turn away from it for this reason) is that they know they will be changed by it. They refuse to listen to it because they don't want to give up their life of sin and death. (John 3:20)

But you are a Christian, and supposedly you *want* to be changed. This book *will* change you, because anybody who comes into God's presence will always be changed. The Bible is the middle ground, so to speak, where God and man meet and talk to each other. Man comes into the presence of light! The experience will affect us like it did Moses, who spoke directly with God at Mt. Sinai. "And we, who with unveiled faces all reflect the Lord's glory, are being transformed into his likeness with ever-increasing glory, which comes from the Lord, who is the Spirit." (2 Corinthians 3:18)

After all, flesh and blood cannot inherit the kingdom of God. (1 Corinthians 15:50) We *have* to be re-made so that we can survive in Heaven; otherwise the experience would kill us! So he starts out a little bit at a time, waking up our souls first and getting us used to living in his presence. Then the day will come when he finishes the transformation and we will step into his full glory ready for the tasks that wait for us there.

• ***He intends to live with you as well.*** If you thought that the kinds of things that the Bible talks about were only for the saints of old, you are mistaken — and you will be surprised. Remember, this history isn't just to entertain you; it is to show you what God intends to do for you as well. The God of Abraham, Isaac and Jacob is *your* God too.

I quoted this verse before, but it is so important that I want to show it to you again:

> LORD, I have heard of your fame; I stand in awe of your deeds, O LORD. Renew them in our day, in our time make them known; in wrath remember mercy. (Habakkuk 3:2)

Where did the prophet hear of God's fame? From his Word! Where did he learn of the deeds that God does? From the Bible! And he thinks to himself, if this is the way God is, then I want the same things. Why should people of past days enjoy all the good things of God and I can only look on with envy? God isn't telling me what he did for people in the past just to make me jealous of them! He wants me to reach out for the *same things*; he wants me to trust him that he will do these things for anybody who will believe in him. The Bible is a description of God and *what he does*. When you start thinking like this (and it will only happen if you *read* the Bible) then the book is working its power on you: you are getting into a good position for the grace of God to pour out of Heaven upon you.

These always happen when revelation is working. It's like plugging an appliance into a wall outlet: electricity makes the thing work the way it was designed to work. Plugging into God makes a sinner into a saint, an ignorant man into a wise man, a coward into a soldier of the cross. The outlet, the place where God's power is ready to surge into us when we plug in, is the Bible.

Ways it reveals him

You need to know, ahead of time, the ways the Bible reveals God. Remember that the Lord didn't lay out his treasures on the surface for just anybody to pick up and fool around with. He doesn't cast his pearls before swine; unbelievers soon become tired trying to make sense of the Bible and turn to other things that interest them more. In the meantime, God's children keep digging in the text and soon start bringing out amazing revelations — because they know *what* they are looking for and they know *how* to get it out.

You've probably been in a museum where they have all sorts of things on display for public viewing. But they don't display everything the same way: some items must not be touched, and are put in glass enclosures. Other things are too big to appreciate without climbing a walkway hanging in midair where people can come right up to the display. Other things are best seen in special lighting.

The Bible does the same thing with God. It has many creative and powerful ways of displaying him. The only difference is that God is living, and what you see here on display is for you to take and use in your life. There are very few "Don't Touch" signs here! Let's look at some of the ways that the Bible reveals God:

- **<u>Doctrine</u>:** There are certain facts you should know about God and his works. Every Christian needs to know a minimum amount of information about God: for example, who saves us? How did he save us? What are we saved from? Why is this world doomed? Why is Heaven our hope? What are God's characteristics? If you don't know the answers to these questions, you either aren't a child of God or you are going to keep running into problems in life that will overwhelm you.

  Some people don't like the word "doctrine" but their fears are unfounded. I know that many churches and denominations put too much emphasis on doctrine, on being able to recite long lists of data about what they believe — in fact, you can't be a member of their church unless you believe in their particular list of doctrines! But their abuse of doctrine doesn't make it less important for the rest of us. What we believe about God makes him different from the gods of other religions, and that is critical to know. You must worship the true God (and not a god of another description) and to do that you have to know something about him — the truth about him, that is. That's all that doctrine really is.

• **History:** As we saw before, history is a large portion of the Bible, so we need to spend some time here. The purpose of history is to show you what God can and will do for his people. We like proof of things: if someone wants to sell me his product, he must show it to me in action. If a politician wants to be re-elected, then he'd better make good on his campaign promises. The Bible's history is just that: showing our God in action, doing what he promised, doing what no other god can do. The histories encourage us to come to God for the same things.

• **Emotions:** Our brains are divided into two sections: the left and right sides. Scientists are beginning to realize that these sections control two very important parts of our personalities: the logical and the emotional. Our logical selves take data and process it to find solutions to problems. Our emotional selves look for happiness and peace and meaningfulness and motivation in life. I'm glad the scientists are catching up to the Bible! There is not only data about God in the Scriptures for our logical selves, but there is also emotion here to feed our emotional selves.

Poetry is for your emotions, and the Psalms especially are the poetry of the Bible. Here the writer displays his love for God, his fear of God, his hopes in God, his hatred for sin, his feelings of helplessness in a crazy world and the joy when God rescues him from it. It doesn't work well to submit the Psalms to a scientific microscope, because he often uses symbolic language to express his emotions. For example, he talks of God having wings (Psalm 91:4) — but logically we know that he doesn't. Emotionally, however, when he covers us and protects us from dangers like a hen sheltering its chicks, those "wings" of God are just as real to us as any that our eyes can see. Ask someone who has felt the protecting power of God if this is true.

• **Wisdom:** The wisdom literature — primarily Proverbs and Ecclesiastes, but also found in smaller pieces in many places in the Bible — tells you the best and most efficient (spiritually speaking) ways of living in God's world. God is here, they are saying, and he is running everything the way he wants to run it. You would be wise if you follow his instructions.

When you are visiting a big city, for instance, and you don't know your way around yet, you ought to keep alert for signs to help you out. Certain lights tell you when to cross the street and when not to. The streets have lines and instructions painted on them. City maps will help you locate the points of interest.

The Bible wants to help you get around in God's kingdom in the same way. A wise man will listen to its clues, he will learn the laws of the kingdom, he will memorize the important principles, so that he can become a good citizen of the city of God. He will be able to work and live there and make a good living, turning a profit in all he does, because he knows how things work there. He won't be a fool with his eyes closed — never knowing just how things work and always being caught off-guard by unexpected events.

• **Faith:** Living in this world requires no more than a level head and at least a few of your senses in good working condition. But living in God's world requires what none of us have naturally, something that the Spirit must give us — faith. Faith is being able to see the world of God (which is invisible to the eyes of flesh) even though this world tends to cloud the vision.

You must have faith to accept the things that the Bible talks about. Very little in it appeals to the natural man. Since it is about God, and since most people don't even want to know about God, it is no surprise that the Bible is not popular reading among unbelievers. Many people only look for things that will appeal to their senses, and the Bible doesn't cater to this attitude. To a person of faith, however, it is a rich feast of things that this world knows nothing about. Miracles galore! Angels ascending and descending! The Son of God appearing in the flesh! Heaven ruling earth! There is enough to keep a spiritual man busy studying all his life.

Only a person of faith will get at this treasure, however, because the Bible is careful to wrap it up in terms of faith. If you don't believe in this kind of God, then you won't get anything from the Bible. If you believe in him, then you are going to find your fulfillment here. There's no earthly reason why you should believe anything in the Bible; but from Heaven's perspective there is every reason to believe it.

• **Contrasts:** One way that the Bible reveals God to us is by contrasting him with several other things. For example, you will find the Bible making comparisons between the God of Israel and the gods of other nations. It does this, of course, so that you can see for yourself which one is the true God. (See 1 Kings 18 for an example) He will not share his glory with another! Israel heard this lesson over and over, and didn't finally learn it until the devastation of Jerusalem and the exile to Babylon. After that, they knew that only God is God, and they quit worshipping false gods.

Another contrast it makes is between God's world and this world. The New Testament spends much time in this area. This is a lesson that we Christians are still trying to learn, because for some reason we think that God wants to give us lots of what *this* world has. We need to pay more attention to the way the Bible passes judgment on this world and how it holds God's world up as the ideal, our hope, our goal.

• **Testaments:** The covenants in the Bible make a fascinating study, but that's not what I'm referring to right now. What I mean is the way the Old and New Testaments balance each other. People often think that the Old Testament was for old times, and the New Testament is the book of the Church today. That's not right. They each have something important to say about the same God, and we must listen to and start using what they both teach.

The Old Testament introduces us to God, through the history of Israel, and spends a lot of time going over basic principles of God and his kingdom. The New Testament's purpose is to record the coming of Christ — that great event when the God of the Old Testament suddenly showed up among his people and accomplished the great work of spiritual salvation that he had been promising for a long time.

Notice, however, that the New Testament doesn't take the time to go over the same things that the Old Testament went over! You will also find the same principle in any other field of study. For example, calculus books don't first review all of basic mathematics; they assume you went through all the basics already, and they just jump into the subject at hand. You must study the Old Testament for what it says about God, then go to the New Testament to find out more things about God. Always keep in mind that the two sections work hand in hand to give you a complete picture of who the Lord is and what he does.

• **Facets:** One last but extremely important way that the Bible reveals God is through what I call facets. A "facet" is a surface on a gem; a diamond, for example, has many flat surfaces cut into it to make it shine the light in beautiful and sparkling ways. To appreciate the whole diamond you must turn it around and look at each facet.

God is so huge, he is so many things, he does so many things, that we just can't understand the whole of him. I have a feeling that we will be spending eternity studying God, and then never get to the bottom of his character. We must keep this in mind when we study about him in the Scriptures. Is God the Judge of all men? He certainly is! But he is more than that — he also has mercy on whom he will have mercy. If you get carried away with him being Judge and forget that he is merciful to whosoever will come to him, you will get dangerously off-balance in your thinking and make the Bible say what it doesn't say at all.

God wears many hats, so to speak. At one point in the Bible we see him rescuing the Israelites from the Egyptians. At another place we see him as the Father who disciplines his wayward children. Here he is the one who saves from sin and death; there he is the one who casts the wicked into the fire of Hell. God is light, he is life, he is the foundation, he is bread, he is our altar, he is treasure, he is the truth — the list of his names goes on and on, and we see him in action doing an infinite variety of things.

Just keep in mind that any single text can't pack in a full description, or even a balanced viewpoint, of God when it deals with one of his acts. Balance that passage with all the other ones that you know about God and you will keep the right perspective on this God who is infinite.

If you get familiar with these ways of revealing God, you will begin to appreciate what the Bible is trying to teach you. For example, some minerals look very plain unless you shine ultraviolet light on them; then they glow eerily in unexpected ways. When the Bible takes a unique approach to showing you something about God, you need to appreciate why it is doing that and pay attention to what is going on. There is always a reason for its methods.

What it reveals

Before I leave it for you to pursue on your own, I want to start looking at some of the things that the Bible reveals to us about God. What does it say about him? What are some of the most important lessons in the Bible about the Lord, things that you really should learn first?

- *__There is a God.__* The Bible assumes God. It calls anybody who thinks there is no God a fool — a stupid person. (Psalm 14:1) The absolutely first, most important, most essential fact that every human being must know and accept is that there is a God. Everything else in life depends on whether you believe this or not.

Everything that happened to Israel came from God; there is just no other way to read the story. He led them and spoke to them and did mighty things among them. He had plans for them and used them among the nations. Whenever someone came along and doubted that Israel's God was real he learned a bitter lesson to the contrary. (2 Kings 19) When the priests in Solomon's day helped build the Temple, they might have thought that the ceremonies there would be uneventful — but they discovered God there in the Temple, so real that they couldn't get into the building. (2 Chronicles 7:1-3) When John the Baptist sent his disciples to Jesus, asking if he was the Messiah to come, Jesus sent back this answer:

> Jesus replied, "Go back and report to John what you hear and see: The blind receive sight, the lame walk, those who have leprosy are cured, the deaf hear, the dead are raised, and the good news is preached to the poor. Blessed is the man who does not fall away on account of me." (Matthew 11:4-6)

In other words, *God* had come down to do miracles, things never before seen among men. This is why Jesus was given the name Immanuel — "God with us." There was no other explanation for the things that he did.

The Bible assumes God, because all of its arguments depend on this being true. *There is a God* — so there is such a thing as right and wrong. God decides what is right and what is wrong, and he won't let us make those decisions for ourselves. (Proverbs 14:12; 16:25) He gave laws to man telling him what he must do to please him. (Exodus 20:1-17; John 15:1-17) And we know in our hearts that he has done this, because our consciences testify against us that there is a God who expects us to do right and avoid wrong. (Hebrews 10:22)

There is a God — so there is meaning to life. He created this world and put us into it for a purpose. We will find fulfillment in life when we get ourselves in line with his purposes (his will, in other words) and get busy doing what he wants us to do. (Psalm 138:8; Ephesians 2:10) He made us in his image, and we will succeed in our lives when we do things that will bring glory to God. (Genesis 1:27) When we devote all our energies and time to ourselves, however, we will find misery and emptiness and nothing in our hands to show for all our efforts at the end of life. (Ecclesiastes 2:17-26) Life means something only when we live for God.

There is a God — so there will be a Judgment Day. All the wrongs will be made right, because God can't stand for anybody to misunderstand what has been happening and accuse him of not being in control of things. (Isaiah 49:22-23) He is going to force sinners to acknowledge him (Philippians 2:9-11). He will reward the righteous (using *his* definition of the word!) and punish the wicked. (Matthew 25:31-46) He will remake the Heavens and the earth and there *will* be a world, finally, that will be honoring to him in every way. (Revelation 21:1-4)

• *__We are his creation.__* We learn this, of course, at the very beginning of the Bible when we read the account of Creation. But do most people realize what the doctrine of Creation means for them? It is more than just the story of how all this world came to be. Because we are God's creation we are always under his eye, under his careful scrutiny, as he ponders what to do with this creation of his.

Creation is arguably one of the two foundation truths in the Bible, the other one being redemption. When we say that God created us, we are saying some important truths: **first,** he made us for a reason. God does things by design, for a purpose, and we humans are the most important part of his design. We were made in his image — which means that we are to display the character and works of God in our natures. As we work, Creation is supposed to be able to see God in us. (1 Peter 2:12) Of course our sin has ruined this image and all that the world sees and feels from us is the fury of wickedness, but that just makes God's agony over us all the more powerful incentive to fix what has been ruined.

Second, God knows us intimately. He made us, so he knows better than we do what we need to live on. (Psalm 139) He provides uncounted physical blessings for every one of us so that we can live and work in the world. (Psalm 145:15-16) He also knows what we need spiritually. We ought to keep this in mind when he speaks to us in his Word about things that we would rather not think about. When he prescribes the way of salvation, no matter what it might take and no matter what kind of discipline and hardship we must meet with along the way, *he knows best.* (Hebrews 12:4-13) Do exactly what he says if you want to be saved.

Third, we live for *his* purposes. We are *not* here to pursue our own interests! (Philippians 2:21) We all forget this and get tied up with affairs of this world, while the kingdom of God goes begging. (Haggai 1:1-

11) The Lord has given us a job to do, talents to multiply, the sick to heal and the prisoner to visit — are we making his work a priority? (Luke 4:18; Matthew 25:32-46) When someone makes an appliance he plugs it in and expects it to do the job it was made for; if it doesn't work then he pitches it out as useless. Remember that God created you for a purpose and he will be just as disgusted if you don't perform to his expectations! (Jeremiah 13:1-11) On the other hand, it is a great comfort to rest in the knowledge that we have God's work to do. We know that if we are doing his will he will provide all that we need to get it done, along with the earthly needs we have. (Philippians 4:13,19; Matthew 6:33) God is faithful if he is anything, and he won't let his children down when they honor him. (Psalm 37:25)

Fourth, he is responsible for us. Don't think that he will go away. He created us and he is going to see this thing through to the end. We might get tired of the program but his purposes are always on his mind. He is constantly checking on us, checking our progress, checking the state of our hearts. (Psalm 121:4-5) When we sleep, he plans. When we take a break he is getting things ready for the next step in his unfolding purposes. (Genesis 50:20) He is tireless, and his kingdom weighs on his heart night and day. He will not rest until you have reached the end of the road (successfully or unsuccessfully) and have turned in your equipment and are ready to receive the last judgment.

• ***He is Master.*** The Bible makes this truth as plain as it can possibly make it. God is Lord, he is Ruler, he is the King of kings, he reigns over the entire earth. (Psalm 2) Everyone and everything must bow down to him in total submission, either willingly now or by force at the Last Day. Even if you don't accept the idea that he is the only Savior, you *will* admit someday that he is your God who has all rights over you. (Isaiah 45:22-24)

Earthly kings rule by the will of their subjects; someone made the decision that this man or woman would make a good ruler and they allowed them to take the seat of authority. For that reason they can depose the king if he turns out to be a rotten apple. God, however, doesn't rule by the will of man — much to our regret. (Psalm 2:1-3) He rules because he has total rights over us, the right of life and death. (Psalm 2:4-12) He rules because we cannot live without him. We can't take the next breath of air without God giving it to us. So he doesn't need man's resources as he rules over man, as earthly kings rely on. He simply speaks the word and creation is made or unmade to suit his will. (Psalm 50:1)

His glory is also from beyond this world. Earthly kings cover themselves with gems and gold and velvet to look glorious; God is glorious because of his own nature, his own power, his own majesty that nothing in this world can add to. He is glorious because his voice thunders over the earth and shakes it to the roots (Job 9:4-8). He is majestic because his light overwhelms even the angels and there is nothing in Heaven or on earth that is so great as he is. (Isaiah 46:9) His glory, in other words, is real — that's why he is the King of kings and will not be trifled with.

When God speaks, all his creatures listen and obey. Angels stand at his throne to do his perfect will. The earth shakes and melts before him as he comes down on mountains and seas. The trees and rivers, it says, clap their hands and praise him. (Psalm 98:8; Isaiah 55:12) All creation exists to do the will of God — nothing else. This is the most important duty of every animate and inanimate part of God's world. And it's not as if he rules by caprice, that he tells us what to do just from the pleasure of seeing us jump. His will made the world the beautiful place it is, and his will is going to make the new Heavens and earth an eternal paradise. He knows what he is doing! For those who obey there will be bliss, pleasure, rest, comfort, food and drink — a life that we cannot understand now. (Revelation 21:1-7)

The one rascal (besides the devil and his crew) in the picture is man, who stands against God in rebellion and refuses to do God's will. Unless he repents, he will take his place in Hell with the rest of the rebels. (Revelation 20:15) If God is of such a nature that our first duty is to obey him at all costs, then disobeying him means certain death. You just do not disobey the King!

• ***What he is like.*** We will learn many things about God's character in the Bible. He is like a multi-faceted jewel that you must look at from many angles to fully appreciate. We call these his *attributes* — descriptions of his divine nature.

Some of his attributes are these: God is *eternal*, which means he had no beginning and will have no ending. (Psalm 102:27) No creature can claim to be eternal because we all need God to exist. God is *self-sufficient*, which means he doesn't need anything outside himself to be what he is; he was perfectly happy before Creation and doesn't need any of it for himself. (Acts 17:25) God is *almighty*, which means that he can do anything that he wants to do — nothing can stand in his way. (Psalm 46) God is *all-knowing*, which means that there is nothing in Creation that isn't open and plain to his sight. (Daniel 2:22) We cannot hide anything from God. And there are many more attributes of God discussed in the Bible.

As you read the Bible, keep your eyes open for the testimony of his attributes. How else can you explain some of the things you find there if God is not like these things? For example, wasn't it his faithfulness that made him keep his promises to Israel, even though they kept breaking his laws? This is what makes him who he is; this is what makes his works so special and meaningful to us. We don't want to turn to other sources for what we need, because our life depends on someone who is not of this world nor is he like anything in this world.

His attributes also set him apart from all other gods. The ancients aren't the only ones who believed in false gods; we have our own versions of them, even though we think ourselves modern and sophisticated. Whenever someone comes up with a definition of God that doesn't agree with what the Bible says he is (and not like his attributes say he is) then they are worshipping a false god, not the God of the Bible. Attributes keep us straight about who God really is.

Also keep in mind that these attributes are going to be our salvation. Thank God he is eternal! That means that he never changes, his mercy is everlasting, that what he did for the saints of old he will do for us now who believe. These aren't just interesting tidbits of information about God, but vital information that will make the difference between life and death. He tells us these things about himself so that we might be saved.

• ***There's more than this world.*** For some reason modern Christians have often approached the Bible for the wrong reasons: they are looking for things that they can have for *this* life. They want to know how to be better parents, better church workers, better businessmen, better leaders, better whatever. As if God is primarily interested in *this* world.

He isn't. The only thing he intends to keep out of this entire creation is *your soul*. When he decides that the time is ripe, he will take all your possessions, all your earthly comforts, all your earthly accomplishments and circumstances and destroy them forever. (Hebrews 12:26-28) Then we will find out that all this was just a temporary stage upon which we acted out our parts. The point wasn't how we got along *here*, but how we got ready for life in the *next world*.

That's why the Bible keeps bringing us back to the vision of Heaven. In the Old Testament you have to read the story with faith (as did the Israelites) or you will miss the point. Was the dusty real estate of Palestine the real goal that God had in mind for Abraham's descendants? No! "Instead, they were longing for a better country — a *heavenly one.*" (Hebrews 11:16) David wasn't God's ultimate choice for a king over God's people; he was a sinner like the rest of us. Rather he was a picture of the more glorious, more powerful, wiser king over all God's kingdom — Christ. (Matthew 22:41-46) Many things in the Old Testament don't make a bit of sense to us unless we interpret them in this light: that there is a Heavenly world behind the physical pictures that we see.

The New Testament strips away the veil and boldly leads us into this spiritual world of God. (2 Corinthians 3:16) There is no apology here for what God thinks of our world; there is nothing here he wants to keep. (2 Peter 3:10-11) He keeps urging us to set our hearts on the things of Heaven. There is where Jesus is now, preparing a place for us to live forever. (Colossians 3:1-4) He urges us to let *him* take care of our needs here while we work on building up the kingdom of Heaven. (Matthew 6:33) We don't have to spend all our time trying to make a living, trying to get ahead in life, when we are employed in his business — he takes care of the rough spots for us when we honor him with our faith.

• **_The ways to please God._** The Bible spends a great deal of time showing us how to please God. Everyone knows this. What we don't know, and what will surprise us when we study it out, is exactly what it has to say about that subject.

Most people will tell you that, to please God, you must follow the Ten Commandments. You must be kind to your neighbor. You must do good deeds to those in need. You will find this kind of thinking in every civilization, every time in history, every religion on earth, in some form or another. They may not call it by the same names, but they mean the same thing. They also assume that we *can* do these things and please God.

The problem is that we can't. God knows this, and you will find that the Bible is merciless when it describes what we can and cannot do. It gives us no credit at all for doing anything that God would be pleased with. (Romans 3:9-20) Real Christianity starts at another point instead of the traditional list of morals and ethics. It assumes that we are sinners, rebellious to the core, dead to the things of God and totally incapable of even knowing God unless he gives us life in our souls. (Ephesians 2:1-10)

God should know what pleases him; he doesn't need us to tell him. (Isaiah 40:12-14) He is in Heaven where things must be perfect to the smallest details, where things must be made of spiritual stuff and not earthly. He is holy, and we are not to bring anything to him with the smallest trace of sin or death in it. He has in mind great things to do, and he isn't interested in child's play — our offerings to him must fit into his eternal plans or they are useless to him.

If all this is true about him, then we should pay careful attention to what the Bible says will please this awesome God. Not anything will do! Aaron's sons found out that even a slight deviation in the offering ceremony was not only useless to God but highly offensive; he destroyed the offering and them too! (Leviticus 10:1-3) We just cannot make assumptions about what he will like. We have to get the details as they are explained in the Bible.

These are some of the more important things that you will learn as you read the Bible. They are important because, unless you understand them and start living by them, you are definitely going to go wrong and end up in deep trouble someday. There will be situations in this life where you will need this information to make a right decision. There are duties you need to perform, which you cannot do in a way that pleases God unless you understand who he is. And on the Last Day your very eternity will hang in the balance depending on how well you knew your God! Many are going to hear to their eternal dismay that they didn't know God *well enough* to pass the final test:

> Not everyone who says to me, 'Lord, Lord,' will enter the kingdom of Heaven, but only he who does the will of my Father who is in Heaven. Many will say to me on that day, 'Lord, Lord, did we not prophesy in your name, and in your name drive out demons and perform many miracles?' Then I will tell them plainly, 'I never knew you. Away from me, you evildoers!' (Matthew 7:21-23)

An Example

Let's look at 1 Samuel 17 for a good example of how to find God in a passage. I can't think of a better example to use for this, because almost all of us have heard the story of David and Goliath since we were young and probably have learned the same lesson from it — the wrong one.

What teachers are usually guilty of, when they teach this story, is turning it into a moralism. Remember that a moralism is what we should or shouldn't do, based on what we learn from the story. We learn that we should be brave, that we should trust in God, that we should fight the good fight of faith, that all it takes sometimes is a few pebbles, that Goliaths can be beaten, and so on. There have been many ingenious as well as stale moralisms pulled out of this story.

The point of the story of David and Goliath, however, is *not* a moralism. Our mistake is that we haven't been looking for God in this story. What is even more ironic is that neither were the Israelites at the time it happened! All they saw was this giant Goliath, and all they knew was defeat, and they were just as amazed as we are that little David brought the giant down so easily. They missed the point too.

But David got the point right away. While Goliath was defying the "ranks of Israel" (verse 10), David was amazed at the gall of the man who would defy "the armies of the *living God*." (verse 26) Did David see something that the others didn't see?

Later he told Saul why he thought he could defeat Goliath: he lists his exploits while defending his father's sheep from wild animals. But did he give *himself* the credit for what happened? No — he said that "the LORD who delivered me from the paw of the lion and the paw of the bear will deliver me from the hand of this Philistine." (verse 37) Saul made a polite and standard reply — "Go, and the LORD be with you" — but probably didn't think that he would.

Then when David approached Goliath he again said what it was that would bring down the giant. He came "in the Name of the LORD Almighty, the God of the armies of Israel, whom you have defied." (verse 45) He says that he will kill Goliath and then the world will know "that there is a God in Israel." Then he says this:

> All those gathered here will know that it is not by sword or spear that the LORD saves; for the battle is the LORD's, and he will give all of you into our hands. (1 Samuel 17:47)

Now think about what all these verses are saying. While the Israelites were worried about Goliath, David shows up and directs their attention to God for a change. *This story teaches us how God saves his people*. There is no other point to the story. For example, these are some things we can learn about God here:

• ***God brings down our enemies.*** David kept saying this over and over. We can't do anything about our enemies; only the Lord can defeat them and give us freedom. As soon as we realize this, we can get out of his way and let him do things his way. Our problem is that we think *we* are called upon to fight the enemies of God, and of course we try using the weapons that we have at hand — the weapons of the world — and we fail. The world is much better at this kind of fighting than we are! What the world *can't* do, however, is fight God, who uses Heavenly weapons against them.

• ***God uses little things in this world to fight his battles.*** He doesn't need lots of people and millions of dollars and all the impressive tricks that the world has in its bag to do his will. He will typically pick the least important person, the smallest "weapon" (Gideon broke jars and sent the Midianites in panic; Samson killed a thousand Philistines with a donkey's jawbone) and accomplish great miracles. He is trying to teach us a lesson in this: the power comes not from the thing used but from God. He can use anything and anybody, and the weaker and more insignificant the better. He is trying to draw everyone's attention to *himself*, because it is *he* that we must fear. Never fear an army of thousands; there's bound to be some way to defeat them. But you'd better run if God comes after you with a few pebbles in the hand of a shepherd boy!

• ***God times his fights.*** Notice that Goliath had the Israelites in terror for quite a while, and David didn't show up until everyone had lost hope and there wasn't anything left to try. To the Lord, timing is everything; usually he will time things so that no hope is left, people despair of anything good happening, and the only thing that could possibly deliver them is a miracle. *Then* he steps on stage, with all eyes on him, and does the miracle for them. If miracles come too soon then people might think that they had somehow done it themselves! But if they come when we have no other hope left, we know that God did it.

• ***God refuses to use the weapons of this world.*** David couldn't use Saul's armor and sword because they were too big for him, and he wasn't used to using them. Neither is God interested in them because they are completely unable to bring about the kind of results that he wants. Who would have been impressed if David had attempted a sword fight with Goliath and somehow delivered a fatal thrust through the giant's armor? They would have praised David, of course, but God would have gotten no glory out of it. But to go up against Goliath with no armor, no sword, and no spear was sheer foolishness! Unless, of course, God is doing the fighting — then we don't need such weapons. Besides, our enemies are highly skilled at weapons of this world and it isn't good strategy to counter with the same kind of weapons; why not use weapons that they don't have? Like weapons from Heaven! Then we will always have the advantage over them — nothing can stand before God's weapons. In this case the weapon that delivered the fatal blow was **faith**.

• *__An insult to God's children is an insult to God.__* David couldn't believe the brazenness of this Philistine! Goliath wasn't just jeering at the Israelites, he was challenging God. Of course the other Israelite soldiers didn't pick up on this because they thought it was *their* fight. But aren't these the Lord's people? Aren't they out there for the Lord's cause? Don't they carry the Lord's Name on them? Then the Lord considers this *his* fight, not theirs, and his glory is on the line. It's his reputation at stake here: either he can take care of his people and defeat his enemies, or he can only stand aside helplessly and watch the pagan Philistines beat up on his people. Goliath challenged the Israelites' God, and the Lord took up the challenge personally and immediately. He wasn't going to let the big fool get away with that! I wish we would see that in our own struggles against our spiritual enemies; the outcome is far more certain than we realize because our God considers himself insulted by the way the world treats us. When we fall down there is war in God's eyes! Someone's head is going to roll for our sufferings.

• *__He trains his people beforehand.__* David was already used to approaching problems this way. Saul had never heard of taking on a giant with just a few pebbles; that's why the Lord didn't use him. David was carefully trained in the ways of God so that when the real crisis came in Israel's history he was able to fill the need and God accomplished another critical goal. While most of us are being trained in the world's ways, to accomplish what the world thinks is worth doing, some people (usually hidden away and unknown) are being trained by God — not the kind of training that gets them a degree or recognition from men! — for that time when *only they* will be able to do the great work of God and save the day for the Church. Count on it, the Lord is not a poor manager. He has his special people in training now so that when those critical spiritual battles come and people's souls are at stake, his special warriors (or workmen) will be able to do what worldly experts cannot do.

• ___He only uses faith, not a lack of faith.___ The victory goes to those who believe in God to do the impossible. The Israelite soldiers didn't believe that much in their God, and so they weren't able to defeat Goliath. David, with a child-like faith that accepted God at his word (this is *his* fight, not theirs, and he will use *his* ways of doing it, not theirs), brought down the giant. Faith in God assures the victory; unbelief always results in defeat. This principle in God's kingdom is much more important than you realize.

It's obvious that David succeeded when the others failed. He brought down Goliath, when the others just stood there in terror of him. Now what does that tell us? Just this: when you focus on God, when you trust in him, when you use his ways, when you train in his school, when you follow him into battle and let the Lord get honor to his own Name, you are going to succeed. The more you know about your God, in other words, the better chance you have of making it.

Let's go one more step, in a direction that has to do with this study: when you study the Bible, *focus on God.* Your life, your salvation, your solutions for problems, and your defense, all depend on how well you understand your God. This is your opportunity to get trained and equipped in God's ways and weapons. Somewhere down the road you are going to hit a real problem that will require so much more of you than you can muster, unless you have done your homework now. Get as much as you can of God now; and later, when you need help, it will be a life-saving knowledge that will give you success.

Questions to ask

If you are going to start looking for God when you read the Bible, here are some questions that will help you find what you are looking for:

- ***What does the passage say about God?*** Look for his nature, the way he does things, what he considers important, what he expects of us and why, the things he uses, what happens when he is around, how people react in his presence, his names, his goals, what his will is, the power of his speaking, the work of the Father, the work of the Son, the work of the Spirit, the prophecies of what he intends to do, the things he does with believers, the things he does with unbelievers, his world-wide influence and reign, the way he controls circumstances, his hidden works, his works that everyone sees, what offends him, what pleases him, what he insists on doing himself, his glory and how it is made known, and many other things!

- ***What is God doing in the passage?*** Back up and look at the great sweep of events in the story. Sometimes you have to look at the entire book or even a whole section of the Bible to see what he is aiming at. How does he do it? What are his methods? Whom does he use, if he does? Did people know what he was doing at the time — or did they not see it until years or centuries later? How does it fit in with the rest of the Bible? How does it apply to us now? Does God still do these things? In the same way? How does this make him different from other gods or powers?

• ***What do the people involved say about God?*** God uses the testimony of man to get glory; it is an important ingredient in the growth of his kingdom. Testimony, or witness, means telling others who God is and what he does; this is something that they have found to be true about God. When does the testimony happen? What makes people want to testify about God? What happens when people testify? How does God use that testimony? Was it just for *their* time, or is the power of that testimony still with us?

• ***What do other passages say about this one?*** Remember that the Bible is its own best interpreter. Many times when you can't understand a certain passage there will be another passage that will help you out. Is this theme discussed in other places in the Bible? Are there key words that are used elsewhere? Is there another passage that seems to contradict it? If so, perhaps you need to dig deeper into both, looking for God in the text, and then the problem will be solved. Keep in mind that the Bible is talking about the same God from beginning to end. He never changes, he has the same goals now that he had thousands of years ago, and "only together with us" will the saints of old finally see the glory of God in the face of Jesus. As you read the Bible it will present this same story to you in many ways, from different angles, with the hope that you will eventually begin to see just how big and yet how ***one*** our God really is. (Deuteronomy 6:4)

Discussion Questions For Key One: Revelation

- Why is God's truth hidden without revelation? *How* is it hidden?

- What things would we have wrong if it were not for the Bible revealing the truth to us?

- How does the Bible fit in with other subject areas?

- What are some signs that people aren't seeing God when they study the Bible?

- Is there truth apart from the Bible?

- Is it possible for anybody to understand the revelation of the Bible?

- Must everybody understand the revelation of the Bible?

- In ministering to others, what are your primary objectives?

Key Two: Miracle

Key Two: Miracle

The Bible is a book of miracles. At the very beginning of Genesis we start seeing astonishing miracles, miracles that no one can explain, and they keep on happening throughout the rest of the book. There are miracles of all kinds — they happened to all kinds of people in all sorts of situations. Some were little miracles for the benefit of an individual and others were huge and affected the course of nations. Miracles occurred in those times in the strangest places, with no advance warning. Sometimes the story could be dry and boring and suddenly a miracle happens, then it returns to its former topic as if nothing out of the ordinary happened. There is probably not another book in the world that is so full of miracles as the Bible.

It's too bad that our generation has taken a skeptical view of miracles. For one thing, science has virtually convinced us that there is no such thing as a miracle — things like that don't happen in our orderly world. There is always some explanation for the mysterious, the scientists tell us. Anybody who tries to tell you differently is just a "magician" who doesn't want you to know the explanation! This attitude keeps most people from believing that the miracles recorded in the Bible actually happened.

Even Christians have problem with miracles. Though they believe that these things really did happen back in Bible times, they usually don't believe that miracles have anything to do with us today. But they are wrong on two counts: first, miracles *are* still going on today among the faithful. Second, miracles are profoundly important for understanding God, and what happened in Bible times — especially the miracles — is absolutely essential for our faith today.

Miracles are much more important to the story of the Bible than we may realize. We often read about a miracle as if it were a magic trick, something that God threw in to entertain and amaze everyone — as if the rest of the story can stand on its own *without* the miracle.

Remember Thomas Jefferson's famous Bible? He cut out everything in it that had a miracle, and was satisfied that what was left was enough to base one's religion on. As if Christianity can stand without its miracles! That's not true at all. Without miracles we have no religion; without miracles we have no doctrines to believe. In fact, we will see that miracles are so important a part of God's way of building his kingdom that *without miracles there is no need for God.* You cannot believe in God without also believing in miracles; and if you want to be saved, you cannot expect anything from God except miracles. Nothing else will do the job.

What is a miracle?

First we want to define very carefully what a miracle is. Many of the problems that people have with miracles would clear up immediately if there is a clear meaning to the word — something that we can see across the entire Bible in the story of every miracle.

We can define a miracle like this:

A miracle is what God does for us directly, apart from natural means.

God is responsible for most of what happens in this world (except for sin — that's *our* fault!). He is always actively involved with whatever happens. At Creation, however, he set things up so that we get what we need from created things, *not* directly from his hand. Let me use an example. We need bread to eat to survive. So we grow the wheat from grain, using the land and good agricultural practices; we harvest and grind the wheat to make flour; we add the right ingredients and bake it. After all these steps we can have bread to eat. Perhaps we buy our bread ready-made at the store, but that only means that someone else went through the steps and we pay for their efforts. Now we give God thanks when we eat the bread — it did come from him, ultimately — but he used many "agents" in this world to get it into our hands.

Now watch God provide bread through a miracle. In Exodus 16 he sends a kind of bread that this world doesn't and can't provide. It was so strange, it appeared in such a startling way that the people asked "what is it?" The Hebrew expression for "what is it?" is *manna* — and the bread got that name forever. Very appropriate — because nobody has been able to duplicate the recipe to this day! God didn't use any normal means of making bread for them, nor did he use materials in this world, nor did he deliver it to them by normal means. This was the finger of God; nobody else can duplicate it.

Jesus, as recorded in the Gospels, brought bread out of thin air in the same way. The disciples wanted to send the crowd back home to get food in the normal way (buying it at the market, cooking, and so on). But Jesus didn't want to do it in the normal way: he wanted to show them that God is capable of providing for them *without using any of the usual means.* (Matthew 14:15-21) In other words, God can call bread into existence just by speaking.

A miracle is something that happens apart from normal means, but it is more than that. A miracle is a direct act of God, something that happens when God himself touches his creation. Mountains smoke, the ocean splits apart, trees wither and die overnight, the dead are raised and the blind see. These are things that the world wishes it could do for us but it can't. When the magicians of Egypt saw what Moses' God could do — something that they themselves could not duplicate — they drew a correct conclusion: "This is the finger of God." (Exodus 8:19) They were amazed; they knew that God himself was touching their land.

There are four elements to every miracle that you ought to memorize and watch for when you read about one in the Bible:

> • ***God does it***. Notice that the miracle is something that *only* God could have done. It should be very clear from the story that the powers at work here are the powers of God, someone who can speak and impossible things happen. If it were unclear exactly how this miracle occurred, it would be no glory to God; so the writer is going to make it obvious to us. The writer sets the stage carefully, because he wants everyone to know that God did this thing. In the Bible, there's never any question about who is responsible for what happened in a miracle.

Remember that the purpose of the Bible is to reveal God to us — because otherwise we wouldn't know many important things about him. One of the first things that we must learn is this fact that he works miracles. This is the way he builds his kingdom. This is his characteristic signature, so to speak, over all his works. He himself will heal and give life and build and destroy. He gives this work to no other creature, because it requires power and wisdom that no other creature has to give. Man's way of doing things is to give the dirty work to someone else to do, while getting all the glory for it. God's way, however, is to roll up his sleeves and do the work himself — every bit of it — not only to get glory but to make sure it is done right.

There's a reason for this. People have to stop looking to the world for their answers and start looking to God for a change. *First*, only he can do the job the way it needs to be done. The requirements are too far beyond our mortal abilities (even if we weren't already sinners!) to accomplish. Our salvation has to last forever! Who is equal to accomplishing just a single step of it? We need God to solve our problems: the one who makes things out of nothing, who destroys invincible armies, who brings back to life. God alone has the answers that humanity needs for its insuperable problems. *Second*, he knows what is really needed. He isn't going to cheat on the steps of salvation or try to get by with doing a second-rate job for us. If it were up to us, we would prefer to skip some areas and spend all our time on things that interest us more. But he is going to make sure that *all* the areas are covered. His workmanship is perfect, to the last degree. *Third*, he wants the credit for being the miracle-working God that he is — he wants everyone to know it. If our problems didn't require miracles to solve, why would we need him? Any god would do! But he wants us to depend on him alone for everything — in other words, to live for miracles. His people honor him by depending on the work of his hands; we are not to fail him in this. He's very jealous of his glory. *Fourth*, only what is founded on his work will last. When God makes a kingdom through miracles, it lasts — the world can't say the same about its works. Try solving your problems without God if you want, but you won't get far. He uses the stuff of Heaven to repair earth's problems. He is a solid foundation; the way he builds his kingdom (through miracle) is a key to his success.

You may not have realized how important it is for your life that God works his miracles in you. They are literally your salvation; you must have them. "Look to the LORD and his strength; seek his face always. Remember the wonders he has done, his miracles, and the judgments he pronounced." (Psalm 105:4-5) You need the special kinds of works that God does if you want salvation at all. If you don't know what they are, this is a good time to learn them so that you can start asking for them.

• ***Man can't do it***. You will also notice in each story of a miracle that man was not responsible for what happened. It is very clear that unless God had done such a thing, it would never have happened. We cannot do what we need. Man is incapable of helping himself overcome certain problems. The sooner we realize this, the sooner we will turn to God for what we need.

Again, this is important for several reasons. *First*, if we aren't convinced of this — that it is no use to try it ourselves — then we will do what we can without him. People are always trying to live without God. Our modern society is perhaps the most guilty of thinking that we can do very well without God: science provides everything we need, government is our savior, education will solve all our problems. Modern man has talked himself into thinking that he doesn't need God for anything! But he's wrong, and it is already showing up in our society that our ways, our works, are only making things worse for everyone. We cannot continue to live without God.

Even in the Church there are too many people who are content to carry on as if God was a story in an old book but has nothing real to do among us today. Thank the Lord that there *are* miracles, things that *are* impossible for us, things that require a God to do, or Christianity would be a disappointing lie — nobody would ever see clear evidence that there *really is* a God. We would preach about a God who used to do miracles for his people, and live as if we need none of them ourselves. The problem with this, again, that it doesn't work. Without God the Church herself will self-destruct — which happens all too often.

Second, nobody ever contributed a thing to any miracle; God alone did the whole thing. A miracle is made in Heaven out of Heavenly treasures and sent down to change the earth. It borrows nothing from us, nor does it need anything from us. We get the wrong idea if we think that man is partly responsible for any miracle. The Bible writers never gave men any credit at all for having anything to do with miracles; that's what is so helpful about their testimony.

If Adam had not sinned against God, we might be able to say that man could do things that would satisfy God. But sin stains our smallest efforts now, and God can use none of our good deeds in his kingdom. Consider the results: if he would use our tainted and weakened spiritual works in the eternal house he is building, could he depend on it for the rest of eternity? Wouldn't he expect to have to replace it a few million years down the road because of its less-than-perfect construction? This will never do!

So you will see, in every story about a miracle, the writer very carefully showing man's complete helplessness in the situation. We are *not* to put our hope in man anymore; if God doesn't work a miracle then the thing won't get done! Science, philosophy, politics, economics, common sense, educational theory, even sheer determination cannot address the basic spiritual needs of man. They never have and they never will. We have to start looking somewhere else for our answers instead of what man (including we ourselves) can do for us.

• *We need it*. It's obvious in most stories about a miracle that the Lord did it to fulfill a need in someone's life. The Israelites, for example, ran out of water in the desert and God performed a miracle of bringing water out of a rock so that they wouldn't die of thirst. (Numbers 20:11) What may not be so obvious, however, is the lesson of each of these stories: *without the miracles of God every one of us is going to die.*

Each miracle addressed a problem that was too much for man to figure out and solve. You may have noticed that the Bible spends almost no time telling us about the day-to-day existence of the Israelites; we know very little about the centuries that passed in relative peace. The stories almost all focus on problem times, national and personal crises that required extraordinary solutions. Not only were people's lives at stake, but the very purposes of God were threatened. If God didn't step in at this critical time and solve the problem, there would be disastrous results. His solution, of course, was to do a work that no power on earth could do because there was no power that could solve it.

Miracles are essential for our survival in this world. Our needs are much more than food and drink, shelter and companionship. The world gives us all these things, but we still obviously have painful needs in our souls. Because we are spiritual creatures, with immortal souls, we have needs that nothing in this world can fulfill. A mother can feed her children food so that their bodies will live, but what will she give them so that their souls will live? We can protect ourselves from the storm and burning sun, but how will we protect ourselves from the wrath of God? When we realize our spiritual needs, and we understand that this world can do nothing for us in this regard, then we see that our help must come from beyond this world. And that's where miracles step in.

There are many people, of course, who say that they don't need these kinds of things. They are enjoying themselves and they choose to ignore the inner cry of their souls. But the conscience, for example, simply will not go away: when life ends, those who refused to think about spiritual matters will finally be forced to deal with them. The experience will be so startling and so real that they will wish a million times over that they had done something about it before then! (Luke 16:19-31)

The Lord made us in such a way that we must get everything we need from him — both indirectly and directly. We are his creatures, and he is our God. We depend on his creation and providence for our physical needs, but we also need him for what this world cannot give us. Not many people are aware of this, or if they are they don't want to admit it. Living without God, however, is like living without purpose or meaning, without wisdom, without goals, without the power to work. Without him we are like machines that have never been plugged in; without him we will die and decay, worthless hulks that never did anything important and never got to live.

• *It works*. God's answers work. While man is still trying to figure out what the problem is, God completely solves the problem in such a way that the person is satisfied and he will never have that problem again.

I don't mean to say that nothing that man does works. In his own domain he is very successful; he can work and learn and accomplish great things, often doing much good for others in the process. Man is the most amazing creature on earth in this respect of working and getting things done. But when it comes to spiritual matters he is helpless and hopeless. He can do nothing to help himself; in fact, he starts out life spiritually dead — and who will expect great things from someone who is dead?

So the Lord insists on providing his own materials, and building the house in his own way, so that it will last and be something that we can all depend on forever. He intends to provide a perfect dwelling for his people; nothing less will do. And he wants us to be perfect too. So only a miracle is going to accomplish what we need.

God's works rebuild the heart corrupted by sin. God's works repair the damage of death. They make the old earth new; they bring something out of nothing. When people despair that any good thing can happen, they find God stepping in with invincible power and wisdom and literally creating the solution out of nothing, and often in the midst of adverse circumstances. The story of the woman suffering from a hemorrhage (Mark 5:25-29) shows the contrast between the best efforts of men trying to solve our problems and the efforts of God. Men fail; God always succeeds. Our answers to life's problems have never worked; God's answers always work. Again, thank the Lord for the Bible's testimony to this truth and how carefully the writers show us how well his miracles address the problems of men.

A Showcase

As you read the Bible, stop at the miracles and study them for a while. Keep in mind that the writer is presenting this miracle to you in a certain way; he is setting up the events in the story with something definite in mind. He wants you to see the point of the miracle, which is this: God can and will do whatever you need, regardless of the limitations that normally stop us.

Miracles in the Bible are showcases, so to speak, that show off what God can and will do for his people. If you visit a museum you will see some displays under glass, carefully arranged and lit from a certain angle so that a viewer can see it best. The writers of Scripture (guided by the Spirit, of course!) took the same pains to present God in the best light for our faith.

So what should we be careful to notice the next time we read about a miracle?

• **_A desperate problem._** Whenever God has to come to the rescue, you will find such a sorry state of affairs that you wonder how people can get themselves into such a mess! We are often tempted to think that *our* problems aren't so bad, that there is still hope; but the Bible shows us people who have no hope at all. Unless God does something for them they will fail or die.

For example, the Israelites, after leaving Egypt, found themselves stuck out in the desert with Pharaoh and his troops hot on their heels and the Red Sea in front of them. They had no idea of what to do. If Pharaoh would catch them, they would have had to go back to Egypt in shame into slavery. It is just at that moment, in their hour of despair, that God stretched out his hand and worked a miracle for them: he split the Red Sea, allowing them to pass through safely, and brought the water back down on Pharaoh's army.

Now the writer *wants* you to ask some questions here. Did they know what to do? No! "They were terrified and cried out to the Lord." (Exodus 14:10) They had no idea what to do; even Moses looked to God and waited for an answer to an unsolveable problem. *Could* they do anything about it? No again. There was no crossing the sea; and they were slaves, not soldiers, and therefore no match for Pharaoh's army. Must they escape? Of course! How could the Lord's promises be fulfilled if Pharaoh recaptured them and

took them back? That would have been a serious
setback to the Lord's plan; so their need was critical.
Also, how would it have looked if Pharaoh managed to
beat Moses' God after all and keep the Israelites from
leaving Egypt? God's honor was at stake here: either
he can take care of his promises and prove himself
greater than Pharaoh's gods, or he can't.

You will find similar circumstances with other
miracles in the Bible. Look at them carefully and ask
questions about them. Notice how the writer makes his
case: someone is in desperate need, he cannot help
himself nor can anybody else help him, and God's honor
is at stake. In other words, if we take the story as it
stands, if this miracle isn't done then real damage will
happen to God's cause!

• ***An amazing solution.*** The Bible loves to glorify
God. The miracles he performed to help his people out
of their predicaments were absolutely astonishing.
Perhaps that's why modern readers don't want to believe
that such things happened, because they seem so
miraculous and lavish!

Watch how the writer presents the miracle. Notice
that it shows clearly that God doesn't need this world's
normal systems to do his work. He touches things
directly and bypasses the normal processes, and that
direct touch of the divine finger creates new things right
on the spot as needed. Most miracles show us the Lord
using something in this world — Balaam's donkey,
trumpets at Jericho, Gideon's three hundred men, Jesus'
spittle — but the thing used didn't contribute anything at
all to the miracle. It was only a vehicle for the miracle
and of no use at all for explaining how in the world God
did such a thing. Didn't John say that God could make
children of Abraham out of rocks? (Luke 3:8)

Note how varied the miracles are. Scan the types of
things that God did and you will see that he really can

do anything; there is nothing he can't do. The needs of man are never-ending and often we think that there is no answer because of the awful mess things are in. But God is never set back by any set of adverse circumstances. He is the Judge of all men and he knows exactly what to do, when to do it, in a way that will perfectly satisfy his Law and fulfill our needs. Then he does it in a big way! He can change water to wine, bring water out of desert rock, make an axehead float, cure leprosy using river water, make the sun go backwards in the sky, burn water with fire from Heaven, call someone out of the grave, calm a storm with a word, walk on water — there isn't anything he can't do when the need arises.

Notice too how God likes to add icing to the cake. When the Israelites grumbled against the Lord in the desert, he sent poisonous snakes among them and many died. When they saw their error they repented (a good move!) and pleaded with God to send the snakes away. He did more than that, though! Not content with just answering their request, he instructed Moses to make a bronze snake and anybody who had been bitten could look at the bronze snake and be healed. The miracle was more than they expected! (Numbers 21:4-9) "Now to him who is able to do *immeasurably more than all we ask or imagine*, according to his power that is at work within us." (Ephesians 3:20)

Don't miss the obvious point of each miracle: **God** did this; there just isn't any other way of explaining what happened. In fact, it is hard to miss this point unless you just aren't awake to the Bible's purpose of glorifying God. Things that happen in our time can be confusing: we don't know whether God did it, or whether it was due to our own genius, or just a happy coincidence. The Bible makes it plain that God does miracles and nobody else can do what he does. He alone gets the credit for helping his people.

Why miracles?

The miracles recorded in the Bible aren't just for our entertainment. If you take the miracles out, our hope is gone — because miracles are what we need from God for our problems. Miracles are a necessity, a foundation for Christianity, without which we have no way at all of rising above the limitations and failures of this world.

When you read about a miracle you will notice that created things could not have done such a thing on their own. Let's take the miracle of Jesus feeding the five thousand as an example. (Luke 9:12-17) Jesus only used five loaves of bread and two fish to feed thousands of people. Obviously the five loaves in themselves were not enough to feed everyone. But the writer (and the Lord!) wants to make that very point plain *to us*: this world *cannot* give us what we need. The disciples thought of turning to the world's ways to solve the problem (Luke 9:12), but Jesus knew that such a thing wasn't God's will at this time. It was not going to answer the problem. The world is so limited in what it can do that we would go hungry if we waited on it, spiritually *and* physically in this case. If these people were going to be fed, the Lord must do something totally alien to the way this world works. In fact, he must bring divine powers and materials to bear on the problem because there is nothing here to work with. And when he does, the people get what they need with no thanks to the world system.

Miracles, then, are a condemnation of this world and a recommendation of God's ways instead. Man has needs that he can *not* find help for in this world — he *must* see that if he wants to be saved. It's like walking out on thin ice in spite of the warning sign! We all do it, and we all fall into trouble when we ignore the Lord's counsel to go *to him* for what we need, not the world.

The second lesson of miracles is to teach us the *way* that God intends to take care of us. He won't quit using natural means to feed and clothe us; we will still work to earn money, and buy our food at the grocery store down the street. Life will go on for us just as it does for anybody else, be they believer or non-believer. But you have many critical needs that this world cannot take care of for you. God promised that he would take care of those needs, however, and he wants to do them by way of miracle. Since the world can't meet our needs, the Lord won't use the world — he will do it himself.

It's the direct hand of God that will help us. When it happens, there is no accounting for what happened except to give God the glory for it. Nothing in this world could have done such a thing. People wonder if miracles still happen in our day. But if they define miracles as things that only God can do, that this world or anything in it cannot do, then certainly miracles happen all the time. We wouldn't have Christianity if it weren't for miracles.

There are good reasons that miracles are recorded for us in the Bible:

•   ___*Not in this world*___ — The world doesn't have what we need. Yes, it provides food and shelter, and our senses are fulfilled to some extent (although we have to eat every day without fail, no matter how much we've eaten in the past — there's no end to it!). But if it's true that we are different from the animals then we need far more than this world can offer us. We need peace in our hearts, which we will never get as long as we are filled with sin that ruins us and burdens our consciences. We need life, but unfortunately we are all headed toward death. We need someone who knows and loves us, which we can't find in this world full of hateful individuals looking after only themselves.

When Jesus did miracles among the Jews, people heard about it from miles around and came running to get *their* miracle too. They had lived their lives in suffering and want and disappointment, not finding what they needed in the world, and now here was someone from outside the world with concrete answers. They didn't need much convincing — they were tired of the world's empty promises. For those of us who read the same stories of what God can do, we won't need much convincing either if we've fed at the husks of the world all of our lives and gotten nowhere.

• **_Glory to God_** — Miracles always turn our attention to God because he is the principal actor. He is the one who does the miracle; this is his special business and he is "advertising," so to speak, to get customers. "Glory" is getting credit for something. He wants everyone to see and understand that not only is he the *only* one who can do this thing, but that *everyone else* should come to him for theirs too. He is the sole source of miracles.

God loves glory not because he's sinfully proud of his abilities, but because he *really is* the only one who can do such things. We are often proud of ourselves and strut our stuff so that everyone can see and admire us. But when God shows off what he can do, he is doing it for our salvation — we will be saved only if we believe what we see and go to him for the same thing. That's always the main point of any miracle: look and believe and wonder at this God who can do such amazing things!

• **_Where to turn for help_** — The last point leads to this one. A miracle is a *testimony*, which means that we are seeing what we need to solve *our* problems. God wants us to know where to go when we need food and protection and peace and strength and wisdom. In other words, this stuff really works — here is proof in front of our eyes — and it's free for the asking.

When John sent his disciples to Jesus to find out if he really was the Messiah, Jesus sent this message back to him:

> Go back and report to John what you hear and see: The blind receive sight, the lame walk, those who have leprosy are cured, the deaf hear, the dead are raised, and the good news is preached to the poor. Blessed is the man who does not fall away on account of me. (Matthew 11:4-5)

His point was that seeing and hearing of these miracles should be enough to make anybody come to the Lord for their own miracle. The Pharisees had their own brand of religion that they expected people to believe and obey. Jesus, however, provided proofs that he was *from God* (who alone can do such things) and, based on those proofs, expected faith from those who saw and heard. He expected a following because of the miracles.

• **_What to expect_** — Be careful when you "believe" that miracles are true. Part of your faith must include the belief that *God will do miracles for you too*.

Let's put this thing together once more. *First*, you have special spiritual needs. *Second*, this world cannot meet those needs. *Third*, God stands ready to meet the needs of any who will come to him. *Fourth*, he will not use this world or its ways to solve those problems, because if the world had the answer in it in the first place we wouldn't have needed to turn to God for the answer! *Therefore*, he will do it himself, without the world. And that's a miracle, when something happens to you that God himself does and there is no other explanation for what happened.

One of the reasons that so many miracles happened in the past is to show us what God intends to keep doing into the future. Some people believe that miracles ceased when the Bible was complete. But they are confusing one kind of miracle with the entire range of miracles. Physical miracles are the finger of God bypassing the normal laws of nature; they seem to be happening much less frequently now than they did then, it is true. But spiritual miracles are *also* the finger of God bypassing normal processes and doing things that are no less impossible — like making a rebel into a child of God! Not only are these kinds of miracles happening now, they *must* happen if the Kingdom of God is to grow! Without miracles there is no Church! The entire work of the Church is due solely to the activity of the

Spirit of God as he gives life, heals wounds, creates new hearts and minds, leads us into Heaven for spiritual worship, and builds a house in which God will live forever.

• *A personal touch* — Keep in mind the heart of the definition of miracle: it is the finger of God that does this thing. When God does something in your heart, you can be sure that he himself came into your life and personally gave you what you needed. He didn't send an angel to do it for him, or command it from way up in Heaven somewhere. He doesn't keep his distance from you when he wants to do you good.

The stories of miracles, especially the Gospel stories, show this clearly. Jesus was God in the flesh, come to personally meet and help those in need. He came and found them; he listened to their cry for help; he touched them and spoke to them. When the Almighty God comes to someone to help them, that sure does make that person feel wanted and loved. We would certainly understand if God was too busy to come personally and he had to send someone else in his place; the miracle itself would be worth getting at any price. But God doesn't let others do his miracles for him (apart from the fact that nobody else *could* do it for him!). They are special gifts for his children. Just like a father who loves to watch his children open their gifts, God enjoys personally giving us his spiritual gifts.

> "For I am the LORD, your God, who takes hold of your right hand and says to you, Do not fear; I will help you. Do not be afraid, O worm Jacob, O little Israel, for I myself will help you," declares the LORD, your Redeemer, the Holy One of Israel. (Isaiah 41:13-14)

Science versus miracle

We modern readers are under a burden that Christians of past ages didn't have to deal with. Due to the discoveries of science we understand how this world works in a far better way than our ancestors and we can often explain things that they thought were miracles. We laugh at their naiveté when they tried to explain how their world worked, and the solutions they invented to take care of their problems. And we are right in this respect: science has certainly given us much understanding and power over the world, and made life much more comfortable and more efficient.

What our scientific knowledge has done to us, however, is make us distrustful of any miracle. We use the word, but we don't mean anything by it. "Miracle of modern medicine," we call things, and "if this works it will be a miracle." But when we read about a genuine miracle in the Bible we say to ourselves, "there must be some scientific explanation to this event; give us some time and we will find the answer and duplicate it."

That's why I was careful to define miracle as I did. I appreciate science as much as anybody else; but when it comes to the kinds of things that God does for his people, ***there is no explanation.*** Science cannot and never will duplicate the miracles of the Bible, for this simple reason: it uses the world to do its work, and God doesn't. Creation is the stuff that science uses to make life more comfortable. It uses matter and energy in ways that follow prescribed laws and comes up with results. God completely bypasses creation and gets his results using absolutely no earthly means whatever. God is not constrained by the laws that constrain us. We work *within* the system (and succeed if we work *with* the system) but God is *over* the system and does things his own way.

So when the Lord did a miracle in the Bible, science stands speechless. Let the best team of scientists gather their most sensitive and complex instruments, and let them study what God did in an effort to understand it; they will never see it. Even if the Lord himself described to them how he did it, they wouldn't understand him. This is the work of the Creator, and created beings can't (by definition) put themselves in his shoes and see it from his perspective. We can understand the creation very well, because we are at its eye-level; we can't understand how God works, though, because he works by command, not through physical laws.

I mention this because well-meaning Christians often try to explain the Bible's miracles in such a way as to make them more appealing to unbelievers. Take the Great Flood at Noah's time, for example. Believers go to great lengths to show how such a thing could have happened: a canopy of water vapor around the earth, continental shift, a meteor passing by to trigger the cataclysm, and so on. But I've noticed in their ingenious explanations of how it could reasonably have happened that they say nothing about God simply reaching down and doing it himself, apart from the world's natural forces. Oh, but he *could* have used natural means, they will say; but that's not what the *Bible* says, I answer. "*I* am going to bring floodwaters on the earth to destroy all life under the heavens" (Genesis 6:17), "Seven days from now *I* will send rain on the earth for forty days and forty nights, and *I* will wipe from the face of the earth every living creature I have made." (Genesis 7:4) The writer makes it plain that God did this; science needs to back off and respect the miracle involved.

If you had been there, would you have been surprised to see him using *no natural process* to bring about the Flood? Using a miracle, in other words, just like the other times when he needed to solve a problem? Yes, he could have tipped some continental plates to bring on the Flood, but the point is that those plates weren't poised for a catastrophe and all it took was a nudge. If that's how he caused the Flood, moving them was no less a miracle than the Flood itself. The Flood was to destroy sinners; natural events don't come about, however, in response to sin — only miracles do.

We moderns are especially prone to the sin of scientific pride. You will often feel that nagging little doubt in the back of your mind when you read a story of a miracle. This can't be true, it will tell you; there must be some plausible, reasonable explanation for what is going on here. They were just naive back then, ignorant and backward, and they called things miracles that we understand very well nowadays. But you can't let yourself be persuaded by these nagging doubts. When the Bible says that something was a miracle, then it was a miracle — by God's definition. If that same thing happened in our day it would be no less of a miracle.

If you allow yourself to doubt what the Bible says, you are giving up the truth — and when you do that you are open to all the attacks that the enemy will throw at you. Our modern Church is almost helpless in the face of countless enemies right now, and a major reason for that is that she gave up the doctrine of the Word of God being *truth* and nothing less than truth. The day will come when everyone will see how wrong science has been about the things of God. It doesn't have the spiritual equipment or categories to understand what the Bible was talking about. We have to hang in there with an unshakable faith in what it says, in spite of what the world wants us to believe.

There is only one proper response to a miracle from God: *believe it*. If understanding the science of a miracle was necessary, then we would all have to be scientists to be believers. And if we can explain a miracle scientifically, then we would be able to duplicate it (theoretically!) — and who then would need God? But if a miracle is something that stymies the experts and brings joy to God's people, then it has an important place in our faith. The least educated saint can know more about what happened than any scientist will.

Kinds of miracles

There are two kinds of miracles that God does:

Physical miracles — These are when God touches the physical world and makes impossible things happen that anybody can see. For example, the miracle of creating the world in six days; the miracle of the Flood; the miracle of splitting apart the Red Sea; the miracle of Jesus walking on water; the miracle of turning water into wine. Everyone who was there when it happened (obviously nobody was at the Creation!) saw it happen and were witnesses that it did happen (sometimes unwilling ones, for example in the case of the Pharisees who witnessed Jesus' miracles).

This kind of miracle is what fascinates everyone, whether they are believers or not. Contrary to all laws of nature, God does something that looks like magic — only it isn't magic at all but the Creator at work. He manipulates his creation the way he wants it to go without being bothered by its laws. And we can't understand how he did it nor can we duplicate what he did, since *we* are bound by natural laws.

The Lord used physical miracles to do all sorts of things, some of which are these:

For creation: God first made the world through miracle, and he continually made things "out of thin air" in the same way throughout Biblical history. If people needed something, and it wasn't available, then God just made it. For example he rained down manna for the Israelites when they were in the desert. (Exodus 16) He made water flow out of a rock for them when they were thirsty. (Numbers 20) He kept meal in the widow's jars until the famine ended. (1 Kings 17:16) Jesus made wine out of water and bread to feed thousands out of five loaves. (Luke 9:12-17)

For judgment: Some miracles were for the purpose of showing God's displeasure on somebody. They were above and beyond the normal trials of life, which everyone experiences, because they were special acts of God against particular sins. The Great Flood in Noah's day was perhaps the most catastrophic judgment against men's sin that this world has ever seen. (Genesis 6-9) Less destructive but just as obvious was the fire and brimstone that God rained down on Sodom and Gomorrah. (Genesis 19) The earth split under Korah and his followers because they rebelled against Moses and God. (Numbers 16) When the Philistines nabbed the ark of the Lord, cancerous tumors broke out among them until they returned it unharmed to the Israelites. (1 Samuel 5-6)

For correction: Some of the miracles that God did were to correct someone's direction or correct a circumstance that was getting in the way. The most notable of these was when he made Balaam's donkey talk. He wanted the man's attention and that was definitely an unnatural way to get it! (Numbers 22) One of the prophets lost a borrowed axehead in the water, and God made the axehead float so that he could get it back again. (2 Kings 6:1-7) During battle, when the day threatened to end too soon for a decisive victory over the enemy, God made the sun and moon stand still to give Joshua and the Israelites more time. (Joshua 10) Jesus walked on water to get to the other side of the lake quickly. (Matthew 14:23-33) He also calmed the storm which otherwise would have swamped the disciples' boat. (Matthew 8:23-27)

For redemption: Many miracles were done to save somebody from trouble. In these instances, the people involved were lost unless God stepped in and rescued them from an otherwise impossible situation. For example, the plagues upon Egypt won the freedom of the Israelites. (Exodus 7-11) And splitting the Red Sea gave them a way of escape from Pharaoh's pursuing army. (Exodus 13-14) The serpent of bronze, which Moses held up during the attack of venomous snakes, spared whoever looked upon it from death. (Numbers 21:9) Samson won amazing victories over the Philistines and took the pressure off the Israelites while he was judge. (Judges 13-16) Elijah was fed by ravens during his stay in the desert. (1 Kings 17:1-6) Elisha and his servant were saved from the enemy by

unseen but powerful forces surrounding the city.
(2 Kings 6:8-23) Shadrach, Meshach, and
Abednego were saved from the fiery furnace.
(Daniel 3) Jesus walked through an angry mob
virtually unseen and unharmed. (Luke 4:28-30)
He rescued people from all kinds of sickness and
even death. And he rescued his disciples from
capture in the garden when the Romans came to
arrest him. (John 18:1-11)

But physical miracles are less important than
spiritual ones because the goal is less glorious. The
story of the ten lepers is a good example. They came to
Jesus for healing, and in mercy the Lord healed them all.
As they walked away free from their disease, *only one*
came back to praise God for what he had done. (Luke
17:12-19) Now what had the healing done for the other
nine men? It only extended their physical lives for a
few years and made them more comfortable in this
world. The man who returned to give thanks was the
only one who experienced a spiritual healing, and we
can assume that he is the only one in Heaven right now
if the others never repented.

Physical miracles are designed to impress us with
the power of God — they are a testimony to God's
attributes — but like other physical phenomena *they do
not save the soul.* We make a mistake when we long for
physical miracles in our day; the Kingdom of God is
built on spiritual works and we do well to long for those
kinds of miracles. Jesus said that workers in the Church
can expect to do greater things than the physical
miracles that he did. (John 14:12)

Spiritual miracles — These happen when God touches
the soul and does things that are impossible to do by any
other means. When God hardened Pharaoh's heart
(Exodus 9:12) he did a miracle, because Egypt was
shuddering under the heavy hand of God and anybody in
their right mind would have gladly let Moses lead the

Israelites out. But God wanted glory, and one of the ways he was going to get it was to make Pharaoh so stupidly stubborn that by the time God was done with him there would be nothing left in Egypt to rule over!

A positive example is in the story of the centurion who came to Jesus for healing for his servant. (Matthew 8:5-13) Jesus marveled at the centurion's faith: here was a Gentile who could see what Jews, supposedly God's special people, couldn't see! He saw Jesus as the Master who could speak and heal from a distance; the Jews only saw a carpenter and a troublemaker. Only God could make this Roman soldier see the glory of Christ. Another example was when Peter testified about the true nature of Christ. (Matthew 16:13-17) Again, this is something that only God could make him see.

Spiritual miracles are much more difficult to do, and much more important. When Jesus healed the paralytic man lowered to him through the roof, the Pharisees grumbled at the way he started out: he *first* forgave the man his sins. Notice how he answers their thoughts:

> "Which is easier: to say to the paralytic, 'Your sins are forgiven,' or to say, 'Get up, take your mat and walk'? But that you may know that the Son of Man has authority on earth to forgive sins...." (Mark 2:9-10)

The spiritual job at hand, when a miracle is necessary, is staggering if you can understand it. To heal a man of his paralysis is one thing; but to turn a sinful rebel into a saint, in such a way that he will never be a rebel again in all eternity, is quite another thing! And to make him into a child of God is an act of creation that far surpasses anything that this physical world has ever witnessed. Yet these are only two of the many, many kinds of spiritual miracles that God is capable of doing, and intends to do, for all his children.

Forgiveness / cleansing: One of the most astonishing acts of forgiveness recorded in the Bible is the time that God forgave David of his sin of adultery and murder. To be a king over God's people, and a "man after God's own heart", and a leader in spiritual worship, and then to be caught red-handed with gross sins like these would have made an ordinary man live with guilt the rest of his life if he didn't actually kill himself! (See Judas' response to *his* crime — Matthew 27:5) But in Psalm 51 we read about the state of David's heart: the Lord caused him to repent and throw himself upon God's mercy, and receive the forgiveness that can only come from God. He got up and went on *guiltless* after this. The finger of God cleansed his soul from his sin so completely that it never got in his way again. There are many people who wish they could get rid of their guilt so easily — but it was the Lord who did it for David.

Knowledge of God: When Jesus asked his disciples who people said he was, he got various answers — all wrong. Peter, however, saw who Jesus really was: the Messiah, the Son of the Living God. Everyone else was expecting a magician or at least a king to start an earthly realm. Peter, however, saw that the One God had come into the flesh and was showing men his Heavenly glory. The only way he could have seen this is if the Father himself opened up his eyes to see it. (Matthew 16:13-17)

Life: While dying on the cross, Jesus reached out to the thief beside him and comforted him with some good news: soon, he told him, you will be with me in Paradise. (Luke 23:39-43) That seems strange for two men who are dying to talk about life! But it was no idle promise: this man who deserved to die was hours away from an undeserved eternal life — made possible by the death of Christ.

Child of God: The story of the Canaanite woman who pled with Jesus to heal her daughter has always fascinated me. (Matthew 15:22-28) At first Jesus seemed to put her off by refusing to give her what he said was only for "the children" — meaning children of Abraham. It was an important point! The Lord gave a covenant to Abraham that was for him and his seed — meaning, as many thought, just the Jews. But Christ here finds a spiritual daughter of Abraham because she displays the *faith* of her *father* (see Romans 4 on this). So Jesus actually *was* keeping the promise of the covenant when he granted her wish: she really was, as it turns out, a child of God. Remember that Jesus said that God could make children of Abraham out of rocks? Well, here he made one out of a Gentile.

Spiritual Gifts: It takes a miracle from Heaven for a man or woman to be able to help build an eternal kingdom. God doesn't want volunteers in his work; he wouldn't entrust such precious work to untrained people. So he picks them and trains them in his ways, with his Spirit, so that they are able to do amazing things that they ordinarily couldn't have done. Take Peter for instance. Starting out as a fisherman, he followed Jesus for at least three years (through many ups and downs!) until the Lord was taken away into Heaven. Discouraged, he returned to fishing. Then suddenly the Spirit comes down on him and he preaches a sermon — and *three thousand people* believe and become the first wave of the new Christian Church. (Acts 2) There is no way to explain such a thing in human terms. It is plain that God made Peter skillful in the work of building a foundation for the Church.

These are the kinds of miracles that you will find throughout the Bible. The common denominator for all these miracles, however, is that God himself did them without the help of the world or its system. What happened was impossible: nobody could duplicate it or even understand it because God bypassed normal processes that we would have used if we were trying it. They were all necessary because the purposes of God required that, at that particular moment in history, something had to be done. The world couldn't do it, men couldn't do it, so God did it.

Results of miracles

As we saw already, God doesn't do miracles just to entertain us. He has good reasons for doing things through miracles instead of through the natural course of events. It boils down to this: when affairs get to a point that something is necessary for the next step in God's plan, and the world can't provide what is necessary, then God himself does it through a miracle.

The Lord certainly doesn't mind that we depend on the world working the way it does, and that we use its normal ways of doing things in order to live. He set it up this way on purpose! He doesn't intend to rain down manna on us as he did the Israelites; in fact, even when *they* got to the Promised Land the manna quit coming. Normal life doesn't need miracles.

But God has plans for us that are far more important than living in and enjoying this world. From the very beginning of man's history God intended to address the problem of sin once and for all. He intended to build a kingdom that is not of this world to replace the fallen one that man so miserably ruined. These are two issues about which he can expect no help at all from earth. So, when he began work on these issues, he kept having to throw in a miracle to move along to the next step of the plan because neither man nor the world was able to contribute to the plan in any way.

For example, when Moses led the Israelites out into the desert (after being freed from Pharaoh and slavery) he brought them to Mt. Sinai where they met with God. Now consider the circumstances: here was a new people about to move north to claim Palestine as their homeland. But they had nothing going for them! They had no idea how to rule themselves. They had been slaves until just weeks ago and were embarrassingly naive when it came to forming a nation. Something had to be done to pull them together and equip them to be the nation that God wanted them to be. A miracle, therefore, was in order. Moses met God on Mt. Sinai and received there two tablets of stone, "inscribed by the finger of God" (Exodus 31:18), and with this Law they became a nation. If God wouldn't have done this for them, there would never have been such a thing as a Jewish nation or King David or even the Lord Jesus himself. The miracle, then, was a critical step in the plan that God had for his people; everything that followed depended on this miracle.

We may not always know why a particular miracle happened, but we can know for sure that God felt it was necessary — things were in a crisis and the world couldn't produce what was necessary. The result, then, of every miracle is another piece of God's plan falling into place. If the Lord would let history run its own course, the Kingdom of Heaven would never come to earth because men don't want it nor can they make it happen if they did want it. In order to override the natural tendency of this world to deteriorate and die, the Lord continually directs affairs with his hand — through miracles, in other words. Then he is assured that all things will be subject to him, and all his purposes will come to pass, and everything will glorify him.

That's the long range reason for miracles. We've already seen some of the short range reasons — his glory, motivation for us to ask for the same things, weaning us from the world, and so on. All of it adds up to building a unique kingdom in which we will live always by the hand of God and won't look to created things anymore for anything we need. In fact, this is the primary characteristic of Heaven — when we finally leave all the earth support system behind and we live directly from the hand of God, with nothing standing between us and him ever again.

Faith and miracles

For as wonderful as miracles seem to be, you wouldn't think that there would be such a problem about them. But there is. It seems that, of all the things in the Bible that most people have problems with, miracles stand at the top of the list. If it weren't for the miracles in it, people would believe the Bible much quicker than they do.

There are many reasons for unbelief. People might not like the way God does things; they might be afraid that they will have to change if they start believing in God; they might not like the unknown — and with God, we are entirely at his mercy and don't know what he might do with us tomorrow. Whatever the reason, perhaps miracles give them the most problem because, in them, God comes so close to us. This isn't doctrine about Someone up in the sky keeping his distance, but the touch of his hand.

Children don't have any problems believing the miracles, and some Christians accept them with the same childlike faith. Whatever the Bible says happened, they believe it — no problems. Jesus demands that kind of faith from all his followers: "I tell you the truth, anyone who will not receive the kingdom of God like a little child will never enter it." (Luke 18:17) And the kingdom runs on miracles — if you are going to be a faithful Christian, you have a lot to get used to in this area of miracles.

Other people who *had* to believe in the miracles were the ones who were there and saw them happen. Sometimes they welcomed the miracle, sometimes they hated and resented it (for example, the Pharisees); but they couldn't argue the fact that it *did* happen.

But most people today have a hard time believing that such incredible things could have happened then. Instead of having a childlike faith, they have typical adult reactions to the story. An adult knows how this world works — he depends on it working the way it does — and he doesn't like anything that would upset *the way* he gets what he needs *from the world*. That's his first problem about miracles. His second problem is that he doesn't like any situation in which he himself isn't in control of things.

The Lord upsets both of these attitudes when he works a miracle. *First*, the miracle shows that God does things the way he wants, not the way we want. Miracles don't depend on anything in this world; God does the impossible without resorting to any of the normal means that we are used to using. We have to turn *away* from this world if we want God's help. *Second*, since the Lord does miracles to solve our real needs, it's not up to us to tell him what to do and when to do it. Adults like to make those decisions for themselves, but God never acts when we think best. We can see that in these stories of miracles and it bothers us that he is so much in control over what he chooses to do. *Third*, the miracles teach us to depend on God alone for what we need. Again, adults don't like to do that — they don't want to have to depend on anybody. They would rather go without than lose face and admit that they need help. In a miracle, however, the Lord does something that we can't do but desperately need. No miracle, no salvation or life! Do without his miracles and you will die.

The presence of God causes sinners to shrink away and hide. Sin means not doing what God said to do, doing what we want instead, and being content to live without God in all things. Sin is destroying us as a result, as you can imagine, since we by nature need the things that God does or we will die. The solution to his dilemma is for a person to have a sudden revelation that he is in desperate need of God, and that God is the very thing that he needs in his sinful state, and then go to the Lord for what he needs. This is faith overriding all the objections and hesitancy and asking for what only God can do. Miracles test the genuineness of a person's faith, not because it's a good intellectual exercise but for this reason: without miracles you will die, and only through faith will you accept miracles.

Let's take the story of Creation for an example. There's no getting around the fact that the text says, in plain English (and it's just as plain in the original Hebrew!) that God created the world in six days. Now there's nothing wrong with that idea. Evolution takes just as much faith to believe as divine Creation! Yet people have come up with all sorts of alternate interpretations of the words and phrases in the story, to blunt the impact of the fabulous miracles described there. Faith says "Yes, that's the way the world came to be; God created it by command." Unbelief can't stand the thought for several reasons: first, it runs opposite to common sense, and we are proud of how wise we are in commonsense matters. Second, it isn't scientific — and our science is able to explain anything for us. Third, it would mean that we aren't masters of the world — and we can't abide the thought that this world belongs to someone else who decides its fate. Fourth, if the world was made so quickly by miracle, then anything could happen *now* in the same way! And people don't like that thought, especially when it comes to the subject of how God intends to *end* the world he made. (2 Peter 3:1-13)

But the story of the Creation is also a shibboleth for people. It's a test to see how you are going to get along with the rest of the Bible. If you can't believe the first story in it without twisting it to suit your taste better, then you aren't going to take the rest of it at face value either. If Creation is too much for you to believe, will the sacrifice of Christ be too much for you also? If you don't like God's explanation for the world around you, what are you going to do in matters of salvation and the Church — which you can't see? I don't think it's accidental that this massive miracle stands at the doorway of the Bible: over its arches is written the message, "Whoever enters here must enter *in faith*."

When and where?

There is one other thing that you need to watch for when reading about a miracle in the Bible; it is subtle and you need to study it to see this. Miracles are like hot-house plants: they need the right conditions in which to grow. God did a miracle when someone was in the right place and time to receive it.

We already saw that the point of a miracle is this: it is something that only God can do. Man can't possibly hope to do it himself, even though he needs it desperately. So when would you expect God to do this thing? When man respectfully stays on his side of the line! If we insist on doing things our own way, God will refuse to do it for us. He will not help those who don't want his help. But if someone knows that only God can do this, and if they *wait* on him until he does it, he will honor their faith and answer their prayers.

For example, the Pharisees had tremendous problems with Jesus. They already had their religion worked out to please themselves, and they considered him to be nothing more than a troublemaker trying to disrupt the system. He, therefore, refused to help them. "It is not the healthy who need a doctor, but the sick. I have not come to call the righteous, but sinners." (Mark 2:17) In another place (his hometown where he grew up and everyone knew him from his childhood) he couldn't do many miracles there — because of their lack of faith. (Matthew 13:54-58) If people don't want God around, if they insist on doing God's work themselves, then he won't do anything for them.

But when someone realizes that he is lost unless God helps him, then the atmosphere is right for a miracle to occur. Faith is a sweet aroma to God; he loves it when he senses it in us. Jesus smelled faith in the Roman centurion right away, and he marveled at this man who could believe when God's own people couldn't. (Matthew 8:5-13) In fact, this story shows very well the awareness of a sinner in need of God's help. The soldier said he understood these matters of authority: Jesus, being Lord, was in the *only* position to command the sickness, and the Roman was respectfully submitting the matter to him and waiting on him. These things must come from the Lord, not ourselves.

Notice, then, in the stories of miracles that the conditions are right for them to happen.

An example

In Numbers 12 we read about a miracle that had both positive and negative results! The story is this: while the Israelites were out in the desert, between Egypt and the Promised Land, Miriam (Moses' sister) and Aaron (Moses' brother) got jealous of their brother. He was the leader of the Israelite nation and was doing many things that made him important in everyone's eyes. Miriam and Aaron wanted some of the glory! They complained about it, and the Lord heard them:

> "Has the LORD spoken only through Moses?" they asked. "Hasn't he also spoken through us?" And the LORD heard this. (Numbers 12:2)

The Lord didn't like it a bit. What they were doing was putting both him and Moses into question! It was bad enough that they wanted to be more important in the community; the bigger problem, however, was that they were making it look as if Moses wasn't very important, that anybody could do his job.

Here was the problem:

Moses' ministry was at stake: What Moses was doing with the Israelites was far more important than anybody realized at the time. Not only did he lead them out of Egypt, he was laying the groundwork for a new nation. To survive in their new land they needed laws to live by, a Temple ceremony to worship God by, a history of where they had been, advice on what they should do and watch out for in the future, and so on. In the meantime he was tied up with being a judge and general and priest and trip leader on their way through the desert. He had a tremendous amount of work to do! Add to this the fact that *all future generations of Israelites* would depend heavily on the work he did during these 40 years, and you can begin to see how important his work was.

Now if Miriam and Aaron could successfully put any of his work into question, how could he have any credibility left for his own and succeeding generations? Why shouldn't others, whenever they wanted and on whatever pretext they chose, decide not to follow Moses and what he wrote? The entire plan of God for the nation of Israel would fall apart before it hardly got started. Think of how much Bible history and doctrine would never have happened if someone took Moses out of the picture!

The glory of God was at stake: Miriam and Aaron weren't only despising Moses' character. They were also saying, in effect, that God's work is something anybody could do and the Lord has to do things the way *we* think best. They were wrong on both counts. First, the person that the Lord chooses to do his work is specially equipped to do that work. God doesn't want volunteers but Spirit-trained people to work in his kingdom. Second, the Lord *alone* decides who will do the important work of the kingdom. He doesn't consult with us, he doesn't do things to please our sense of justice, and he doesn't intend to bless our work (even if done in his Name) when we stick ourselves out there on the limb without his authorization.

Moses was doing all this work in God's Name — which means he had God's orders, God's authority, God's wisdom, God's power. This was God's work from first to last. It wasn't something that Moses was making up for his own glory! This wasn't a game that anybody can play the way they want. These two rebels had to be taught to fear God because, when it comes right down to it, it was the Lord they were despising.

So a miracle was definitely in order. Moses had no answer for them except to wait on the Lord. Anything he would have said or done would have looked bad on him, because he was the one under discussion. What if he would have come to his own defense? Everyone would have said that he was acting out of pride and actually wanted his brother and sister out of the picture, so that he would get all the glory. And of course he could work no miracle on his own, to dazzle them with his power, since he knew very well that only God could do such a thing. So he was helpless in the face of this personal attack. But something had to be done or real damage would happen to God's cause and Moses' credibility among the Israelites, as well as to later generations.

God's anger burned against them, and the cloud that was over the Tent of Meeting rose and left them. There stood Miriam covered with leprosy! All Israel witnessed the event. Leprosy, as you probably know, was the plague of plagues in those days; nobody was allowed near a leper and the leper was under orders to leave the camp before he infected anybody else with the disease. This was a staggering blow against Miriam, something that she would never live down for the rest of her life. She did have to leave the camp, but only for seven days, because the Lord healed her of it after that and she returned to the camp.

How did this miracle happen? Nobody can say! One minute she was OK, and the next she was covered with leprosy. Leprosy doesn't happen that quickly, not under any conceivable circumstances. This was, obviously, the hand of God and nothing else. Moses couldn't have done it, the virus that causes it couldn't have brought it on so quickly — there just isn't any reasonable explanation other than God gave it to her instantly. There it is.

What were the results of this miracle?

Moses' reputation shot up immediately. *First*, the miracle proved to them that they were wrong in this matter and Moses was right. Moses was specially chosen for this work; they weren't. *Second*, God further explained to them just how special Moses was. I wish I had a chance to get into this subject more, but it's not very pertinent to our point of miracles. Moses was a special kind of prophet: no other Israelite prophet was like him except for the Lord Jesus. Only the two of them could claim to see the Lord and hear his voice. *Third*, look who Aaron turns to for the next miracle of undoing what the first one did! He pleaded with Moses (whom he had just despised a few minutes before) to intercede with God and take away this curse on their sister. *Now* he has a proper attitude toward this man of God, brother though he be. From now on he will look at Moses with a profound respect and be ready to listen to whatever he tells him. So will all the succeeding generations of Israelites when they read this story.

They repented of their sin. Notice their immediate reaction when the miracle occurred: they realized, probably because God was so powerfully there among them and he is *holy*, that they had primarily offended *God* with their sinful attitudes. But they didn't want to leave things that way. They wanted God to forgive them of their sin and cleanse their hearts so that they would never say or do such things again. This miracle, though a physical one, had spiritual results.

They turned to God. God got glory this day. The miracle pointed out the fact that the Lord was working through Moses, making all the decisions and claiming all the credit. The Lord was the one behind it all. The Israelites only saw Moses, and only heard what he said. But when Moses claimed that he was speaking the very Word of the Lord, it was true — and woe to that person who didn't believe that. The purpose of the miracles that God worked through Moses was to show plainly that this was not a religion of man's doing, but something that God made from beginning to end. It should strengthen *our* faith too, since Jesus is called "the author and perfecter of our faith." (Hebrews 12:2) Our Christianity is of God, not man; it is based on miracle, not on the natural events and processes of this world.

Questions to ask

You have to get used to asking questions when you study the Bible. If you just read the story and move on to the next one, you will miss most if not all the important truths that the story contains. Just like any other subject that we can apply our minds to, only the *diligent* student will find useful information in the Bible.

When studying a miracle you should find out all the details involved. Ask these kinds of questions:

- *What are all the circumstances?* Who was involved? When did it happen? What did the miracle consist of? What part of Biblical history did it occur in? (There seemed to be periods when miracles happened more frequently, and they seem to be associated with particular people.)

- *Why was the miracle necessary?* What events brought it about? What problem did it address? Was someone in need, or was it another piece of God's overall plan? Was God's glory at stake? Did man's sin make it necessary, or was it something that was needed that the world couldn't provide?

- *Why wouldn't it do to let man take care of the problem?* Remember that a miracle is something that God does, not man; for some reason God didn't want man to take care of this problem — hence the miracle.

- *What happened after the miracle?* What were the results? Did men change — for better or worse? Was there an act of judgment in it? Did revelation occur, or salvation, or punishment, or blessing? And what happened to God's glory and kingdom because of the miracle?

- *What did God use in bringing about the miracle?* Did he use the obedience or disobedience of man? Did he use things of this world? Or did he do it out of nothing? If he did use something, did it really contribute anything to the miracle itself or was it just a springboard for an impossibility — in other words, could it have happened apart from the thing used just as easily? If so, why do you think God used it in the first place?

- *Show proofs that this miracle came from God and had no help at all from created things.* Demonstrate that the answer needed for the problem cannot be found in creation, nor in the wisdom or abilities of man; show also that God does have those abilities and wisdom needed. Find details in the story that purposely point to the impossibility of the thing.

- *How is this miracle different from the way we would have tried to solve the problem?* What would we have used? How would we have gone about it? What part of the problem would we have tried to solve (if not all of it, since we *may* realize our limitations!)? How successful are we at trying to do this same thing our own way? Do we still try anyway?

- *What does this miracle teach us about God?* What kinds of things does he want to work on? What problems does he address with a miracle? How does he solve problems in this world — can you categorize the problem with the kinds of miracle he used to solve them? Does it tell you anything specific about his insight, power, skill, patience, ways, anger, love?

- *Does this miracle have any application to your own life?* Do you have those same problems? Are you looking to yourself or some authority or power in this world for the answer instead of looking to God? Is this story trying to persuade you to look to the Lord instead? What can you expect from the Lord if you wait on him for the answer?

Discussion Questions For Miracle

- Why are miracles always associated with God?

- What are the deceits of the enemy? (See Matthew 24:24)

- What do we need that this world doesn't have?

- How do you know that it is God doing the miracle?

- What kinds of things in the Church should be miraculous events? How could you tell when they happen?

- What is happening in a miracle that science can't grasp or explain? And what enables scientists to do their work that miracles bypass?

- Have physical miracles ceased since the days of the apostles? If so, how do you account for many modern "miracles"? What could be a test to determine their genuineness?

- Must we believe anyone's claim that a miracle has occurred based on Matthew 12:22-32?

- Do we need physical miracles now? If not, what do we need?

- What are the spiritual miracles? How do these happen in the Church today?

- **Why is the modern Church so embarrassed when talking about miracles to unbelievers?**

- **Why do unbelievers need to hear about miracles?**

Key Three: Ways

Key Three: Ways

Probably very few people have considered what God is like from the point of view of personality. They learn the things he has done, and the attributes that describe him (like being eternal, holy, righteous, and so on) but they don't know much about him *as a person*. So they read the stories in the Bible as if they are only history lessons about someone who is far away and strange to us.

Well, the Lord *is* strange to us — not the least because he is God and we are only his creatures. We will never understand things from his point of view, since we will never be him. But we *can* get some fascinating insights into his personality. He opened himself up in his **ways** so that we can understand what kind of person he is. This revelation wasn't accidental, nor is it hard to discover if you are keeping your eyes open. The ways of the Lord draw us closer to him than just memorizing data about him.

Strangely enough, this subject has been little studied. You won't find an entry in Naves Topical Bible, for example, for "the ways of the Lord." Yet it is one of the most powerful principles in the Scriptures for understanding and working with God. It deserves close attention.

The Lord has ways

The Lord has ways of doing things. So do you — you prefer to go at things in a certain way, and you like your surroundings to be a certain way. God is a person, more than an impersonal force that guides the universe along. We should expect to see characteristics in him that make him more personal to us.

When we speak of "ways", what we mean is this: the *road* that we take to reach a goal, or the *method* that we use to achieve a certain end. It isn't the goal or the end that we want to look at here, but the *means* of getting there.

The Bible actually says a lot about the ways of the Lord:

> *As for God, his way is perfect.* (Psalm 18:30)

> *The way of the Lord is a refuge for the righteous.* (Proverbs 10:29)

> *Show me your ways, O* LORD, *teach me your paths.* (Psalm 25:4)

> *As the heavens are higher than the earth, so are my ways higher than your ways and my thoughts than your thoughts.* (Isaiah 55:9)

God has unique traits that distinguish him from everyone else. He has opinions about things that explain why he does things the way he does. He uses certain methods for achieving his goals, for doing his works. We ought to be able to see these kinds of things about him when we read the Bible, since he wants to make his ways known to us.

But this knowledge also comes from living with him. For example, if you knew someone's name and address you could say that you knew something about that person. But if you went and lived with that person, then you would, over time, learn much more about them than just facts! You could observe them in action, how they arranged their home, what they liked and didn't like. You would get to know them well enough to predict what they would do in a particular situation. In fact, if you lived by the rules of the house, you would probably have to change your ways and preferences to get along with them in their house!

When you study God from the standpoint of his ways, you are going to find out these kinds of things about him. Suddenly you begin to see patterns in his works, common elements across all the stories that show you the same traits over and over. You begin to see that God prefers certain ways of doing things. It is also obvious that, being the Master of the house, he expects everyone to do things his way! You can see then the importance of learning what his ways are so that you can get in step with him.

Knowing his ways gives you a deeper understanding of God than just knowing doctrines about God. The doctrines are good, and you must know who he is so that you don't mix him up with false gods. But knowing his ways means you are getting close to him, you are living with him, you are walking with him and working with him. This comes from an intimate acquaintance, not just textbook learning.

Where will you learn his ways? From the Bible! The Scriptures show you his ways in action. It won't always be spelled out in so many words, but you are supposed to dig deeper than a superficial level. After a long string of lessons in the desert, for example, the Israelites were supposed to understand the way God liked to do things. Anybody with spiritual insight would have begun to see patterns in the work he was doing. Did they?

> Do not harden your hearts as you did in the rebellion, during the time of testing in the desert, where your fathers tested and tried me and for forty years saw what I did. That is why I was angry with that generation, and I said, "Their hearts are always going astray, *and they have not known my ways.*" So I declared on oath in my anger, "They shall never enter my rest." (Hebrews 3:8-11)

Let's look at what happened when they didn't know God's ways. When they arrived at Canaan they still didn't understand the way God does things, even though he had been teaching them his ways; they rebelled at his command to go in and take the land. So instead of letting them into the Promised Land, he turned them away at the edge of Canaan and sent them back out into the desert for another 40 years *to die there*. It was that lack of understanding that so angered God. You can read about it in Numbers 13-14.

Notice too that the New Testament repeats this warning. That means that we Christians are supposed to learn his ways! He will keep *us* away from the Promised Land too, if we are so ignorant as to miss the lesson in the stories that we have recorded for us in the Scriptures.

So we must learn his ways: they will be life to us, the key that unlocks the power in following God as he leads us through this dark world. Those who walk in the ways of the Lord will succeed against impossible odds and against all conventional wisdom.

Characteristics of his ways

The Lord's ways are not like the ways we do things. As it says in Isaiah, his ways are higher than our ways. (Isaiah 55:9) This means that we are dealing with something that we're not used to seeing. We will have trouble not only understanding his ways, but accepting them!

God's ways reflect his character. When we say that God is holy, this means that he is holy and everything he does is holy. It also means that the way he does things is holy. He is always true to his character, and we should be able to detect this in all of his ways. So we can describe his ways like this:

• ***They are perfect.*** We rely on God so little that our tendency is to not trust him. For one thing, we aren't familiar with his ways or his value system or his goals. So we don't understand him. Another reason we don't trust him is that we don't believe that his way of doing things really works.

But "as for God, his way is perfect; the Word of the LORD is flawless." (2 Samuel 22:31) There just isn't a better answer to our problems. He has a way of creating and providing and caring and bringing to fruition that leaves one in absolute wonder. He knows how everything has to fit together. He knows the danger we are in and has taken measures to protect us. He reckons what it will take to save us, to bring us out of sin and death and lift us up to his kingdom of light. If we could see how wise he is, how interested he is in us, how painstakingly he moves everything around for our sake, we would feel more like Paul did about God's ways: "I know whom I have believed, and am convinced that he is able to guard what I have entrusted to him for that day." (2 Timothy 1:12) And that was in spite of the suffering and persecution that he had to endure during his ministry.

The Lord has perfect ways to finish the job of sanctification in you — he wants you to be perfect, not flawed. His ways are painful at times, which makes us think that he doesn't know what he is doing or that he doesn't have our best interest in mind. But faith knows better: a Christian has to hang in there as God works out his ways in us. "Perseverance must finish its work so that you may be mature and complete, not lacking anything." (James 1:4) God knows what he is doing even when we are so caught up in the pain and trial that we can't see our Father's steady hand.

The Lord brings good things out of an otherwise unpromising sinner; only he knows how to do that. It's his Word, after all, that is the miracle worker. Of course we don't have much faith in what God is doing! All we know is the imperfect and powerless world system that we are a part of. We don't know much about this power from Heaven that changes the world. But "as the rain and the snow come down from Heaven, and do not return to it without watering the earth and making it bud and flourish, so that it yields seed for the sower and bread for the eater, so is my Word that goes out of my mouth: it will not return to me empty." (Isaiah 55:10-11) A power from Heaven! It "overcomes the world" and achieves everything that God wants to see in you. You wouldn't think that a book has the power to change a sinful heart to a heart full of grace, but that's the way God likes to do it.

• ***They are precious.*** God's treasures aren't like the empty promises of this world; we will find in him real, satisfying solutions to our problems. We just have to get used to seeing treasures in strange dress!

For example, Christ claimed that our lives couldn't be built on anything more solid than God's ways. "Everyone who hears these words of mine and puts them into practice is like a wise man who builds his house on a rock." (Matthew 7:24) No storm that the world can throw at you will upset you if you are doing things God's way. Even death can't take away your reward. And God's ways are what Jesus had been talking about in this passage — Matthew 5-7.

"I walk in the way of righteousness, along the paths of justice, bestowing wealth on those who love me and making their treasuries full." (Proverbs 8:20-21) The Lord's ways are worth following because they lead to a full and joyful life — not as the world counts joy, but the eternal joy that we have when we discover the Kingdom of God in our hearts. God plants his spiritual blessings there when we walk in his ways.

When God teaches us his ways, when we sit at his feet and determine to know God's ways instead of our own, he "forgives us our iniquity," he "confides in us," he "releases our feet from the snare," he "guards our lives," he "redeems Israel from all her troubles." (Psalm 25:8-22) Are these things worth having?

Listen to Jesus as he expertly guides you toward what you really want. "If anyone would come after me, he must deny himself and take up his cross and follow me." (Matthew 16:24) Does that make sense? Is death so valuable? Isn't life what we would rather have? But Jesus continues: "For whoever wants to save his life will lose it, but whoever loses his life for me will find it." (Matthew 16:25) He is telling us that the *only way* to keep your life is to lose it for his sake — living as he tells you to live. His way of saving life sounds impossible and ridiculous, but his way will guarantee that you will live again, forever — the world can't make that promise.

"Endure hardship as discipline; God is treating you as sons." (Hebrews 12:7) None of us like to go through hard and difficult times, but faith sees something here that is precious to us — "a harvest of righteousness and peace for those who have been trained by it." (Hebrews 12:11) Once we understand what God is doing, we wouldn't trade his ways for anything else in the world. They make us more pleasing in God's sight.

• ***They are just and holy.*** The closer you get to God, the more obvious it will be to you that he is profoundly holy. "Holy, holy, holy is the LORD God Almighty!" (Isaiah 6:3) But in normal life this is perhaps the least understood and most surprising thing about God's ways. We have a tendency to look for practical solutions, because our problems are very practical. How can I get ahead in the world? How can I make sure that I have enough to eat? Where is my next appointment? Whom must I avoid, and whose favor should I be getting?

But God doesn't see the world in practical terms; he sees it in terms of the gross immorality that fills it. The goals he wants are holiness and justice. He isn't concerned so much with what comfort level we are living at, but whether our hearts are pure. And I mean *pure*! We don't know what purity is until we see him. "Our God is a consuming fire." (Hebrews 12:29) When we get a good view of God, suddenly we understand what life in the kingdom is all about; our priorities change drastically. "'Woe is me!' I cried. 'I am ruined! For I am a man of unclean lips, and I live among a people of unclean lips, and my eyes have seen the King, the LORD Almighty." (Isaiah 6:5)

The Lord pushes his program of sanctification on us whether we like it or not. We will be judged by the state of our hearts, not by our accomplishments. He expects to see righteousness and justice between us, not a superficial peace that allows each person to pursue his own goals of worldly comforts at the expense of others. He has uncomfortable demands on us, in fact, demands that gnaw at the conscience until we either turn away from him or turn to him for relief. The more you know about him, the closer you are to him, the more you can expect a moral change in your life — a change of heart — instead of a change of outward circumstances.

The disciples thought at first that being Christ's follower was going to be a great picnic — here was the fulfillment of all the old prophecies and they were in on it! But as time went on they realized that Christ wasn't interested at all in worldly kingdoms and fame and fortune. The way he went about doing things, in fact, ruined his chances of ever being great in the world's eyes! In the end they ran from him, denying that they even knew him, never realizing that his ways led him to life and victory. The course he chose, however, was by way of the cross, which is a necessary element for all who would follow him.

The Lord is no respecter of persons, and that becomes more evident the more we walk with him. "I now realize how true it is that God does not show favoritism ..." (Acts 10:34) There aren't going to be special favors for you; you won't be allowed to shortcut God's ways when others have to take the long road. He has as much to do in your life, and *through* you to the world and the Church, as anybody else. Don't expect that the closer you get to him the less you will have to bear for his sake, or the less hardship you will have to go through. It may be that he will lead you through easier times than somebody else, or it may be that he will put you through fire. You have to submit yourself to his sense of justice and forget your own ideas of what is fair. (John 21:20-23) Whenever everyone receives the same wages, no matter what they had to suffer through or how long, they grumble against God. But he answers, and justly so,

> Friend, I am not being unfair to you. Didn't you agree to work for a denarius? Take your pay and go. I want to give the man who was hired last the same as I gave you. Don't I have the right to do what I want with my own money? Or are you envious because I am generous? (Matthew 20:13-15)

• ***They lead us to him.*** You will find, as you get to know God's ways better, that they lead you to him. He isn't leading you off into the wilderness somewhere to live on your own; he is leading you out of darkness into the kingdom of light. The shepherd leads his sheep beside quiet waters — the Lord's peaceful kingdom. "I am the way and the truth and the life. No one comes to the Father except through me." (John 14:6) Expect to see your path lead you into God's presence more and more.

Paul prayed that the Ephesians would have the "Spirit of wisdom and revelation, so that you may know him [*the Father*] better." (Ephesians 1:17) Paul says about himself that he wants to "press on toward the goal to win the prize for which God has called me Heavenward in Christ Jesus." (Philippians 3:14) We probably consider such statements to be more fanatical than practical. Religion is good in small doses, we feel, but when it takes over our lives so completely then we aren't any good for the affairs of this world. But we grossly misunderstand the point. It's not a question of *how much* of our lives are assigned to God's business; he has already laid claim on us! We are totally his now, and *everything* we do is for him. We have no options. What we do apart from his expressed will is gross negligence. He isn't interested in anything we do except as it brings us closer to him. Someday he will destroy all our works, except those that were done for Christ — which will survive the fires of Judgment. (1 Corinthians 3:10-15)

"So whether you eat or drink or whatever you do, do it all for the glory of God." (1 Corinthians 10:31) There is some aspect of whatever you are involved in right now that can lead you to God, whether trust in him or hatred of what he hates or pushing for his goals or *something.* This isn't saying the same thing that some pagan groups that claim that "all roads lead to God." Many roads do lead to God, but we don't like to walk them. Sin isn't the way to God, but hatred of sin is. Love isn't the way to God, but love for the true God and for man the image of God is. Man's glory isn't the way to God, but man glorifying God is. God's world touches us everywhere in life, and everything in life is a way to God if we see it from the Bible's perspective.

The better we know his ways, the more we realize how much God is in control of our situation. This God is really King! Paul was in awe of God's ways: "Oh, the depths of the riches of the wisdom and knowledge of God! How unsearchable his judgments, and his paths beyond tracing out!" (Romans 11:33) As his mind staggered in the knowledge of God's ways, he realized how much God's rule extended throughout creation: "For from him and through him and to him are all things." (Romans 11:36) We all live to serve him. All the events in our lives point us to him. We use his borrowed world. Everything we have, we will have to turn back over to him and give an account of what we've done with it to his satisfaction. Our souls belong to him, and so do our children. We are serfs in the kingdom of God, to whom we owe everything. This feeling grows on us the better we know God.

Some of the ways of the Lord

Let's take a careful look now at some of his ways. We won't be able to exhaustively study all his ways, nor will we have time to find all the times that the Bible shows us God working in any particular way. But we can get a good sense of what some of his ways are — and perhaps be more convinced that his ways are different from ours and very powerful.

• ***He works through his people***. There are two kinds of work going on in the world right now: God's work, and everything else. As man is busy building empires and making life more comfortable for himself, the Lord is busy building a new world out of the ashes of the old. The two streams of activity run parallel to each other, and some people can see both sides; but most people can't.

Man is busy doing his work and has little or no time for God's works. He is busy accumulating wealth, building communities and nations (with all the attending governments), building monuments to himself, and seeking pleasure. People are running after food and drink and clothing. (Matthew 6:32) They hate God, they love what this world offers them, and they are pursuing their dreams thinking that they *can* reach them.

The shame of it all is that they think that they are really accomplishing something with all their hard work! They don't want to work on God's kingdom, nor do they want anything to do with spiritual matters. So, as long as they have the will to throw their lives into this world, God lets them work on that while he assigns his children to the really important work!

God's little children are the nobodies, the people who don't amount to anything when it comes to the world's achievements. God's people have been called to work on a far more important job than the unbelievers are working on. In fact, they just don't have the time to make a name for themselves in the world's eyes because God's work takes up so much of their time.

What have they been called to do? *First,* God has given them the task to build the Kingdom of God. God's Kingdom is eternal, it is made up of redeemed souls who will live with God forever, and it doesn't depend on or need anything from this world that we live in now. It runs on the commands of God; he is king there. Once that kingdom is completely built, the Lord intends to destroy this world with all its works and replace it with the newly finished kingdom that his children and he have been working on for thousands of years.

Second, they are building a house for the Lord to live in. The fruit of the Spirit welds the saints together into a place where God loves to live. As the Church grows, as Christians all around the world find their one purpose in the Lord and discover reasons to love each other, we become the garden that God enjoys to walk in. (Song of Songs 4:12 - 5:1)

Third, they are preparing for the day of Judgment. There is a lot that has to be done before that day. Souls must be saved, people have to learn the truth, the enemy has to be fought. The children of God are busy night and day with all their available strength and time to prepare themselves for the Last Day and the great unveiling of God's justice and glory.

This is all going on alongside the world's work, though the unbelievers don't see it. They think that we are wasting our time, dreaming imaginary things like children playing. Only on Judgment Day will they be convinced that we really *were* working on something real!

Now there are certain qualifications that a person has to have before he can work on such important jobs! Not just anybody can volunteer for this work. They have to have the *Spirit of God*, so that they know what to do and can have the strength to do this impossible work. They have to know the *truth* so that they might have unerring judgment. They must live by *faith*, because nobody will even attempt such work unless they can see the spiritual hope on the other side of this dark and discouraging world. They must be *humble*, because they have to ask God for every single thing they need — no room for boasting here! And they must have the *graces* that God provides (love, joy, peace, etc.) because only to the pure in heart will he entrust his precious resources and share his counsel. As you can easily see, the people of the world, no matter how great they are, have none of these qualities and therefore cannot be entrusted with God's work.

Let's look at some examples. While Babylon was busy building empires that would affect the lives of millions and end up in every history book ever written since that time, the Lord chose **Abraham** and sent him to a far-away land to start what seemed at the time an insignificant project. Abraham was a nobody; he could easily leave Ur and nobody would notice. Yet his project was the beginning of the line of Israel, of the Christ himself, and the eternal Church. Who will not realize the greatness of the task that God gave Abraham compared to the mighty kingdoms of men, when that holy race one day rules the universe!

Joseph's life started out on a bad note, it seems, when his brothers sold him into slavery. Being the next to youngest brother didn't put him in a very good position for having anything to say about family affairs! But it turned out that God had far greater things in mind for Joseph, so far above the little affairs of Jacob's family that nobody would have dreamed the critical role that he ended up playing in the events of history. It was Joseph who saved not only Egypt from starvation but all Jacob's family, and because of his important position they had a new home in Egypt to grow into a nation. Pharaoh thought that the Lord put Joseph in Egypt to save the Egyptians. But really the Lord had greater things in mind for the future nation of Israelites who would one day march out by the millions to go to their new home in Palestine.

Moses was brought up and trained for royalty under his adopted parents in Egypt. But the Lord had something much different in mind for this greatest of all the prophets — the foundation, teaching, and leading of the people of God. He left all the glitter of the world's powers and pomp behind to identify with God's people, to take up their cause, even though nobody could understand that. But without Moses there would have been no nation Israel!

Joshua moved the Israelites into Canaan and in the process destroyed most of the people already living there. The Canaanites might have thought that what they were doing was important, certainly more important than whatever this wandering tribe of nomads called Israelites could have wanted. But they learned the hard way that what God wants, man cannot argue with nor even get in the way of. All that we do must take second place to his priorities, and we may even be shoved aside or eliminated to make way for his plans.

One would never have suspected that a lonely widow's life would have much effect on history. Yet God worked strange events in **Ruth's** life and brought her a husband, who turned out to be an ancestor of the greatest of Israel's kings and an important ancestor of Christ. Again we see the Lord using an "insignificant" child of his to bring about the greatest events of the Church.

We could go on, but you can look up the stories of such people as Samuel, the shepherd boy David, Hezekiah as he stood against the great Sennacherib, Ezra the scribe, the despised Jeremiah, the tax collector Matthew, the fishermen James, John and Peter, and Paul the radical Jew. Each of these and many more were pulled out of the mainstream of the world's history — where they may or may not have made a name for themselves — and set to work on God's kingdom. There they accomplished great and lasting results that affected the lives of millions of God's children and will be engraved on the memorials of eternity. The kingdom they built will last forever. The prize that they fought for was our eternal life. They will sit at God's right hand and help rule the universe because of their faithfulness to the cause.

What happens when God's children work on God's kingdom? They get real results! The world's workers accomplish almost nothing for all their hard work; their labor is meaningless and has to be repeated from one generation to the next. (Ecclesiastes 1:8-11) All their wealth disappears when they die; they aren't remembered by the following generation; nothing they do will last for long. Every age insists on doing things their way, as if nobody before them had ever existed and all wisdom is only with them. It's a senseless rat race.

But God's children get *results*. People are brought from death to life; the ignorant are convinced that their lives are meaningless if not lived for God; sinners leave their sin and live in righteousness for a change; the selfish start to see the needs of others and do something about meeting those needs. The work of Christians brings about miracles of grace in the hearts of those who feel the hand of God transforming and remolding the wrecks of our society. Like the touch of Midas, believers are spreading the life of God among those who are dead. The Kingdom of God has come among us and it will never go away; it will still be here when the world ends.

• *__He uses time to ripen__*. Time is a tough thing to try to define, probably because it is one of the most precious and necessary things about life. We have no idea what life would be like without time! It carries us from one event to the next. It separates us from what has happened in the past, and forces us to wait for what will happen in the future. Nobody escapes from the constraints of time, and often we enjoy its benefits.

But God has no need of time. He isn't limited by what limits us; to him, all times are the same. "With the Lord a day is like a thousand years, and a thousand years are like a day." (2 Peter 3:8) He is the Creator of time and he uses it however he pleases without being limited by it at all.

He does, however, use time with great effect in our lives — in fact he purposely does things over time instead of doing them instantly. We, however, would often like to eliminate time, and we don't appreciate the wisdom behind the way the Lord uses time in our lives.

Some of the ways he uses time in our lives are these: **first,** he uses time to give us opportunities. "Bear in mind that our Lord's patience means salvation." (2 Peter 3:15) Right now is the time for the Gospel. Instead of dealing out justice now for what sinners have done against him, he is patient with us and allows us the opportunity to take care of our sin — and get right with him. Instead of weeding out all sinners from the Church, he allows things to continue as they are so he doesn't damage the Christians who also keep sinning against him. (Matthew 13:29) Though many people take his patience for granted (Ecclesiastes 8:11), some take the opportunity he is allowing them and grow spiritually while conditions are ripe. (Hosea 10:12)

Second, he uses time to develop circumstances. He won't usually arrange things right away in our lives. He usually moves things around (sometimes *very* slowly!) over time until the time is ripe for the thing we really want from him. Prayer is a good example of this: Jesus encouraged us to keep praying, even though he doesn't immediately answer us (Luke 18:2-8), mainly because the circumstances just aren't in place yet for him to feel good about giving us what we want. Look at Joseph's life for another example of how God slowly moves the pieces of a person's life until the right time comes for the fulfillment of his promise to them. It just wouldn't have worked any other way! (Genesis 37-47)

Third, he uses time to strengthen faith. All God's people must learn to live by faith. (Romans 1:17) Faith is being able to see spiritual realities in Heaven and live by that, instead of following the lies and deceits of this dark world. What God has for his children is completely different from the things that we usually depend on in this world. It takes a great deal of faith to turn one's back on the life that is so familiar to us and trust in things that we can't see and are still largely untried by us. But the Lord tests our faith (James 1:2-3) to see if it is genuine — to see if it is the kind of faith that will reject the worldly and hold fast to the spiritual. The way he often tests it is over time, through trying circumstances that won't go away even after many prayers. He will answer our prayers, there's no doubt about that. But he won't often answer them right away because of this need to test the quality of our faith. Faith shows its colors the best when it hangs on during trial.

Fourth, God specializes in growth. He sees things as living and part of the whole, and he doesn't like to take a piecemeal approach to anything. Look at how he created the world and the way everything depends on everything else! Take one single thing out of the picture and everything else is in danger of collapse. He is a master at *whole systems*, making a living organism out of many separate parts that couldn't be used by themselves to accomplish what the system does. So when he works in the lives of his people, he will do it in a way that plugs them together with others into a body (1 Corinthians 12:12-30). He puts individuals together into the Church which will one day be presented to him as a beautiful bride. (Ephesians 5:25-27) So be patient, because as he answers your prayers he is also fitting you into the bigger scheme that he has in mind over a vast period of time affecting many more people than just yourself.

Once you start seeing that he insists on doing things over time, the lesson you need to learn about that is to *wait on him*. That's the lesson across the entire Bible, as the following passages will testify:

Psalm 25:3 — those who wait won't be ashamed
Psalm 37:7 — wait patiently on the Lord
Psalm 59:9 — we wait for his strength
Psalm 62:5 — wait only on God
Psalm 65:1 — praise waits for the Lord
Psalm 69:3,6 — my eyes fail waiting on God
Psalm 123:2 — our eyes wait on the Lord
Psalm 130:5 — my soul waits on the Lord
Psalm 130:6 — wait more than watchmen for the morning
Proverbs 20:22 — wait on the Lord and he will save you
Isaiah 25:9 — we have waited and are glad
Isaiah 30:18 — blessed are those who wait on the Lord
Isaiah 40:31 — those who wait on him will renew their
                          strength
Lamentations 3:25 — the Lord is good to them who wait
Hosea 12:6 — wait on the Lord continually
Habakkuk 2:3 — though God's answer tarries, wait on it
Acts 1:4 — wait for the promise of the Father
Romans 8:23 — we are waiting for our adoption
Galatians 5:5 — we wait for our hope of righteousness
1 Thessalonians 1:10 — wait for the Son from Heaven

• ***He wins by losing***. We don't like to lose at anything. In fact, we will do anything to keep from losing! Losing shows weakness; it means that we can't have what we want. Someone has to lose, of course, when there is competition, but we can't stand a never-ending losing streak! Politicians fight for office, businesses fight for the market, students fight for academic honors, and we all fight to get what we can out of life without falling helplessly into failure.

But God has a peculiar way about him: he willingly loses in order to win. The loss isn't just an appearance, either; his loss of honor and glory are real and devastating to the kingdom. But like a shrewd chess player, his loss will soon prove to be a win when the whole story plays itself out. With God, we can put up with some temporary losses when we know that the end of the road will make everything right again.

Consider, for example, the history of the Jewish nation. When Moses led them out of Egypt and into the Promised Land, they had everything going in their favor and a bright future ahead of them. The Lord finally had a people who would glorify and worship him. Not only was this new life a joy to them, the Lord was laying on them a responsibility to be his people — which means that they had to obey his commands or else. God's glory to the other nations was on the line: by the obedience of the Israelites, the pagans could see that God did live among them and bless them. There was a lot at stake here.

But as you can read in the story, they continually failed God and worshipped other gods instead. They refused to obey him. They brought sacrifices to the Temple and yet continued to sin against him. Finally, he had had enough of their hypocrisy and wickedness and sent them off to Babylon in exile. The experiment had failed; God's Name was in disgrace, and the nations laughed at Israel and her God. "By the rivers of

Babylon we sat and wept when we remembered Zion."
(Psalm 137:1)

I believe that if you review the events of the Old
Testament you would see that God's cause has run into
failure and setback throughout history. Many hopeful
starts, and many embarrassing setbacks. Not that God
himself couldn't do what was right and necessary, but
his people have proved false and undependable over and
over. This rate of failure is what the world points to
when they despise the things of the Lord. And the
failures are still happening! Now is supposed to be the
age of the Church, when the Spirit is building the eternal
kingdom from people with renewed hearts and minds.
Love, patience, unity — the Lord promised all sorts of
things in this age. But we run into failure after failure!
It seems that the Church is the place where the *exact
opposite* of Christ's intentions can best be found. These
are real losses among the people of God, and shouldn't
be happening, and yet they are. What is the
explanation?

Yet we can't believe that God isn't in control!
Somehow he is winning even in these failures; we just
have to back up and see the bigger picture. For
example, God must have **glory** — that is the highest
priority in the Kingdom of God, and must be had at all
costs. So he resorts to defeat in order to get glory!
Christ goes to the cross in utter shame and a victim of
man's injustice and wickedness, and what happens?
"Just as Moses lifted up the snake in the desert, so the
Son of Man must be lifted up, that everyone who
believes in him may have eternal life." (John 3:14-15)
In his very shame we see the glory of the Savior dying
for the salvation of his people — whoever will look on
him *there*, in his *death*, will find *life*.

God wants our **souls** — so he bids us take up our
crosses. In order to live, we must die! "What you sow
does not come to life unless it dies." (1 Corinthians

15:36) The old self must die and get out of the way, and in so doing will make room for the new self to come to life and grow strong.

God wants to build a **kingdom**, a holy nation of kings and priests who will honor and obey and worship him. So he scatters the Church! The disciples were scattered soon after Christ's death and resurrection; churches are scattered around the world. There is no visible head for the Church of God and seemingly no organization to any of it — certainly not our way of bringing about a kingdom on earth! Yet we will see, on Judgment Day, a perfect Church that was painstakingly assembled over thousands of years even against all the forces that kept it from being a success in worldly terms.

God wants **justice**; he loves justice. "Let justice roll on like a river, righteousness like a never-failing stream!" (Amos 5:24) Yet even this he willingly puts aside for now, and he lets the wicked get away with murder every day. It seems as if there is no justice in this world! But it's not as if God has changed his standards: someday all the injustices that people have committed *will* be judged and put to right. It's just that now is the day for salvation, and he is unwilling to deal justice to the wicked while the righteous are among them. (Matthew 13:29) But justice is coming, and we will see then that the wicked dug their own graves when they thought they were getting away with something.

So watch the Lord as he uses apparent failure to reach his goals. He isn't out of control; he knows what he is doing. You have to trust him, though, while he leads you through failure and loss and embarrassment and persecution and even death. These are the ways to life and success, whether you can see it or not. For example, Paul learned that the thorn in the flesh was for good reason and he quit pleading with God to take it away when he saw how good it would be for him. (2 Corinthians 12:7-8) It's not that the failure itself was all that good, but that it will lead to greater good. (2 Corinthians 12:9-10)

Besides, failure shows us where the answers really are. They are not in ourselves, they are not in the world where we keep wanting to win. It is a small victory to get more out of life when we have so much waiting for us in Heaven. It is a small success to have one's reputation intact with men when there is greater reward in pleasing God. "What is more, I consider everything a loss compared to the surpassing greatness of knowing Christ Jesus my Lord, for whose sake I have lost all things. I consider them rubbish, that I may gain Christ." (Philippians 3:8) When we feel the sting of defeat and loss, we need to consider that perhaps the Lord is teaching us that we had our hearts set on *the wrong thing* — and we need to change our ways and strive for higher goals.

Losing is often unthinkable, and some Christians are ready to fight for their rights rather than accept failure in their lives. But this is often the way that God works in the world. He allows failure to happen; he allows his people to suffer humiliating defeat. If you win this world you will probably lose your soul in the process. For their own good and the sake of his growing spiritual kingdom, defeat in this world is often the best fertilizer for the tender plants of God's holy people. The foundation of the Heavenly Jerusalem is build on the blood of the martyrs. (Revelation 6:9-11)

• **_He uses a little to accomplish a lot_**. We are easily impressed with big things. We love to look at mountains; we fear the massive power of the atom bomb; we read with fascination the history of the United States as it waged war with powers on both sides of the globe and won; we fear what would happen in our lives if the nation's banking system collapsed. Man loves — and fears — to deal with things bigger than himself; there's so much potential for fast, permanent change.

But God isn't impressed with what impresses us. He created the world, after all, and he is bigger than all of it put together! All the things that impresses us make little difference to him. In fact, what he considers to be big things we take little or no interest in.

A small thing is something we don't notice — or don't want to notice. It has no power of its own, it is helpless, it can't do important work. It has no place in our plans or goals; we find little use for it. And yet these small, insignificant things that we don't want to waste time on may be the most important things we could possibly deal with. Ignoring them may be disastrous!

For example, we consider our sin to be a small thing, of no importance in the great scheme of things. Yet God sees our sin like a huge neon sign flashing in his face and can't see anything else in us. (Isaiah 29:13) We consider God's Word to be a small thing and not worth studying, yet it describes the eternal life that we will need so desperately when this short life is over. (John 17:17) We think that God's grace is a small thing and we can do well enough with the goodness that is in our own hearts, not knowing that our "goodness" is like filthy rags and of no use whatever to God or others. (Isaiah 64:6) We think that our neighbor is of little importance, yet on Judgment Day we will be judged on the basis of how we treated him! (Matthew 25:31-46)

Ironically the things that are big and important to us are insignificant and unimportant to God. Money, comfort, esteem and respect, accomplishments, dangers — God tells us not to worry about any of these things; they aren't worth living for. Jesus told us to give away our money (Luke 16:9). While we work for comfort, God prepares to bring us to death and judgment. (Luke

12:16-21) Working for esteem from men means you will get none from God. (Matthew 6:1-8) None of our accomplishments will achieve what we hope from them, and they will all disappear after our deaths anyway. (Ecclesiastes 2:17-26) And dangers that loom large in this world are nothing to those who find God at their backs. (Romans 8:31)

So, what are the important things to God? He wants a kingdom of righteousness; he wants to defeat the enemy; he wants to save sinners; he wants glory. How is he going to achieve all these jobs? Any one of them are way beyond our little capacities; man has been trying to do things like these from the beginning of time and has miserably failed. How will God do them? With huge budgets? With the great and powerful leaders of the earth? Through cosmic processes that will sweep through puny men's lives and force results upon them?

Strangely, he isn't going to do these things through any big and impressive means. He prefers to use little things, insignificant things that we would never have thought could do the job. For instance, he likes to use **little people** to do his work. Paul refers to this in his letter to the Corinthians:

> Brothers, think of what you were when you were called. Not many of you were wise by human standards; not many were influential; not many were of noble birth. But God chose the foolish things of the world to shame the wise; God chose the weak things of the world to shame the strong. He chose the lowly things of this world and the despised things — and the things that are not — to nullify the things that are, so that no one may boast before him. (1 Corinthians 1:26-29)

Yet through the slaves and women and fishermen of the early church God built a foundation that collapsed imperial Rome and still supports the people of God 2000 years later! He used Abraham, a nobody in Ur, to be the father of the Jewish nation and the father of the eternal covenant given to him and all the faithful. He used David, the runt of the family of Jesse, to be the king of Israel who was the model of the Messiah to come. He used Gideon and his little band of Israelites to defeat the entire army of Midianites. He used a left-handed man (Ehud) to get into the enemy's stronghold when no right-handed man could have done it.

God works through **small things** too. He not only made the massive galaxies in space (that have little to do with us on earth) but also the microscopic germs that keep killing people. We also need to focus our spiritual microscopes on tiny sins that are capable of killing us spiritually; any of those little sins that normally we take no notice of can keep us from fellowship with God. (Psalm 24:3-4; Matthew 5:20; James 4:8-10; Revelation 20:15)

More examples: a little word spoken at just the right time will bring joy and peace to someone's heart. (Proverbs 25:11) A little act of kindness will be your ticket into Heaven. (Matthew 25:40) There are only two things that you need in your religion, both seemingly small and unimportant. (James 1:27)

The Lord works in **small ways**. He builds his kingdom from small beginnings, while nobody is noticing, using little people doing little things, until the world suddenly realizes that God has an unstoppable force that they must reckon with. (Matthew 13:31-33) He wins enemy territory city by city, mile by mile, until it all belongs to him. (Joshua) He helps us conquer our sins one at a time, over periods of time, so that we aren't overwhelmed by obligations and failures. (1 Corinthians 10:13)

While the Lord is using small people and small things, doing his work in small ways, the world takes no notice of what he is doing — because they are only impressed with big things. But someday the small steps of the Kingdom of God will suddenly step out of the shadows as a full-blown, powerful, and overwhelming force that will utterly throw down all the "big" things of this world and set up rule forever. That will be a surprise for those who weren't used to looking for little things.

• ***He works through his Spirit***. The ways of God are mysterious and hard to understand, and perhaps this is true all the more because he prefers to work through his Spirit. We don't know much about the Spirit, and we would have expected God to do things in a more open, physical way that we can understand. But our ignorance of the Spirit's ways is unfortunate: until we learn *how* he goes about doing things, we will see little or nothing of God's works and will never be able to follow him in his ways.

If God had asked our opinion about things, we would have told him to work in these ways: through angels, through physical means, and through us. Angels we can understand, and they make an impressive show in any story. Since we are physical, we understand the laws of how things work in this world and can appreciate what we see happening on that level — we look forward to physical results and are impressed by them. And we love to be the key player in the action: we expect that God will need us to do many things for him.

But actually none of these ways of doing things will work, as far as God is concerned. He wants spiritual results, and neither angels nor physical laws nor man can build a spiritual kingdom. He intends to completely destroy our world at the end of time (2 Peter 3:10); how, then, can he depend on and use any work done by those who are so much a part of this world?

The only way a spiritual kingdom can be built is through the Holy Spirit. If you are paying attention you will notice the Holy Spirit "behind the scenes" all through the Bible; he first shows up, as a matter of fact, at Creation! (Genesis 1:2) When the Lord told Moses to set up the Tabernacle, which was going to be the means of their forgiveness and acceptance with God, he gave the Spirit to the builders of the Tabernacle so that they could make it like the Heavenly Temple. (Exodus 31:1-11; Hebrews 8:5) David, understanding that his role of king was crucial to the life of Israel, pleaded that the Lord not take away his Spirit. (Psalm 51:11)

The Spirit of God does many important things for us that we may not appreciate. He guarantees our inheritance (Ephesians 1:14); he gives us access to the Father (Ephesians 2:18); he reveals the mystery of God (Ephesians 3:5-6); he makes unity in the Church (Ephesians 4:3); he fills God's people with divine blessings (Ephesians 5:18-19); he defends God's people from the enemy (Ephesians 6:17-18) There are many more things he is doing for us; the sum of it all is that he is building a kingdom that "cannot be shaken" (Hebrews 12:27) because it is built on a solid spiritual foundation.

There are two main things that the Spirit of God does: first, *he reveals the world of God to us.* "This is what we speak, not in words taught us by human wisdom but in words taught by the Spirit, expressing spiritual truths in spiritual words." (1 Corinthians 2:13) What used to be hidden and mysterious to us, the Spirit reveals and makes plain and easy to understand. There is much about God that we desperately need to know: for example, his holiness, his power, his wisdom, his love, his wrath against sinners, and so on. We would never know any of this if the Spirit didn't reveal the truth to us and convince us of its truth. Just look at all the people who "know the truth" about God and still sin against him anyway! They are blind to the truth of God and headed down the road to destruction. But those who have the Spirit of God know these truths and have a chance of getting in a better position to please him.

We can't do anything with that knowledge, however, unless someone helps us. That's where the Spirit does the second thing for us: *he gives us power to live in God's world*. When we can't pray, the Spirit helps us to pray in a way that will be pleasing to God. (Romans 8:26) When we can't live a holy and righteous life, the Spirit will give us the graces of God and enable to walk in that way. (Galatians 5:22-25) When we can't fight against the enemy on our own strength, the Spirit will fight the battle for us. (Zechariah 4:6)

As you read through the Bible take notice of all the places where the Spirit of God is mentioned. You will find that he was there at all the important times making possible the critical things in the building of the Kingdom of God. The Spirit was there at Creation bringing order out of chaos. The Spirit moved Moses and his helpers to put together a nation that God would call his own. The Spirit directed Samuel in the choice of David as king of Israel. The Spirit showed Isaiah the vision of Heaven and gave him his calling. The Spirit showed the rest of the prophets the future Messiah. The Spirit came down on Jesus at the beginning of his ministry. The Spirit came down on the apostles at the beginning of the Church. The Spirit continues to come down on God's people, making it possible for them to live in God's graces and do the spiritual work necessary to build the spiritual Temple of God. And the Spirit showed John the glory of Christ and the times to come, when all things in Heaven and on earth will be wrapped up and the Lord will judge all nations. Finally, as the Bible began with the Spirit, it appropriately ends with the testimony of the Spirit. (Revelation 22:17)

As you read about these things, keep in mind that the Lord purposely did them through the Spirit — instead of using the physical means that we would have expected or preferred.

God has many more ways of doing things, though we don't have the time and space here to explore them all. Keep your eyes open for these kinds of things: he uses our faith to do big jobs; he builds up instead of tears down; he uses man; he keeps things simple; he keeps things in balance; he uses variation and creativity; he loves tradition and ceremony (his own!); he hates pride. The more you learn about the way he does things, the better you will know him personally.

Problems about learning his ways

The ways of the Lord give us sinful humans many problems. They are harder to learn than one would think! They don't appeal to our senses nor to our reason, and therefore we end up either not knowing what they are (which is displeasing to him, because he *expects* us to know them) or not wanting to do things his way.

- *__They aren't what we would have expected.__* When we are faced with a problem, we think that we know how to solve it; solving problems is what humans love to do. But it's impossible to solve our spiritual problems in the same way that we solve every-day situations. We are dealing with dangers and damage that sinners can't do anything about. When we try, we only get things more tangled up.

   Then God reveals his way of doing it — and it completely surprises us. We weren't expecting to hear him say that! The rich young ruler figured that he had the answer to eternal life; but when Jesus told him that he must sell everything he owned and follow Jesus, that stopped him. (Matthew 19:16-22) When Naaman wanted to be healed of his leprosy, he couldn't believe that the cure was to dip in the Jordan River seven times! (2 Kings 5) When the Israelites heard that there were giants in Canaan, they figured it was time to turn around; yet here was God telling them to go on in and take the land! (Numbers 13-14)

The main reason that God's ways are surprising to us is that they are based on an invisible reality — God's world. If we could see that (and we won't without the Spirit of God who reveals it to us) then we have no problem stepping out onto thin air, as it appears when we walk in faith. All God's ways are plain when we see the spiritual foundation under them.

• ***They don't sit well with us.*** We don't particularly like the way God does things. God's ways spell trouble for our life of sin; they have a way of homing in on the real problem in our hearts.   When the Pharisees complained about Jesus' disciples eating with unwashed hands (he always did seem to break their traditions!) he answered that the problem was the sin in the heart, not dirty hands. (Matthew 15:17-20)

We won't be able to have our own way if we accept his. He is going to kill our sin and deny our flesh if we listen to him and do things his way.   He told his disciples that the way he was going would crucify the flesh — if they wanted to follow him, they must take up their crosses first. (Matthew 16:24) He said that we must forget trying to build up our treasures here on earth and focus on piling up treasures in Heaven. (Matthew 6:19-20) None of this appeals to our flesh, naturally.

We feel cornered with nobody to help us when God gets close and works on our hearts. We don't know what he is up to or how he is going to work on us, but we don't like the feel of things. God's ways spell doom to the old man.

• ***They are spiritual, we are physical.*** We can define "spiritual" like this: whatever will still be here after Judgment Day. At that time the Lord intends to destroy everything physical, everything of the world, and keep only the spiritual things. We are spiritual creatures because of our souls, but because we were born spiritually dead we cannot appreciate the spiritual side of things. Sin has perverted us so that we can only appreciate what *this* world offers us, the physical side of life.

When Jesus fed the 5000 he had many new followers — but they were only after more physical bread, not the bread from Heaven. (John 6:26-27) God, of course, is Spirit — and his ways rip huge holes in our comfortable little worlds, like an invasion into enemy territory. (Matthew 12:22-23) There is no contest between Heaven and earth; when God moves among us there is a fierce spiritual battle and we must choose sides based on principles that have been strange to us in the past. (Joshua 24:15)

• ***They are holy, we are sinful.*** We are at an immediate disadvantage when we try to do anything in life: our sin trips us up. No matter what we do, it will violate something that God has commanded us. We are doomed to fail from the start; the smell of death (the natural result of all sin) hangs over everything we do. But God is holiness itself, the Law itself. His nature is completely and awesomely holy. His righteousness shocks the world. So whenever he becomes involved in something his holiness immediately comes to the front and is obvious to everyone. That's what offends us so much about his ways: he is aiming at what pleases his holy nature, and we are aiming at what pleases our sinful nature. When the sons of Aaron decided to offer a sacrifice to the Lord, even though it wasn't something that he specifically commanded, he killed them on the spot — and without any apologies offered this explanation for his action:

> Among those who approach me I will show myself holy; in the sight of all the people I will be honored. (Leviticus 10:3)

• ***Our ways head in the opposite direction.*** We couldn't be any more opposite to what the Lord demands of us if we tried! Whatever God wants in our lives, we want the direct opposite. And we aren't standing still, waiting for some occasion to contradict God; we are even now traveling as fast as we can in the opposite direction from God! All our ways are designed to offend God, to try to frustrate his will, to deny the truth of God, to lead others away from God — and usually *before* God has a chance to tell us the right way to go. When Moses came down from Mt. Sinai with the Law of God in his hands, he found all the Israelites — including his brother Aaron the high priest! — worshipping a golden idol. (Exodus 32) Of all things to be doing when God is forming them into *his people*!

• ***We don't understand his ways.*** We have been so long captive to the deceits of our own ways of doing things that we can't get the point when we read God's Word, no matter how many times we read it and no matter how much we try to fit into God's ways. They are beyond us! If we were perfect and had deep spiritual knowledge, we would understand the ways of the Lord. But because we were born in sin and were naturally ignorant of spiritual things, the Lord confuses us with his ways and we can't understand them unless he explains them to us. The disciples just couldn't understand why Jesus kept talking about being killed. (Matthew 16:21-22) The Israelites panicked when the came up to the Red Sea with Pharaoh hot in pursuit; they accused Moses of murder by leading them out into such a predicament. (Exodus 14:10-12) They just didn't understand the Lord's ways of doing things.

You will see one or more of these problems in yourself as you study God's ways. It's bound to happen; don't be surprised when you see it. The point is that you must learn to overcome your resistance to them and train yourself to work with him, not against him. Your ways will never work; his always do.

Reasons we need to know his ways

You may wonder *why* you need to know the ways of God. Isn't he higher than we are? Doesn't he do things his own way without our help? Do we need to know how he goes about things when all we have to do is believe that it will all turn out as he wants it?

For one thing, he doesn't allow us to be ignorant of his ways. "Ignorance is bliss" may work for some things, but not in God's camp! There are many important reasons for knowing God's ways, but perhaps the most fearful one is the threat he holds against those who refuse to learn them. I just can't get away from the warning about this in Hebrews 3:7-11. This is the warning given to Christians, in the age of the Church; it's not just history.

- ***We have to work with his ways.*** There is such a thing as working *with* God instead of against him. If you don't know what is going on, you are probably getting in his way and aren't of any use to him. For example, Peter got in Christ's way because he didn't understand the way Christ was taking to life. When he rebuked Jesus for talking about getting killed, Jesus brought him up sharply: "Get behind me, Satan! You are a stumbling block to me; you do not have in mind the things of God, but the things of men." (Matthew 16:23) Instead of helping Jesus, Peter was getting in the way.

- ***We must avoid our ways.*** Our ways most certainly lead to sin and death. We have had our chance to make the world better: for the last few thousand years that's what man has been trying to do, and failing miserably in the attempt. It's time we stepped aside and let God do it his way. We can get into trouble acting on our first impulses, or according to what seems reasonable to us. For example, "Man's anger does not bring about the righteous life that God desires." (James 1:20) And yet we keep resorting to different kinds of anger and vengeance when we want to stop others from doing what we don't like. This will never lead to life and peace; only God knows how to bring someone to justice without doing a lot of unnecessary damage in the process.

• *His ways are life.* The Lord isn't trying to irritate us with his ways of doing things; it isn't as if he is just an eccentric old man that we have to learn to get along with. He knows what he is doing. When he says that the way to life is through the cross of persecution and affliction, he knows what he is talking about. He has been there already! And when he insists that we be patient and wait on him, while he arranges circumstances slowly to suit his purposes, we will only get ourselves into trouble and do damage to his cause if we jump the gun and do it our own way. Abraham, for example, got tired of waiting on the Lord to fulfill his promise about a son and tried to do it through Hagar. But that wasn't the son of promise, the miracle baby that Isaac was. (Genesis 17:17-21) Ishmael could never be the heir to the covenant. (Galatians 4:28-31)

• *His ways override the world's system.* God steamrolls through the world when he does anything, mainly because he throws us all off track with his strange and startling ways. It's no wonder that Jesus made the claim, "Take heart! I have overcome the world." (John 16:33) It's not that he is going to destroy the world *now* (that will come later) or change the way it works; but he will override its effects in us. What is poison to an unbeliever will become sweet food to the believer. The cross that kills the body will lift the children of God to Heaven. As the wicked do their work of sin and death among us, they dig a grave for themselves on Judgment Day. Though Paul suffered terribly through his years of work for the Lord, he recognized it as the "marks of Jesus" that was helping to advance the kingdom of God. (Galatians 6:17)

• *His ways explain providence.* Once you understand the way that God does things, you won't be so confused about what you see in daily circumstances. For example, by all appearances this world is winning the fight against God; we don't see or hear of God's glory much these days anymore. But since God wins by losing, we shouldn't be so discouraged about the setbacks and failures in the struggle between Church and world, because no doubt the failures are making some thinking Christians review the situation and fall back on more spiritual weapons instead of relying on the world's weapons. (2 Corinthians 10:4) Losing a few battles tends to make determined soldiers look for more effective ways to win the next battle.

An Example

Read the story of 1 Samuel 3-6. Eli, the high priest at the time, was in deep trouble with the Lord concerning his lax oversight of the Israelites and especially his own sons. God cursed Eli and his household with terrifying words: "The guilt of Eli's house will never be atoned for by sacrifice or offering." (1 Samuel 3:14)

Right after this the Israelites, discouraged because of their repeated defeats at the hands of the Philistines, decided to take the ark of the covenant with them into the next battle. (1 Samuel 3:4) They should have asked God first if he intended to fight for them! The battle was a rout: the Israelites lost 30,000 men to the Philistine army. What followed was even worse: the Philistines captured the ark of the covenant! Such a thing had never happened to Israel; it was unthinkable that their God was at the mercy of the heathen. When news of the defeat reached Eli, he fell back in his chair and broke his neck. His sons were killed in battle, and the curse against Eli's house came to pass. It was a dark day in Israel's history. "The glory has departed from Israel, for the ark of God has been captured." (1 Samuel 4:22)

So it seems as if the Lord and his people fell under crushing defeat. But now the story gets interesting! The Philistines took their booty back home and set it up in their temple as a captured god. The next morning they found the image of *their* god, Dagon, face down on the floor before the ark of Israel! They set it back up only to find it smashed the next morning. Something was going on here that they didn't like.

Then the Philistines started breaking out in tumors and dying, and whichever town they moved the ark to, the people who lived there developed tumors. They finally in panic put the ark on a cart, hitched up some cows to it, pointed it in the direction of Israel, and bade it a willing good-bye!

This is a beautiful story about how God pulls a decisive victory out of a crushing defeat. He was never out of control of the situation. Yes, the Israelites had to learn a lesson and they suffered real harm because of their sin. Yes, the Philistines won the day and shamed the hosts of the Lord, even taking God's holy ark into their unholy temple. But they should never have touched that ark! They didn't know that when God falls back in seeming failure, he pulls his opponent down with him, like a Judo expert, and throws him over his head. Of course the Israelites didn't know that either because they didn't understand his ways themselves.

Questions to ask

It's not the easiest thing in the world to discover the ways of the Lord when you are reading the Bible. It requires the Spirit guiding you into all truth, and some determination on your part to keep looking until you uncover his methods. So when you read a passage about something that God did, ask yourself these questions:

- *Is there something going on here that I've seen somewhere else in the Bible?* God keeps using his ways, in many different circumstances, because his ways always work. He is "the same yesterday and today and forever" (Hebrews 13:8) — which means that the ways he started out using early in the Bible, you will see repeatedly throughout the Bible. This is perhaps the biggest help in learning his ways, because it gives us a chance to see them happen in many different circumstances and it shows us that he *does* like to use a particular way when he keeps resorting to it.

- *Is he going about this thing in such a way that it bothers me?*   This is a sure sign that you have uncovered one of the ways of God. God's ways are not like our ways, and he is going to insist that we change our ways to conform to his.   He is challenging us: he wants us to quit doing it our way and listen and watch him for a change. Our ways of doing things don't touch the problem in our hearts like his does; our ways don't save. God's ways work remarkably well in the spiritual areas that we need the most help.

- *What do I need to change to conform to his way?* You are going to see how ineffective you are in your way of doing things, and the proper response is to *quit* doing it your way. It's time to retrain; it's time to change your priorities. Don't do things the way the world always does things. Learn God's ways. Of course this will take a great deal of faith, like Peter stepping out on the water when Jesus called him. But when we see how solid the realities of God are under our feet then we will be more willing to burn our bridges behind us and do it his way for a change.

- *Does it work?*   Go ahead and ask the question, because God wants to prove to you that his ways *do* work — against all predictions to the contrary. Let him prove to you that when you trust him in these ways of his, and do it his way, you can expect his kinds of results. The ways of the Lord always work and they solve the problem completely.

Discussion questions for Ways

- How do we know that God has personality?

- If we learn God's ways by living with him, how do we live with God?

- How are his ways and his works related?

- How can you predict what God will do in a given circumstance? How much of it can you predict?

- What do the ways of the Lord mean for the wicked?

- What do the ways of the Lord mean for the righteous?

- Show how the Lord would do each of these in a local church:

     He works through his people:

     He uses time to ripen:

     He wins by losing:

     He uses a little to accomplish a lot:

     He works through his Spirit:

- Who can learn God's ways?

- **How do you think that success in the Christian ministry relates to knowing God's ways?**

Key Four: Works

Key Four: Works

One of the most obvious truths in the Bible is the fact that God has done many things throughout history. The Bible is the record of God's works; it is a history book from God's point of view. Someone observed once that to study the works of the Lord, one would have to study the entire Bible! But this truth is, perhaps, one of the more subtle points about the Bible's many lessons. Although we can easily read about the works of God, we don't often get the point that it is trying to make about them.

The point is this: we need to know what God's works are because *they tell us what kind of God he is*. Watching him in action does many things for us that are important: it teaches us the truth about him, it increases our faith in him, it teaches us what to expect from him, it warns us not to try such things ourselves, and many more things. What Christian would want to stay in the dark about something that tells him so much about God? Therefore we must learn about his works if we want to please him and if we want to get good things from him.

God's works

It's an interesting thing that, even though we know that the Bible spends much time on God's works, we don't think about God working *now* very much. Our works are much more important to us! Even in our church work we think that what *we* are doing is most important. We don't think in terms of God doing anything in particular, except perhaps blessing the whole thing for us — like sprinkling holy water on our offerings — so that things go better.

But God's works are far more important than that. In fact, without God's works our works mean nothing and accomplish nothing. "Unless the LORD builds the house, its builders labor in vain. Unless

the LORD watches over the city, the watchmen stand guard in vain."
(Psalm 127:1)

The Bible tells us many times that we must learn the what the
works of the Lord are:

> For you make me glad by your deeds, O LORD; I sing
> for joy at the works of your hands. How great are your
> works, O LORD, how profound your thoughts! (Psalm
> 92:4-5)

> Great are the works of the LORD; they are pondered by
> all who delight in them. (Psalm 111:2)

> They have harps and lyres at their banquets,
> tambourines and flutes and wine, but they have no
> regard for the deeds of the LORD, no respect for the
> work of his hands. (Isaiah 5:12)

> LORD, I have heard of your fame; I stand in awe of your
> deeds, O LORD. Renew them in our day, in our time
> make them known; in wrath remember mercy.
> (Habakkuk 3:2)

> And we know that in all things God works for the good
> of those who love him, who have been called according
> to his purpose. (Romans 8:28)

> For it is God who works in you to will and to act
> according to his good purpose. (Philippians 2:13)

> Great and marvelous are your deeds, Lord God
> Almighty. Just and true are your ways, King of the ages.
> (Revelation 15:3)

"Work" means using materials and a method to reach a goal.
That can range anywhere from using wood and an ax to make a log
cabin, to using computers and programs to calculate interest at a bank.
We understand what it takes to do work because we have done it: it

takes time, it usually takes money, it takes much physical or mental effort, but it is the only way we can achieve our goals.

God's work is the same kind of thing. He either uses the materials of this world (providence) or he doesn't (miracle). He uses time to move the project along, and he uses certain methods to carry out his plans. His work proceeds according to his wisdom, and he is skillful at getting certain jobs done. The result is something that he wants to see.

Now there are two things about his works that we have to look at here: **first**, only faith is going to *correctly identify his work*. Unbelievers can see much of God's works, or at least the results of his working, but they don't think that it was God who did it. They call it Mother Nature, luck, chance, evolution, fairy tales, superstition, false religion, and all kinds of other things instead of what it really is. But believers — since they know their God — will be able to recognize God's handiwork and correctly identify him as the author.

Second, these things that God does are things that *only he can do*. Nobody else can do what God does. In fact, that's why God did these things: man was struggling on his own without getting anywhere, sinking deeper into sin and failure and death, and God stepped in like a rescuer and lifted man out of the impossible situation he was in. The stories about God's works are supposed to impress us with how unique God is, and how much we need him; without him and his works, we have no hope.

The source of our information about God's works is the Bible, as you would expect. But even this isn't appreciated as it ought to be. Too often people form their own opinions on who God is, and they tend to make him into a God who will wink at their sins and give them the desire of their (lustful) hearts. They certainly didn't get their strange ideas from the Bible! Let's get serious about the God of the Bible. If we say that we believe in God, then let's use *only* the Bible and *all* the Bible to find out what to believe about him. It's not fair to use the names "God" and "Christian" if we aren't willing to believe what he says about himself, even when it doesn't suit our opinions. So the Bible is going to tell us *what God does*. We have to start there, getting the truth straight about him, so that we can draw the correct conclusions and believe the right things about him.

The reason we have to make this point is that we are awash with the works of man: everywhere we turn, man is on center stage and what he is doing is getting all the attention. You would think that God has nothing to do with this world! Even in the Church people are getting all the attention: we rely on God *so little* and work so hard at *our* jobs that we are an age without miracle, without the works of Heaven under and over us. That will prove to be disastrous for us when we need a divinely built wall between us and the forces of darkness that are threatening to overrun us.

What are his works?

We can see at least seven categories of God's works in the Bible. As we look at each kind of work that God does, notice that the obvious lesson is this: **only God can do such a thing**. He never requires these things from us, nor does he accept our good intentions when we try to do his work. His work is special to him, unique to him, and nobody can nor should try to do what God does. Otherwise, there would be more gods than him! If we could do it, why turn to the Lord? He will never be pleased with such a situation: "For my own sake, for my own sake, I do this. How can I let myself be defamed? I will not yield my glory to another." (Isaiah 48:11)

- **Creation and Providence.** We start, of course, where the Bible starts — God made the world and everything in it. We have to start here, because we find out some critical things that we need to know:

  We find out the agenda for the world. The way that a thing is designed will tell you its purpose. God doesn't do anything without reason and purpose. What he intended for the world was built into it from the beginning and is still there; nothing in life makes any sense unless we study his blueprints.

  We find out to whom all this belongs. He who makes, owns; and he who determines, rules. If God made everything, then he certainly has the right as well as the ability to determine the outcome of it all. Creation shows us what he expected to see in his new world.

We find out man's part in the scheme of things. Once you realize who is running the show, you can better see your own position in the situation. Creation tells us what we are doing here. Not only do we find out God's intentions for making us, but we also find out our right relationship to the world.

At the very least we can say that God made the world; but we need to know more than that, because even unbelievers will be willing to admit that. What we want to know is, why did it take *God* to make the world? Why can nobody else do what he did?

God made the world out of nothing. "By faith we understand that the universe was formed at God's command, so that what is seen was not made out what was visible." (Hebrews 11:3) This is the fundamental doctrine of Creation, and the toughest thing for unbelievers to accept. If God made everything out of nothing, that means he has unimaginable power, infinite wisdom, and total control over everything. And it means that nothing is impossible for him. It also means that he needs nothing from the world (especially from us!) to do his works.

God brought order out of chaos. "Now the earth was formless and empty, darkness was over the surface of the deep, and the Spirit of God was hovering over the waters." (Genesis 1:2) The raw materials of the universe will never, by themselves, align themselves into neat little rows and become aware of themselves. It takes God to put the elements together into meaningful creations and give them life and purpose and motion. He has design and purpose in everything he does in this world — and that's the opposite of what happens when God isn't involved in something.

God made it all very good. "God saw all that he had
made, and it was very good." (Genesis 1:31) "Good"
means that it will perfectly fulfill the requirements;
evidently God was pleased with what he had made
because with it he could achieve his goals. But "good"
also means that the creation itself was a complete
harmony, in which each part contributed to the whole.
As long as everyone and everything kept its place and
did its job (in other words, the scheme can't be
improved upon!) then everything and everybody would
exist in perfect peace and joy.

The whole creation obeys God. "Have you ever given
orders to the morning, or shown the dawn its place?"
(Job 38:12) If you would read this section of Job —
chapters 38 to 41 — you would see that God
commanded each part of creation into existence and
demands that it do its duty as designed. Every creature
lives and moves in a way that God first determined for it
ahead of time — it can't help living that way. His
instructions are etched into its brain or structure beyond
the reach of reason, into the instinct. Man is the only
one who has reason and therefore the ability to disobey
God; but even man is expected and commanded to
obey. It's just that man is to obey with his reason, a
more glorious job than the rest of creation.

God made man in his image. "So God created man in
his own image, in the image of God he created him;
male and female he created them." (Genesis 1:27) Man
was created to bear the image of God in the world. That
means the world should be able to see God in us! We
are his representatives here; we carry a profound
responsibility to carry out his will through our actions.
This assumes that we know God so well that we *can* do
work here that will both glorify him and carry out his
purposes for the world.

*God never meant for creation to fulfill man's deepest
needs.* "The eye never has enough of seeing, or the ear

its fill of hearing." (Ecclesiastes 1:8) There is no end to man's hunger, physical and psychological and spiritual; he gobbles up what he needs today and then starts over the next day, hungry again. People wonder why the good times don't last, and success wasn't as sweet as one hoped, and money doesn't satisfy. The reason is that the Lord didn't make this world to satisfy man's heart; everything here is of a passing, temporary nature. We are more than creatures of physical sense: we straddle two worlds, this one and the spiritual world. This world is only a means to a more important end; we cannot find our destiny here.

Providence, the other side of how God deals with the world, is the description of how he keeps things running. Some people think that God has nothing to do with the world, that it runs on its own now and it is up to us to keep things together. But the Scripture teaches the opposite — Providence shows us that if God would pull his hand away then everything, *everything*, would collapse.

He keeps the world in existence. "He is before all things, and in him all things hold together." (Colossians 1:17) It looks to us as if the world stays together by itself, that the laws which govern its behavior are built into existence and obvious. But the Bible attributes everything that happens in the world to God's direction: rain is his doing (Psalm 147:8), the sun moving or not moving is his doing (Joshua 10:13), "seedtime and harvest, cold and heat, summer and winter, day and night" are all his doing (Genesis 8:22). We can explain and understand creation from our side (science), but we cannot explain the most fundamental connections that the world has with its Sustainer.

He provides for the daily needs of every creature. "The eyes of all look to you, and you give them their food at the proper time." (Psalm 145:15) By design God made all creatures totally dependent on him. They constantly have needs and the drive to fulfill those needs take up most of their waking hours. He also designed the system so that only he can fulfill those needs. Only God is good (Mark 10:18), and if you want good things then you must go to him. And notice God's intentions — we may sometimes wonder if God really wants to do us good, yet here is the Bible testifying that God fully intends to do us good. We worry and hoard up and sweat to hedge our bet, thinking that if we don't look out for ourselves then nobody will; yet that isn't true at all. God has our interests at heart more than we thought.

When you learn about how much God had to do with creation and providence, you should get a whole new view on things. The world isn't a product of random occurrences and aimless wanderings; God is closely supervising all aspects of the world and we should be glad of that when we think about it. Who else would we rather have as our Creator and Provider?

• **The making of Israel.** Creation wasn't the uppermost thing on God's mind when he made the world. He of course knew how man would react to his command in the Garden, and he could see the vast destructive force of sin on the entire human race. His new world was in for some hard times. But God doesn't take pleasure in the death of man (Ezekiel 18:23,32), even though death is the Lord's punishment of man's sin. He began preparing for a grand rescue long before it was needed, because he loves to forgive and restore and bring from darkness into light. The Bible says that God is love because of the special work that he loves to do.

The work of grace is no small task, however. You will better understand the nature of the remedy if you know what sin has done to you first:

Sin separates us from God. We are all interested in God, but not in the God of the Bible. This is a universal characteristic of all sinners. We prefer to make our own gods so that we can do what we want, with nobody ruling over us. (Psalm 2:1-3) The Bible's God is holy, just, good, wise, powerful, and many other things that make us uncomfortable in his presence. We prefer the darkness rather than coming to this God.

Sin obscures the image of God. The Lord made us in such a way that we reflect his glory in what we do and say. What happens instead, due to our rebellion against his Law, is that we dishonor his Name. We break his plain commands and then brazenly claim his Name over what we do! Instead of others getting to see God working in us, they are seeing the effects of God *not* being here — death and destruction instead of life and peace.

Sin leads to death. "For when you eat of it you will surely die." (Genesis 2:17) Death is the most certain thing that will happen to all of us, because it is driven and executed by God's determined will. It is a terrible fate, something that man wasn't meant to experience. It pronounces a sentence of futility and hardship over everything that he does; it seems pointless and counter-productive. But it is God's just revenge on our willful rebellion against him.

God intended for us to work with him and enjoy life, but sin has ruined a good thing. Paul tells us that the spirit of rebellion has been "at work" in us to thoroughly ruin God's creation. (Ephesians 2:2) It has certainly succeeded! But God launched a tremendous program to reverse the effects of sin forever; the result must be *total freedom from any trace or effect of sin.* This is certainly an enormous task and something only God could do.

He made a covenant of faith. "Abraham believed the Lord, and he credited it to him as righteousness." (Genesis 15:6) This one verse is the key to the entire plan of salvation, all the way from Abraham's time to our own and to the end of time. With one stroke of genius the Lord put our salvation on a firm footing, entirely avoiding the issue of man trying to solve the problem of sin on his own.

God was committing himself to solve the issue of sin, instead of expecting us to solve it. In Genesis 15 we read about the oath that God swore: that he would keep the covenant for both himself and man. He knew that man would never be able to keep his side of the bargain. None of us can keep the demands of the Law. So the Lord shouldered the demands of the Law upon himself — in fact, it happened when Jesus came — and by doing that declared all his people righteous and heirs of the covenant with Abraham. Thus the whole history of Israel is the process of God working out all the necessary details of salvation so that, when Jesus finally arrived, God would fit the critical piece into the picture and save his people from their sin.

Abraham, contrary to human nature, received this free grace from the Lord. He laid aside all his own natural inclinations to make himself better; he could see that his own efforts would not do him any good. Only God can save us. Paul calls Abraham "the father of all who believe" (Romans 4:11) because this is the basis that all Christians are on with God: *he* saves, we trust him for it.

He made a nation of his own. "Has any god ever tried to take for himself one nation out of another nation, by testings, by miraculous signs and wonders, by war, by a mighty hand and an outstretched arm, or by great and awesome deeds, like all the things the LORD your God did for you in Egypt before your very eyes?" (Deuteronomy 4:34)

You have to know a little bit of Israelite history to appreciate this question. When the Israelites were trapped as slaves in Egypt, the Lord sent Moses to Pharaoh to demand their release. Pharaoh, of course, refused. But after Egypt suffered the shock of ten devastating plagues at the Lord's hand in punishment, they willingly let the Israelites go. After Moses led the

people out he took them to Mt. Sinai for their meeting
with the God who delivered them.

They found out that God intended to be their king as
well as deliverer. He "laid the Law down" in the form
of stone tablets and instructions to Moses, which we
have in the books Exodus, Leviticus, Numbers and
Deuteronomy. What is more important, however, is that
he was establishing himself as the Lord of the Israelites.
They were his nation, and he was their governing head.
That has never changed since then. It established what
God's people can expect from him as he rules over
them, and what they are responsible to him for.

Can you imagine ruling over a people (sinful at that!)
and doing the job so well that there isn't one thing about
God's Kingdom that a man can find fault with? Surely
the Lord rules in perfection and wisdom.

He gave them a land. "Leave this place, you and the
people you brought up out of Egypt, and go up to the
land I promised on oath to Abraham, Isaac and Jacob,
saying, 'I will give it to your descendants.'" (Exodus
33:1) The Israelites probably thought, "Easier said than
done!" when God promised to give them the land of
Canaan: the reports were that it was filled with giants
and would be impossible to take. But when they finally
did go in with Joshua, the place fell miraculously at their
feet — just as God had promised.

He had told Abraham that he himself would give his
descendants this land. And once they arrived, he kept
them there, in spite of the threats and pressures from
other nations around them. Even when they were
deported to Babylon during Jeremiah's time, they
eventually returned 70 years later because, in God's
eyes, this was their home.

There were some important reasons for giving the
Israelites this land. God wanted one place on earth

where people could find him and worship him: at Jerusalem, in the Temple. Also, it would be a visible proof that the Lord takes care of his people. Finally, he wanted a place where Christ could come and work out the final stages of salvation, for all the world to see, in the middle of his people. Canaan was an important part of God's overall plan. It is even the symbol of the Heavenly land that is being prepared for the Church of Christ.

He set up the Temple economy. "Make this tabernacle and all its furnishings exactly like the pattern that I will show you." (Exodus 25:9) The entire blueprint for the Temple was the brainchild of the Lord, not any man. First, only the Lord knows what is necessary for true worship. The complexity of the system is bewildering to the uninitiated. Who knows but God what will take away sin? How can we know all the requirements of meeting God in his house? It was a mercy that he revealed all these secrets to Israel, and to the Church, because now we have the right and the knowledge of access to the Holy of Holies to gain our salvation.

Second, the thing works. God makes it work as we use it in obedience and faith. The Israelites discovered that their sacrifices brought forgiveness, while the pagan nations (with all their false religion and sacrifices) were fodder for destruction at God's hands. God worked miracles among them. He came close to them and heard their prayers.

We little appreciate the vast preparation and work that went into the Temple system, though we need to learn it better. That ancient system was the support for the Church as it is today: Solomon's Temple was an earthly picture of the Heavenly Temple where all God's children must come for grace. (Hebrews 10:19-23) So God's Temple work supports the entire Church, Old Testament and New Testament.

• **Judgment.** People often misunderstand what judgment really is. It isn't a matter of the judge handing down a sentence for a crime committed; if that was all that there was to it, the policeman who arrested the person could look up the crime in the law books and hand out a sentence on the spot! The purpose of a judge is to have someone who can *decide what really happened.* Since people rarely tell the truth, and everybody thinks they are not guilty, we have to have someone who can study all the evidence and give an impartial judgment on the truth of the situation. Then the sentence itself is based on that impartial judgment.

God of course is the final judge of all men and situations. An earthly judge will miss many of the details of a case simply because he isn't all-knowing nor all-wise. God is both, and whoever escapes earthly justice will be caught in God's infinite justice in the end. We can't judge a person's heart, because we can't see what is in their heart. (Matthew 7:1) But God does — "He knew what was in a man." (John 2:25)

The Lord has a purpose for this world and he wants to make sure that everything fits into his plans perfectly; not a single thing can be out of place. So he is careful, always, to analyze each person and work as he "works out everything in conformity with the purpose of his will." (Ephesians 1:11) Everything that survives the coming day of fire *will* be pure and holy and upright and will reflect God's glory perfectly. Since this *must* be the case, he is constantly judging each situation so that all things will be ready for that day.

> *He judges the thoughts and intents of the heart.* "For the word of God is living and active. Sharper than any double-edged sword, it penetrates even to dividing soul and spirit, joints and marrow; it judges the thoughts and attitudes of the heart." (Hebrews 4:12) Only God can know us like this. It is a penetrating look deep into us that so unnerves us when he does it to us. Adam and Eve hid from him because of it (Genesis 3:8); Isaiah cried out in anguish when God looked into his soul (Isaiah 6:5); Peter wept bitterly when Jesus looked into

him (Luke 22:61); John fell down on his face "as though dead" when Jesus turned his "eyes like blazing fire" upon him. (Revelation 1:17)

The Lord will not allow you any privacy. He knows what you are at all times, even when nobody else knows the truth about you. "Where can I go from your Spirit? Where can I flee from your presence?" (Psalm 139:7) You are the one thing in his orderly universe that has the power and inclination to mess things up for him; he's got to keep an eye on you! If for no other reason, he has to protect others from the sin you are so prone to do.

But there is a positive reason for his constant watch over you: your sanctification. This is a full-time job too, because the least sin can run through your heart like wildfire. "We take captive every thought to make it obedient to Christ." (2 Corinthians 10:5) This, of course, is where the Word of God comes in. Unbelievers hate to read it because it reads *them* so accurately; but for Christians it is our very life with God who knows how to save us and what to save us from. "Come, see a man who told me everything I ever did. Could this be the Christ?" (John 4:29) Thank God for his judgment of me!

He judges by the standard. "He will judge the world in righteousness; he will govern the peoples with justice." (Psalm 9:8) You will not find a fairer piece of legislation to judge the world with than the Law of God. It perfectly glorifies God and his nature in its requirements, it demands no more and no less from us than what is our duty as God's creatures, and the penalties and rewards that it recommends are entirely fitting.

A judge has to judge fairly by the accepted standard or everyone will cry out in protest that justice was not done. He must not play fast and loose with the standards, because the welfare of the entire community depends on the standards staying firm. "When the righteous prosper, the city rejoices; when the wicked perish, there are shouts of joy." (Proverbs 11:10)

The reason that God is so interested to judge us by his Law is that it describes his own nature. The Law is just a description of God and his perfect kingdom; it's no wonder it is higher than we are. "Be perfect, as your Heavenly Father is perfect." (Matthew 5:48) God can't tolerate the very smell of sin; "Your eyes are too pure to look on evil; you cannot tolerate wrong." (Habakkuk 1:13) "Such people are a smoke in my nostrils, a fire that keeps burning all day." (Isaiah 65:5) God wants his surroundings to be of a high quality, that's all; and he uses the Law to determine what and who might be allowed to be part of his environment.

He works on the conscience. "At this, those who heard began to go away one at a time, the older ones first, until only Jesus was left, with the woman still standing there." (John 8:9) In this story we see men who couldn't bear up under the shame they felt in Jesus' presence. The conscience is a powerful tool in God's hand to bring us down to the dust in repentance.

God wisely made us with a conscience because it will keep us in line when nothing else will. We all have the Law of God etched into our hearts: "The requirements of the Law are written on their hearts, their conscience also bearing witness, and their thoughts now accusing, now even defending them." (Romans 2:15) A man can live with all sorts of physical punishments easier than he can live with a wounded conscience. "A rebuke impresses a man of discernment more than a hundred lashes a fool." (Proverbs 17:10)

There are witnesses. "On the testimony of two or three witnesses a man shall be put to death, but no one shall be put to death on the testimony of only one witness." (Deuteronomy 17:6) And so the Lord, according to his own law, is preparing witnesses against us in preparation for Judgment Day. Of course he knows all things already, and additional witnesses are really unnecessary. But won't it be uncomfortable to see these others who also saw our sin come out of our past and accuse us?

On Judgment Day we will finally realize that the life that God gave us affected many other people, and we failed them too. The enormity of our responsibility is going to hit us when God calls witness after witness against us. Even the earth and the Heavens will be called to witness against us! (Deuteronomy 30:19) Where does it all stop? How much am I responsible to do in my life? Who is my brother, that I have been accountable to him? Was my every step, my every word, a burden to others, a cross in their lives, that I was never aware of? How much of this would I have avoided if I had taken God more seriously in life?

Judgment is a very public affair. We haven't lived in a vacuum all our lives. What we have done and said, even though in secrecy, "will be proclaimed from the housetops" (Luke 12:3) so that all the universe will know the truth about us.

Fitting reward, fitting punishment. "Your eyes are open to all the ways of men; you reward everyone according to his conduct and as his deeds deserve." (Jeremiah 32:19) When God pronounces his verdict over us, then comes the fitting sentence. Man has always known that there are rewards and punishments in God's kingdom, though he has been confused about how God decides the merits of each case.

God is preparing something for the wicked, which ought to put fear in their heart; instead they joke about Hell. Such terrible plans that God has for them! God will, in wrath, hurl every rebellious soul into the "eternal fire prepared for the devil and his angels" (Matthew 25:41) who would not have him to be their God. Hell is no laughing matter; it is sobering to think that it is no more and no less than a sinner deserves — it is a just God's answer to the way they broke his Law.

God is also preparing something for his faithful servants. "I am going there to prepare a place for you." (John 14:2) What he is doing there now, and why it takes all this time to prepare it, we have no idea; but we know that God does all things well and that reward will be worth waiting for. Remember however that God is just, and Heaven will be according to our righteousness — which is provided by Jesus, not ourselves. Thank God that we have what Jesus deserves!

• **The coming of Christ.** This was the biggest event of the history of the world. It was thousands of years in the making, involving millions of people. There were all sorts of prophecies made about him, and hopes ran high that, upon his arrival, the Jews would experience the height of the kingdom of God on earth.

But it never happened as people expected. Jesus came and went in almost total obscurity — his life ended in apparent failure and the Jews were pretty much at the same point after his life as they were before he lived. For some reason nobody got the significance of who he really was. They had the Scriptures that testified of him (John 5:39), but they couldn't match up the *Word* with the *Work*. They didn't understand the massive amount of preparation and work that went into making Jesus' life possible.

O Jerusalem, Jerusalem, you who kill the prophets and stone those sent to you, how often I have longed to gather your children together, as a hen gathers her chicks under her wings, but you were not willing. (Matthew 23:37)

If you can see the hand of God as he works, you will be able to pick up on all the work that the Lord did to prepare for Jesus' coming, work extending over thousands of years and in almost every story in the Old Testament. You will also be able to see God finishing his work and carrying out his purposes in Christ's life and death and resurrection.

Preparation through the Jews: "And who is like your people Israel — the one nation on earth that God went out to redeem as a people for himself, and to make a name for himself, and to perform great and awesome wonders by driving out nations and their gods from before your people, whom you redeemed from Egypt?" (2 Samuel 7:23) Until the Lord started working with Israel, men and nations all around the world were ignorant of who God really was. But through Israel the Lord showed his true nature. Here, in their history and the Law that was given to them, we learn that God isn't like the other gods; he shows us what he will do to sinners and to saints.

God worked out the doctrines of who he is through the nation Israel. All the things that we believe about him *now* come from the experiences recorded *in the Old Testament* where people learned over time, through real events, the truth about him. God was preparing the way for the Messiah: when Jesus showed up, the Jews should have recognized their God because their Scriptures carefully describe him.

Preparation of the Temple system: "It was necessary, then, for the copies of the heavenly things to be purified with these sacrifices, but the heavenly things themselves with better sacrifices than these." (Hebrews 9:23) Here is the heart of the Old Testament system of salvation and, for those who can see it, the heart of the salvation that is in Christ. The Lord put a great deal of work and thought into the Temple and all its ceremonies, because it had significance not only for the Jews in their day but for the entire Church of Christ. We depend right now on the finished work of Christ in the Heavenly Temple.

The different parts of the Temple represent profound realities of God's kingdom and the way he saves sinners. For example, the Lord instructed Solomon to use enormous amounts of gold on the inside walls of the Temple: this shows the immense wealth of the salvation in Christ, and it overwhelms us with its glory.

The Temple dealt with man's root problem: sin. Here was the difference between life and death for us, and God didn't scrimp on the work he put into it. He said that his eyes and ears are always open in the Temple, ready to receive all who come there for spiritual help. (2 Chronicles 7:15-16) And Jesus came to make our entrance into the Temple in Heaven even more sure and certain: he led the way into the Holy of Holies and expects us to follow him there to get our grace from God.

Preparation of revelation: "These are the Scriptures that testify about me." (John 5:39) The Lord also put an immense amount of time and effort in the written revelation that described Christ's ministry so well. Every significant event about Jesus' life and work was described long before he came; but only the ones with spiritual insight would be able to read the record and get the point. In fact, the Old Testament is *God's* explanation of the work of Christ: he wants us to learn there the importance and the meaning of his son's coming. Just reading the New Testament will not give you an accurate understanding of Jesus.

The Old Testament is so full of Christ that the New Testament doesn't bother to go over the same material again; that would be needless duplication. It's no use repeating the same lessons! This means that many important things that we need to know about Christ will only be found in the Old Testament. The apostles used the Old Testament to teach people the truth about Christ. Paul says that the Scriptures (and they were, to him, the Old Testament) "are able to make you *wise for salvation* through faith *in Christ Jesus*." (2 Timothy 3:14-17) This is a remarkable statement about a book that most modern Christians know almost nothing about!

The birth and growing up: "The virgin will be with child and will give birth to a son, and they will call him Immanuel — which means, 'God with us.'" (Matthew 1:23) Of all the miracles that God ever did, the incarnation of Christ — that is, God becoming man — surely tops the list. It sets the stage for a person and ministry that would shake the very foundations of man's work and replace it with God's work of salvation.

Jesus' earthly life started out just as ours does: nine months in the womb, a birth, growing up under the care and authority of his parents, learning and experiencing the world around him. In starting life the hard way (you little appreciate what he left in Heaven to do things this way!) he was doing the will of the Father; this is how he *had* to start life if the plan of salvation was going to succeed.

It took thirty years to prepare the Messiah for his short earthly ministry, but it was a work of perfection that only God could do. Jesus would have to be able to handle a crushing burden, a work load that no other man in history had been able to carry. And this on top of the constant fighting against the Pharisees, teaching and encouraging, doing miracles, and training the disciples to carry on after he left. It's no wonder that people were amazed and said, "Where did this man get this wisdom and these miraculous powers?" (Matthew 13:54) God did a perfect job of getting Jesus ready for everything that he had to do.

The ministry: "The words I say to you are not just my own. Rather, it is the Father, living in me, who is doing his work." (John 14:10) Jesus was always careful to disclaim any originality in what he did or said. All this was from the Father, not him. It seems strange that he would insist on this, since he is God's Son and certainly deserves glory alongside the Father. But there was an important reason for this: Jesus was doing the work of *God.* There is only *one God*, and there is only *one work* that we can say is God's work. This is, in fact, the same work that God had been doing since the "foundation of the world" — the work that he did which the Old Testament records. It is all one plan, and has only one end in view.

In other words, there is nothing new in the ministry of Christ, nothing that isn't already in the Old Testament either in symbol or prophecy or historical event. Jesus was always careful to do things according to the Scripture because he, being the God of the Old Testament, must do the *same work* in this New Testament age. The doctrine of salvation had already been worked out in the old days, and now he came to fulfill it in men's souls. There must not be any difference between the two teachings; otherwise all God's work until this point will have been useless, and the work of Christ — being a "new" thing — would be suspect.

And for those who had the faith to follow him, he proved that he was their God; after all, only *he* could do the *work of God* in their hearts. He was the Counselor, the Savior, the Lord, the Teacher, the Captain, the Rock, the elder Brother, the Light and Bread from Heaven and many other things that the Old Testament says God will do for us. Jesus' promise wasn't an empty one.

The death and resurrection: "That power is like the working of his mighty strength, which he exerted in Christ when he raised him from the dead." (Ephesians 1:19-20) God didn't just snap his fingers and Jesus walked out of the grave. Sin put him in the grave, and sin has tremendous powers of destruction. The Scriptures speak of God's *battle* against the powers of darkness. If we were trying to solve this problem ourselves we would never make it; it would be completely beyond our powers to overcome.

But God has the power to overcome sin and death; he can reverse any damage that sin does. From the unspeakable tragedy of a dead Savior, the Father reached down and lifted up a living, triumphant Savior. It was a stunning victory against all the forces of darkness that put him in the grave. Now Christ has a life that cannot die, an eternal life that is completely safe from all the power of sin and darkness. In it is a new power that we also will share if we are one with him. And it took the power of God to do this thing: in that one act he achieved what thousands of years of man's efforts have failed to achieve.

The ascension: "And seated him at his right hand in the heavenly realms, far above all rule and authority, power and dominion, and every title that can be given, not only in the present age but also in the one to come." (Ephesians 1:20-21) We almost never think about the ascension of Christ, yet it is one of the most important doctrines of the Church; without it we have no salvation.

If Jesus had only come back to life, where would we be now? Our hope isn't to live *here* with Christ but in Heaven! When he went back to the Father he assumed his throne in Heaven; from there he rules over all the world and is the Head of the Church. He sent the Spirit right away and started the Church. He started getting our place there in Heaven ready for us. He is even now putting the nations under his feet, getting everything ready for Judgment Day when he will turn it all over to the Father. He is speaking from Heaven through his Word and saving souls. In other words, we have a real hope — now that Jesus has been raised on high.

The glorification: "Therefore God exalted him to the highest place and gave him a name that is above every name." (Philippians 2:9) There is a note of irony in this statement. If you consider what Jesus was when he came to earth the *first* time, you will marvel that the people of earth would change their opinion of him so completely when he comes the *second* time.

If there ever was a man in history that has been misunderstood it is Jesus Christ. The Jews (his own people) missed the point about him; the Romans mocked him; the Greeks were only willing to put him alongside their hundreds of other gods; modern man uses him for an idol, a curse word, an excuse to indulge in Christmas materialism. Even Christians little realize how much they need him for everything in their lives.

This will change, however. Now that Jesus has been restored to his place of glory, the Father is working, right now, on how he will reveal the true glory that is in his only Son. More on this later.

• **Building up the kingdom.** While men and nations are busy building up their own kingdoms (which never survive long, but they keep working at it anyway!) the Lord is building his own kingdom "on the side" — in a way that most people never know what is happening. We think that everything that we do is so important; but when time is no more and everyone is brought before the Judgment seat of Christ, we will realize then that *his* kingdom was the important work, and ours had little or no value.

Jesus came preaching the coming of the Kingdom of God. (Mark 1:15) Some were given the knowledge of the secrets of that kingdom. (Matthew 13:11-13) Not everyone, however, sees the Lord's kingdom! "I tell you the truth, no one can see the kingdom of God unless he is born again." (John 3:3) And if we can see it, we are in a good position to help build it.

It is a real kingdom: "The LORD is king for ever and ever." (Psalm 10:16) A king rules over his subjects; he is no king who has no people to rule. The Lord rules over all the earth! The whole world is his kingdom, mainly because he made it and has the right and wisdom to do just things with it.

A king has several responsibilities: first, he must make the laws for his people to go by. Second, he must provide for his people and see to their needs. Third, he must protect his people from their enemies. Fourth, the king enjoys his kingdom and loves to be around his people. These are all true about God. He gave us laws to live by (Deuteronomy 4:5-6); he cares for our needs (1 Peter 5:7); he protects us from our enemies (Psalm 23:4-5); he judges his people fairly (Psalm 139:1-4); and he enjoys his kingdom. (Isaiah 5:7) We can find many other passages in the Bible that show us God carrying out the functions of a king over all his subjects around the world.

It is a spiritual kingdom: "My kingdom is not of this world. If it were, my servants would fight to prevent my arrest by the Jews. But now my kingdom is from another place." (John 18:36) Jesus himself made this distinction between "physical" and "spiritual" and we have to be very clear about it. "Physical" means whatever won't be here after Judgment Day. That includes the world, organizations, money, flesh and blood, and everything else that we are familiar with. "Spiritual" refers to the unseen world of God that will be here after Judgment: this includes God himself, the angels, our souls, the devil and his demons, and the "new heavens and a new earth." (Isaiah 65:17)

Though most people are completely unaware of the reality of the spiritual world, it is real nonetheless. An unbeliever thinks it is so much nonsense because he can't see it or understand it. (1 Corinthians 2:14) But a believer knows that there is a God, and that he is accountable to God, and that the Spirit of God is dealing with men about their souls.

The work that is going on right now in God's kingdom is spiritual work. Church buildings and committees and finances contribute absolutely nothing to God's kingdom, since they are materials of this world. The body of Christ, fellowship in the Spirit, and the treasures of Heaven are extremely important to the Lord's kingdom, however, and God's people deal in these things daily to achieve God's goals.

It is an unshakable kingdom: "Therefore, since we are receiving a kingdom that cannot be shaken ..." (Hebrews 12:28) If you shake a pine tree that has snow on it, the snow comes off and reveals the dark green branches underneath. This is how God will shake all things at the end of time: the physical will fall off, and the spiritual — his perfect work that has been going on for ages — will be revealed in all its beauty.

This passage teaches us two important things: *first*, this world is doomed to destruction. The Lord uses it now for his purposes, but someday he will no longer need it and he will throw it away. We make a terrible mistake basing our lives and setting our hearts on what God is going to throw away. He didn't make it to last forever, and he doesn't want us to spend all our time making treasures out of it.

Second, the kingdom of God is unshakable. Things last there. When God gives you comfort, you are comforted forever. God's wisdom enables you to see the eternal truth and it will change your entire outlook on life. Spiritual love doesn't cool off like physical love, but carries you through any amount of hardship until you see the one who loves you face to face; you can feel his arms around you even in the hardest times. The kinds of things that God does to your soul will give you direction in life and give you the steel in your backbone to keep on going until God gives you all his promises.

It is virtually unnoticed: "The kingdom of heaven is like yeast that a woman took and mixed into a large amount of flour until it worked all through the dough." (Matthew 13:33) At first the yeast doesn't appear to do anything to the dough; but after a while, slowly at first, the bread puffs out and gets bigger. That is the way God's kingdom works: at first we don't think that the Word got through to someone's heart, or we think that the enemy really has won the field. Later, however, that person who heard the Word changes his life and we discover that something real happened. We see our enemy crumble under the weight of his sins and pride, unable to make good on his boasting, and the righteous have the victory in the end.

The work of God is always unimpressive at first. You will find a nobody, a little person, ministering in God's Name, and people despise the work of the Church because of it. But perhaps more good has come out of those nobodies working faithfully than whole seminaries of preachers and professors! And God uses little things to build his kingdom: for example, he made man out of dust, he fed thousands with a few loaves of bread, he brought powerful Egypt to its knees through a humble Moses, he brought down Goliath with a stone — over and over he shows us that, while at first we think nothing will come of it, he knows exactly what he is doing. There is never any doubt about the outcome once the Lord starts his work.

It is a perfect kingdom: "He will wipe every tear from their eyes. There will be no more death or mourning or crying or pain, for the old order of things has passed away." (Revelation 21:4) Perfection is a powerful word. It means that all that *must* be done, *will* be done, to God's exacting specifications. The past will be fully judged and no sin unaccounted for. The righteous will be rewarded for every act of faithfulness. Nothing will be missed: God will wrap everything together at the end of time and everyone will be satisfied with the result.

You know that the Lord has to have profound wisdom, and unimaginable power, to be in such control of things that it will all end perfectly! Nothing is ever out of his sight, and everything fits perfectly into his plans. "And we know that *in all things* God works for the good of those who love him, who have been called according to his purpose." (Romans 8:28) We can't possibly control the events of our lives in such a way that it pleases even ourselves, let alone others. God, however, from the beginning of the world all through history until the very end, carefully builds a kingdom that will last forever. He has unerring skill.

• **The Last Day.** Most people don't think that there will be a last day. They think that the world — and man! — will just continue on as always. They *want* to think this because they dread the implications involved if there really will be a Last Day as the Bible claims!

We live in a borrowed world: this is God's world, not ours, and he is only letting us use this world for the time being. We need to rewrite our history books with that in mind. All of history is headed for the closing chapter when God will end the works of men, and all the suffering and injustices they caused, and make things *new*.

The culmination of his work here: "Then the end will come, when he hands over the kingdom to God the Father after he has destroyed all dominion, authority and power. For he must reign until he has put all his enemies under his feet. The last enemy to be destroyed is death." (1 Corinthians 15:24-26) This passage tells us what the Lord is busy doing right now. We often think that the Lord is losing the fight! But he isn't — even when men become the most wicked, and seem to win the battle, they are only tightening the noose around their necks. Occasionally the Bible gives us little clues that the Lord has everything in control.

The work going on in the Church now seems very slow and not making much headway. But even there the Lord is getting more done than we may realize; he isn't interested in doing something that would impress us as a stunning victory over the world. The little victories that we think aren't worth noticing are the cause of great rejoicing in Heaven. (Luke 15:10)

Unveiling the great work: "... Into an inheritance that can never perish, spoil or fade — kept in Heaven for you, who through faith are shielded by God's power until the coming of the salvation that is ready to be revealed in the last time." (1 Peter 1:4-5) None of us have gotten a full sight of what God is working on. Like an artist who keeps the painting under wraps until it is done, we see only little glimpses of it here and there. Someday, however, the Lord is going to take the wraps off his kingdom and we will all see this thing that he has been making.

The Lord is looking forward to that day. Right now people don't see the glory of Christ, or why he deserves great honor and worship from us. But on that day "every knee will bow ... and every tongue will confess that Jesus Christ is Lord." (Philippians 2:10-11) People don't think that their sins will be discovered; but "because of your stubbornness and your unrepentant heart, you are storing up wrath against yourself for the day of God's wrath, when his righteous judgment will be revealed. God will give to each person according to what he has done." (Romans 2:5-6) God's little people think that they are nobodies, especially since the world treats them like that. But on that day God will call each one of them "you who are highly esteemed!" (Daniel 10:11)

The war is over: "I will take away the chariots from Ephraim and the war-horses from Jerusalem, and the battle bow will be broken. He will proclaim peace to the nations. His rule will extend from sea to sea and from the River to the ends of the earth." (Zechariah 9:10) Since the fall of Adam and Eve the forces of Heaven have been involved in a full scale war. We might not appreciate the extent or the fierceness of this conflict, but millions of men, women and children have been saved out of darkness and brought into the Kingdom of light. At the end of time we will see the entire Church together around God's throne; what a vision of victory over sin and death! That will be a powerful testimony of God's saving grace that can save even the most wretched sinner.

On that day we will lay our weapons down because God will destroy all our enemies — even death — and provide us with all the treasures and joy and peace that we could ever want. There will be no more sin or suffering. The wicked will be gone forever. Believers all long for that day to come, and we should take heart that the Lord is working right now, through the Spirit and through his people, to bring about that final victory.

The highest glory: "Praise be to the LORD God, the God of Israel, who alone does marvelous deeds. Praise be to his glorious name forever; may the whole earth be filled with his glory. Amen and Amen." (Psalm 72:18-19) "Glory" means this: the one who gets the credit. On that Last Day the Lord will finally get the credit for everything that he was responsible for. Man won't be the center of attention anymore; we will all crowd around God and give him the credit due him for all his works.

Right now God gets credit for very little, except when we complain about our circumstances! But we don't need to feel sorry for him, because he is keeping notes of all the things that he does for us that we forget to thank him for. He intends to let every person know on that Last Day just how involved he was in guiding every detail of their lives.

The fullness of time: "To be put into effect when the times will have reached their fulfillment — to bring all things in heaven and on earth together under one head, even Christ." (Ephesians 1:10) God almost never does something immediately. He usually works through periods of time to do his works. He could snap his fingers and do something in an instant, but he has reasons for not doing it that way: one is so that we will develop patience as we wait on him. Another is so that we will get in step with him, working in such a way as to contribute something useful to the Kingdom. He honors us when he calls us "fellow workers"! (1 Corinthians 3:9)

So as the Lord slowly unfolds his plan, wait on him. Trust him to do it his way, and you will see things turn out for the best. The Bible itself shows us this in a very powerful way since it was written over long periods of time; notice that some things that the Lord did extended over hundreds or thousands of years! Yet they all turned out exactly according to plan and couldn't have been done better.

A whole new mode of existence: "There will be no more death or mourning or crying or pain, for the old order of things has passed away. He who was seated on the throne said, 'I am making everything new!'" (Revelation 21:4-5) Perhaps every child of God has tried to imagine what it will be like to be in Heaven, with earth and history and sin and death behind us. But words and ideas fail us when we try to imagine it: Paul said that he saw "inexpressible things, things that man is not permitted to tell." (2 Corinthians 12:4)

In other words, the works that God has been doing in *this* world isn't the whole picture! He has been doing other works that we have no idea of, in order to prepare Heaven for the arrival of his people. "In my Father's house are many rooms; if it were not so, I would have told you. I am going there to prepare a place for you.

And if I go and prepare a place for you, I will come back and take you to be with me that you also may be where I am." (John 14:2-3) We can only imagine what the place will be like. Surely it will make all the hardships that we had to go through in this world well worth the effort. "For our light and momentary troubles are achieving for us an eternal glory that far outweighs them all." (2 Corinthians 4:17) God is "able to do immeasurably more than all we ask or imagine" (Ephesians 3:20) — and he is right now preparing that "immeasurably more" for his people.

- **Scripture.** We need to look at one last thing about the works of God — the Bible itself. It's nothing less than a miracle that we have the Word of God in our hands. How such a precious treasure from Heaven has survived the ravages of time and men's sins makes a fascinating story, but we can only tell a little bit of it here.

The Scriptures are the truth of God put into the words of men, so that they can have the opportunity to know the Lord. To take advantage of a truth, one must first learn the truth. But the Bible is more than just a fact book about God — through these spiritual words the Spirit will bring you into God's presence and you will be changed, conformed into his likeness, and made fit to live with him forever. The Bible is a tremendous opportunity to get the most important issues of life taken care of.

What has God done for us in the Bible?

> *Preserved the truth for his people.* Men of all nations and of all times have claimed to know the truth about ourselves and the world; the problem is that they were all wrong. God alone knows the truth — he made us, he keeps us going, and he is building his own kingdom that will replace all earthly kingdoms. When the Lord had the old saints write down the words of the Old and New Testaments, he was giving every child of God something that the wisest of all philosophers and the most powerful of kings have never had: the truth.

The Old Testament is just as much the truth as the New Testament. Here we learn who God is, his works, his ways, his plans and purposes, his wrath and his mercy. And in the New Testament we read about this God who came to earth to display his glory to us and proved that the truths that we learned in the Old Testament were absolutely correct!

We must believe that this is the truth about the Lord because if it isn't, if one single thing is wrong, then we can't trust any of it. Either it is the Word of God or it isn't; it is truth from outside man's limited perspective or it is the dreams and imaginations of men. Most people think it is the work of men; that's why they aren't saved by it. But a few recognize it for what it really is:

> And we also thank God continually because, when you received the word of God, which you heard from us, you accepted it not as the word of men, but as it actually is, the Word of God, which is at work in you who believe. (1 Thessalonians 2:13)

Revealed himself. The Bible is a revelation, an uncovering of what we couldn't see before. When a sculptor takes away the covering from his creation, others can see for the first time what he made. You will find this idea throughout the Bible: prophets got visions and dreams; angels came and declared the thoughts of God; people were transported to Heaven and saw things there that nobody knew about previously; the veil was lifted from a person's appearance and others saw God working through him.

When the Lord revealed himself he spoke in words that we would understand, and showed us things that our senses could take in. Although God is higher than we are — he is Spirit and we are physical, he is the Creator and we are the created — he accommodates himself to our level *so that we can understand.* This is very important. If he would have spoken in the language of Heaven in ways that a creature could never grasp, what good would that have been? But he has our good at heart: he knows that we are dust, and he wants us to live, not die.

Preserved the manuscripts. This makes a fascinating story. There is more to the Bible than Moses and Isaiah and Matthew writing an account and saving it for us to read. It's been 4000 years since Abraham's day; that's a long time to keep a story intact! It can only be the hand of God behind the accuracy and reliability of the Scriptures that we have today.

The Jews were almost fanatical (thankfully!) in their methods to ensure strict accuracy when they made copies of the Scriptures. And though we unfortunately don't have any original manuscripts from Bible authors, we currently have thousands of copies that almost all agree with each other about what the very first one must have read like. The Bible and its manuscripts are more reliable than any other ancient manuscript in all history!

Guided translators. Translation is a tricky business at best. The Old Testament was written first in Hebrew; for an example, here is Genesis 1:1 —

בְּרֵאשִׁית בָּרָא אֱלֹהִים אֵת הַשָּׁמַיִם וְאֵת הָאָרֶץ:

And the New Testament was written in Greek; here is John 1:1 —

Ἐν ἀρχῇ ἦν ὁ λόγος, καὶ ὁ λόγος ἦν πρὸς τὸν θεόν, καὶ θεὸς ἦν ὁ λόγος.

Any translator knows that there is no single right way to translate the Bible; one can translate most verses in several ways and be correct.

Not all translations are equally reliable. Unfortunately men sometimes subject the truth of God to *their* notions of what is truth, which are wrong, and the translation will come out wrong too. But most versions of the Bible have at least enough of the truth for faith and life. None of them are perfect; the only perfect Scriptures are the Greek and Hebrew originals! Most of the versions, however, will give us an adequate understanding of what God wants us to know about him and ourselves, and the only way to salvation. If a version's imperfections really bother you, there are plenty of language helps available for you to explore the original texts yourself.

Provided a defense against our enemies. From the very beginning, Satan has been attacking God's Word. "Did God really say ... ?" (Genesis 3:1) He just hates for people to take it seriously and base their lives on it. He would much prefer that we believe his lies and ignore God's truth.

Especially in our day it is the fashion to laugh at the naive Bible and all those who believe in it. Almost nobody believes all of it! Even Christians have those parts that they just can't accept, because it goes against the modern trends and knowledge and ways of doing things.

But God isn't worried. He has all the defenses he needs against his enemies in his Word. When Satan attacked Jesus in his temptations, he found a warrior ready with the truth of God and was thoroughly beaten with *just that*. Paul understood the power in God's Word:

> The weapons we fight with are not the weapons of the world. On the contrary, they have divine power to demolish strongholds. We demolish arguments and every pretension that sets itself up against the knowledge of God, and

we take captive every thought to make it
obedient to Christ. (2 Corinthians 10:4-5)

When this generation is long gone and all its glories are
laid in the dust, the Word of God will still be here
saving people and giving them hope and explaining the
truth to them. There is nothing that threatens or destroys
the truth: "The grass withers and the flowers fall, but
the Word of our God stands forever." (Isaiah 40:8)

I know that we have spent a lot of time going over the
works of God; but I wanted you to see how much time *the Bible*
spends talking about God's works. They are important! These are
things that we absolutely have to know about; we cannot do these
things ourselves, and it should be good news that God does them
for us.

The important point about the whole subject is that **only
God can do these things**. If this is what you want, now you know
where to go for it. You make a terrible mistake when you try to do
any of this on your own. It's true that God expects a lot from you;
but he doesn't expect you to do any of his special work. He is the
only one who has the wisdom and power and goodness needed.
God will be God, and we need to learn to be creatures and depend
on him to provide us with what we need instead of turning our
backs on him and trying to get along without him.

What we have to do is learn his works, so that we know
what to ask him for. The works of God are materials for prayer.
These things aren't just interesting stories in an ancient history
book; they were written for us, so that we would believe in the God
who does these things for his people. The Lord knows that we are
getting the right idea about his works when we pray for them.
"LORD, I have heard of your fame; I stand in awe of *your deeds*, O
LORD. Renew them in our day, in our time make them known; in
wrath remember mercy." (Habakkuk 3:2)

Why should we know his works?

We are not wasting time to learn the works of God. This is precious knowledge that every Christian needs; in fact, we can trace much if not most of our spiritual problems back to ignorance about what God does. If we don't know these things about him, how can we trust in what he does? How can we possibly work with him? Like children who don't know their parents' work — they wait for food to get on the table three times a day without knowing how it happens — we Christians often don't know any more about God's hard work for our sake than that.

Why do we need to know about the Lord's works? *First*, **they reveal him.** If you have spiritual eyes and ears to learn such things, you can find out a lot about what kind of God you have just by watching what he does. Other gods don't do what the God of the Bible does! That's because the Lord is unique, and he does things according to his nature.

For one thing, you will find out what is important to him. He doesn't do what he isn't interested in doing. Since he has never dropped bags of gold from the sky, you can conclude that he doesn't want to do that — even if you ask for it. We work on what interests us, on things that we think are important, because we don't have the time or resources to waste on unimportant things. And in the same way, there are certain things that are extremely important to him — like our salvation, his glory, spreading his Truth, finishing his plans for the earth, Judgment, preparing a place in Heaven for his saints — and he simply doesn't have time or interest to do other things. Don't expect him to change his priorities, either, for your sake.

For another thing, they are always holy and just. God works to set up a holy kingdom, a holy people, and the wicked are going to find out that they are being cut out of the picture. All that the Lord is doing will boil down to two things: he is saving his people from their sins (Matthew 1:21) and he is holding the wicked for the day of judgment. (2 Peter 2:9) Since he is so serious about setting up righteousness and punishing the wicked — to the point that we can't get him to do anything else! — what does that tell us about what *our* priorities should be? What should we be praying for?

God's works also reveal his other "attributes" (characteristics of his nature). His works are eternal, they are perfect, they are according to profound wisdom, they are good. They are all these things because God is this way; we can't expect any other kind of work from him.

Second, **they accomplish his will.** We make two fatal errors concerning the works of God: we underestimate them, and we ignore them. We don't think that God is doing anything significant in the world, and we are much more taken up with our own works than with his works. But we do God a terrible injustice when we think this way, because his works are powerful principles that have always been working in the world and still continue to work in our day. Without the work of God, our world would fall apart! Our salvation would be impossible. We would have no hope that life has any meaning at all if God were not doing the lion's share of keeping the world and the Church going from day to day.

The better you get to know God's works, the clearer his purposes will become to you. When you watch someone start a project you don't always know what they are going to build; the first stages are sketches, a framework, nails and joints and rough lumber. But if you keep watching you will see a method behind the movements, and the skill of the workman as things fit together perfectly. You will see a transformation as what started out in the workman's mind becomes a finished product. Study God's work and you will begin to appreciate that he had something in mind from the beginning: "I make known the end from the beginning, from ancient times, what is still to come. I say: My purpose will stand, and I will do all that I please." (Isaiah 46:10)

Third, **they support his people.** We little appreciate everything that God has done for us. If we think that all that we need are a few sacrifices that Jesus made for us, we are like babies who know almost nothing about our Father. God has done an enormous amount of work for us. He didn't do these things for himself! He doesn't need Heaven; it is all for us. He didn't make the earth for himself to live in; he made the earth for us. All the work that he did in Abraham's family — the millions of men and women involved, the Law at Sinai, the prophets he sent, the wars and kings along the way, the years of teaching and persecutions that the apostles went through —

all this was for our sake. He did all these things so that we might live; every part of the whole project was important for him to do because we need it all.

If you don't know anything about construction you will probably take for granted the office that you work in or the home that you live in. You didn't know, perhaps, that the foundation had to be made in *just the right way* or the entire building would collapse. It takes a lot of skill, a lot of effort, and a lot of time to make a good foundation. And that's only a single part of the entire building!

God's building — history itself, the Heavens and the earth, all mankind, the eternal Temple — requires far more wisdom and skill and energy than any creature can imagine. Take a single thing out of the picture and it would be less than perfect, and therefore useless to us. Whether we know it or not, we depend heavily on everything that God does, down to the smallest detail.

***Fourth*, they are much different from man's works.** God doesn't do what man does, and man doesn't and can't do what God does. This is very important to know and would clear up much confusion about what people claim to be doing "in God's Name." If you know exactly what it is that God does, you can test any situation to see if God really is present in it doing his work. Whatever doesn't match the Bible's description of God's work is not God at work.

Jesus never resented it when people wondered if he was the Messiah; he willingly provided proof that he was by the work that he was doing. When John the Baptist wondered if Jesus was the one to come, Jesus sent back this message to him:

> Go back and report to John what you hear and see: The blind receive sight, the lame walk, those who have leprosy are cured, the deaf hear, the dead are raised, and the good news is preached to the poor. Blessed is the man who does not fall away on account of me. (Matthew 11:4-6)

In other words, this is the work that the Messiah does — so that means that Jesus is the Messiah! No mere man could do what Jesus did. To clear up any confusion, just check the list of the special works that only God can do, see if that is indeed what is happening, and you can know for sure whether God is involved.

Men claim all sorts of things to get others to follow them. "Ministries" done in the Name of the Lord aren't always with God's blessing, however, because it is very possible that God is not involved in it! He didn't send them! (Deuteronomy 18:20) It would be foolish to accept their word — just because they claim that God is working through them doesn't mean that he really is — when the simple proof lies in the Bible. If we can't test men's claims with the plain and simple truth, then no wonder that we are like "infants, tossed back and forth by the waves, and blown here and there by every wind of teaching and by the cunning and craftiness of men in their deceitful scheming." (Ephesians 4:14) It's a mercy that the Bible makes the truth about God very plain to us.

Fifth, it's handy knowledge to have. The Bible tells us to **_remember_** the works of the Lord; this assumes, of course, that you first spent time to learn them! You can't remember what you never did learn. But if you spent some quality time studying what God's works are, there will be many times when that knowledge will come in handy. You will be thankful that you know these things about how he works.

> Remember these things, O Jacob, for you are my
> servant, O Israel. I have made you, you are my servant;
> O Israel, I will not forget you. (Isaiah 44:21)

When David came to fight against Goliath, he remembered how God defeated his enemies in the past and used the same technique in this situation. (1 Samuel 17:34-36) When Moses appeared before Pharaoh to get the Israelites released from slavery, he remembered that God turned his staff into a snake and did the same miracle in front of the Egyptians. (Exodus 7:9-12) The prophets constantly reminded the Israelites of God's Law. Jesus reminded the Jews of the miracles that God did in the Old Testament as proof that he was doing God's work too. (John 6:31)

When you remember God's works, several things will happen: first, your faith in God will strengthen. If you know that he did certain things in times past for his people, then certainly he will do the same thing for you when you face the same needs and circumstances. Second, you won't try to do those things yourself. If this is something that only God does (and how can you know that unless you first study it and remember it?) then wait on him to do it for you. You have plenty of other things to do in obedience to him without trying to be your own God!

<u>Sixth</u>, they are just what the situation needs. If you understand the works of God, you will get good at predicting what he will do in any situation. If God wants to fill a need *in a particular way*, then he isn't going to change tactics just to suit us! He will do it that way every time. We can depend on him for it. It takes care of the problem in a way that glorifies him the most and makes us dependent on him.

For example, how many times did the Lord miraculously provide food "out of thin air" for his people? Perhaps more times than you realized! He gave the Israelites manna in the desert, he stretched 20 loaves of bread to feed a hundred men, he filled many empty jars with oil out of one jar, he fed crowds of people on two occasions with only a few loaves of bread and several fish. These happened because the time was ripe, the people were there with God, in his will, and in need, and the world couldn't provide for their needs. Jesus acted as if the disciples should have known what God would do in such circumstances! They *would* have if they had known God's works better.

<u>Seventh</u>, we need to focus on God's works for a change. All we seem to hear about these days is man and what man can do. We almost never hear about God's works, which accounts for the tremendous problems that our society has — and the Church itself. There is no help in man! We enjoy our works, we love to do things, we think that what we are busy doing is the most important thing in the world, *but there is no salvation in that*. Where is our God? It's time to turn back to the Bible and read what God has done. It's time to go to him for what only he can do. We need to learn more about *him*, and start waiting on him to do *his* works among us; then we can claim the privileges of being his people since he will get glory among us.

Using this knowledge

You may wonder if there is any practical value in knowing God's works. Why learn them? Why do we need to know what they are? Will this help me in my Christian walk? The answer is — you can't do anything right unless you do know them! To even take the first step of faith, to believe in Jesus as the Savior, requires that you know *what* he did and *why* he did it. Every step of faith after that also requires knowledge of his works. The works of God are the starting point and foundation for everything in Christianity.

So we are obligated to learn them. As you will find in the following list, the more we know of what God does, the wiser we become and the more useful we will be in the Church.

- **_Test someone's claim._** "Dear friends, do not believe every spirit, but test the spirits to see whether they are from God, because many false prophets have gone out into the world." (1 John 4:1) When you know what the God of the Bible does, you have the necessary knowledge to test whether he is at work in a particular situation. As we mentioned above, people will make all kinds of claims so that you will follow them; they aren't all right, however! Perhaps they are trying to deceive you. Maybe they don't know themselves that God isn't behind what they are doing. You, however, don't have to stay in the dark about it. The simple thing to do is to check what is going on against what the Bible says God actually does.

- **_Work with God, not against him._** "Since we live by the Spirit, let us keep in step with the Spirit." (Galatians 5:25) When two work together, and one person tears down what the other one is building up, they aren't a very efficient team, are they? Yet that's exactly what we end up doing when we don't know what God is doing and we are busy doing what we want instead. There must be communication between us! And he isn't going to change his plans: *we* must change, and we must conform to what he wants done. But if we know what he wants to do then we become valuable servants to him. He entrusts us with more work, more responsibilities, more opportunities, because we "have in mind the things of God." (Matthew 16:23)

• ***Praise him.*** "Declare his glory among the nations, his marvelous deeds among all peoples." (Psalm 96:3) The Lord not only does wonderful works, he wants everyone to know about them. You are his "advertising agent", so to speak: through your testimony of his works others will hear about him and come to him for the same things. When your neighbor sees that God made such a difference in your life, he will either be turned off (his sin won't let him approach the God who did these things to you!) or become interested in the Lord himself. This means that you have to change what you talk about to others: instead of directing their attention to you, you must start talking about what God did for you. After all, though others may be interested in you as a person, it's what God did for you that is going to help them. All that you have is a gift from God.

• ***Let him do his work — you stick to yours.*** This is the hardest part about learning God's works. It may come as a surprise that some things that you thought *you* were responsible for in your salvation were really God's doing. Don't take God's glory away from him; only he can do certain things for you. If necessary, make a list of the things that only God can do and make another list of the things that he expects of you. (Be sure to get your list from clear statements in the Bible!) Then **wait** on him to do his part, and you stick to your list. Your waiting on him proves that you are really convinced that this is God's job, not yours.

• ***Pray for these things.*** "LORD, I have heard of your fame; I stand in awe of your deeds, O LORD. Renew them in our day, in our time make them known; in wrath remember mercy." (Habakkuk 3:2) When you learn what God does, by reading the record of what he has done in the past, ask for the same things. This pleases the Lord; it means that you are getting the point. Prayer means asking God for what you read in his Word. "Do good to your servant according to your Word, O LORD." (Psalm 119:65) This shows him that you liked what you saw and value them above what your heart would want. And you ask for these special works of God because you see that only they will solve the problems you live with.

An example

To see God in action, let's look at some examples of Jesus building the kingdom of God. Jesus did the *work of God* because he is the *Son of God*. He claimed this privilege many times and expected us to trust in what he did just as much as what the Father does. "Trust in God. Trust also in me." (John 14:1) The point here isn't that we trust in two Gods, but that both the Father and the Son do the *same work*. This means that Jesus was working on the same Kingdom of God that the Old Testament promised.

We must first realize that Jesus himself is that King that the Old Testament promised. The Israelites looked forward to the coming of the Messiah — a Hebrew word that means "the anointed one." It refers to the practice of pouring oil over the head of the chosen king. Just as David was anointed king over Israel, so the Messiah (who would sit on David's throne) would be King over God's people. Read about the formal ceremony that made Jesus King in Psalm 2.

If Jesus was king, we should be able to see him acting like a king as we read the Gospels. In other words, he did the *work* of a king:

> ***He proclaimed the coming of the kingdom.*** He started out his ministry with these words: "The time has come ... The kingdom of God is near. Repent and believe the good news!" (Mark 1:15) He evidently felt that this was to be his main purpose on earth, his most important work. Everything that followed was to be kingdom work. He came already chosen as king, he had subjects to gather together, he had solutions for their problems,

he had laws to issue — the picture here is that Jesus rolled his sleeves up, so to speak, and got busy building his kingdom that he had been looking forward to for so long.

He fed his people. A good king provides for his subjects. On two occasions Jesus felt the need to give bread to those who were following him. (Matthew 14:15-21, Matthew 15:32-38) When you think about it, why did he think that this was *his* responsibility? Would anybody else have thought to do it? This reveals his thinking to us: a king has the resources that he needs to take care of his people, and he feels the responsibility to help them in their need. Another person could neither provide for them nor would he feel obligated to.

He protected his people from their enemies. When the Pharisees brought a woman accused of adultery to Jesus for condemnation, he had mercy on her; not because she deserved it (the Pharisees were right — the Law was strict about adultery) but because he chose to. But first he must rescue her from her accusers! They were really after him, of course, but they wouldn't have thought twice about killing her to make their point against him. He wasn't just a private individual doing whatever he could to help. Only the King had the *right* to free her from the demands of the Law, and the *power* to release her from determined men. The Lord very skillfully sent them all away in shame and let the woman go free. (John 8:2-11)

He laid the law down. In Matthew 5-7 is the Sermon on the Mount in which the King outlines the rules to his new kingdom. The backdrop was the mountain, a symbol of kingship that the Jews wouldn't have missed who saw him there. He sat down to pronounce his Law; and though it wasn't a literal throne, faith can see the King seated in power and authority with all his subjects gathered around his feet. He took several laws from the Old Testament and gave them deeper power and meaning, which only the Lawgiver had the right to do. And they had to please *him,* the King, with their obedience, not themselves or someone else.

___He judged.___   A king examines the evidence and pronounces the verdict based on what he thinks is really going on. When the Pharisees harassed Jesus, they did their best to portray themselves as righteous and doing God's will. They didn't fool him, however.

> At this, some of the teachers of the law said to themselves, "This fellow is blaspheming!" Knowing their thoughts, Jesus said, "Why do you entertain evil thoughts in your hearts?" (Matthew 9:3-4)

He was able to read men's minds and hearts because doing his job well depended on knowing what kind of people he had to work with. "He knew all men. He did not need man's testimony about man, for he knew what was in a man." (John 2:24-25) The king *must* know what is going on so that he can make sure that justice gets done!

___He set up a spiritual kingdom.___ Remember that Jesus had a certain kind of kingdom in mind; he wasn't out to make another kingdom as the world understands but a spiritual one. When Pilate asked Jesus if he was a king, the Lord answered that, yes, he was a king — but not of a kingdom in *this* world. "My kingdom is not of this world. If it were, my servants would fight to prevent my arrest by the Jews. But now my kingdom is from another place." (John 18:36) This explains why he did such strange things — instead of building an army, he trained disciples; instead of sitting on a throne and living in a palace, he wandered through the countryside teaching and doing miracles; instead of punishing his enemies on the spot, he dusted off his feet and went to the next town. In other words, the goal dictated the means; a spiritual kingdom means working toward spiritual results using spiritual methods.

The reason the Gospels record his work is that here was the first and only successful attempt at building the eternal Kingdom of God. Only he knew what to do, and how to do it; only he got results that pleased God. Everything he did worked! The kingdom grew under his hands, and when he was gone he left instructions and power for the disciples to carry on what he started. In other words, here is someone who knows what they are doing for a change and getting real results. Don't miss the point, however: he is the Son of God, who alone can do the works of the kingdom. Everyone went to Jesus for what they needed because only he could give it to them.

Questions to ask

There are many things that you need that you cannot do for yourself. That's why the Bible is such an encouragement: it shows us God working on those very issues for you, so that you will live and not die. So when you study the Bible, focus on what God is doing in the story. Ask yourself these questions:

- What exactly did God do? Why was it necessary for him to do this? Why couldn't man do it for himself? What happened when God did it? If man tried to do it without God, what happened?

- What does this work show us about what God is like? Did he do it for believers or unbelievers — or both? Did men trust in God when they saw it happen? Do God's works go basically unnoticed? What does God think about that? Was it a physical or spiritual work? How does it tie into other works that God did?

- Does man have imitations of God's work? Why aren't they good enough? What does God think of them? How can you tell the difference between God's works and man's works? What are man's works designed to do? What do people usually try to do with them?

- What are the works of God the Father, God the Son, and God the Spirit? What works does God do in the Church? Are these different from works that he did among the Israelites in the Old Testament? When the Scriptures teach that we should rest from our works and trust in God's works, what does that mean? How do our obedience and faith fit into that idea?

- How are God's works made known? Who or what makes them known? How does worship do this? How does the testimony of the people of God relate to the works of God?

- How does one ask for the works of God? When should we ask for them? What exactly should we ask for — an exact repeat of what he did in the past, or a new version, or an entirely new thing? What does this say about the role of the Bible in prayer?

Discussion Questions For Works

- Is the Bible the record of all the works of God? Give Scripture to prove your point.

- How much of our salvation is God's doing?

- What do the works of the Lord tell you about him?

- What will happen if you don't know God's works? What will happen if you do?

- Find modern examples of the seven kinds of work that God does:

> Creation and providence
> The making of Israel
> Judgment
> The coming of Christ
> Building up the Kingdom
> The Last Day
> Scripture

- When someone claims that God is working in them or through them, what should you do? Why?

- God works by his Spirit. (Zechariah 4:6) Give an example of this principle for each of the seven kinds of work (give references).

- If these are God's works, what are man's works? That is, if the Lord told us that *he* will do *these* things, what does he expect from us?

- **How can you use this knowledge of God's works when you are ministering to others?**

Key Five: Glory

Key Five: Glory

The driving force behind everything that God does is *glory*. To him it is the most important result of all his works: it must happen, no matter what the cost. He plans things in order to get glory, he does things in a way that gets glory, and he expects all the glory after the work is done. If somewhere along the line he doesn't get the glory he thinks he deserves, he gets positively angry. The purpose of Judgment Day is that God will finally get the glory he deserves.

This isn't an overstatement of how seriously God takes the subject of his glory. His glory is far more important than we realize. Just because we can't see his glory — and therefore aren't much concerned with it — doesn't mean that *he* isn't continually thinking about it! It's because of his glory that the important parts of the kingdom of God exist. Hell exists (as terrible as the Scriptures describe it) because of God's glory. There *must* be a Judgment Day because his glory demands it. Heaven will center not on our happiness primarily but on God's glory.

The point of the entire Bible, as a matter of fact, is the glory of God. Here you will see him in his full glory (as much as you can see without being in Heaven, that is!). The Bible glorifies him in all its stories, through history and praise and doctrine. If after reading it you aren't completely amazed at who God is, what he is, the kinds of things he has done and will always do — if God doesn't become bigger and greater in your eyes through reading the Scriptures — then he isn't getting glory and something is seriously wrong. And since he is jealous of his glory, you can be sure that your thinking about him will change, either now or at Judgment Day, until you give him the glory he deserves.

Let's look at what the Bible has to say about God's glory.

What does glory mean?

In Hebrew the word for "glory" comes from the word "to be heavy." It is used sometimes in connection with gold (see Psalm 45:13, where the word that is translated "glorious" also means "heavy") as you can well imagine, because gold is both heavy and very precious in appearance and worth.

Kings used to dress themselves in royal robes and cover themselves with jewels and gold. They did this to impress their subjects with seemingly limitless wealth, absolute power at their command, and the importance of their persons. The trouble was that they themselves might not have been all that impressive! They might have been no more than fools playing a game, which many of them turned out to be. But their dress and surroundings at least brought them some measure of respect from anybody who wanted to approach them for a favor.

God, however, needs none of the baubles that we value so highly. "What is highly valued among men is detestable in God's sight." (Luke 16:15) He is impressive without using robes or gold or jewels. When someone comes before God, or when God comes before them, they shake in fear at the sight of a holy God (if he has been gracious enough to keep them from dying in his presence, which would happen naturally if he didn't protect them from himself!). God grips the heart, rivets the eyes upon him, makes the heart race with fear and awe. When someone sees God, there is nothing else he can imagine more fierce and beautiful and holy and huge at the same time. You know when you have been in the presence of God — it's an experience that you will never, ever forget.

That's the overwhelming presence of God, which is one meaning of the word "glory." The other meaning is this: *who gets the credit*. For example, if someone scores during a ball game, he wants to make sure that everyone knows he did it! He wants the credit for making the point. In the same way, when God does something that man needs to know about, he wants to *make sure* man finds out about it. The Lord has ways of making sure we hear about what he did: he publishes the news of his works somewhere where we will see it and get the point that *he* was the one who did this thing. This is the purpose of the Bible.

So when we speak of God having glory, we mean two things by it: first, that he is so overpowering in his presence that all creation immediately falls prostrate before him; and second, he wants credit for what he did.

The Bible is where we learn about God's glory. For example, the following Scriptures teach us important things about his glory:

➤ His Names show us his glory, especially the Name that is arguably the most important Name in the entire Bible. *(Exodus 33:18)*

➤ God's glory filled the Temple so overwhelmingly that the worshipers couldn't go in. (*2 Chronicles 7:1*)

➤ The heavens declare his glory to us. (*Psalm 19:1*)

➤ We are supposed to glorify the Lord because of what his Names teach us about him. (*Psalm 29:2*)

➤ The whole earth is filled with the glory of God. (*Psalm 72:19*)

➤ God gets himself glory through his works. (*Isaiah 26:15*)

➤ God refuses to let others get the glory that should be his alone. (*Isaiah 42:8*)

➤ The Lord is going to send his people all over the earth with news of his glory. (*Isaiah 66:19*)

➤ When God's glory left the Temple, that was the worst thing that could have possibly happened to the Israelites. (*Ezekiel 10*)

➔ When God's glory came back to the Temple, that was the best thing that could have possibly happened to the Israelites. (*Ezekiel 43*)

➔ We have seen the glory of God in Christ. (*John 1:14*)

➔ Jesus glorified the Father in everything he did. (*John 17:4*)

➔ God is behind everything (except sin), and therefore he deserves glory for it all. (*Romans 11:36*)

➔ Christians are to reflect God's glory in their lives. (*2 Corinthians 3:18*)

➔ Christ is the radiance of God's glory — which means that we see the glory of God best in him. (*Hebrews 1:3*)

➔ Heaven is a place where people continually give God glory. (*Revelation 4-5*)

As you can see, the Bible is full of the glory of God. No other book gives God the credit that he deserves. That's not surprising, because the Lord was behind the writing of the Bible and he *made sure* that he would get proper credit for what he did. It would be a shame if we read it and missed the point — unfortunately, that does happen. Some people are so blind that they can't see the glory of God in the very thing that glorifies him the most!

Probably the biggest reason that God doesn't get glory is that it's not very obvious when he is involved in something. God is Spirit, and it takes spiritual eyes to follow him as he works. All that we see are the results, not the causes. And an unbeliever is, of course, going to claim that those results happened not because God did them but because of other causes. Psychologists think that a person becomes a Christian because of events in his childhood or the environment. Evolutionists think that the world came to exist through chance and accident. Few people see that God did all these things, so of course he doesn't get any credit for them. That makes the Bible even more important to us: it pulls away the veil so that we *can* see who is really behind all these events. The Bible alone shows us the truth about God.

Does God get glory?

We may ask the question, *why* does God bring glory to himself? Isn't that like "tooting your own horn" or patting oneself on the back? We hate to see people do that (though they often do!) because it doesn't look very good. Paul warned us not to think more of ourselves than we ought. (Romans 12:3) Why, then, is it OK if God does it?

There are two answers to that question: *first*, God really is what he claims to be. A proud person who struts his stuff and shows off before others may or may not be able to back up those claims of greatness. The Lord, however, has made claims about himself that even the proudest man on earth would never think of making — and then backed them up with hard facts. When God challenged Job by asking if he had made all the creatures of the earth, he was showing Job that only the Lord *could* do such a thing. (Job 38-41) The evidence is all around us that God is the Creator, that Genesis 1-2 tells the story of someone who knew what he was doing and could do what no other power in the universe could even attempt. So if God can and does do these things, what's wrong with saying so? It's the truth!

Second, when he shows us his glory, he isn't trying to make us feel bad or inferior — like an arrogant person would do. God glorifies himself *so that we might be saved.* The wonderful things about God that he shows to us are solutions to our problems. They are *good news*, the medicine for our ills, the very things we were hoping would be true about him. It's an advertisement, so to speak, of a great product that we desperately need. His glory isn't meant to drive us away, but to draw us closer to him for fulfillment of our deep spiritual needs. When we see the glory of God, or hear about it through the Word, that's a signal to us that it's time to reach out and take what he is offering us: himself.

> How, then, can they call on the one they have not believed in? And how can they believe in the one of whom they have not heard? And how can they hear without someone preaching to them? And how can they

preach unless they are sent? As it is written, "How beautiful are the feet of those who bring good news!" (Romans 10:14-15)

So God richly deserves glory. The problem is that he usually gets no credit at all for being what he is. He ought to get lots of glory, but he doesn't. We are strangely reluctant to give God the credit he deserves. God has been the most misunderstood person in history! People have claimed to know all about him, when really they didn't know a thing about him; they describe him in ways that completely contradict the way the Bible describes him. The things that people say about God borders on the absurd! In fact, that's the reason we have so many other gods in our religions: everyone has their own idea of who "God" is, and usually no two people are agreed on it.

When we look around for someone to save us, we *don't know* that God can and will save us if we go to him and ask for it — in other words, we don't give him the credit for being the Savior. When we need an explanation for why circumstances turn out the way they do, we *don't know* that God was behind it working out his purposes — and we come up with nonsense trying to explain the way the world works. So, God is like an expert that we should be using but nobody knows about. The Lord gets no credit at all for being what he is, and we continue to shuffle along without him. Most of the time we act as if he wasn't even real!

The result is that "my people are destroyed from lack of knowledge." (Hosea 4:6). This confusion can't continue; the Lord wants everyone to know the truth about him. He wants a kingdom in which all eyes are on him and he does everything for them that they need. He wants a people who trust in him completely. He wants sinners to fear him. He will be pleased only when we start to take him seriously.

Things he deserves glory for

The Lord wants to get glory for a change. He wants credit for being what he is, not what he isn't. The first step in seeing the glory of God in the Bible is to learn some basics about him, some concepts that we must believe — or else everything that we believe about him will be perverted and wrong.

The problem is that these basics are "hot spots" for us — we didn't think that these things were true about God. Our preconceived notions of God keep him safely at arm's length, in some safe place away from us so that we have room to be ourselves and decide our own fate. There are some rights that we cherish too much to give over to God's control! But our notions of who God is just aren't true, and we are in for a surprise when we read the Bible. The purpose of God's revelation is to destroy those myths of ours and force us to see the truth about God — and then our lives are going to change drastically as a result. (Remember, the more credit God gets for what he does, the better for us — his glory is our salvation!)

- ***There are some things that only God can do.*** "Do not be afraid, O worm Jacob, O little Israel, for I myself will help you, declares the LORD, your Redeemer, the Holy One of Israel." (Isaiah 41:14) Did you catch the word "worm" in this verse? It's to show us that we are completely helpless if God doesn't help us. There are many things that we need that only God can do. He knows that only he can do it, and he won't let anybody else do the work for him; it *can't* be done by anybody else. When we finally admit that, we are giving God the glory he deserves.

What are these things? We are willing to give him credit for doing a few things — for example, many will allow the fact that God made the world — but we don't often think through what that means. If he is the Creator, that means that only he knows what this world is, and what it needs, and where it is going, and how everyone fits into it, and how to take care of it. It means that we are needy creatures who depend on God to take care of *all* our needs. He must feed us, he must protect us, he must give us everything we need to live, or we will die. "The earth is the LORD's, and everything in it, the world, and all who live in it." (Psalm 24:1) "The eyes of all look to you, and you give them their food at the proper time. You open your hand and satisfy the desires of every living thing." (Psalm 145:15-16) If it wasn't for God's constant care we would all die.

But does he get the credit for being our provider? Not very often! We might say a quick "thanks" but, like little children, too often we take all the good things in life for granted, as if they just showed up on the table (we don't really care how) and we have a right to these things. The result is that God doesn't get the glory that he deserves — we don't really believe that he gives us all these things that we take for granted.

Only God can give you what you need, and he will — if you give him the credit for being able to. "For the pagans run after all these things, and your heavenly Father knows that you need them. But seek first his kingdom and his righteousness, and all these things will be given to you as well." (Matthew 6:32-33) The trouble is that we just hate to take that step of faith that God can and will do this for us; in other words, we don't want to give him glory.

There are many other things that only God can do. He alone can save man from sin; he alone can see the end from the beginning and make sure that events take the right road to that end; he alone can protect us from our enemies; he alone can make the Church strong; he alone can work miracles. We have seen some of these things in former chapters. The Israelites got a wonderful lesson on all this when the Lord led them out of Egypt, out of slavery, through the desert into the Promised Land. "You were shown these things so that you might know that the LORD is God; besides him there is no other." (Deuteronomy 4:35) This was the whole point of the Exodus: God got glory in the entire process.

• ***He knows what he is doing.*** "I make known the end from the beginning, from ancient times, what is still to come. I say: My purpose will stand, and I will do all that I please." (Isaiah 46:10) Never underestimate the wisdom of God. We might not think he knows what he is doing — circumstances often seem to be confused and things go from better to worse — but events always prove him right. He is in control over everything.

He knows what he is doing because he has unfathomable wisdom. There is no end to God's knowledge and insight. Man's puny efforts at understanding the world, even though they look impressive when they fill whole libraries of knowledge, are only a drop in the bucket compared to God's knowledge of his creation. And that doesn't begin to cover his wisdom — there is an eternal world that is far bigger than the physical universe, and he rules over that as well!

But the way some people talk, they make God out to be a fool; they seem to know better than he does what is necessary and right. They evidently think that they would do a better job at running the world! "If there is a God," they say, "why then is there misery and suffering? Why does the Church fail? Why do the wicked rule?" In an effort to make sense of the contradiction — that God is good and yet his world is bad — they say things about God that just aren't true.

We need to start off on the right foot by giving the Lord his due: this is his world, he is completely responsible for what happens in it, and he knows exactly what he's doing — in spite of our misgivings. History is proceeding just as he planned, and this whole business will end exactly as he conceived it at the beginning. And he isn't surprised or confused or frustrated by anything along the way!

We of course don't understand what God is doing, and we doubt his wisdom. David looked at how well the wicked were doing in life and couldn't understand why God could let such a thing happen. He thought that God had made a mistake! But the Lord graciously showed him the truth:

> When I tried to understand all this, it was oppressive to me till I entered the sanctuary of God; then I understood their final destiny. (Psalm 73:16-17)

He found out that the wicked weren't going to get away with anything. Though they lived long lives and prospered, the day of reckoning was sure and certain.

By the way, the sanctuary in those days was the place where God *revealed* himself to his people. It was only there that David learned the real truth about what was going on. In our day it is the Bible; only when you read the Word and believe it will you start to understand that the Lord really does know what he is doing in the otherwise confusing circumstances in your life.

Perhaps the best known example of this principle is the story of the blind man in John 9. The disciples wondered *why* the man was born blind; in their mind, it made sense that it was the man's own fault he was deformed. But Jesus told them that they were wrong:

> "Neither this man nor his parents sinned," said Jesus, "but this happened so that the work of God might be displayed in his life." (John 9:3)

Do you get the significance of what Jesus is saying? The man's blindness wasn't chance, or genetic, or even due to sin: God did it so that this miracle could take place. How many times during his life must this man have wondered *why* he had to be blind? He never knew that God did it to him, as step one, in preparation for step two — the healing. "When times are good, be happy; but when times are bad, consider: God has made the one as well as the other." (Ecclesiastes 7:14) People don't like to believe this about God, so he doesn't get the glory he deserves.

• *__He knows best.__* "Our fathers disciplined us for a little while as they thought best; but God disciplines us for our good, that we may share in his holiness." (Hebrews 12:10) The last point is related to this one: if we give him the credit for knowing what he is doing, we also have to believe that he has our well-being in mind. Whatever he does is for our good; we have no cause to complain of his treatment of us.

> And we know that in all things God works for the good of those who love him, who have been called according to his purpose. (Romans 8:28)

He knows how the world works (of course, since he made all things!), he knows what we need, he knows our hearts, he knows all the dangers around us, he knows what it will take to make us fit to live with him, he knows what will destroy us, he knows what roads are safe and what roads are dangerous — he knows it all. So how foolish we appear when we come to this one who is all-knowing and pretend to tell him how to run his kingdom! "Guard your steps when you go to the house of God. Go near to listen rather than to offer the sacrifice of fools, who do not know that they do wrong." (Ecclesiastes 5:1)

When he led the Israelites out into the desert where there was no food or water, the people thought he was leading them to their deaths.

> Why did you bring the LORD's community into this desert, that we and our livestock should die here? Why did you bring us up out of Egypt to this

terrible place? It has no grain or figs,
grapevines or pomegranates. And there is
no water to drink! (Numbers 20:4-5)

This is typical human nature. We are never
satisfied with how life is going for us, and we usually
blame God for our problems. What they didn't
understand, however, was that the Lord was training
them to live by faith — a rare and precious skill that no
other nation had the privilege of learning. If someone
can live by faith, he has all the treasures of Heaven at
his disposal, let alone the treasures of earth! The Lord
made them go without some of the more immediate
comforts in life so that they might gain invaluable
experience in how to live by faith.

We almost never learn this. Unfortunately the
Israelites complained all the way to the Promised Land,
doubting God's good intentions the whole way. We do
the same when life treats us roughly. Someone has to
take the blame! Since God claims to be taking care of
us, he is the natural one to blame: why can't he take
better care of us? But when we accuse him of not doing
what is best for us (or at least more to our liking) we
aren't giving him the credit for knowing what *is* best for
us.

For an example of someone who knew how to
give God glory, see Joseph. There was a man who
suffered through unbelievable oppression and rejection
for no good reason! Yet he could say to his brothers,
"You intended to harm me, but God intended it for good
to accomplish what is now being done, the saving of
many lives." (Genesis 50:20) Joseph gave God credit
for knowing what was best for all concerned.

• ***He is powerful.*** "For nothing is impossible with
God." (Luke 1:37) God does the impossible; we saw
that when we studied miracles. He loves it when people
believe that and turn to him for impossible things.

In light of this truth, it's amazing how people continue to think that God can't do certain things. When the wicked gain the upper hand in society and they are the ones that rule, the righteous panic: now all is lost, they think, and things are going to go from bad to worse. They forget that "surely the nations are like a drop in a bucket; they are regarded as dust on the scales; he weighs the islands as though they were fine dust." (Isaiah 40:15) When the food in the cupboard runs out, people panic: they lose all hope when they can't provide for themselves. They forget that the Lord promised, "Never will I leave you; never will I forsake you." (Hebrews 13:5)

We might question whether God *will* do something, but it's never a question whether he *can* do it. He can do anything he wants to do! If he doesn't do it, the problem is with us instead: there is either sin in our heart, or we don't believe he can do it, or it isn't the right time for it. It's not fair to lay the blame on God when he isn't doing great things in our lives!

The one time that we reveal exactly what we think of God's abilities is when we pray. What do we ask for? If we ask for little things, we aren't giving God much credit for being able to do the impossible. If we ask the Creator of the world for just a "blessing" — without being specific about what particular blessing we need — isn't that wasting a golden opportunity? The one who can do *anything* has granted you the privilege of access to his throne, and he told you to ask for *anything* in his Name! "I tell you the truth, my Father will give you whatever you ask in my name." (John 16:23)

Some people don't hesitate to honor God with big requests. Gideon, for example, asked for something he knew was impossible; if such a thing happened, he reasoned, then truly he was in touch with the God of

Israel. (Judges 6:36-40) On the other hand, some people don't think that God can do big things, so they scale down their requests to something safer. Even if God doesn't answer with a miracle, they reason, the thing I ask for could very well happen on its own — and I'll accept that as an "answer" to my prayer. The king of Israel, for example, struck the ground only three times for victory, not believing enough in God's power to ask for six victories. For such unbelief he was rebuked. (2 Kings 13:18)

The Lord wants credit for being able to do the impossible. We've got to start giving him glory for being able to do *all things*, because we desperately need those works of almighty power to solve some of the problems that we have.

• ***He is the only resource***. "Every good and perfect gift is from above, coming down from the Father of the heavenly lights, who does not change like shifting shadows." (James 1:17) We tend to think that we can get all that we need from the world around us, or from people we know, or even from our own efforts. But that's not true — God alone is the source of all that we receive, whether we know it or not or even if we appreciate it or not. Our mistake is this: we don't realize that the world is only the medium, the "chute", so to speak, through which God gives us what we need. He is the real source of everything.

It's no use turning to the world for what we need, because the world's promises are hollow and deceitful. It *can't* give us what we really need; it is only God's "servant" that contains the storehouse that he stocked for our use. God, however, is a never-ending source of supply and protection: we will never go hungry if we depend on the Lord. The Bible gives us plenty of testimony that this is true. "I was young and now I am old, yet I have never seen the righteous forsaken or their children begging bread." (Psalm 37:25)

"For the pagans run after all these things, and your heavenly Father knows that you need them. But seek first his kingdom and his righteousness, and all these things will be given to you as well." (Matthew 6:32-33) The Lord fed the Israelites for forty years in the desert, with manna from Heaven, when they had no other source of food to draw from. (Deuteronomy 2:7) Jesus fed over 5000 men, as well as the women and children, with a few loaves of bread. (Matthew 14:14-21) He also provided the tax that he and Peter owed in the mouth of a fish. (Matthew 17:27) Paul found him to be completely sufficient: "I can do everything through him who gives me strength." (Philippians 4:13)

If we don't know this to be true in our lives it's only because we haven't tried it — we don't want to trust him for it, perhaps. It's not because he can't provide for us! It stands to reason that the Creator of the entire universe can surely give us what we need no matter what that may be. All his world is at his disposal, and he promised to take care of all his creatures.

More important, however, is the fact that he *will* give us what we need spiritually. Our souls have desperate needs that only God can provide for: "My soul yearns, even faints, for the courts of the LORD; my heart and my flesh cry out for the living God." (Psalm 84:2) Spiritually we need *him*; we can't live without him. Of course he knows this, and he will give us himself to feed on:

> Whoever eats my flesh and drinks my blood has eternal life, and I will raise him up at the last day. For my flesh is real food and my blood is real drink. Whoever eats my flesh and drinks my blood remains in me, and I in him. (John 6:54-56)

Our problem, however, is that we rarely turn to God for anything. We too often turn to every resource *except* him when we are in need. James noted that "You do not have, because you do not ask God." (James 4:2) And we do not ask God because we think that something else will be able to take care of our needs better than he can. So we do him a dishonor, saying that he isn't our *only* source of good.

• *He is the explanation.* "When times are good, be happy; but when times are bad, consider: God has made the one as well as the other. Therefore, a man cannot discover anything about his future." (Ecclesiastes 7:14) It's a surprise to most people that God is behind most of what goes on in this world. They like to think that he wound the world up like a clock and then went off to do other things, leaving us on our own to figure out life alone. They wish! God has no such intention of letting his creation follow its own directions. He has a purpose for it all! And it can't fulfill his purpose unless he is there, every step of the way, guiding it along his paths.

The only thing that God won't take responsibility for is sin — man and the devil alone are responsible for that. But the penalty for sin *is* due to God: "You must not eat from the tree of the knowledge of good and evil, for when you eat of it you will surely die." Genesis 2:17) God is responsible for the first massive judgment of sinners (Genesis 6-8), the scattering of the races (Genesis 11:1-9), the rise of the holy family of Abraham (Genesis 12), the destruction of Sodom and Gomorrah (Genesis 19), the protection of Jacob's family in Egypt (Genesis 46-50), the deliverance of the Israelites from Egypt through Moses (Exodus 12), the Israelites entering the promised Land under Joshua (Joshua), the rise of David as king over Israel and model of the Messiah (2 Samuel) — we can go on and on because the list of things that God did is huge. He was behind all these events, both good and bad, though people may not have known it at the time. Often they didn't know it until years or centuries later when the Word of God came with an explanation of what happened to their fathers in former years.

There are three important reasons for knowing the truth about this. *First*, if we think that nature takes care of our needs, that "fate" is behind the way circumstances turn out, then we won't rely on God for these things, will we? We will turn to other "gods" to take care of us instead of the one who alone can take care of us. That takes away from his glory! No other god can do what we need, nor will the Lord allow any other power to pretend to take his place. Either we believe that or we don't. But someday the veil will be taken away and we will see that there were no other gods involved, that the Lord God Almighty was behind everything that happened, whether people believed that or not, and help was only a call away if they had taken the trouble to turn to him.

Second, if we don't think that God is behind all the events of history, then what *do* we think about him? It can't be flattering! Is he helplessly standing by while his creation runs crazily on its own? Is he a fool, that he set a world into motion and made men only to have the whole thing explode into sin and rebellion in his face — did he really not know what he was doing in the beginning? Is he irresponsible, that he lets wickedness and "chance" and misery and death and meaninglessness happen without lifting a finger to do anything about it? We can't think such things about our God! To avoid believing blasphemy about him, we have to give him credit for knowing what he is doing and being in control of things. Even if we don't understand *how* he could direct all things to his glory, we must believe that he does — the alternative is unthinkable.

The *third* reason that we must believe that God is behind all things is that, if we don't, we will get a confused notion of who God really is. If we believe that

God only does loving things, we won't believe that he is the Judge of all men and the punisher of the wicked — which he is. If we believe that God lets circumstances take their own course, we won't believe that the Lord works all things to the good of them who love him. (Romans 8:28) Something in our understanding of God is going to suffer if we don't accept *everything* the Bible teaches us about his wide range of activities. He is bigger than our understandings; it's always a mistake to limit the Lord to what we can logically grasp. The human mind can't fully comprehend the infinite God and all the things he does. So we can't focus on just one passage: we have to believe *all* the things that the Bible says about him, even if we don't understand how it all fits together. He knows how it does, and that should be good enough for us.

These particular points are the areas where God deserves the most glory, and unfortunately they are also the areas where we have the most trouble giving him that glory. That's typical when sinners read the Bible: he demands credit for being what he is, but we don't like what we see about him there and so we refuse to believe it. There will always be a battle between the Lord and us over these issues.

How does he get glory?

In order to get glory, God has to get our attention. We are so engrossed with our personal lives that we tend to think that the whole world revolves around *us*! We forget that there is a God. We can't see him, much of what we do can be done without him, and therefore he just isn't very real to us. Only on Sundays do we ever think about him, and even there he seems remote and distant — a story from long ago. Since we live without God so much, before God can do anything for us he first has to appear in person and show us that we can't afford to live without him any longer.

Christianity takes two to work: the Lord, and you. False religions do very well without their gods, which is a good thing because their gods don't exit! But our God exists; he is real. We just cannot continue to do "religion" without the Lord. We have problems that can't be solved unless he steps in personally and takes care of them himself. And that's how the Lord gets glory — by stepping into our lives and doing things that only God can do. When there are suddenly answers to our problems that nobody can account for, all eyes turn to the Lord; it's plain then that he must be real.

God gets glory in these ways:

• ***When he overrules men's works*** — Man is a determined creature and he usually does what he wants to do. He is a problem-solver: if he can't solve the problem one way, he will usually try a different approach and succeed by doing it another way. Mountains can't even stand in the way of men if they decide they want a road there instead.

But if the Lord decides that he doesn't want man to do something, *he* steps in our way and becomes an obstacle that nobody can move. There are times when the Lord overrules and man *can't* do what he wants — under any circumstances. Instead, what happens is what *God* wants, and man can't do a thing about it. For example, read the story of the Tower of Babel in Genesis 11:1-9. The point here is that men usually can find a way to achieve whatever they want to do, if they can get cooperation between themselves. There was no reason to expect the project to fail. But the Lord didn't want them to do this thing. "If as one people speaking the same language they have begun to do this, then nothing they plan to do will be impossible for them." (Genesis 11:6) So he stopped them! In an unexpected way, he confused their language so that they could never again attempt such a project and hope to succeed with it. God was a barrier to them that they neither expected nor could they overcome.

The Lord also stopped Balaam from cursing the Israelites. (Numbers 22:21-35) He brought the giant waves of the Red Sea crashing down on the Egyptian soldiers who were chasing the Israelites. He blinded a false prophet who was making a lot of trouble for Paul. (Acts 13:6-12) There are many examples in Scripture that show the Lord frustrating the plans of the wicked and doing his own will instead.

When the Lord has something to do, he is like a steamroller that smashes through all of man's plans. When the schemes of men suddenly stop, for no accountable reason, and sinners are frustrated from carrying out their purposes, and Satan is forced to retreat, it is plain that God is there tearing down the kingdoms of men and setting up his kingdom in their place.

• ***When he rescues*** — The Lord rescues his people in amazing ways. He seems to take delight in *how* he rescues them, as if he wants to prove beyond any doubt that only he could do such a thing. His rescues are fantastic displays of his infinite wisdom and power, and are primary ways that he gets glory.

For example, the most famous rescue in the Old Testament was the time that Moses led the Israelites out of Egypt. (Exodus 7-14) First the Lord hammered the Egyptians with ten plagues, with the result that the most powerful nation on earth was beaten down into the dust helpless, and the Israelites didn't have to do anything to help. Next the Lord opened up the Red Sea and brought his people through safely while the walls of water towered on both sides over them. The Egyptian soldiers who followed them in were, of course, drowned when the Lord let the water crash down on them.

We read the story almost disinterestedly as if it were no more than a fable. But the Israelites who witnessed it were struck with wonder at what they saw; they never imagined that God could do such a thing. God was there, in power, holding his hand over them and striking their enemy. They had heard about God in the past through stories that their elders told them, but here was that God in person working for their benefit! They never forgot the miracle, which they continue to tell their children to this day, more than 3000 years after it happened.

This is a good example of how the Lord works an awesome miracle to deliver his people out of the trouble they are in and gets glory from it. They are usually in the kind of trouble that nobody *could* help them with: for instance, when the Philistines kept pounding away at the helpless Israelite tribes, or when Sennacherib showed up at Jerusalem's gates with hundreds of thousands of invincible soldiers. What God did to get them out of the mess was miraculous, unexpected, nothing that anybody else could have done, and it *worked*. It's a wonderful testimony for us who need help with our own problems. When he saves us in such amazing ways, there is no doubt that there is a power present that can't be explained in earthly terms.

• ***When people try it his way*** — When Naaman was told that he could wash in the Jordan River to get rid of his leprosy, he scorned the very idea: he thought that the great rivers back home were more worthy of such honor than this little Israelite stream. But unless he humbled himself and did what the Lord told him, he was going to remain a leper — there was no healing anywhere else except where the Lord directed him. (2 Kings 5)

This strikes at our pride, our attitude that we ought to know better what we really need. Since Adam and Eve first ate the forbidden fruit in the garden, we have all formed our own opinions on what is right and wrong and what we want to do with our lives. But as we have already seen, our ways are not God's ways — the difference is that our ways *do not* work and his *always* work. When we put our ways aside and do it his way for a change (not reluctantly but in faith), we find life — and, of course, he gets credit for having ways that work.

There are many examples of this principle. The Israelites did as God said and marched around Jericho seven days, shouting and blowing their trumpets; on the seventh day the city fell without a single man touching the walls. (Joshua 6) When Gideon wanted to take a large army against the Midianites, the Lord instructed him to prune down the size of his force until there were only 300 left — and armed with torches and clay pots they routed the entire enemy army. (Judges 7) When Peter resisted the Spirit who was telling him to go to the gentile Cornelius with the gospel, the Lord *insisted*; Peter came back amazed that Cornelius believed and the Spirit came into him just as the Jewish Christians had experienced. (Acts 10) What did Peter expect would happen, anyway, when the Lord was behind it!

In these and many more instances, God shows that "he knows best." We never believe him at first; but when we do what he says, and things start working for a change, then we get a new appreciation for our God and the kinds of things he can do. This is what "glory" means.

• *When the wicked are destroyed* — God gets glory from the most terrible events in human history as well as positive events. We don't like to think about such things — if we admit that he gets glory from punishing men for their sins, then any of us could find his sword of vengeance hanging over *our* heads for *our* sins. That's too close for comfort! It means that we have to be careful how we live and do things in such a way that would please *him*, not ourselves. It means that God will not hesitate to finally draw the line and put an end to man's wickedness with severe and irreversible punishment, with no hope of anybody rescuing us from his hands. When it comes time to punish, the God whom everyone thought was just a story from the past shows up in person, in glory, and does terrifying things.

Glory is always God's goal, and punishing the wicked brings him glory too. It shows that he means business when he tells us how to live. It shows that he intends to reward those who are righteous and who turn away from their sin. If the wicked get away with rebellion, how fair would that be to those who obey? So when the Lord destroys the wicked, he is showing us some of his most precious characteristics, things that believers hope are true about him: his righteousness, his holiness, his justice, his power, his love for his own, his ability to know all things, and so on.

Sodom and Gomorrah found this out the hard way. If you go to that part of the world today, you will find nothing there that even hints that those cities used to exist. God finally had enough of their wickedness and destroyed them completely. Did it bring him glory? Yes — the event was plainly recorded for all history to read and learn from. He showed in an unmistakable way that he will not put up with men's sins forever, but will finally bring them to account for their rebellion against him. "He condemned the cities of Sodom and Gomorrah by burning them to ashes, and made them an example of what is going to happen to the ungodly." (2 Peter 2:6) When you read what he did to the wicked in story after story, you eventually learn that you had better not cross him. "The fear of the LORD is the beginning of knowledge." (Proverbs 1:7) God is real, he exists — and "our God is a consuming fire." (Hebrews 12:29) Don't make the mistake that most do, thinking that he won't do anything about your sin. He certainly will.

• ***When he takes care of everything*** — God is like a parent who watches over his foolish children. We think that we can take care of ourselves and handle most any problem in life that we have. Meanwhile the Lord (who knows that we *can't* take care of ourselves) makes sure that we have everything that we need, often giving us things that we didn't realize that we needed. He has such a huge perspective on the world that it's a good thing he's taking care of us or we wouldn't survive long!

When the Israelites were in the desert, the Lord thought of everything. He saw to it that they got the obvious necessities, like food and water. He also provided things that they didn't think about: like protection from their enemies, and directions to the next stop, and capable leaders. He gave them laws to live by, covering all the aspects of life that none of them could foresee in the future — like the Temple worship and what to do with prophets. He also knew what they needed spiritually: he spelled out all the sins they *could* do against him (and would do!), as well as the necessary sacrifices for forgiveness of those sins. No other nation had the benefit of God watching over their every need! They just never realized how well he was taking care of them.

Other examples: when Jesus was teaching the people out in the mountains and providing their souls with spiritual food, he took care of their physical needs while he was at it and fed them with bread and fish to eat. (Matthew 14:15-21; Matthew 15:32-38) When Jacob was working for his uncle Laban, the Lord made sure that he increased in wealth and family over the years so that he returned home a much richer man and ready to launch the twelve tribes of Israel into history. (Genesis 29-31) Ruth, unknown to herself, was led by God in every (seemingly chance) circumstance as she found a husband in Boaz — the forefather of King David. (Ruth)

Usually we only know part of what is going on around us; when a desperate need hits us, it surprises us because we just didn't expect to get hit with those kinds of circumstances. The Lord always knows what is needed, however, long before the need comes up — and he is always there when the time comes with the necessary answer. "And God is faithful; he will not let you be tempted beyond what you can bear. But when you are tempted, he will also provide a way out so that you can stand up under it." (1 Corinthians 10:13) He isn't surprised by anything. Paul got so used to the Lord's never-failing mercies that he could say with confidence, "I have learned the secret of being content in any and every situation, whether well fed or hungry, whether living in plenty or in want. I can do everything through him who gives me strength." (Philippians 4:12-13) Here is the kind of glory that draws people from an undependable world and gives them hope in God instead.

• ***When we pray*** — The Lord gets profound glory when we turn to him for what we need. Prayer is the highlight of the Kingdom of God; it is far more important and powerful than we realize. In Heaven, a prayer is like a bell that signals everyone there that someone from earth has come to lay claim to the promises of God. It rarely happens, though, because so few people believe that those treasures are lying there for the asking.

Prayer reaches out for the God who is real. Only faith is going to see God: "Anyone who comes to him must believe that he exists and that he rewards those who earnestly seek him." (Hebrews 11:6) Remember that God's glory means his presence among us, the overwhelming sense that we are in touch with the Creator and Redeemer. When someone prays, they believe (or they should!) that the God of the Bible is real and he is ready to receive all who come to him with special requests. When we find him, he proves himself real by making us aware of himself — we know we are in his presence, and that both terrifies us because of our sin (Isaiah 6) and encourages us to ask for his mercy. (Hebrews 10:19-23)

Prayer shows that we *know* that God is the only one who can help us. We have given up trying to do it ourselves and now we are asking him to do it for us. And when he answers us and gives us what we ask for, that gives him credit in a powerful way: no other gods ever answered *their* followers! People see these answers and wish they could have them too — soon others are looking into the reason for our faith, because it's obvious that we are praying to the living God when we get answers.

We pray for what we can't do. We can fry ourselves breakfast, and drive the car, and study for a test; it doesn't make sense to ask the Lord to do things that we can do for ourselves. But there are many things that we can't do and *shouldn't* do. We aren't allowed to try, because that would mean that God isn't the answer and we don't need him! He expects people to turn to him when they need victory over sin; that's something that sinners can't do and shouldn't try on their own. They can't live forever unless he gives them life; they can't ease their conscience until he forgives them; they can't go to Heaven unless he takes them there.

Hezekiah knew, when the overwhelming army of the Assyrians surrounded Jerusalem, that unless the Lord did a miracle for them they were all lost. So he did what few people do in his situation (for proof of this, read about most of the other Israelite kings and what *they* did when they were in trouble!), but the very thing that honors God the most: he went to God in prayer. That's all that the Lord was waiting for — it was an open door of invitation through which he could do good for his people. He got glory that day when he killed 185,000 of the enemy soldiers as they slept. (2 Kings 19) The enemy felt the burden of the Almighty that night!

Prayer is an opportunity to God as well as to ourselves. We gain the treasures of Heaven, and the Lord gains glory. He will never miss an opportunity to answer a prayer of faith. That's why Jesus insisted that we ask for whatever we wanted from the Father. "And I will do whatever you ask in my Name, so that the Son may bring glory to the Father. You may ask me for anything in my Name, and I will do it." (John 14:13-14) You see, your prayer tells the world that you *actually believe* what the Bible says about God! He isn't going to let this golden opportunity slide by. He is going to answer that prayer and show the world how real he is, and what someone can expect from him if they would come to him too.

• ***When we believe*** — Our faith is another golden opportunity for God to "show off" what he can do for his people. It moves us to pray for his promises, to wait patiently on the answer, and to obey him even when circumstances make it hard.

Faith is the ability to get past the false appearances that this world puts in our way and see the reality of God's world. When Peter stepped out of the boat and started walking on the water, he knew Jesus was holding him up — though no scientist could have seen how he did it. That story tells us the kinds of things Jesus can do for those who trust in him. (Matthew 14:28-32) When Abraham laid his son Isaac on the altar and raised his knife to kill him in obedience to the Lord's command, the Lord told him that —

> I swear by myself, declares the LORD, that because you have done this and have not withheld your son, your only son, I will surely bless you and make your descendants as numerous as the stars in the sky and as the sand on the seashore. Your descendants will take possession of the cities of their enemies, and through your offspring all nations on earth will be blessed, because you have obeyed me. (Genesis 22:16-18)

Abraham knew, since there was nothing in this world to encourage him in his faith, that all the circumstances were against the promise of God. But he also knew that the Lord could and would bring good out of this desperate situation in spite of the impossibility of it. (Hebrews 11:17-19) Faith can see what unbelief can't see — the reality of God, which is another way of saying the glory of God.

When God requires obedience and faith from us, we will sometimes understand why he expects these things from us — but we will *always* find it hard to do because of the difficulties it causes us in this world. That's why faith honors God so much — it says that in spite of the difficulties, he can more than make up for all those problems with the rewards he has in store for us.

• ***In the Church*** — The Church is the special place on earth where the glory of God is broadcast — we could say "advertised" — to all who come to hear and see. He is the center of attraction in the Church. All eyes are directed to him and we find out who he is and what he does.

Or at least the Church ought to be this way. Too often it is a stage for man to show off and do his own thing. The Lord often has little to do in churches because people are doing it all instead. They won't turn to him for what only he can do; they want to do it themselves — or they think that God won't do it and they *must* do it themselves. So of course they are going to live with the results of their own efforts, and that is like starving to death on worthless husks. But they don't seem to mind this life of failure and doing without God.

This isn't the purpose of the Church. Here of all places is where people ought to see the glory of God: he is there, in a way that is special and unique on earth. "For where two or three come together in my name, there am I with them." (Matthew 18:20) If anybody wants to see God at work, building his eternal Kingdom and saving souls, they should be able to witness such things in the Church.

How does this happen? The leaders preach and teach the Word which tells us about God and what he does; sinners see their only hope in him; witnesses tell of what he did for them; people bend the knee before him and pray for what only he can give them; the Lord issues his orders (since he *is* the head of the Church!) and willing servants go out into the world to follow his commands. The whole experience of church should make everyone "fall down and worship God, exclaiming, 'God is really among you!' " (1 Corinthians 14:25)

When the Christians in Jerusalem had a problem with persecution they were getting from the Jews, they went to God and honored him in their prayer (they used his Word, they called on his Name, they turned to him for what only he could do, and other things). The building shook from the power of the Spirit that came down on them. He heard, he saw them honoring him, and he responded in power. (Acts 4:24-31) God was *there among them*, in power, in his glory, and he filled them with power to go out and do miraculous things. Only when a church experiences unearthly things, things that can't be explained in any way except God himself did it, will it be a church that he is pleased with.

Who will glorify God?

God will get glory — but from whom? Who will tell the world what God is like? Who will draw men's attention to the Lord for a change and make us to see how wise and powerful he is, how much we all need him?

The newspapers aren't going to. They give him no credit at all for what happens in the world, nor do they report on the spiritual progress of the Church — although there certainly is progress (the Lord is seeing to that) and it is changing people's lives. The government isn't going to glorify God because they think *they* are what the public needs, that *they* have all the answers. Yet, "the king's heart is in the hand of the LORD; he directs it like a watercourse wherever he pleases." (Proverbs 21:1) The military depends on its own arm of strength and it won't look to God to deliver them. But that's a mistake: "No king is saved by the size of his army; no warrior escapes by his great strength. A horse is a vain hope for deliverance; despite all its great strength it cannot save." (Psalm 33:16-17) Even the schools, while they are seeking knowledge, studiously avoid the Truth of the Word of God — out of principle. But, "Where is the wise man? Where is the scholar? Where is the philosopher of this age? Has not God made foolish the wisdom of the world?" (1 Corinthians 1:20) You would think that the way the world is going these days, nobody will glorify him.

But God isn't going to let that happen. He *must* get glory! And since he is bigger than we are, he is going to force the issue and make us glorify him. So you will see him getting credit for things from many different and unexpected places.

God glorifies himself, of course, and the place he does that is **in his Word**. There were times when he showed up in person, (for example, when he rescued the Israelites, and when the Lord Jesus performed miracles) but that's not how he primarily works nowadays. The first and most important place we will see the glory of God is in the Bible.

What is very unfortunate about our generation is that we have virtually closed the book and we aren't paying attention to what it says anymore. Not only has our godless generation rejected the Bible, too many Christians have found "better" sources for wisdom and guidance than the Word of God. How will we know the truth about God unless we study the material he gave us that teaches us about him? There is no other source of knowledge about God. Men's books about God are only true if they ground themselves solidly in the Scriptures;

otherwise they are deceived and no more than blind guides.

The reason that the Lord gave us the Bible is to teach us the kinds of things he can do *for* those who love him and *against* those who hate him. He is showing us that he is real, and if we take him seriously and trust in him then he will start taking us seriously and fulfill his amazing promises for us. Then the cold words of the book will become powerful and exciting realities for us.

All the world will glorify the Lord at some point or another. "Holy, holy, holy is the LORD Almighty; the whole earth is full of his glory." (Isaiah 6:3) God made this world; you can tell by the traces left behind. The creation glorifies him by showing off his wisdom and handiwork: "The heavens declare the glory of God; the skies proclaim the work of his hands." (Psalm 19:1) You can also tell that this is God's world by the way it keeps running — according to wisdom and purpose. He hasn't gone off somewhere to let it run on its own; everything that happens is due to his continued work and masterful hand. And the new heavens and new earth that will come after the destruction of this one will also show off God's glory, because it too will be entirely his doing.

Witnesses will glorify the Lord — those who have tried the Lord and found him to be everything the Word says he is. "Anyone who comes to him must believe that he exists and that he rewards those who earnestly seek him." (Hebrews 11:6) Their testimony is valuable for this reason: they are "advertising", so to speak, and telling us things about God that we also can use if we will go to him. God isn't just a story in an ancient book: he still lives to keep his promises to anyone who comes (*now*) to him.

We are ready to listen to people that we can identify with — people who had the same problems that we have. When their problems are solved, that makes us think that the solution that they found would be good for us too. That's how we should use the testimony of the Bible. Moses glorified God after the Lord delivered the Israelites out of Egypt (Exodus 15:1-18): he told of what he saw and experienced that day, and this helped the Israelites remember that story for thousands of years. The Jews still recite it at their worship services! God was real to them that day, and it keeps alive the hope that he will come again and rescue them. David wrote scores of psalms telling about the spiritual riches he found at the table of the Lord; these are what give Christians hope as they approach God for the same things.

Enemies will also glorify God. This might seem strange, but even those who have no love at all for God will be forced to admit that God deserves credit for being the only God. When Moses started doing miracles that Pharaoh's own experts couldn't duplicate, the Egyptians said to Pharaoh: "This is the finger of God." (Exodus 8:19) They were forced to admit that they were dealing with a power here that they couldn't keep up with. The Israelites' God was real! Balaam was forced to glorify God and he couldn't curse the Israelites, as he was hired to do, (Numbers 23-24), though he was no friend of God or God's people, as events proved later. God came in person and overruled what Balaam would have liked to have done. It's especially satisfying to see people who hate God being forced to admit that there really is a God, and that he won.

Every knee will someday bow before the Lord and give him the glory he deserves. (Philippians 2:10-11) For thousands of years the Lord has patiently waited for the credit he ought to have had, being more concerned with saving sinners than clearing his Name at this time. He purposely hid himself behind circumstances, so that most people to this day think that he doesn't really exist. But he won't wait forever.

Those who rebelled against him through all the periods of Israel's history and got away with it will be brought forcibly to the throne of God and made to admit that he was right and they were wrong. "They will look on me, the one they have pierced." (Zechariah 12:10) All the people who did wrong in the history of the Church and refused to do things God's way will someday bend their knee before the Head of the Church — Jesus Christ — and made to admit to their wrongdoing and admit that his way was right after all. God is determined to get glory on the Last Day.

Christ glorifies God, of course, both during his ministry on earth and his present ministry in Heaven. He *is* God, but he refused to glorify himself (John 8:54) because he didn't come to do that the first time around. He came to reveal Israel's God and show them that all good things come from the Father. His name is *Immanuel* — "God with us." "Anyone who has seen me has seen the Father." (John 14:7) When people were around Jesus, they felt the reality of God in a way that they had never felt before. He finally tore away the veil that hid the Father and even now invites all those who will to approach the throne of grace; he wants us to believe that the Father forgives sinners and intends to call out children to live with him forever. He is displaying the Father, you see, and showing us that the things we read in the Old Testament about him *are true*. God is a living God — we know that when we are around Jesus.

The **Spirit** also glorifies God. He too is God, but he also doesn't bring glory to himself but to the Son of God. "But the Counselor, the Holy Spirit, whom the Father will send in my Name, will teach you all things and will remind you of everything I have said to you." (John 14:26) He does this because there is life in Christ's Name, Christ's counsel is good, his death gives life to us, he is the Prince of Peace, he restores justice and righteousness — all the Old Testament promises about him are true. The Spirit makes us see this in him when we read the Gospels. The Spirit brings us into his presence, there in Heaven, so that we can be face to face with our God and we can communicate with him. "Yet a time is coming and has now come when the true worshipers will worship the Father in Spirit and truth, for they are the kind of worshipers the Father seeks." (John 4:23) The Spirit will make these things happen among us as he builds Christ's kingdom on earth. Of course the world doesn't see Christ's glory until the Spirit opens their eyes to see the truth about him.

All these people, and God himself, are giving God the credit he deserves. The purpose is that we might be saved; the more we know about our God and what he can do for us, the better for us.

When will God get glory?

That is an interesting question. In some ways the Lord is always getting glory: for example, right now in Heaven. And his creation is continually glorifying him, even if nobody appreciates it.

In other ways the Lord isn't getting the glory he deserves. When it depends on sinners to give glory to God, it usually doesn't get done. The Lord has been very patient for these thousands of years. He could have insisted that we glorify him in *everything* we do, from the very beginning of time, and he could have severely punished people for not glorifying him. Instead he chose to let it slide for now until a better time.

The Bible records many times when he did get glory. These stories are lessons that teach us important truths about God. In other words, in a particular time and place the Lord did a miracle or spoke to someone or changed the course of human events in such a way that got him lasting glory, and he recorded it for the benefit of the rest of the Church to read and consider. But that doesn't mean that every time that same situation comes up, he will step in and do the same thing he did back then. For example, when the time came to deal with Sodom and Gomorrah, he completely destroyed them as a lesson to the rest of humanity that we mustn't take his commands lightly. We either do as he says, or he is going to destroy us. That got him glory for the rest of history, which for the time being was all he was after. There have been many other cities as wicked as those two, and they also fully deserved being destroyed! Yet he tolerated them, not giving them the punishment they deserved, and in the meantime going without the glory that he deserves.

When God waits to get glory, you really ought to take advantage of the situation and get your own relationship with him straightened out. "Bear in mind that our Lord's patience means salvation." (2 Peter 3:15) He has the right to demand glory right now — if he doesn't, he is giving you a chance to see the error of your ways and learn how to glorify him willingly. If you don't, he will someday force you to do it. (Philippians 2:10-11) So even his patience with us, and willingness to forego his glory for now, is a credit to his character and our means of salvation.

Most of the credit that the world owes God won't come out in plain view until Judgment Day. That last day will be a day of glory, to be sure; it will be then that the Lord brings back everything that happened throughout history, in the life of every human being, in the actions of every nation on earth, and settles accounts once for all. He is determined to get all the glory that we owe him on that day. He won't miss a single thing, because if he doesn't dig it all out and straighten out the record then someone will wonder if he really is almighty and all-wise as he claimed he was.

The reasons for glorifying God

This thing about giving God glory is not an option. We *must* do it; we were created to glorify him, and if we don't then there is something wrong with us. Just as an engineer expects his machine to do the job it was created for, God expects us to glorify him. All the rest of creation glorifies God; and man was specially made to glorify him in the highest ways. Many catechisms state that man's chief end is to "glorify God"; that's the only reason we are here on this earth. We can't fail him.

If you need some motivation for glorifying God, here are some important reasons why you must start doing it. As you can see, so much hangs in the balance; it would be unthinkable if we failed to give him glory!

• *He is behind everything but sin.* God isn't limited as we are. He isn't weak, he isn't ignorant, he isn't stupid. He is God, the Almighty who made all things and does what he wants to do. We need to start believing what the Bible says about him, instead of the countless theories of men that try to take away God's glory. The only thing he won't take credit for is sin; that alone is our doing. But everything else is under his control: he is carefully guiding all things (even our sin, by the way) toward the Last Day when every injustice will be made right and every mark of death reversed into life. If the least little thing was left up to chance or our caprice, the Lord couldn't guarantee the outcome at the end! But the Word says that "all things serve you" (Psalm 119:91) and all things will glorify him: "For from him and through him and to him are all things; to him be the glory forever! Amen." (Romans 11:36) He couldn't guarantee this if there was anything not under his complete control.

• *He doesn't get credit for anything until we do glorify him.* There is a sense in which God is glorious without anybody having to say so; before there was an earth, or humans living on it, God lived in total glory. He doesn't need anybody to tell him how glorious he is! But if there are going to be creatures, they all *must* see the truth about him and give him glory. If a single creature refuses to acknowledge that he *is* the only God and the only good thing there is, there is trouble in Heaven.

This is speculation, but I wonder if the reason there are so many demons (fallen angels) is because Lucifer (the devil, who was at first the chief of the angels) refused to glorify God. His rebellion possibly led to their rebellion. Something that *isn't* speculation is that a bad apple spoils the whole barrel, as the saying goes. When one person dishonors God, all sorts of bad things happen: others who see this are made bold to sin against God too, and as the wicked gain power the righteous have to hide to avoid persecution, and things deteriorate. Although God could destroy the wicked and force people to glorify him, he doesn't; for the time being, he puts up with people mocking him and denying him the credit he deserves. On Judgment Day we will find out how much damage was done and how deserving certain people are of punishment. But then it will be too late for them!

• *__We are prone to look to other gods.__* We must glorify God because, if we don't, we won't believe that only God can save us and give us what we need spiritually. People already look to every source of pleasure and good *except* God! When the priests, and especially the kings, of Israel drifted away from directing the people toward God, the entire nation turned to the false gods of their neighbors. After all, the Temple worship wasn't bringing any concrete results! The priests couldn't show them a real God, and the Canaanites could. So the people went where the action was. The same thing happens in our day when the God of the Bible is just a dusty concept that is outdated and doesn't fit into our modern culture. People *will* listen, however, when you show them a God who changes lives and stops the wicked in their tracks.

• *__He has what you need.__* Go to him. The source of all good things is God. People need to know that, if for no other reason than to keep them from going to the world and dying on the poison that the devil feeds them there. The world is no place to go for peace of mind, or relief of the conscience! The news has to get out that God has life, abundant life, and those who come to him will find freedom from their sins and joy and peace and a purpose for living. The way to God is rarely traveled; most people are headed the opposite direction to eternal misery. It's about time we made the way to God plain again, so that people can know exactly what to do to find the true God.

• ___Fear.___ There is also the other side of the coin — God not only rewards, he punishes too: he won't tolerate our sin *at all*. That has to be made plain to the world. The more we learn about God, the more we realize that we are dealing with someone here who isn't playing games. He even destroyed people for a *lack of faith*, let alone for the grosser sins that we thought were the only punishable offenses. "Let us be thankful, and so worship God acceptably with reverence and awe, for our God is a consuming fire." (Hebrews 12:28-29) One of the sure marks that God is getting glory is when people straighten up and start doing what he says to do. They don't want to sin anymore, because that offends God; they want to do what pleases him, and they are sensitive to anything that might interfere with their relationship with him. In other words, the *holy* God is real to them now.

• ___He runs the show.___ The Lord especially gets glory when people understand that *he* is the Lord — not them. This strikes at the heart of man's root problem; we do not want to submit to God in any way. We want to do our own thing, not what he tells us to do. But as long as we hold that attitude, the world is going to keep suffering in sin and death and misery and failure. There is no life when man runs things, because we use the wrong standards to judge what is right and wrong. (1 John 2:16) Life and joy and peace and success only happen when the Lord rules. Besides, even in our sin the Lord overrules and works out his purposes. "The LORD works out everything for his own ends — even the wicked for a day of disaster." (Proverbs 16:4) There is no escaping the fact that God rules over us in every way. You will especially know that you understand this when you pray; don't tell *him* what to do, but come and find out from him what *he* wants to do, and what he wants *you* to do. Prayer is for listening, not for telling. God is the Lord; we aren't.

> Guard your steps when you go to the house of God. Go near to listen rather than to offer the sacrifice of fools, who do not know that they do wrong. Do not be quick with your mouth, do not be hasty in your heart to utter anything before God. God is in Heaven and you are on earth, so let your words be few. (Ecclesiastes 5:1-2)

• *Use his wisdom.* The Lord has unfathomable wisdom, and it's a shame to waste it! Imagine, being able to access the very wisdom that made the world! The wisdom that successfully analyzes man's heart and has come up with the cure for its deadly sickness. The man who can read this knowledge has at his fingertips the answers to all the problems of life, as well as the knowledge to all the infinite treasures of Heaven. What fools we are to waste our time searching in man's wisdom, as good as it might sound, for truth — when only God really knows the truth. It's time the news got out that God alone knows what is going on in our world; only he knows the solutions to our most serious problems. That wisdom, of course, is the Bible — and it will be a glorious day when Christians take it seriously and study it for a change! When they become *experts* in the Word (it says a "workman" in 2 Timothy 2:15), that proves that they think it's worth knowing.

• *His purposes, ends.* Another thing that the world needs to hear is what God has in mind for it. We are not masters of our own fate! The Lord has already decided our fate. Instead of keeping that knowledge to himself, however, he has graciously told us ahead of time what to expect in the future. So many people read the prophetic writings of the Bible as if they were no more than comic book thrillers! That isn't why the Lord told us what Judgment Day would be like. He warns us of the destruction of the world, the judgment of all humans, the punishment of the wicked and the reward of the righteous, the new Heavens and the new earth, *so that we might be saved.* The focus is on him, not the events; we need to know why he is going to do all this, what he is after, and how we can please him so that when it does happen we will be ready spiritually for his coming!

• ***Quality of life.*** If nothing else motivates you to glorify God, this reason may — because it seems that we are most interested in how comfortable we are in our circumstances. But even this won't appeal to those whose interests are only in the things of this world. The Lord promises to honor those who honor him — "Those who honor me I will honor, but those who despise me will be disdained." (1 Samuel 2:30) In him is life — abundant life. Man little knows the precious things in store for him when he enters the halls of Heaven! All the wealth and joys of this world are nothing in comparison to the treasures that God has for those who glorify him. Though we must wait until later for most of that, we can taste those good things now, and that taste keeps us plodding on even in difficult times in the hope that the Lord will give it *all* to us as an inheritance someday.

If we don't glorify God ...

As we mentioned above, God is glorious even when nobody knows it. But the fact remains that he created us for the sole purpose of *bringing him glory.* If we don't do that, something is terribly wrong and God *will* fix the problem, one way or another.

It is not only possible to fail to glorify God, it is commonplace. He gets almost no credit for anything that he does! Usually we get the glory ourselves; we "steal the show" and make sure people see how smart and strong and clever we are. We don't realize (or perhaps we don't want to think about the fact) that everything we have, we got from God.

Probably the most important reason for learning to glorify God is this: when we don't, something gets damaged. God isn't hurt, of course, because there is nothing that man can do to hurt God. But there are many things in God's creation that we *can* hurt when we refuse to glorify him! All you have to do is *do nothing* — and that in itself will be enough to mark you as a troublemaker. The Lord requires glory from *every* creature, especially man, and any person who refuses to participate in the Divine plan is a stumbling block to others and must be removed. And if we actually take away from his glory, that makes him positively angry! (If you would like an example of how he feels when we carelessly destroy others through our ignorant ways, read Mark 9:42.)

If we don't glorify God, this is what is going to happen instead:

- *__We will get the glory instead.__* This is called **pride**, and God hates it. What happened in the Garden of Eden is the explanation for the way people act today. We set ourselves up as equal to God, capable of deciding right or wrong on our own, never turning to him for anything but relying on ourselves instead. As if we could save ourselves from death! Man has tremendous problems on his hands that he can't do a thing about; unless he turns to God he will surely die: "if you do not believe that I am the one I claim to be, you will indeed die in your sins." (John 8:24) You can easily see the effect of pride in our culture: there are monuments to man everywhere, as everyone promises us happiness if we just put our faith in men and their great works. It's as if God has nothing to do with the world, as if he wasn't even an option for answers.

- *__People won't go to the Lord to be saved.__* If he doesn't get credit for being the *only* Savior, people are going to go to all sorts of other gods instead, looking for help in time of need. That's the reason for the confusion during the early years of the Israelite nation. They were supposed to get rid of all the Canaanites living in Palestine. They didn't, however, and the result was that their ungodly neighbors showed off their pagan gods and what those gods could do for anybody who worshipped them — so the Israelites started worshipping false idols as well as the Lord. If they needed rain, they asked Baal for it; if they wanted children, they asked Ashtoreth. In the meantime the prophets were trying to get the people to forget those other gods and go to the Lord for *everything*. It was such a mess that only by sending the nation into exile did the Lord finally break the back of idol worship and get their full attention. *There are no other gods but the Lord.*

• ***Problems won't get solved.*** If people don't think that God alone is their help, they are going to go to other sources of "help" and find *nothing*. Governments and schools and businesses are all trying to find solutions to their problems apart from God, and they are all going to fail. Our society — and the Church too, unfortunately — is worsening as a result. Only God is our strength and help in time of need; if we don't believe that, we are going to fail miserably. When Judah turned to Egypt for help against the invading Babylonians, they made a serious error: the Egyptians helped them, but at a terrible price. And the Babylonians ended up invading them later anyway. (Ezekiel 17) As if the Israelites' own God wasn't enough to defeat the enemy!

The Lord isn't going to tolerate all this confusion. He didn't create this world just for us to ruin it by our stubbornness, and he didn't create us in his image just for us to snuff out that image and steal his glory. On Judgment Day he is going to make all these wrongs right: he is going to take back the glory that we stole from him and he will once again rule over his creation in the full glory that he deserves. He is going to *destroy* all his competition. Anybody who dared to claim that they could do what only God can do, is going to be ground into the dust like the fools they are and the world is going to see the truth of the situation at last. The point of the sermon of the Last Day is this: *there is only one God.*

Most people don't really know the purpose of Judgment Day. They think that it will be the day when God just punishes the wicked and rewards the righteous. That's true, but that's not all. There will be a much more important thing on God's mind than just rewards and punishments. Some people heard about Christ and rejected him; they refused to give Jesus the glory he deserved, and for that they will be punished. Some people never heard anything about Christ; but they did see God's glory in his creation (Romans 1:18-20) and they knew the requirements of God's holiness in their conscience — and they rejected it. They too refused to give God the glory he deserves (Romans 1:21-23), and for that they will be punished. The biggest issue of that day will be God's glory, and everyone will have to face it.

Unless the Lord is gracious to us and opens our eyes to his glory, we will all refuse to glorify him. Hell, as terrible as it is, is God's way of dealing with everyone who will not acknowledge that *he is the God he says he is in his Word.* It is necessary, for the sake of his glory, that God have the final word about this matter — that's what Judgment Day is all about.

An Example

We should be able to take any passage of Scripture and, with the Spirit's help, see the glory of God in it. The purpose of the entire Bible is to glorify God! Let's look at Psalm 62 for an example.

In this Psalm we see that God is a far better refuge than what people usually put their trust in. It's a comparison between the Lord and this world's common solutions to our problems. David starts out by telling us of his complete confidence in the Lord:

> My soul finds rest in God alone; my salvation comes
> from him. He alone is my rock and my salvation; he is
> my fortress, I will never be shaken. (Psalm 62:1-2)

There is a reason for his confidence: he found the Lord to be everything he needed. David had tremendous problems, which you can read about in the history of his life and reign in the books of Samuel. He had problems in his family, among his trusted advisors, in the ranks of his army, among the people he ruled, and on every border of the country in the form of desperate enemies. Though we all have problems, he was in a greater difficulty than the average believer — he had tremendous responsibilities on his shoulders since he was the king and role model for the nation, as well as the symbol of the coming Messiah who would rule over the entire Church. Every step he took was critical for the well-being of *all* of God's people!

He could not afford to make any mistakes. He had to find something that would solve all his problems, in a way that would satisfy the demands of his job and fill the needs of his people. He found that fullness in God. David's life was not only filled with problems, it is an exciting record of the Lord *solving* problems. Everything that David touched succeeded — he lived with God, and as a result his problems never defeated him. That's the purpose of this Psalm — to tell us about the powerful answers that he found in the Lord. David counsels us to forget the usual things that we take refuge in, things that we turn to when we need help: men (both lowborn and highborn, they are all unable to help us), crime, and wealth. These are what most people turn to when they have needs. Instead, the Lord will protect everyone who takes refuge in him. If we hide ourselves in him, and let him protect us, there is nothing that this world can do to hurt us. God is a safe and secure place; nothing can move us if we are in him.

This is an example of giving God glory. David makes it perfectly plain what God is and the kinds of things he can and will do for his people. This is Divine "advertisement" intended to make more people interested in what the Lord can do for them. God gets credit for being a *better* refuge than anything else we usually turn to for help. He doesn't get this glory simply to show off, but that we might turn to him and be saved. That's the purpose of the glory of God: that we might see his glory and reach out for what he offers us in it.

So this psalm is presenting you with a dilemma. As is usual with the glory of God, your heart naturally turns away from it and prefers to trust in things you can see: the fear of man, the temptation of sin, and the love of money. David is telling you that God is far more secure and dependable than those things are. He is giving the Lord credit for being what we all so desperately need. Will *you* give him that credit? Do *you* believe this truth about him? If so, you will act on it and bring him glory for being what he says he is. If not, you will dishonor him; you are saying that he isn't as good as the other solutions, that he can't help you as well as they can. I guarantee you that he will not allow you to continue in that belief much longer; he *will not* share his glory with another. He will either change your thinking about him so that you trust in him alone, or he is going to let you stand on that rotten foundation that you are so fond of — and fall to your ruin in the end, because nothing else can compare to him. On the last day, however, you will look upon the one you rejected and, with dismay, realize that he *was* your only hope.

Questions to ask

We are going to have problems seeing the glory of God. Paul tells us that "now we see but a poor reflection." (1 Corinthians 13:12) We live in a dark world and our minds are dark; sometimes the Lord shines his light on us and we see the truth, but not until we stand in Heaven will we "see face to face." If we could see God's full glory now, we wouldn't need books or teachers or preachers or witnesses anymore — we would know the truth about him without needing anybody to tell us. But since we can't see his glory, we still have great need of someone to tell us the truth about him and increase our faith in this God who deserves glory.

That's the primary purpose of the Bible: to glorify God. When you are reading the Bible, be sure that you don't miss the point. Most people do! They tend to see what they want to see, and make the Bible say what it doesn't say; the result is that they don't see God there and therefore he isn't real to them. You know that you are getting results from Bible study when God becomes more real to you, when you depend on him more for what the Word says he will do for those who come to him in faith.

Remember these things about God's glory as you study the Bible:

- **The Bible always glorifies God.** How does this story glorify God? What does it say about him specifically? To whom did he glorify himself? Did he *tell* them something about himself, or was it through his *works*? Did he show up in person and overwhelm someone with his presence, or did he claim credit for something? Why did he need to glorify himself? Did his glory come through someone's witness about him? Or was it through historical events, or the creation, or even from his enemies?

- **God rarely gets the glory he deserves.** What was the reaction of those to whom God glorified himself? Since people usually either miss the point about God, or they don't want to listen to it, you will probably find the people in the story turning a deaf ear to the glory of God. They don't want to give him the credit he deserves. Why did they react that way? Did their disinterest anger God? Notice carefully what he was angry about: he is most often angry when people won't give him credit for being what he is — in other words, when they refuse to glorify him. Is that what is going on here? Or did someone get the point and give God credit for a change? How did they do that? Why did they do that?

- **God has more to do with the world than we can imagine.** Since a big part of the idea of glory means getting the credit for something, you will discover that God deserves credit for much more than we possibly imagined. What is he claiming credit for in this story? Why doesn't he usually get credit for it? What do people usually think about this — since they don't give God credit for it? Does it bother you that God does this? Does this change your views on who God is and what he does? Does it fit in with other things you already know about him?

- **God's glory is our salvation.** When God insists on getting credit for something, he has our good in mind. Is that obvious in this passage? Is it something we need? Is he proclaiming it, "advertising" the things he can do, so that people will see and come to him for those things? Is he disappointed when people don't take advantage of it? Did he reward those who saw and heard and believed? Did those who refused to come miss out on something important? Most important, is Jesus the same way? Remember that he is the glory of God and the salvation of God — the two are combined in him. Anything we read about God in the rest of the Bible is most clearly seen in him, and we also ought to see the usefulness of it in him.

- **God alone deserves the glory for what he claims.** In this passage you are studying, is it obvious that God's claims are unique — that there is no other god that can claim to be what God is? Does God himself make a point about that? Sometimes he proves his claims by showing up in person — the presence of God convinces even the most hard-hearted that God deserves glory. Did he do that here? Were there other gods, or men, or nations, that tried to take away from God's glory? Did they claim to be able to do those things that only God can do? What did God do in response to them? If not anything immediately, did he promise to do something in the future?

- **God will make his glory known to us.** The Lord is jealous about his glory; he doesn't want to completely set aside his glory until a future day. He does often wait for it, though — is that obvious in this passage? Or perhaps we need to back up and see the bigger picture. The point of the Bible is to glorify God. Did he really wait, or was he careful to give himself credit — in this passage? Was it enough for him to record it this once in the Bible so that you and I can read it and get the point about him? Will people really have an excuse on Judgment Day, saying that they didn't know the truth about him, when the Bible was so careful to teach us the truth? In other words, this may be our one chance to get it right!

Discussion Questions For Glory

- Who can truly glorify God?

- How do we know when God is near us — or when we are near him?

- What is the purpose of witnessing to others?

- What kinds of things should God get credit for but doesn't? Why?

- What is Heaven like?

- Man was made in God's image, so that he would truly glorify God on earth. How was that supposed to work?

- A Christian has the ability and opportunity to do what people have never been able to do since the fall of man: glorify God. How does that work?

- In what can we see the glory of God in our world today?

- Why isn't God getting glory in our world today?

- Is God justified in punishing the wicked and rewarding the righteous on the basis of whether they gave him glory?

Key Six: Faith

Key Six: Faith

Christians are people of faith. Our religion requires that we "live by faith" (Romans 1:17) — and the reason for that is the nature of our God and the works that he does. Other religions have visible gods, idols of stone and wood and the imaginations of man, and it doesn't take faith to believe in what you can see and touch and think up on your own. But we believe in what we *don't* see: "blessed are those who have not seen and yet have believed." (John 20:29)

Faith is a profound and mysterious experience. Not everyone who claims to have faith really has faith! The Bible clearly defines what true faith is; there is no mystery in that. The problem is that someone just can't step into faith whenever they like. It's a spiritual experience, it touches the world of God, it deals with things that you can't see with your physical eyes. It is the one sign that proves that you are in touch with God. It is, perhaps, the most important characteristic of a Christian because it makes a new creature out of him, and separates him from all other people who don't have faith.

As far as God is concerned, there isn't another thing that we could do that would please him as much as simple faith. He loves to see faith in us, and he will give us whatever we ask for if we just ask him in faith. (John 16:23) Faith has the power to move mountains — it moves God to do miracles for us. This simple yet powerful characteristic of a Christian is the key that unlocks the treasuries of Heaven. But it isn't something that just anybody can do! True faith is a rare jewel, even in today's Church, and you won't see it as often as you might expect. Jesus was surprised to see it in a Roman centurion. The Jews, he said, who ought to have had it, showed no signs of faith. (Matthew 8:10)

Faith is so characteristic of God's people that, once we understand what it is, we are going to see it all through the Bible. The Bible is the book of faith telling about the people of faith. It describes a new spiritual world where faith is the only way of communicating with God. At the very beginning of the works of God, as he first started building a spiritual kingdom for his people (in the Old Testament, where most Christians wouldn't have thought that faith would be so important!), the Lord set it down as a principle that his people would *live by faith*. Only the saints who did live by faith inherited the promises — both in the Old Testament and the New Testament.

A definition of faith

You could say that faith is the currency of the Kingdom of God. With it, you can get whatever you want from him; without it, you are spiritually poor and can't expect to get anywhere with God. But also like money, there is a counterfeit variety of faith that our enemy has produced in the hearts of many people; and at first glance it can fool us into thinking that it is genuine.

The "faith" that most people have is this: they just believe in something very strongly — it doesn't matter what. The common expression is that "it doesn't matter *what* you believe, just that you *do* believe." That's wrong on at least two counts, however: *first*, it's obvious that you can't believe in lies! If you are content with just believing the things you want to believe in, you are an easy target for whoever wants to spread his propaganda around — like the devil. There really is such a thing as the truth, and if you don't believe in that then your faith isn't worth anything. In God's universe there is one truth: what *he* says is true. If you don't believe that, then you are believing in lies. Ignorance is *not* bliss; it is the first step toward death. This is *God's* world, and there is only *one* truth; whoever believes in lies are the children of the father of lies (John 8:44) and will someday share in his destruction. (Revelation 20:15)

Second, even if you believe the Bible (which, by the way, is the *only* truth — "Your Word is truth." — John 17:17) that doesn't mean that you are automatically a Christian. For example, some believe that there is a God, and they feel that they are doing God a favor in that. "You believe that there is one God. Good! Even the demons believe that — and shudder." (James 2:19) You see, you are in bad company if all you believe are a few facts about God! You believe that Jesus was a real man, who lived among men and preached the truth about God. Good! You believe the history books then; but that doesn't make you a Christian. Whenever you hear a sermon about a particular passage or read a book that discusses some part of the Bible, it seems reasonable to you and you accept it as true. Good! But the Bible has sounded very reasonable to people of many religions and nationalities; most of them, however, were never Christians and never even claimed to be.

So faith isn't just a matter of believing what the Bible says; it's true that you must believe what it says to have true faith, but you must also do *more* than that. This is why so many people are deceived into thinking that they are believers when really they don't have any faith at all.

The writer of Hebrews tells us what true faith is:

Now faith is being sure of what we hope for and certain of what we do not see. This is what the ancients were commended for. (Hebrews 11:1)

We could put it like this:

Faith is living in the light of God's world.

Faith is the special ability to see things as God sees them (with spiritual eyes — our physical eyes can't see them, as Hebrews 11:1 says). From where he is in Heaven, he can see this world in its entire scope, through the mists that normally cloud our eyes from seeing things clearly. God's world is all light, and whoever has that light can see all things as they really are. Faith is walking in the searchlight of Heaven that casts no shadows, that clearly lights the way in front of you.

When you have true faith, you see things that others can't see. For instance, you can see the realities of Heaven itself — God is there, in all his glory, surrounded by angels and other creatures who continually praise him. He sits on his throne, in the Temple, and the sacrifice for sins that Jesus made is forever on the altar there. There are the treasures that God has for his people, waiting for them and their arrival. With faith these things are visible spiritually, they are real —

they aren't just a story or even a wishful hope. That's why the writer of Hebrews paints such a vivid picture of what it is like in Heaven right now — because it is something that both he and we can see through faith:

> But you have come to Mount Zion, to the heavenly Jerusalem, the city of the living God. You have come to thousands upon thousands of angels in joyful assembly, to the church of the firstborn, whose names are written in heaven. You have come to God, the judge of all men, to the spirits of righteous men made perfect, to Jesus the mediator of a new covenant, and to the sprinkled blood that speaks a better word than the blood of Abel. (Hebrews 12:22-24)

This passage is all the more significant because it is in the book of faith, right after the famous chapter of faith (Hebrews 11). In that chapter we have the testimony of many saints who saw the promises of God. In other words, faith *sees* God's real world.

Faith is designed to address a specific problem that all people suffer with. From the day we were born, we were blind, ignorant, and totally unaware of the spiritual world of God. We can know our world only on the physical level, with our senses; but we have never been able to discern the spiritual level of existence. That's why unbelievers still think that there is no God — they can't see him. They think that this world is running on its own, as if it were a clock that somehow got wound up and will run for a long time until it decides to unwind. They see no more purpose to life than to eat, drink and be merry — for nothing means anything anyway.

The downside of this theory is that they don't have anybody but themselves to look to when trouble comes. If there is no God, then how will we solve our problems? Only by our own strength and cleverness — until that runs out, and then we just fail and die. There's no hope in this "belief" of how the world works; it's with profound truth that Paul says these people are "without hope and without God in the world." (Ephesians 2:12)

What they lack is spiritual insight — the ability to see the "other dimension" to the world. That's faith: seeing that there is more to this world than just physical things. Faith sees that God created this world, and therefore it has meaning and purpose. Faith sees what kind of God he is and why we need to live in such a way as to please him. Faith sees that this world is destined for destruction and therefore we need to put our hope on an inheritance that will never fade — a Heavenly treasure.

Someone isn't going to get this spiritual insight simply by wishing it. We are blind and ignorant of the truth because we are *dead spiritually* — that is the tragic truth of all humanity. We don't have time to get into a full discussion here of our natural spiritual state. But we are *all*, since we are descendants of Adam and Eve (who first died when they ate of the fruit of the tree of the knowledge of good and evil), dead to God and all spiritual things. We are alive for a while to the physical side of the world, but we are completely dead to the reality of God and our souls. If we get faith it's because God reaches down and touches our dead souls and makes us alive to him:

> But because of his great love for us, God, who is rich in mercy, made us alive with Christ even when we were dead in transgressions — it is by grace you have been saved. (Ephesians 2:4-5)

Just as a baby that takes its first breath in the world and opens its eyes to the light of day, a new-born Christian opens his eyes of faith and sees things that he didn't see before. He sees his Father (and the rest of the family of God!), he sees food, he sees his soul, he sees many more things that don't make sense to him right away. As he grows and develops he learns more about how this spiritual world works and how he can best get around in it. The analogy is exactly the same between physical and spiritual birth, and would make a fruitful study in the Scriptures for you sometime (start with John 3). This is the life of faith.

When a person lives in faith, it's as if a strong searchlight shone down from Heaven and lit his surroundings so that he can see. He is aware that God is there above him, guiding him with light and life. He sees that the issues of life are spiritual. He sees what sin is, and why it is such a curse on man. He sees the emptiness of this world and the glory of the next. That sight of spiritual realities is what makes him live as he does. In fact, it's frustrating when one talks to an unbeliever who doesn't see these things. It's not just an argument or an idea, as it is to them — it's real, and we know it. We can't be talked out of it any more than of our own existence! But the unbeliever doesn't see any of it.

Faith knows that God exists and that all the spiritual truths that the Bible talks about are real. And you can also see why someone who doesn't have faith will never please God: "And without faith it is impossible to please God, because anyone who comes to him must believe that he exists and that he rewards those who earnestly seek him." (Hebrews 11:6) Without faith we will never know him, we will never hear or obey him, we will never go to him with the right requests — none of our "religion" will work without true faith. But with faith, everything becomes plain and we can go about our spiritual duties with complete confidence.

The steps of faith

Faith doesn't come naturally to someone; it isn't an easy thing to do. Faith is an extraordinary ability to do what a blind sinner cannot do on his own. As with all of God's works, faith follows certain prescribed steps that make it different from anything else that men call "faith". The works of God (and faith is one of them, since he gives us the ability to see — Ephesians 2:8) are clearly distinguished from the works of man by the way they come about. Here is how the Bible says true faith will occur:

- *__Faith starts with God's Word.__* You must start here. God speaks to us first, *then* we believe. It has always worked like that and it always will. This first step is what separates true faith from what many people think is faith. The "faith" of many is just a belief in their own ideas, not what God told them in his Word.

    The Bible is our window into Heaven; if it wasn't for God's Word we wouldn't have any idea of what the spiritual world is like. Though men have come up with all kinds of philosophies and religions over the millennia, and thought they were right — they were in fact wrong about everything that has to do with God. The gods they described don't exist. They were only guessing about what the spiritual world is like. But those who read the Bible know exactly what it looks like, because in it they see a true picture of God's world.

It is also the true description of man and this world that we live in. We don't have to guess what man is like, or what he really needs, or how to solve our problems. The Bible tells us all these things so that we can know the truth. Here is where God speaks to us; it's no use looking for another source of "truth" because there isn't any.

The Bible is God's spoken word to man, telling him things he wouldn't have known otherwise. Unbelief always rejects what God says, however, mainly because it doesn't see the reality of it. When the Bible says there is a God, and he is like such and such, and these are his works, many people don't see it and therefore don't believe it. They can hardly be said to have true faith, then, if they don't believe what God himself says about his kingdom!

The father of lies started us doubting God's Word in the Garden of Eden. The root of all sin is that we don't believe what God said, and we substitute some other truth in its place. If people say they believe in God, yet they don't believe what the Word plainly says about something, then they don't have true faith. You will find that it is impossible to "prove" the Bible to someone who doesn't have any faith already. The Bible isn't a matter of human reason or common sense, but revelation from Heaven — and those who don't have eyes to see the things of God will never believe God's Word. "The man without the Spirit does not accept the things that come from the Spirit of God, for they are foolishness to him, and he cannot understand them, because they are spiritually discerned." (1 Corinthians 2:14)

You will notice in the Scriptures that the Lord always initiated things; he first *spoke* to someone, and *then* they believed. That seems so simple, yet it seems to escape so many people. He has to tell us what to believe first! He spoke to Moses out of the burning bush and taught him the truth about himself, including his right Name. He spoke to Hezekiah when the Assyrians threatened Jerusalem; it was because of what the Lord told him that Hezekiah waited confidently for the outcome, in spite of the odds. God spoke to Rahab the prostitute in Jericho through the Israelite spies, and she decided to switch sides. He spoke to Balaam through the donkey and gave the pagan prophet something new to think about. In the Bible, faith never invents what it wants to believe about God; rather it responds to what God *says*. "And how can they believe in the one of whom they have not heard? And how can they hear without someone preaching to them?" (Romans 10:14)

There is one very good reason for insisting that faith starts with God's Word: it is the *only truth*. You can't just make up what you want to believe. Saul did that when he decided that it was time to get moving and quit waiting around for God's instructions, and for that he lost his kingdom. (1 Samuel 13:1-14) We have to listen carefully to what the Lord says in the Bible and believe in *that*, not our own version of the "truth" even if it does sound good. When Aaron's sons changed the Lord's instructions a little and offered a well-meaning sacrifice that didn't conform exactly to the Lord's commands, they thought they were acting in faith — but it was only presumption, because it wasn't based on what the Word said to do. The Lord killed them for that presumption. (Leviticus 10:1-3) So God isn't playing around; we either take his Word seriously or quit claiming that we are "believers."

There is another problem about faith and the Word of God. There are some people who don't want what the Bible says — they want more than that. Since God doesn't offer them what they want, they therefore claim that the Bible isn't the *only* truth to believe in! They say that God gives them "revelations" and insights that are more appealing to "itching ears" nowadays. But when you press them about it, those revelations of theirs didn't come from the Bible and, in their view, don't have to. That's never a safe approach to faith. We were instructed to stay close to the testimony of the apostles and prophets — the Book that they wrote — so that we know we are always dealing with the truth. (2 Peter 3:2; Ephesians 3:5; Ephesians 2:20) "But as for you, continue in what you have learned and have become convinced of, because you know those from whom you learned it." (2 Timothy 3:14) We know the Bible is right; we don't know for sure, however, about any other revelation, because it may have come from a deluding spirit. So this is how you can best tell that you have true faith: you want what God has promised in his Word. Anything else is suspect.

• ***Faith wants what God promised.*** God promises, in his Word, an alternative to this world — and what an alternative! The world of God is completely different from our world: in his world there is only light and life and joy and peace and righteousness and holiness. In his world, God rules over all and everything glorifies him. His power brings him glory, because he does things that no creature can do. His love comforts and heals and binds up wounds and draws us close to him. And his justice is terrifying, with the result that there is *no sin* in the presence of God. Everything conforms exactly to God's expectations. This is the kind of world that God reveals to us in his Word, and his people want this more than anything else.

Faith is never "blind faith." God shows us something real, and he offers us more than just a hope that things in our lives will get better. This world is so discouraging, it is so full of failure and misery and death, that we *need* news from another world that there is something better to live for. So when the Lord shows us that place, that vision lifts up our souls up in joy and expectation: so there *really is* hope!

And our hope isn't imaginary; it is real. The Spirit of God reveals to us the things of God so that we can see and know their reality:

> We have not received the spirit of the world but the Spirit who is from God, that we may understand what God has freely given us. This is what we speak, not in words taught us by human wisdom but in words taught by the Spirit, expressing spiritual truths in spiritual words. (1 Corinthians 2:12-13)

The only problem is that it isn't *here*, in this world, yet. We can only look on from a distance and wait for these things.

There are many examples of this in the Bible. When David committed adultery and murder, he found no consolation in this world; he knew that there was no forgiveness for his sin except with God. But he could not face the rest of his life in guilt! He desperately wanted forgiveness from the God of Israel, because he knew that when God forgives he lifts the burden from the conscience forever and replaces it with an everlasting love and acceptance. How did he know that? God showed him! David did find that forgiveness — he walked away with no guilt left on his conscience, and a full confidence that God accepted him. (Psalm 51) When Moses grew up in Pharaoh's court, he had all that he could have wanted in life; yet he chose to identify with the despised Israelites because he wanted the riches of the kingdom of God instead of Egypt's riches. Evidently he saw how much more valuable God's spiritual kingdom is than what Pharaoh could offer him. (Hebrews 11:24-26)

The words of Scripture are only words until the Spirit makes them real to you. They *are* the truth whether we believe them or not; but until we believe them and see that they are the truth, they will do us no good at all. Many people read the Bible and walk away unimpressed; it's not as real to them as this world, and they don't feel any conviction at all. But someone with faith reads those words and sees a new, powerful, wonderful reality that puts this world to shame. When that happens, faith happens naturally: he wants what he sees, and he turns his back on this world.

• ***Faith faces and overcomes the impossibility of it.***
The first thing that we notice when the Lord tells us his promise is this: it just couldn't happen. There is no way under the sun that such a thing could be, not in our world. What God is promising to do is not only beyond the capability of anything in this world to produce, it goes against the grain of all of life. Even if we wanted it to happen, that's just not the way things work here.

This is an extremely important step of true faith. Of course it's impossible! But God deals in impossibilities, not things that our world can do. If anybody else than God could do such a thing, then we wouldn't turn to God for it, would we? And we shouldn't be surprised that God's miracles run contrary to the way the world normally does things; he made the world, so he can certainly bypass its laws whenever he wants.

The world is going to argue that it can't be done, it isn't reasonable, it isn't the way everyone else does it, you won't be accepted if it happens — in other words, the world is *against* God and all his ways and works.

You must see that, and then consciously *turn away* from the world and turn to what God is telling you. "Therefore come out from them and be separate, says the Lord." (2 Corinthians 6:17) It's like stepping off a sinking ship onto a safe and steady ship. Turning your back on the world's lies is the first half of your salvation from sin and death.

When Peter heard Jesus invite him to step out onto the water, he knew very well that the water couldn't hold him up; he was no dreamer but a practical fisherman. But in that realization he decided that the word of Christ was far more solid and dependable than concrete, and he could safely venture out on what another person would have considered suicide. (Matthew 14:25-29) When Gideon led 300 men against the entire Midianite army, he surely realized that this would mean the end of him and his little band under any other circumstances. But since the Lord commanded him to do it and promised that he would be with them, Gideon walked right into the danger without fear. (Judges 7) "If God is for us, who can be against us?" (Romans 8:31) When the Israelites were about to cross the Jordan River in its flood-stage, they surely didn't march into it with their eyes closed! When they set their feet into the water's edge, even while the river was still raging past them, they knew what would happen if the Lord didn't perform a miracle and do it fast! (Joshua 3-4)

To face the facts, to realize that God's promise is contrary to nature, to fully realize that unless God steps in with a full-scale miracle we are about to step into thin air — and in light of this knowledge to *trust God anyway* because we know that his promise always overcomes the barriers of the world — *that* is the heart of true faith. It proves that we see something more real than this world. Faith looks *beyond* this world to a world where anything that God says can happen.

• *Faith won't try it on its own*. The last point naturally leads into this one. If you are convinced that what God promised could never happen on its own, not in this world, then (if you really want this thing) you are faced with two choices: turn to God to do it (if you have faith in him) or try to work something out on your own (if you don't believe he can do it). Those who don't believe in God's Word will try to work out something by themselves to solve their problems.

For example, when the Israelites came to the borders of Canaan, the Lord told them to go ahead in and defeat the inhabitants living there and take over the land. After all, this was the Promised Land that he had been telling them about since they left their slavery in Egypt; now they were ready to receive the promise. But they balked: the spies brought back reports that there were giants living in the Promised Land! So the people refused to go in. This is a good example of looking at the impossibility and *not* having faith! But when the Lord got angry and sent them back out into the desert to die there instead of inheriting the Promised Land, the people panicked. With the prospect of the promise slipping through their fingers, they changed their minds and told him they would go in after all. No good, said the Lord; you lost your chance. If you go now you will go without me. But since they were people with *no faith*, this didn't sound like a serious problem to them. They did go in, without God, and they got soundly whipped by these giants that they couldn't defeat without God's help. This was an example of people trying to do things on their own because they didn't have the necessary faith in God to do it for them. (Numbers 13-14)

For some reason we think that we can do very well *without* God. Aren't most people in this world trying to do that very thing? They want to solve their own problems, do their own will, soothe their own conscience, decide their own future, decide for themselves what truth is and what is right and wrong — all these are things that only God can do. Yet people don't want God to interfere with them in these areas. They don't like God's solutions for them, so they would rather do it themselves. The problem is that their solutions never will work; God's solutions always do. Anybody with faith can see that plainly.

• ***Faith waits on God***. The Lord has ways of doing things (as we have already seen) and one of those ways is this: he works through *time*. Although he promises you a certain thing, he may not give it to you right away; he may choose to wait until a more appropriate time. Faith will wait on him no matter how long it takes — because, of course, his answers are worth waiting for!

Some of the things that God promised people didn't take long at all. For example, Naaman's healing took seven dips in the Jordan River; the deliverance of the Israelites at the Red Sea was only a matter of a couple of days; Sennacherib and his great army were defeated overnight. But some things took years and even centuries before they happened: the promise of the Messiah, for instance, was first given in the Garden of Eden and not fulfilled until thousands of years later. The Israelites in exile in Babylon had to wait 70 years before they could go back to Jerusalem. David waited between 15-20 years before the promise that he would become king over Israel was fulfilled. To wait this long for what God promised, you really have to believe that it is real and nothing in this world is a good substitute for it.

When someone waits on God's promises, that shows several things: *first*, they know that no other answer is good enough for what they need; they know that only God's work is good enough for them. And if they have to wait to get it, then they'll wait. *Second*, waiting on God means resisting the world when it tries to get you to change your mind. The unbelievers, who do not see what you see, will "think it strange that you do not plunge with them into the same flood of dissipation, and they heap abuse on you." (1 Peter 4:4) You aren't going to make any friends in the world when you wait for your spiritual reward, while they are taking their physical rewards now. *Third*, waiting on God pleases him greatly. To him it means that he has a humble child, willing to let him rule over them, willing to wait for whatever he has for them. He can use such a faithful saint with great effect as he builds his Kingdom. The kind of work that Christians must do in the Church requires the skill of sowing the seed and faithfully *waiting* on God for results, in his good time.

Abraham: the father of us all

Abraham was one of the patriarchs of Israel, which means he was the forefather of the Israelite race. In fact, he was their *first* important ancestor; the Lord called him out of Ur and led him to Canaan to become the beginning of God's special people (somewhere around 2000 BC). For that reason he is held in high honor among the Jews even today. They are all his children by natural descent.

But Abraham has a much more important role in God's plans than just being the forefather of the Jews. As is usual in the way the Lord works, the first instance of God dealing with a person in the Bible is usually the pattern for the rest to follow. It is in the story of Abraham that we first find the subject of faith; and, according to Paul, Abraham's faith is the pattern for the *entire Christian Church*.

In Romans 4 Paul discusses the story of Abraham. Before you read that, however, you need to go back and read the story as it unfolds from Genesis 12 to Genesis 25. When you read it you will see these things happening:

- *God calls Abraham out of Ur and into Canaan*
- *God promises Abraham a son*

- *God promises to make Abraham into a great nation, and give him and his descendants the land of Canaan*

- *God expects Abraham's obedience and requires circumcision*

There is much more to the story than this, of course, but this is the idea. But more than anything else, the story about Abraham is about faith — the kind of faith that pleases God. This is the model, the blueprint of true faith as God sees it.

The point is that the Lord wants *us* to have the *same kind* of faith that Abraham had; it must work the *same way* if we are to claim God's promises for ourselves. The ingredients in his faith must also be in ours. Whatever steps that Abraham took when he learned the skill of faith, we also must take if we want to please God. "And without faith it is impossible to please God." (Hebrews 11:6) What kind of faith must we have? "The promise comes ... to those who are of the faith of Abraham." (Romans 4:16) That's the point that Paul is making in Romans 4.

Abraham, then, according to Paul, is "the father of us all" (Romans 4:16) — one of the most remarkable statements made in Scripture. We prove that we are children of Abraham, of the same faith as Abraham, and therefore heirs of the promises given to Abraham, when we believe *exactly as he did*. So, at the very beginning of the Church, the Lord set up the pattern for true faith that he wants *all* his children to follow. There is no other kind of acceptable faith in God's eyes.

Let's follow through the steps of faith in Abraham's life:

- ***He heard the word of the Lord.*** The Lord called Abraham while he was living in Ur and told him to move to Canaan, a place that his descendants would eventually inherit. (Genesis 12:7) He also told Abraham to expect a son. (Genesis 15:4) All of Abraham's actions from this point on were based on what God said, not things that Abraham made up. Faith is always a reaction to the Word of God. And the Lord kept repeating those same promises to Abraham over the years.

Furthermore, Abraham *saw* those spiritual realities. They weren't just physical promises to him but spiritual promises: "Your father Abraham rejoiced at the thought of seeing my day; he saw it and was glad." (John 8:56) "For he was looking forward to the city with foundations, whose architect and builder is God." (Hebrews 11:10)

• *__He set his heart on God's promise.__* For Abraham to leave his city of birth, his work, his neighbors and family, and set out for an unknown land and an uncertain future was asking more of him than most people would be willing to give. But Abraham saw something in God's promise that was worth far more than whatever he had in this world; it was worth leaving everything behind and living as a nomad for the rest of his life. God's promise became more precious to him than anything else he had in life. That's what motivated him to have so little interest in what others would never give up, and base his entire life on what others couldn't see.

• *__He faced the impossibility of it.__* When God told him that he and his descendants would inherit the land of Canaan, it wasn't hard to see that such a thing would require a miracle! The Canaanites always treated Abraham with suspicion and as an alien; a lot would have to happen to get rid of these determined people. And Abraham was only one man! He couldn't possibly get rid of all the Canaanites, no matter how many servants he could muster together to help him. Furthermore, the promise of a son was, in the world's eyes, even more ridiculous. His wife Sarah was beyond the years of childbearing; it was biologically impossible for her to have any children. Nevertheless,

Without weakening in his faith, he faced the fact that his body was as good as dead — since he was about a hundred years old — and that Sarah's womb was also dead. Yet he did not waver through unbelief regarding the promise of God, but was strengthened in his faith and gave glory to God, being fully persuaded that God had power to do what he had promised. (Romans 4:19-21)

In other words, it strengthened his faith to see how impossible the promise was. If God can do this, as impossible as it looks, then he is the God I want to trust in for everything.

• ***He believed in God.*** Even when he saw that God's promise was impossible, he believed God could do it. That takes true faith. Instead of doubting that God could do such a thing, he believed the exact opposite: God evidently can do whatever he wants! There are no limits, no barriers to God. "For nothing is impossible with God." (Luke 1:37) Later when the Lord told Abraham to sacrifice his only son, the very boy that God had promised to make a nation out of, Abraham obediently went out to sacrifice him. "Abraham reasoned that God could raise the dead, and figuratively speaking, he did receive Isaac back from death." (Hebrews 11:19)

Adults don't naturally understand this kind of faith. They know how the world works, and they know how impossible God's promises are — so they have a lot of problems believing them. Children, however, who don't yet know that the world is fixed and unchangeable, will believe anything that God tells them. That's why Jesus told us that "I tell you the truth, unless you change and become like little children, you will never enter the kingdom of Heaven." (Matthew 18:3) We must believe that God can and will do whatever he wants to do in this world, and nothing is going to stop him. *Nothing*, no matter how far-fetched it sounds, is impossible to God.

• *He failed in one point: he tried it his own way*. At one point Abraham felt that perhaps God's promise was a little too miraculous to hope for! How could his wife have a son at her age? So he listened to his wife's solution of having a son by their servant girl, which in those days was an acceptable solution for passing on one's inheritance. In that one instance Abraham failed the Lord; instead of waiting for a miracle, he tried taking a more reasonable approach. But you will see in the story that the Lord didn't consider that to be a good solution. Our ways never work; only his ways work. We can see that now — hindsight is clearer than foresight — because Paul demonstrates clearly that Ishmael could never have been the solution that God had promised. (Galatians 4:21-31) But at the time, Abraham had problems seeing that. So the Lord rejected Abraham's solution and told him to wait for the miracle. Since God has in mind a kingdom that rests on miracles, it wouldn't do to start things off with man's works!

• *He waited on God*. Once Abraham learned his lesson, he settled down and waited on God for what he had promised. Abraham waited 25 years for that son! When Isaac was finally born, Abraham's faith shone like a jewel among the testimonials of God's people: he proved that God was as good as his word, that the "miracle baby" was much more satisfactory than the son born to the slave woman, and that the Lord prefers to build his kingdom on miracles. And he learned that God will often wait until all hope is gone that any such thing could ever happen, and then wait even longer! It seems that he gets more glory the longer we wait on him; when it finally does happen, we have to admit that *only* God could have done such a thing. So Abraham's faith resulted in great glory for God.

This is the kind of faith that all Christians must have. All the saints in the Bible had it; you will see these same steps in their circumstances as they struggled against a world that opposes the unseen things of God. Someday father Abraham will sit in Heaven surrounded by all his children — all those who heard God's Word and believed it in spite of the difficulties that this world threw in their way. "So those who have faith are blessed along with Abraham, the man of faith." (Galatians 3:9)

The power of faith

Faith works. Jesus tried to get us to realize the power of faith when he said,

> I tell you the truth, if you have faith and do not doubt, not only can you do what was done to the fig tree, but also you can say to this mountain, 'Go, throw yourself into the sea,' and it will be done. If you believe, you will receive whatever you ask for in prayer. (Matthew 21:21-22)

I hope you realize that faith in itself has no power; by "power" I mean that God rewards faith immediately and eagerly. It is, as I said before, the currency of Heaven: show up before God with faith, and he will give you whatever you ask. Faith gets results with God when nothing else will. There are some basic reasons for this:

- **_Faith came before the Law._** Many people are confused about whether the Law or faith is what pleases God. To make it very plain, Paul tells us that Abraham's righteousness was credited to him *before* circumcision (which is a matter of the Law), not after circumcision. (Romans 4:10) What he means is this: *faith* is the foundation of God's kingdom, not righteousness by the Law. Anybody who wants to please God has to start with faith, not Law. What God did through Abraham is the model for us all. So Jews (the physical descendants of Abraham) and believing Gentiles (the spiritual descendants) both have to approach God in the same way; there aren't two ways to Heaven but only one.

For example, long before the Law was ever given, people were living by faith in the Lord and getting his promises. Abraham, of course, discovered the principles of faith — about 500 years before the Law. His descendants Isaac and Jacob both had faith in God and received promises from God. Joseph believed in God even when his life turned into a personal disaster; at the end he could see the hand of God leading every single event for his glory. Moses, interestingly enough, the man who gave God's Law to Israel, saw the glory of God and believed *before* he received that Law.

This makes perfect sense when we remember the definition of faith: walking in the light of God's world. When we see that the things of God are real, *then* we are in a position to obey God's commands and do what he wants us to do. When someone meets God, that puts a whole different perspective on life! Morals aren't something we could do if we want; we must do right or we will be punished by this real God. Our worship changes from dry ceremony and ritual to excitement and wonder. A real God makes a real and satisfying faith. So to put life into the Law, he based even the Old Testament kingdom on faith — the Jews were to obey the Lord, through the Law, not out of drudgery but because they had seen him — he lived among them.

God first calls a person, *then* he fits them into his kingdom. Faith is always the first step, then obedience. This has caused many problems in the Church! People who already believe and are comfortably obeying the Lord's commands are often upset when they see the Lord being good to a careless sinner; how could the Lord set his own rules aside like that? The older son in the story of the prodigal son felt the same way. (Luke 15:11-32) They don't understand that the Lord starts with faith to bring sinners in, and then steers them into the ways of obedience. If he didn't have mercy first, none of us would be saved!

The Law was first given to his own people — the Jews. It was the rules of the government of his kingdom over them. But the Lord gave faith to many people outside of the community — people who weren't part of the Jewish nation and who really had no reason to expect they could ever be accepted with God. Their faith made them acceptable with God — and in that, we see that faith is more important to have than even the Law itself. For example, David came from a race of people that were absolutely forbidden in Israel — the Moabites. His great grandmother Ruth was a Moabite widow who had no right and no hope of ever being one of the people of God, according to the rules. (Deuteronomy 23:3) But the Lord gives faith to whosoever he wills, not always according to the rules; so Ruth and all her offspring were included in the community of Israel.

This is true about many other people in the Old Testament as well as the New Testament. The Lord dealt with them through faith, apart from the Law. Abraham himself could very well have been a worshiper of false gods when the Lord called him and gave him faith. Naaman, though he was a hated Syrian enemy, through faith received the Lord's blessing. The widow in Zarephath, a foreigner, was the only one who received food during the three and a half year famine sweeping across Israel. (1 Kings 17:10-16) Rahab the Jericho prostitute was spared when the Israelites destroyed the rest of the city. There are many more examples in the Old Testament of the Lord dealing with people through their faith, not by the Law, and it didn't violate his sense of justice at all.

In the New Testament we see this more and more. The Roman centurion, the Canaanite woman, Cornelius, and finally the opening up of the Church to the Gentiles all show the priority of faith over the Law.

Faith brought them into God's favor; *after* that, they received details about how to live obediently in his kingdom.

Perhaps the most striking example of this is the Israelites themselves. It's easy to miss the point of their early history, but we have to back up and look carefully at what exactly happened to them. *First* they were delivered; *then* they received the Law. Salvation first, then obedience! The Lord delivered them (don't forget that they were Abraham's children!) out of Egypt, destroyed their enemies, then he brought them to Mt. Sinai to receive the rules for living in this new nation that he just created. So even in the case of the people who had the Law, faith took priority over the Law.

• ***Faith gets hold of God's world.*** Another fact that makes faith so powerful is that it enables us to reach beyond this world and touch the world of God. If we remained bound to the earth forever, then we could expect no better life than the animals; but since God called us to him and gave us a way to get there, we can walk in places we never expected to be in. We can see and know and touch the things of God, and that is certainly going to add new dimensions to life that nothing on earth could do for us.

This world gives us no clue at all that there is another world to be known and explored. It is like a shroud around our eyes, a curtain, and we can't see out — all we can see is what our senses tell us about. But there *is* another world — God's world — and we must get through to it if we hope to enjoy the things that God promises us. He never intended the things of this world to fill our souls. Therefore he is not very interested in making sure we have plenty of them, and he doesn't want us to spend all of our time pursuing such things.

What he is interested in is giving us spiritual treasures. The Spirit of God is the key here: he tears away the veil of this world so that we can see Heaven, we can see the Lord in his glory, and we can actually go there — in Spirit, but real nevertheless — to experience God's world. When, for example, the Israelites were instructed to build the Tabernacle, God first gave the Spirit to the chief workmen — Bezalel and Oholiab — so that they could *see* the Temple in Heaven and pattern the earthly Tabernacle after it. (Exodus 35:30 - 36:1) "This is why Moses was warned when he was about to build the tabernacle: 'See to it that you make everything according to the pattern *shown* you on the mountain.' " (Hebrews 8:5)

Things are still the same in the New Testament. It is by the Spirit of God that we push this world aside and enter Heaven, where our salvation is. Jesus tore the curtain of the eternal Temple in two and made it possible for us to go in. (Hebrews 10:19-22) And what will we see when we enter Heaven?

> But you have come to Mount Zion, to the heavenly Jerusalem, the city of the living God. You have come to thousands upon thousands of angels in joyful assembly, to the church of the firstborn, whose names are written in Heaven. You have come to God, the judge of all men, to the spirits of righteous men made perfect, to Jesus the mediator of a new covenant, and to the sprinkled blood that speaks a better word than the blood of Abel. (Hebrews 12:22-24)

Ask whatever you want there, take whatever you see, use the opportunity to fill your mind and heart with spiritual treasures that are all promised to you and laid out in front of you. Faith is the only way you will get into Heaven to see the *certainty* of God's promises.

• *Faith is the channel for Heaven's treasures.* People struggle every day with problems they can't solve; they just do the best they can with what they have. Life is often like a persistent fire that we are trying to put out before it destroys us, but we don't seem to be getting anywhere putting out the problems — our answers, which we thought would work, don't.

But the Lord has solutions that can put any problem fire out! The treasures of Heaven are astonishingly effective at solving the problems of life. The only problem is getting those solutions *here* where the problems are! That's where faith comes in: when we believe in God's promises, he unleashes the floods of the fullness of the Spirit, and sends them down into our souls where they become like water to thirsty and parched land. Then the Old Testament prophecy comes true:

Water will gush forth in the wilderness and streams in the desert. The burning sand will become a pool, the thirsty ground bubbling springs. (Isaiah 35:6-7)

Jesus said that this refers to the Spirit of God, bringing refreshing life to the thirsty soul who turns to God in faith: "Whoever believes in me, as the Scripture has said, streams of living water will flow from within him." (John 7:38)

If you remember any Roman history, you will know that they built stone channels, called aqueducts, that brought the water from the mountains down to Rome many miles away. Faith is just like that: it is a channel that reaches up into Heaven and extends down to our lives. As we reach out to God, he fills the channel with good things. So faith in itself won't save us, but it will bring us those things of God that will.

For example, Abraham's faith brought down many solutions from Heaven. **First,** his nephew Lot twice ended up in dangerous territory. The first time Abraham had to go rescue him from an army;   the second time Abraham prayed that the Lord would spare him from the destruction of Sodom. Both times the Lord answered Abraham's faith with miracles. Lot owed a lot to Abraham's faith! **Second,** Abraham also believed in the Lord concerning a son. You have to appreciate the situation to understand what a timely miracle this was. In those days, a son inherited the father's entire estate upon his father's death. Not only that, Abraham was responsible for the welfare of the entire community that traveled with him — his wife, his slaves and hired hands — and when he died, who would take care of them all? When he had no son, his chief servant was the only choice; but when Isaac was born that solved many potential and real problems. Again, through his faith in God he got *good* answers to his life's problems.

New Testament and Old Testament

You mustn't think that faith is a principle found only in the New Testament. We've seen that the way that God dealt with Abraham is the model for us all, whether we are physical descendants of Abraham or spiritual descendants. Faith is the main requirement for all those who live in God's eternal Kingdom.

The list of faithful saints in Hebrews 11 is, you will notice, taken from the Old Testament — a book that many Christians consider to be only about Law. And since faith is seeing God's spiritual world, this means that these Old Testament saints believed in the *same spiritual kingdom* that we New Testament Christians believe in.

For he was looking forward to the city with foundations, whose architect and builder is God. (Hebrews 11:10)

Instead, they were longing for a better country — a Heavenly one. Therefore God is not ashamed to be called their God, for he has prepared a city for them. (Hebrews 11:16)

He regarded disgrace for the sake of Christ as of greater value than the treasures of Egypt, because he was looking ahead to his reward. (Hebrews 11:26)

These were all commended for their faith, yet none of them received what had been promised. God had planned something better for us so that only together with us would they be made perfect. (Hebrews 11:39-40)

That certainly does put a different light on things when we go back to read the stories in the Old Testament! Faith was a requirement then just as it is now. All the other nations were content to live with whatever they could get out of life, with whatever the world gave them. The Israelites, however, were to look up — to Heaven where God lives. They were to long for the things that only God could give them. They were to wait for the hand of God to *change* the world, not to accept it in its wickedness and darkness. They knew about and hoped in the Kingdom of God that would come down to earth.

Everything that God did for them demanded faith:

First, even the physical miracles were the acts of a spiritual God. Who could account for such things except that there really was a God in Heaven who did whatever he liked with his creation? Faith knew that these things didn't just happen on their own! Other gods could claim to do miracles for their followers, but only God could produce miracles. Unbelievers would see the miracles that the Lord did for Israel, and even give him credit for being a miracle worker (as Nebuchadnezzar did many times — see the stories in Daniel). But only Israel knew personally the God who did the miracles — through their faith.

Second, all the Old Testament themes had a spiritual dimension. Although they appeared to be on the physical level, they were really shadows, or "types" of the more important realities of Heaven. A "type" is a physical reality that points to a spiritual one. For example, the Tabernacle that the Lord instructed Moses to build was a *type* of the Temple that is in Heaven. Hebrews called it a "shadow" of the reality (Hebrews 8:5; 10:1); if we could see the two side by side, we would immediately notice the similarities. These aren't accidental, either: the type was given to Israel to teach them, in a sort of picture lesson, what the spiritual reality was that they were supposed to believe in. Faith is how they connected the two.

There are many types in the Old Testament. The sacrifices in the Law were types of the sacrifice that Christ makes for his people. David was a type of the Messiah, who is Christ, showing us what the King of God's people would be like when he ruled over them. Joseph was a type of how Christ would rise above his brothers and save them from destruction. The manna in the desert was a type of the spiritual bread that God the Father would send down — Jesus. Canaan, the Promised Land, was a type of Heaven, the true Promised Land for God's people.

Third, the Jews of the Old Testament were supposed to get the spiritual point of what the Lord was doing with them. The story of the Old Testament *leads to Christ*; there is no other way to understand what God was doing then. One wonders whether they *could* get the point, however, considering the fact that we ourselves only know about the spiritual themes of the Old Testament because we have the New Testament's explanation of them — they, of course, didn't have the New Testament yet. In a way that is true; only Christians know the whole story about what God was doing in the Old Testament. But the Israelites could have gotten the point to *some* degree. Some did! Jesus said that "Your father Abraham rejoiced at the thought of seeing my day; he saw it and was glad." (John 8:56) Hebrews 11 tells us about other saints of the Old Testament that saw the spiritual work of God behind the physical circumstances.

Furthermore, the Israelites should have realized that those physical circumstances surely weren't what God ultimately had in mind. Canaan, in spite of all the initial excitement during Joshua's conquest, didn't turn out to be a land of rest and "milk and honey" for everyone who has lived there! The blood of bulls and goats did not cleanse the conscience, and the Israelites should have known that. The fact that they continued in sin showed that their hearts needed more than animal's blood. Something else had to happen to fulfill what God was promising — if they were living by faith, they would have continued to look for something better. The prophets did: "I have no pleasure in the blood of bulls and lambs and goats ... Stop bringing meaningless offerings! ... wash and make yourselves clean. Take your evil deeds out of my sight! Stop doing wrong, learn to do right! Seek justice, encourage the oppressed. Defend the cause of the fatherless, plead the case of the widow." (Isaiah 1:11,13,16-17)

In the New Testament we don't have much problem tracing the story of faith. At first the ministry of Christ is very physical: people are healed, the dead are raised, thousands are fed, and so on. Again, this just shows that God was among them doing what no earthly power could do for them; he was changing the laws of his creation to suit his purposes. Faith knew that this was Israel's God at work. But eventually the physical level drops away (which Jesus foretold over and over) and the spiritual world assumes the center of attention, especially when the apostles spread out and the Church grows among the Gentiles. The letters of Paul, for example, deal with issues of the soul far more than they deal with physical promises. Physical miracles aren't as important now as the spiritual miracles of rebirth, walking in the Spirit, cleansing the heart of its sin, adoption as God's sons, and other things. Now we are almost completely walking by faith, not by sight. God's children are grown up now and don't need the props that the Old Testament Israelites needed for their faith.

The struggle between faith and sight

It would be nice if we would all just believe whatever God says and live that way. But unfortunately that rarely happens. Either we don't know what he said or we don't like what he said; but the fact is that we are usually not much different after we have heard the Word than before we heard it. Why is it that the Bible makes such little impression on us? Probably the single most important reason for our unbelief is this: *we tend to believe only what we can see.* "Seeing is believing," as the saying goes. We can see *this* world very well; we know how things work here, and we are used to it, since we have so many years of experience. A human being feels most comfortable with what he knows the best. But when God starts talking about things that we can't see, the words go in one ear and out the other. Such things are fine for Sunday worship service, but you can't base your life on impractical spiritual fantasies — or so we think.

The fact is that there *is* another world besides this one, and that world will affect you much more than this life will. Right now the war councils of Heaven are making plans to protect you against future enemies; your future life is charted out step by step because God knows "the end from the beginning" (Isaiah 46:10); Jesus is praying for your soul and applying his blood against your sins; the Spirit is sending you daily provisions for your soul; the work you are doing in the Lord's Name is constructing a house in which the Lord intends to live someday; Jesus is getting a place ready for you to live when you go to Heaven; and many other things. The petty affairs of this life don't compare in importance to what is going on in God's world! But since we don't see any of that going on, it is hard to take it very seriously; that's why we don't walk by faith.

Paul knew a lot about that other world — he was torn in his heart about it because he wanted to be there, not here! This world held no appeal for him; the only reason he was content to stay here was that he could continue to preach the name of Christ to the Gentiles and help expand the Church. His heart and spirit, though, roamed the streets of God's city through unceasing prayer — the prayers of faith. "We live by faith, not by sight." (2 Corinthians 5:7) The truths and realities of Heaven guided Paul in the steps he took in this world. Since he had a hope there, he put no hope in anything here; since Christ is the head of the Body, Paul labored to bring more saints into the Church and complete the Body of Christ on earth;   since God gets all glory in Heaven, Paul gave all glory to him wherever he went on earth.   To Paul, everyone here was a potential convert or an enemy of the Gospel of Christ:

> So from now on we regard no one from a worldly point
> of view. Though we once regarded Christ in this way,
> we do so no longer. (2 Corinthians 5:16)

His last remark there is interesting.   The last thing that the world remembers about Jesus Christ was that he was dead on the cross and then buried in the tomb.   As far as unbelievers are concerned, he is only a story from a long time ago.   But Christians who live by faith — in other words, who have the spiritual eyes to see into Heaven — know that he is very much alive and in control of things.   Christ didn't disappear for good!   He rules over all nations now, he is the King of kings, and he is both guiding the building of the Church and laying the groundwork for the judgment of the entire world.   Jesus' present position of glory and power is a far cry from the days when he was a carpenter's son!   John, the apostle whom Jesus especially loved while on earth, discovered Jesus to be a fearful God and fell down at his feet terrified! (Revelation 1:12-18)   Paul, who lived by faith, lived according to what he saw in Jesus through the Word;   the world and all its children of unbelief are still living as if Jesus is dead. Time will tell who were the wise ones.

The rewards of faith

Another thing that you should notice as you read the Bible is this: everyone who lived by faith were glad they did.   They were rewarded for their faith.   And their story was recorded for our benefit, to encourage us to take this thing about faith seriously.

You just don't realize how much God loves to see faith in us. When Abraham believed what God promised him, the Lord "credited it to him as *righteousness*." (Genesis 15:6)   What an amazing statement! While millions of people worry about how to do right and live ethically and please God, a few have the faith to see what *really* pleases God — it's not what most people think. "Righteousness" means "acceptable to

God" — and that means *perfect*, someone that the Law cannot condemn in any way. Who would have thought that the one sure way of making God happy with us is to just believe what he tells us? As far as the Lord is concerned, a person with true faith is more acceptable than the person who has lived by the Law all his life. (Matthew 19:16-22)

Most of the Jews never understood this. They thought that their righteousness would come through obeying the Law. Of course none of them succeeded! Even the smallest sin ruins the effort of a whole lifetime. They should have seen that the Law was impossible for imperfect man to keep, and looked for someone else (who *was* perfect) to keep it instead. Some of them did see it, however — like David, who spent all his time at the Lord's feet in humility and faith instead of relying on his own "righteousness."

The root idea of faith is being able to see the spiritual world of God. Think about this a minute: this is the very thing that unbelievers don't see. When you can't see God, you don't fear him and of course you don't do what he requires. So it stands to reason that you are going to get more and more into trouble with him! But if you have seen him, if you know he exists, if you are convinced that he is actively at work in the world — then you are going to live in an entirely different way. You aren't going to sin against him, you are going to rely on him for things, you are going to give him credit when he deserves it, and so on. This is going to make you and the Lord an effective team, and you have his mercy and love to look forward to in the relationship. Living as if there really is a God is so novel among sinful men that the Lord is careful to reward it and hold it up for all to see.

God doesn't want us to miss the point about faith; that's why he made sure the stories in the Bible of living by faith are so carefully described and clear. You will never find, in the Bible, someone successfully living by the Law (except Christ, of course); you will never read about someone living happily in wickedness and getting away with it; you will never see someone worshipping false gods and getting answers to prayers; you will never see someone who loves money get healing for their souls; you will never read about someone who loved this world living forever. You will never see these things because they are not true, and God wants you to know that. You *will* see, again and again, people hearing the Word of God and believing it, and things getting straightened out in their lives. He rewards those who have faith.

The Bible also shows you what happens when you don't have faith. When Jesus went to his hometown to preach the Gospel, his former friends and neighbors despised him.

> "Where did this man get this wisdom and these miraculous powers?" they asked. "Isn't this the carpenter's son? Isn't his mother's name Mary, and aren't his brothers James, Joseph, Simon and Judas? Aren't all his sisters with us? Where then did this man get all these things?" And they took offense at him. (Matthew 13:54-57)

When they refused to believe in him and his words, *no miracles happened.* "And he did not do many miracles there because of their lack of faith." (Matthew 13:58) Without faith we offend God; he will not help us, nor have mercy on us, if we don't believe what he is telling us in the Bible. In a way those stories are a testimony too, because they were written for us to think about and take seriously. We can't expect to get anything from God unless we live by faith.

An example

During the exile in Babylon, while the Israelites were being punished for their worship of false gods, there were a number of Israelites who had a believing heart and lived for the glory of God — even in a foreign land, far away from the Temple that they loved. In Daniel 3 we read about three of them: Shadrach, Meshach and Abednego. Since they were hard workers and trustworthy, King Nebuchadnezzar set them in positions of importance in his government. But one day they got in trouble because of their Jewish worship: when the king issued a decree that all of his subjects must worship an image of gold, these three refused and continued to worship the Lord. Someone reported them to the king.

When they were brought before Nebuchadnezzar and he demanded an accounting from them, they made this answer:

O Nebuchadnezzar, we do not need to defend ourselves before you in this matter. If we are thrown into the blazing furnace, the God we serve is able to save us from it, and he will rescue us from your hand, O king. But even if he does not, we want you to know, O king, that we will not serve your gods or worship the image of gold you have set up. (Daniel 3:16-18)

Now they made two very remarkable statements here. **First,** they *knew* that God could save them from the king's furnace — no matter how hot he made it. They weren't just guessing about this either! They knew their Scriptures and the kinds of things that God had done with his people in the past. They were convinced that God made all the world in six days. They remembered the miracles in Abraham's life, the miracles done during the Exodus from Egypt, and the times that Joshua and the Israelites took Canaan and defeated the giants there. They remembered the story of David and Goliath and what the Lord did then. They knew how Hezekiah and Jerusalem were saved from Sennacherib's giant army. All this information about what their God could do wasn't lost on these three young men; Nebuchadnezzar was nothing compared to the Lord. They knew he could save them, because the Spirit of God showed them a powerful God before whom no enemy could stand, and would let no harm come to his people. When you are facing death, as they were, you need more than some Bible memory verses to stay so cool! You need the Spirit making real the things of God in your heart.

Second, they stood defiant of the king's order no matter what happened. Notice that they wouldn't be so presumptuous as to say that God *would* save them, only that he *could* if he wanted to. What they *did* say for sure was that they weren't going to worship a false god. Why were they so adamant about this? Especially in light of the fact that the Lord might not save them, and Nebuchadnezzar was furious at this point and on the verge of throwing them into the furnace, wouldn't it have made more sense to be cautious and say something that would de-fuse the situation? At least until the king's temper cooled off and they could tell him about their God?

They never even gave such a thing a thought, and here is why: there is another thing they saw about God somewhere along the line — his holiness. Perhaps the Spirit brought some past memories to mind, things they heard from the priests when they were children in Jerusalem. Perhaps it was some passage of Scripture that described God in his wrath against sinners. They must have seen, again because of the Spirit revealing it to them, that it was far more dangerous to turn away from God than to defy Nebuchadnezzar. To live by sight — in other words, to fear the king and do this simple act of worship toward a gold idol, which wasn't a hard thing to do — would have meant certain punishment from the King of all kings. They knew that hell is much worse than any earthly furnace since it burns the soul and not just the body. "The fear of the LORD is the beginning of knowledge." (Proverbs 1:7)

Nebuchadnezzar had no idea what these three men saw in the God they believed in. He was mystified by their behavior, because he thought the threat of death would make any sensible man change his mind and bow in submission. He didn't understand them because he had no faith. They had faith, however, and they couldn't deny what they had seen and heard in God. The Lord was more real to them than this unfortunate circumstance they found themselves in. All problems will pass away eventually, but we must someday stand before the Judgment Seat of Christ and give an account for all our actions. Fortunately, these three responded in faith to what they saw and heard in God's Word and became witnesses to the power and results of living by faith.

Questions to ask

Every person in the Bible either lived by faith or didn't. Whether they were plain old pagans who heard the Word of God for the first time, or whether they were Jews who knew the Law already, each responded in some way to God's Word. That response is what we are interested in here. When you read the stories, ask the following questions to help you learn more about how faith works.

- **What problem were they having?** God promises to help those in need — spiritual need. What was the nature of their problem? Why couldn't they solve it themselves? Why couldn't someone other than God help them? Does this help you understand their real need — that no other god could do anything for them? What did God have that could solve the problem easily? How long had they had this problem? How did it come about? (You will usually find that the false promises of the world are responsible for the problems that we struggle with; it's through fellowship with the world — or living by sight, as Paul calls it — that we get ourselves into the fixes we are in.)

- **What did God say to them?** Since he always starts with his Word, we can always expect to see this in the story. Was it a vision, a prophecy, a rebuke, a Scripture, a witness? Was it just for them, or for others — or for us too? What did he promise to do? What did he actually say? Many people think they have faith when they believe *most* of what it says, when actually the part they weren't careful to read puts a whole new light on things. For example, we love to quote the following verse: "And we know that in all things God works for the good" — and stop there. We should read the rest of the verse! " ... *of those who love him, who have been called according to his purpose.*" (Romans 8:28) But subconsciously we quit paying attention when we get to those words. Therefore our "faith" isn't based on his Word, only on our shortsightedness.

- **What did they see in God's world?** Faith doesn't hope in something that *might* be real, it hopes in something that *is* real. The Spirit reveals the things of God to us (1 Corinthians 2:12) so that we can live by faith — the certainty that what we believe is true. What was it in God's spiritual world that the person heard about? How did the Spirit reveal it to him? Do we have the record of that special vision, or must we assume that he saw it? How was the reality in God's world so much better than the temptations, or dangers, that the world showed them?

- **When did they turn to God?** Did they immediately believe when God spoke to them? Or did they take their time at it? Did God tell them everything about the promise at once or did he spread it out over time? Did faith grow with each new piece of information? Was their sin holding them back from believing in God's Word?

- **Was there a temptation to ignore God's Word?** Faith is never a simple matter; there are too many pressures and temptations to turn away from God (who seems to be taking his time about giving us what he promised) and turn to the world's answers instead. If they turned away, did the world give them what they really needed? If they didn't turn away, how difficult was the struggle? What would have happened if they had given up? What kinds of sins make it tougher to live by faith? What kinds of things in the world make it tougher?

- **Did they wait on God's promise?** Did they *ever* get what God promised? Were they satisfied in waiting, or were they impatient? Did the Lord ever say *why* he was making them wait? Did the waiting strengthen their faith? What happened during the wait — more temptation, more sin, more pressure to turn away from God? Or did they get encouragement to wait? If encouragement, of what sort was it? Why were they willing to wait? This is often the truest test of faith.

Discussion Questions for Faith

- What's the difference between a strong faith and a weak faith?

- Can someone have faith without the Bible — for example, someone in a land where nobody has ever taken the Bible to them yet?

- When you tell someone to "believe the Gospel," what are you actually saying to them?

- If one person says that he believes one thing, and someone else says that they believe another thing, and the two views are contradictory — can such a thing be?

- We use many physical things in our worship services and personal devotions; we call them "aids to our faith." How much of that is really helping our faith, and how much actually gets in the way of faith? How little of the things of this world can you have and still worship in true faith? What does this say about our "aids"?

- If you live by faith in all things, how different will your life look from others who don't? Give some examples.

- Faith is waiting on God to do his work; but the Lord still expects us to work too. How do faith and works fit together? What happens if we don't do the work he commanded us to do?

- Has anybody really seen the world of God and not had faith as a result?

Key Seven: Name

Key Seven: Name

When God made the world, he made everything unique and good — which means that he decided what it looks like, how it works and how it fits in with the rest of the world. But he gave man the job of *naming* all the things he had made. (Genesis 2:19-20) Ever since then we've been fascinated with the science of names.

Someone once said that man's knowledge is mostly a matter of naming things. When we give something a name, we are really describing it and giving it an identity that shows how it is different from everything else. Names turn little understood and useless objects into useful tools that we can use to enrich our lives. When we name something a "fish tank", for example, everyone knows what to do with it.

God also has names, but he didn't wait for man to give him his names. That's not our job! He reveals his names to us in his Word. His names hold precious and rare insights into his nature and work. They describe what he is, and they give us the ability to know him and take advantage of that knowledge. His names are literally a key that opens up formerly locked doors to the world of God. Unlock those doors, and you will know the God that most of humanity has never seen or heard.

Since the names of God fill the Bible, we want to find out more about them and how to use them. They are recorded there for a reason! The most important thing that the Lord wants us to learn from studying his names is this: *we are to call upon the Name of God.* Do that, and like turning a key in a door, the way into Heaven will swing wide open and you will see the God you have called by name.

Names mean something

When we name our children we don't usually pay much attention to what the name means; usually we like the sound of the name, or perhaps we name the child after another family member. But whether the name means anything in particular or not, each child gets a name for several important reasons: **first,** the name will make him unique among other children. If everyone was called Robert, it would be hard to get the attention of just one of them! **Second,** over the years this child will either be a blessing or a curse to other people. When they speak of him, it will be by his name — and everyone will associate the personality (good or bad) with the name. The name *becomes* the person, in a way.

We name objects for the same purposes: to make each one unique with its own identifying name, and to help us talk about an object by name so that everyone will understand the characteristics of the object without having to describe it every time. For example, whenever I use the word "chair" I don't have to explain to you what a chair is like or what it is used for, because the name is so well understood by everyone.

So names do these jobs for us: they **identify** something, making it unique from everything else; they **describe** the thing, either the name reflecting what it's like (the name "glasses", for example, already tells us what the thing is made of) or associated with what it does (for example, a computer computes). In the case of people, names give us the ability to **call** someone by their name and get their attention.

God's names

God's names perform the same functions. This isn't a happy accident but quite on purpose: the Lord wants us to know his names so that we can use them just as we would names for things on earth. His names make a spiritual God very understandable to physical creatures; they bring the Almighty down to our level where we can see and take advantage of his goodness. In other words, he revealed his names to us *so that we might be saved.*

The **first** thing to consider is that God *reveals* his names to us. Just as we learned earlier that the Bible reveals God to us, one of the most important ways it does that is to tell us what his names are. We would never know who God really is if he didn't reveal his names. People have made up all kinds of names for him, and they call on those names that they invented — but he is like none of the names that man can dream up. Baal, Ashtoreth, Molech, Zeus and Thor are some of the fanciful names that people have called God in the past; nowadays it is Allah, Vishnu, Brahman, the God of Love who would never punish someone, the God who changes, the God who allows sin, the American Dream. These are all wrong; they do not sufficiently describe what God is like.

Remember, man is given the job of naming created things, but he is never allowed to dream up his own names for God. God has to open man's mind to realities in Heaven that he never imagined, because man on his own would never know the truth about God without the Spirit's enlightenment. "For who among men knows the thoughts of a man except the man's spirit within him? In the same way no one knows the thoughts of God except the Spirit of God." (1 Corinthians 2:11) God is beyond the ability of man to understand. "Clouds and thick darkness surround him." (Psalm 97:2) God is not of this earth, and man can't know who God is — not even his name — until God reveals himself to him.

The Lord reveals his names either by announcing them, or by giving a detailed description of them, or by showing the kinds of things he does (in other words, through events in history), or through someone's testimony of him. He *announced* and *defined* his name Yahweh to Moses; he *demonstrated* his name of Deliverer when he brought Israel out of Egypt; David *testified* to the fact that God is a Refuge. You need to reread the Bible with this in mind: in every story about God you will learn some new name, or something new about an old name, that he wants you to remember and use for yourself.

We need to be taught these things about his names! In the first place, the Lord doesn't want us to get it wrong; he wants us to know the truth about him, not what the world makes up about him. So he will teach us personally: "All your sons will be taught by the LORD, and great will be your children's peace." (Isaiah 54:13) Who better to teach us about God than God himself! Second, sin darkens our minds and the world confuses us with lies and ignorance, so much so that we need some help if we are going to find out what God is really like. We can't put any faith in everyone's opinions about God, not even in our own feelings. If God is like what *we* wanted him to be, he would let us get away with sin — and he will never do that! Third, too much is at stake here. If we don't know what he is, then we won't get what he has for us; if we don't know what to ask for, of course we won't get what we need. He can't allow that to happen to his people. He wants to save us, he wants to give us his inheritance, to open the doors of Heaven and shower his goodness upon us. He wants to deliver us from our sins and rescue us from this evil world. He can't leave us in ignorance about the one thing that will save us. Knowledge is power, the saying goes, and in the world of God, the knowledge of his names is a tremendous source of power for the believer. Armed with this knowledge, he can overcome all circumstances and problems in a way that no other "solution" on earth can hope to achieve.

The **second** thing to consider about his names is this: the Lord is giving us great advantages by showing his names to us. These names are doors into Heaven, bells that call God's attention to our needs. They are passwords known only to the family of God, allowing them to go in where even angels dare not go. Again, you can't even know what these passwords are until the Lord reveals them to you. Who will know what God's names are until he reveals himself to them? Once someone has this knowledge, it will prove to be the advantage that he needed in life. While others are struggling with their problems and calling on a God they don't know (and will never find, until they call him by name), you will be opening the doors to God's house and approaching the Almighty himself, calling his name as you come in like someone showing a pass that gives the bearer of it the privilege to enter.

The **third** thing to consider is that God's names mean something. Our names don't necessarily mean anything special, but God's names do. They are either special Hebrew or Greek words that have particular meanings, or they are descriptions of his character or work. Every name of God has a meaning that we must study and meditate on. There is a reason for his name: either there is a problem in our lives that the name will solve, or it is a weapon that we can use against our enemies, or it is a source of strength and nourishment that we aren't getting from the world. We can't afford to miss *any* of his names, any more than we can do without a well-balanced diet. We might not know how to use a particular name yet, but rest assured that it has a use and we will need it someday. Jacob, for example, needed the "God of Abraham and the God of Isaac" for the kinds of trials he was about to face and the lessons he needed to learn. (Genesis 28:13)

What are the names of God? The Bible is full of them — the problem is deciding which names to take time out to study! Here are some of the more important names and what they mean.

> ***The LORD*** — When God called the Israelites out of Egypt and brought them to Mt. Sinai, the first thing he revealed to them was this special name of his. *This is the most important name of God in the Bible.* It is a special Hebrew name:ⵀⵀⵀⵀⵀ — which he revealed to Moses and the Israelites. The English Bible translates this word as either **LORD** (with all capital letters), or **Jehovah**, or **Yahweh**.

So that nobody would be mixed up about what this name means, the Lord gave a full definition of it to Moses:

> The LORD, the LORD, the compassionate and gracious God, slow to anger, abounding in love and faithfulness, maintaining love to thousands, and forgiving wickedness, rebellion and sin. Yet he does not leave the guilty unpunished; he punishes the children and their children for the sin of the fathers to the third and fourth generation. (Exodus 34:6-7)

This isn't what language experts would have thought the name means, but it is what God wants us to know about it. It describes the most important truths about the God of Israel, the things that make him different from every other god, the things that he wants all his people to think about when they trust him and go to him for something. There are so many aspects to God that we could never learn everything about him; but if we don't learn anything else about him, we must learn this name if we want to be saved and part of his kingdom.

Notice that the other authors of the Bible books use the *same* name when they talk about the God of Israel and his works of salvation among them. They even refer back to this very definition: it's as if the Exodus 34 passage is a formula that God wants us to memorize, a Scripture that he wants us to learn by heart, because we will be referring back to it again and again in our daily needs. For example, when Nehemiah was praying for the Israelites who were newly returned from exile, he remembered how the Lord treated their wicked forefathers: not in vengeance, but according to his name. "But you are a forgiving God, gracious and compassionate, slow to anger and abounding in love. Therefore you did not desert them." (Nehemiah 9:17) When David needed help against his enemies, he turned to the Lord and called his special name — for a purpose: he wanted what that name described. "But you, O Lord, are a compassionate and gracious God, slow to anger, abounding in love and faithfulness. Turn to me and have mercy on me; grant your strength to your servant and save the son of your maidservant." (Psalm 86:15-16) Even Jonah knew, much to his dismay, that the Lord would probably have mercy on the city of Nineveh because that idea was in his name. "I knew that you are a gracious and compassionate God, slow to anger and abounding in love, a God who relents from sending calamity." (Jonah 4:2) You will find other writers referring to this same formula; for example, see Psalm 103:8; Psalm 145:8; Joel 2:13.

__Adonai__ — This name means "master" or "Lord" (with small letters), and it is not only applied to God but also to human masters, such as kings or slave-owners. In God's case it means that he is King of kings and the supreme master over everything in creation. He owns everything, and everything must submit to his will.

Elohim — This Hebrew word means "God" without saying anything special about him. Other religions in that day also used this name for their god. It usually occurs along with another of God's names, however, which of course narrows down which God the writer is talking about in the text: the God *of Israel*, God *Almighty*, and so on. One interesting thing about this name is that it's in the plural, as if to say "Gods" instead of one God. Yet we know the Jews firmly believed in only one God, in spite of this perplexing fact. You will see this name, for example, in Genesis 1 where it says "Then God [*Elohim, plural*] said, 'Let *us* make man in *our* image ...'" (Genesis 1:26) Christians have long believed that it refers to the Trinity of God: the Father, the Son, and the Holy Spirit, three Persons, all one God.

El Shaddai — "El" is the short form for Elohim, and "Shaddai" is a fascinating name in itself. It comes from the word "breast" — and most Bible students feel that this teaches how God provides for all the needs of his people. He takes care of them through miracle (we've already seen that miracles are the foundation of God's kingdom), which means that he forces the world to do things it wasn't made to do. This is why the name is usually translated "Almighty" as in *God Almighty*. The name can be found in places like Genesis 17:1, Genesis 28:3, Genesis 48:3, and Exodus 6:3.

The God of Abraham, Isaac and Jacob — The Lord especially wants us to remember him by this name. He told Moses to teach the Israelites this name:

> God also said to Moses, "Say to the Israelites, 'The LORD, the God of your fathers — the God of Abraham, the God of Isaac and the God of Jacob — has sent me to you.' This is my name forever, the name by which I am to be

remembered from generation to generation."
(Exodus 3:15)

There were some extremely important things he did with Abraham, Isaac and Jacob that affect the existence and operation of the entire Church — both Old Testament and New Testament saints of faith. We need to go back to those stories and study what he did *through* them *for* us; that's why he wants to be known by this name.

The LORD Almighty — This word "Almighty" is a different Hebrew word than the one we just looked at. The Hebrew word is "Sebaoth", which comes from the word meaning "to wage war." In some versions it is translated *Lord of Hosts*. Our God is one who leads the hosts of Heaven against the forces of the world who hate him; he will destroy their kingdoms and set up his in their place.

> The LORD Almighty is with us; the God of Jacob is our fortress. Come and see the works of the LORD, the desolations he has brought on the earth. He makes wars cease to the ends of the earth; he breaks the bow and shatters the spear, he burns the shields with fire. (Psalm 46:7-9)

The prophets talked a lot about God's future activities using this special name, which we will see in the next chapter on Prophecy. They looked forward to the time when God would set up his kingdom and do away with all other powers, and they warned the people to get themselves ready for this event.

The LORD our Righteousness — This name teaches us how we will become righteous: through his work, not ours. The prophet Jeremiah predicted the day when God's people would be brought back in safety from exile, and they wouldn't be an unrighteous people anymore. How would he make them into a holy people?

His name tells the story: "This is the name by which he will be called: The LORD Our Righteousness." (Jeremiah 23:6) He would be holy for them, and they would enjoy the benefits of his holiness. This of course points right to Christ who came to do that very thing.

A fortress — This is an example of a name that describes one of God's characteristics. When David was in need of protection — when someone was after him, threatening him with death — he ran to God and discovered that the Lord was a great place to hide inside. Nobody could reach him when he hid in God! In fact, while David rested in the Lord, the Lord fought his enemies for him and personally defended David from all their attacks. David's fight became God's fight. You can get a wonderful picture of this in Psalm 18.

There are many more names for God in the Old Testament; but that's only half the story. In the New Testament we learn new names for God — the Son of God came especially for the purpose of revealing God's name to his people.

I have *revealed your Name* to those whom you gave me out of the world ... I have *made your Name known* to them, and will continue to make you known in order that the love you have for me may be in them and that I myself may be in them. (John 17:6, 26) *

The names of Christ can be found both in the Old Testament and the New Testament. They of course describe who he is and what he does just as God's names do.

Messiah — This special Hebrew word means "the anointed one." It refers to the way a king was called and

---

* The NIV, generally an adequate translation, failed miserably at this point. The Greek original has the word "name" in both these verses, but for some reason the NIV leaves the word out completely. But if the names of God are so important for the life of the Church, and if indeed Jesus came with the intent of revealing those names to his people, then we must insist that the English translation include the words.

prepared for office: someone would pour oil over his head (we don't understand this custom in our day, but it meant a lot to them!) as a ceremony of taking office. David was anointed into office as Israel's king. But even the Jews realized that someone would come to sit on David's throne again who was anointed from on high — anointed with the Spirit of God — who would be king over Israel and defeat their enemies. Jesus did that very thing: his anointing took place at the beginning of his ministry (Matthew 3:16) and he sat down in the throne of God to rule over the earth, especially his people. (Hebrews 1:3)

Son of God — This name irritated the Jews, because they knew exactly what it meant. God is one God, and we aren't polytheists (believers in many gods). "Hear, O Israel: The LORD our God, the LORD is one." (Deuteronomy 6:4) But God himself reveals in the New Testament that believing in God the Father, God the Son, and God the Spirit is not believing in three Gods. How that is true, nobody knows but him; but we must believe it if he says so. "This is my Son, whom I love. Listen to him!" (Mark 9:7) This means that whatever Jesus says is the very Word of God, and whatever he does is the work of God; he, therefore, really is the Savior of men.

Wonderful Counselor — We get this name from Isaiah's prophecy which was given long before Jesus came: "And he will be called Wonderful Counselor." (Isaiah 9:6) Jesus had the words of life. Whoever would listen to him would find life and peace and joy, but whoever ignored his words of counsel would only find death and failure. A counselor knows what he is talking about and he is in the business of helping others solve their problems with his knowledge. Christ is the ultimate counselor: "The words I have spoken to you are spirit and they are life." (John 6:63) There are other passages that teach the importance of Christ's counsel to men: John 6:68; John 12:47-48; John 14:24; John 15:7.

Shepherd — Everyone knows this name of Christ, if for no other reason than we have seen the picture of the gentle Shepherd on the walls of our churches. It teaches us how helpless God's people are to take care of themselves, and how carefully and completely Jesus provides for all their needs.

The Gate — This name also irritates many people, because it means that there is only *one way* into Heaven — through the gate that God provided. "I am the gate; whoever enters through me will be saved." (John 10:7) "Salvation is found in no one else, for there is no other name under heaven given to men by which we must be saved." (Acts 4:12)

Cornerstone — Every building needs a point of reference: a fixed spot from which the builders can determine where the rest of the stones will extend. Jesus is the point of reference in the Church, the building that God is making for his home. Christians rely on Christ for truth, for direction, for purpose, and for strength.

> Consequently, you are no longer foreigners and aliens, but fellow citizens with God's people and members of God's household, built on the foundation of the apostles and prophets, with Christ Jesus himself as the chief cornerstone. In him the whole building is joined together and rises to become a holy temple in the Lord. (Ephesians 2:19-21)

God the Spirit also has names that reflect what he does for us:

The Holy Spirit — If you would see God face to face, the single thing about him that would strike you the most is his holiness. That's what Isaiah saw and heard when he came before the throne of God. "Holy, holy, holy is the LORD Almighty; the whole earth is full of his glory." (Isaiah 6:3) And when God calls someone and makes that person into a child of God, he sends his Spirit into them — so that they will live in the presence of his holiness at all times, day and night, in whatever they do. That means that *they* are going to be holy too!

The Spirit of truth — God the Spirit is always working to get the truth into us. That's one of his primary jobs, mainly because we are so ignorant and in need of truth. We live in a world full of darkness and lies, and we have been trained in the world's lies since we were born. We have much to learn about God! If we are going to learn anything about God and be saved from sin and death, the Spirit must reveal new things to us that we never knew before, information that we won't get anywhere else. He doesn't come up with absolutely new information, however; he teaches us the words of God. "When the Counselor comes, whom I will send to you from the Father, the Spirit of truth who goes out from the Father, he will testify about me." (John 15:26) He opens our eyes so that we can see the realities of Heaven, and see this world in the light from Heaven. We can walk by faith (see the last Key) because of what the Spirit helps us see.

The Comforter — The Spirit also comforts those who need a soothing touch to their hearts. It's a difficult thing to grow a tender flower in a howling desert. It's also not easy for a new-born Christian to live in a hostile world, surrounded by enemies (who may even be those of your own household!), called to do impossible tasks, hoping for a reward that he can't see. So the Spirit provides much-needed comfort in the face of this adversity, encouraging the believer that he isn't working *for no reason* and that the promises of God are certain in Christ (2 Corinthians 1:20).

There are so many names for God in the Bible that we can't even mention them all here. Look for these as you read: the Holy One of Israel, the God of the living not the dead, the Fear of Isaac, the Son of Man, the Ancient of Days, the Deliverer, the Judge of all the earth, the resurrection and the life, the First and the Last, the Living One, and many more. Each of these names is full of meaning and is designed to teach you what God is like.

There are three things that we must notice about these names of God: *first*, he has always had these names, and he always will. He didn't reveal his names all at once at the beginning of history, because man wouldn't have been able to learn that much about him in such a short time; most if not all of it would have gone right over his head. Besides, most of his names need some explanation and demonstration, which requires using the lives of men and the flow of history — and all that takes time. But whenever he did reveal a name to someone, it was a revelation of what he is *already like* — he was always this way, even though they didn't know his name before. Of course he was revealing this name at this point because he wanted to be remembered by it in later generations. He is an unchanging God, and all his names describe him as he is in every age, now as well as when he first revealed them.

Second, no other god has these names. The Lord alone, the God of Israel, the God of the Church, has the honor of being what these names describe. False gods would like to claim some of these characteristics — like being almighty, the wise one, the beginning and the ending, the creator, the savior — but in fact they are disappointing liars. People make a great mistake going after false gods for what they need in their lives.

Most people in a civilized society don't intentionally turn to a god when they need help. They turn to books or counselors or teachers or presidents or money or possessions or reputation or something that seems to hold a promise of help or encouragement. Even in religion, people don't usually turn to God in their trouble — they try to find some relief from their burdened consciences in other people or lots of activity or doing good deeds or denying themselves like monks. But all this is, in a way, looking to other gods for what only the Lord of the Church can do; we are making other things into gods and bowing down to them in an effort to get some help. It will never work. We might put a sign on something in this world with "almighty" written on it, but that name doesn't make it true. When the Israelites under Ahab chose to worship Baal, Elijah challenged their "faith" with a showdown of the gods. The one who really is God, he said, will burn the sacrifice with fire from Heaven; the fake will not be able to do it. Baal turned out to be a lie because he wasn't really a god, no matter how much the people called him one. (1 Kings 18:16-40) The names of God are true because he *is* what the name says. You would do well to review his names and think about how well he does what the name describes, and how futile it is that any other power on earth would even try to take that name for itself.

Third, we have to remember not to get carried away with just one or two of God's names. To understand God completely, we have to look at *all* his names, not just a few. God is so big, so complex, so beyond the mind of man to comprehend, that it takes all these names to do him justice. You might say that he wears many hats. In one circumstance he appears as a Judge, in another the Savior, in another the Holy God of Israel, and so forth. But when some people only focus on a few characteristics of God they are going to come up with a skewed picture of what he really is. In fact, this is probably the main reason for most off-balanced ministries in today's churches: they teach a small bit of truth about the Lord without bringing in a balanced view of all his characteristics and works. It may look like a big job to study all his names to fully understand him, but unless you do you will risk getting your information about him wrong — and end up creating a false god of your own. At the very least, you ought to humble yourself before this huge God and not be so dogmatic whenever you talk about him, as if you know exactly what he is like!

Call on God's name

It would certainly be enough if we knew the names of God — enough, that is, for us to praise him and appreciate him for what he is. It's much better knowing the truth about God than being in the dark about him. The other religions of the world are still in the dark about the true God because they don't know his names like we Christians do. That puts us ahead in our knowledge. But he didn't reveal his names to us just so that we can know who he is; he revealed them to us so that we can *use* them. His names are not only his glory, but our salvation.

The third of the Ten Commandments shows us how important the Lord's name is to him:

You shall not misuse the name of the LORD your God,
for the LORD will not hold anyone guiltless who misuses
his name. (Exodus 20:7)

This was right before he told Moses the meaning of his special
name (Exodus 34), as if to get them ready for the holiness and awe that
surrounds his name. Some translations (like the KJV) have this: "You
shall not take the name of the LORD your God *in vain*." Either way
reflects what the original Hebrew word means, which is to do
something to *no purpose*, or to be *worthless, empty*, the same as *doing
nothing at all*. Do you see what he is saying here about his name? If
we use it as if there is no meaning to it, as if he could just as well have
any other name and not be any different, then we are using his name in
vain, we are misusing the gift that he has given us. And that, he says
here in this verse, he will *not* tolerate.

If you use a hammer to fix a china plate, or use a clock to
shovel snow, it's obvious that you don't understand how to use the tool
in your hands nor how to get the job done. You are misusing your
equipment; you may as well be doing nothing as trying to solve the
problem with the wrong tool. In the same way, when we approach the
Lord and use his names ignorantly, without knowing what they mean,
and not even asking for the very things that his name teaches us, then
we are misusing his name. We are using a power tool without plugging
it in when we call on God's name with no intention of using what the
name describes. Worse yet, we might be using a holy and precious
thing for our personal lusts. We are supposed to be experts at this! Not
only does our ignorance disappoint him (he went to all that trouble to
reveal his name to us so that we *could* use it with success) but he gets
angry at our arrogance. How can we hope to please him if we refuse to
use what he has *provided* to please him? Will we please him with our
sin? With our "wisdom"? Even with our good intentions? Or will we
please him only by doing his will and *honoring his name*?

Many people think that this commandment only means not to
use God's name while swearing. It certainly does mean that; I can't
imagine what it will be like for those fools who thought that God was
only a handy swear-word and then have to face him in his wrath on
Judgment Day! But this isn't the only thing it means, nor do I believe
is it the primary meaning. Considering how important his name is

throughout the Bible, and how he keeps stressing that his people learn and use his name correctly in life and in worship, it seems that the main thing that he is getting at here is to get *his own people* to take his name more seriously. It's a rebuke to believers who aren't using the gift that God has given them. Jesus himself had to rebuke the disciples for this same neglect: "Until now you have not asked for anything in my name. Ask and you will receive, and your joy will be complete." (John 16:24)

One of the most interesting passages about the name of God is in connection with the Temple that Solomon built. Many years of work and planning went into the Temple, because it had to be built to God's exacting specifications; it had to do the job that he intended for it. When it was all done, Solomon and the Israelites came together to dedicate it to the Lord. But it occurred to Solomon that, in a way, it was futile to expect the Lord to live in a house made with human hands.

> But will God really dwell on earth with men? The heavens, even the highest heavens, cannot contain you. How much less this temple I have built! (2 Chronicles 6:18)

Pagan religions might think that their gods lived in the temples they built for them, but Solomon wasn't so foolish. Rather, he asked the Lord to do something special for them concerning the Temple:

> May your eyes be open toward this temple day and night, this place of which you said *you would put your Name there.* May you hear the prayer your servant prays toward this place. (2 Chronicles 6:20)

In some way unknown to the human mind, the Name of God came down in power and filled the Temple, so much so that it says —

> When Solomon finished praying, fire came down from heaven and consumed the burnt offering and the sacrifices, and the glory of the LORD filled the temple. The priests could not enter the temple of the LORD because the glory of the LORD filled it. (2 Chronicles 7:1-2)

Now, when the Israelites had something to say to their God, they turned to the Temple and called his Name. That would get their God's immediate attention (because, remember, no other god can lay claim to that name) and he would honor his name among them by answering their prayer. It was a wonderful solution for all their problems.

This story shows how God intended for us to use his names. They aren't just for show, but for us to grab hold of and swing open the doors into Heaven. When he hears his name being called, he answers the call. Now do you see why he forbids using his name to no purpose? Anybody who calls on the power of Heaven had better be ready to meet that power! It's the same thing as our telephone system: if we call someone by phone, and they answer, and then we don't say anything to them, we are wasting their time and ours too. The call was to no purpose. When we call on God by his special name, we are calling a *certain* God by name and looking for the particular thing that the name describes, and we should expect to get answered by the God with this name — not by some other god. Believe me, there are plenty of the devil's henchmen waiting to answer whatever prayer you send their way, if you are so careless as to send out a prayer with no name attached. Be careful to name the God you want first! Nobody else should be reading your mail to Heaven; so address it to your Father alone.

This is what you will learn about how the people in Bible times used God's names. They wanted something in particular, and God's name gave them reason to hope that they would find it in him. Abraham called him "the Judge of all the earth" (Genesis 18:25) and for good reason: he was pleading for the lives of the righteous in Sodom and Gomorrah (he knew of at least one!) and he appealed to one of God's names so that he could get a fair judgment. Jacob learned one of God's names — the God of Abraham and the God of Isaac (Genesis 28:13) and decided that he wanted the Lord to be his God too, in the same way that he was God to his fathers. We have already seen how the Lord revealed his special name to the Israelites (Yahweh) and he expected them to memorize its definition and come to him for what that name describes: forgiveness, long-suffering, mercy, abundant in goodness and truth. (Exodus 34:6-7) Samuel, David, Jeremiah, Isaiah, all the apostles — they knew the power in God's many names and they never lost the opportunity to grab hold of the names when they needed the Lord's help.

When Nehemiah was in Babylon during the Exile, he heard that some of the Jews had returned to Jerusalem and were having a bad time of it. Jerusalem was on the heart of every good Jew, and Nehemiah was no exception. He immediately went to God about the matter. But he *started* his prayer with the name he wanted to focus on, the God who had the power to help in this particular problem. He didn't wait till the end of the prayer and stick God's name on as an afterthought as we do! Here is how he started his prayer:

> O LORD, God of heaven, the great and awesome God,
> who keeps his covenant of love with those who love him
> and obey his commands. (Nehemiah 1:5)

He wanted somebody in particular: not the Babylonian gods, not the false idols that they used to worship in Canaan, but *this* God — the one he described by name. He could depend on the Lord (as described in Exodus 34) to be merciful to sinners such as they were. The God of Heaven had the authority to release the captives from their Babylonian masters. The "great and awesome" God could do the miracles that would be needed to get the Jews back to Israel and restore the land. And notice that he *knows* he got God's attention after calling him by name: "Let your ear be attentive and your eyes open to hear the prayer your servant is praying before you day and night for your servants, the people of Israel." (Nehemiah 1:6) This is the very idea behind the Temple! He ends his prayer by asking for success, being so bold as to assume the Lord will answer him, because he delights to revere the Lord's Name. (Nehemiah 1:9)

When you use one of God's special names, what you are actually doing is pointing at the God you want. You are being specific about the thing in God that you see, that you want and need for your problem. And you aren't being presumptuous at all: he revealed these things for you so that you *can* point and ask for what you see. Imagine a smorgasbord meal where all kinds of dishes are laid out for you to pick. Each food has a little sign beside it giving its name, and perhaps what it is made of. You can pick the thing that looks like it would taste the best, or fill you up, or whatever you want. Seeing God in the Bible is much like that: here you read a name of his that describes something he can do, there you see another name, and more and more names. The feast is rich! Which one will you pick? Which one do you need the most? Call on the God you need and you will be filled with the fullness that the name promises.

Is God the same now that he was back then? Can we expect to find the same answers, the same promises, the same comfort and wisdom, the same power and miracles that we read about in the Bible? Most people think not; they think that he has changed over the centuries and he doesn't do things now the way he did them then. But they are mistaken about him: God is the Unchanging God: "I the LORD do not change." (Malachi 3:6) His names have never changed, which should tell us that he himself hasn't changed either. He is still "the God of Abraham, Isaac and Jacob." He is still the Redeemer of Israel. He is still the LORD who has mercy on sinners, and punishes the wicked. If you call on him by those "ancient" names that are recorded in the Bible, you will find him to be very much alive and still like what those names describe. When the Sadducees challenged Jesus about the doctrine of the resurrection, he answered their unbelief with this very point. God said he was the God of their forefathers, so that means he is *always* the God of their forefathers: "Have you not read what God said to you, 'I am the God of Abraham, the God of Isaac, and the God of Jacob'? He is not the God of the dead but of the living." (Matthew 22:32) Not only are the three Patriarchs still living, but God is still their God! His names should be giving you hope that *you* still have a chance to enjoy the blessings that he promised long ago to the saints.

One of the most incredible events that ever happened in Jewish history concerns the name Yahweh. Around 400 BC the Jews were trying their best to follow the letter of the Law: They had just come back from exile in Babylon, having been sent there as punishment for their idolatry, and they were trying to behave themselves for a change. They took another look at the Third Commandment and decided that perhaps they weren't obeying it with all their hearts. So they *quit using* the name of the Lord in daily conversation; they didn't want to risk offending him with a useless reference to him. Soon they quit using it even in religious services, claiming that the sinful lips of men ought not to profane the holy Name under *any* circumstances. They came up with all sorts of clever ways around having to pronounce the Name when reading the Scriptures. For example, they often substituted another word, like Adonai, in its place so they wouldn't have to pronounce the holy Name that was written in the text.

You should know a little thing about Hebrew at this point. Written Hebrew was for a long time a language of consonants only; they never wrote the vowels in the text. It's as if we would write the first sentence in this paragraph like this: **Y shld knw lttl thng bt Hbrw t ths pnt**. As you can see, most of the words are fairly easy to make out, but you probably would have trouble with some of them. The Jews didn't need written vowels, however, because everyone knew how to pronounce the words already.

The problem is that, since nobody was allowed to pronounce it, after a while they *all*, even the priests, forgot how to pronounce the special name of God! The consonants are these: YHWH. You can put in several different vowel combinations and they would work; but to this day nobody knows for sure how the Lord first pronounced it to Moses.

That's not the worst of it, however. Because of their over-zealous attitude about keeping the Law, they shut the door to the most powerful resource they had at their disposal. *They refused to call upon the name of the Lord* — and therefore denied themselves all the good things that are in that name, and the privileges that come from honoring God's name. And this was in spite of the plain promise that God gave them about it: "And everyone who calls on the name of the LORD will be saved." (Joel 2:32) Instead of laying hold of the very thing that would save them, they turned away from it (it's no matter whether they did it from stubbornness, superstition, or "reverence for the Name", because it amounts to the same thing) and died spiritually as a result. Long before Christ was born the Jews were wasting away because of their obstinacy; the prophecy about them came true:

> No one calls on your name or strives to lay hold of you;
> for you have hidden your face from us and made us
> waste away because of our sins. (Isaiah 64:7)

When Jesus dealt with the Jews he found a people slavishly following the letter of the Law, getting nowhere, straining out gnats and swallowing camels because they didn't understand the spiritual meaning of their Scriptures. All this because they refused to call on God's name. So when the very embodiment of the name in Exodus 34:6-7 stood before them in the person of Christ, they neither recognized him nor wanted him. (John 1:10-11) They had quit calling on him long before then, and now he was only an unwanted intrusion in their lives. They even killed him to get him out of the way!

So the main thing to keep in mind about the names of God is this: ***call on him by his name***. That's what the names were designed for, as doorknobs that you can grab and pull open the door of Heaven. Name the God you want when you pray, and you will find him responding to you.

The Lord's special Name

Let's look again at the special name that the Lord revealed to Israel through Moses. It is so rich, and it shows us the very heart of our God, that we don't want to miss anything important about it. Besides, it will be a good exercise to study this name, because we are going to let the meaning of the Name tell us the truth about God and show how our ideas of him could very well have been wrong. All his names are like that.

The name Yahweh (or LORD) is a name that only the God of Israel, the God of the Christian Church, has. No other god or power in Heaven or earth can lay claim to what that name means. When he first told Moses what it meant, he was letting the Israelites in on a mystery that no other nation was allowed to know. The history of the nations has proved that this is true, because in their struggles to understand divine things they have gotten everything wrong about God; their gods don't resemble Yahweh in the least.

Remember that his name Yahweh means this:

The LORD, the LORD, the compassionate and gracious God, slow to anger, abounding in love and faithfulness, maintaining love to thousands, and forgiving wickedness, rebellion and sin. Yet he does not leave the guilty unpunished; he punishes the children and their children for the sin of the fathers to the third and fourth generation. (Exodus 34:6-7)

What is the Lord saying about himself in this definition?

• **_He has a serious view of sin._** Sin is sin, as far as God is concerned. He will never change his mind about the terrible nature of sin and rebellion; he hates it and he always will. The Law is the only definition of what sin is — we can't substitute our own definitions for it (we would water it down so that we could get away with something!). When God gave the Law to the Israelites he did it for a good reason: to end all questions as to why man is so guilty, and show what the penalty will surely be for any who break that Law. This definition of his name doesn't give us any freedom to think he has changed his ideas about sin. What it does say is this: in light of the problem of sin, since it has to be dealt with in some way that is satisfying to God's high standard of righteousness, there is another way besides destroying all sinners. He isn't going to change the Law, but change the sinner. There is a lot of difference. For those sinners who refuse to be changed, they will find the Law waiting for them on Judgment Day.

• **_He welcomes those who come to repent of their sin._** Our God is astonishing when it comes to forgiving sinners. When we consider how zealous he is about holiness, how severe the Law is against the least rule that is broken, and how much damage our sin has done to God's creation, we can't understand how he can so completely forgive hardened sinners and forget what they have done against him.

But it's easier to understand this miracle when we look at *how* he intends to solve this problem of ours. He is going to change us. He is going to make our hearts do what they couldn't do before: walk in the way of the

Spirit of God, in true holiness. *He* will work the miracle; we don't have to. He can undo the worst damage, he can make the hardest heart love him — but they *have* to come to him for help. He can turn a Christian-hating Saul into the Church's greatest apostle; nothing is impossible for him. But he will do nothing for a person if they don't come to him with their hearts open, ready for him to work on them.

This is why he is so open and free with his forgiveness. He knows he can change a sinner's heart from obstinate rebellion to loving obedience. Whereas we would have doubts that so and so deserves to be forgiven, because we have a feeling he is just going to go back to his sin after his "confession", the Lord has no such doubts. All he needs is for them to come within range of his grace and they *will* be saved from their sin. So when a sinner comes to God for forgiveness, he always finds a loving Father who puts the past away forever and welcomes his child home. This is the love of God, a love that we can't understand but is the very heart of the Gospel.

- *He has a dim view of the wicked*. Notice that while the Lord shows such an amazing willingness to forgive some sinners, he gets angry about others and promises to destroy them. How can he have such opposite feelings about people? The answer is, again, in the fact that some people will not come to him for cleansing. *Not coming* is what makes him so angry. They are called the "wicked" not because of their sin (the righteous are also sinners when they first come to him!) but because they don't want God to work the miracle of grace in their hearts. They want to remain sinners and rebels against God. The Lord has no feelings of pity or love for such people, only plans to destroy them in wrath. He will not have rebels running loose in his kingdom.

After they learned his special name, the Israelites were about to find out the depth of the meaning of the Lord's Name in the upcoming years and centuries. Through good times and bad times, hardships and trials, victories and successes, the Lord led them into deeper knowledge of himself as he used various circumstances to teach them. Their entire history was a lesson on the meaning of this name Yahweh.

Notice that at the very beginning they received the Law. First things first: God is a holy God, and he absolutely demands that his environment and his people are perfectly righteous and holy as he is. The standard is set and he refuses to lower the standards. The second thing to get straight is that they have a serious problem: they are sinners. Although the Lord told them that they must obey the Law, every one of them knew, if they were honest, that they couldn't possibly hope to keep the Law as God intended — not to the depth that the Law reaches. Besides, they were already Law-breakers before they started! Once they admit that, they can get down to business and get the problem solved; until they do, they are wasting their time and the Lord's too.

The way that the Lord intended to solve the problem is through a system of sacrifices and the Tabernacle. The Law condemned them as sinners, and in the Temple they found deliverance from that condemnation. This was the way out, the escape from condemnation, that they needed. And this is what the name Yahweh was all about. Only to the children of Abraham would there be forgiveness of sin, welcoming arms, amazing love — they found that in the Tabernacle when they were allowed to approach the very throne of God and ask him for forgiveness. The whole idea of the Tabernacle (and later the Temple) was to make sure the Israelites could get forgiveness for their sins. No other nation had that privilege!

We can also see the name Yahweh demonstrated in how the Lord dealt with the Israelites throughout their history. For example, during the times of the Judges, the Israelites would sway back and forth in their loyalty to the Lord. Sometimes they would worship the false idols of their Canaanite neighbors. But when they started getting persecuted by those neighbors, they swung back to the Lord again and pleaded with him to save them from their enemies. If *we* were leading them, we would probably have just let the enemy have them! When someone keeps going back into sin, and then running back to God when things get tough, you wonder whether their heart is right and whether they deserve to be rescued. The Lord, however, true to his special name, kept forgiving them. Though they were incorrigible sinners, he valued their coming back to him; the degree of sin doesn't worry him like it does us. His heart always melted when his little wayward children ran to him for help.

David is probably the best example of a person who trusted in the Name of the Lord when it comes to forgiveness of sin. He was the king of Israel, their spiritual and political leader, and he was also the model of the Messiah to come. A lot of responsibility lay on his shoulders! He was an important servant of the Lord. So when he committed adultery with Bathsheba and murdered Uriah her husband, we are staggered at the enormity of his crime. If it were up to us, he would have lost his position of authority — at least his standing as a religious leader — and melted back into history in shame. But that's not what happened. He, knowing the meaning of the name Yahweh, went straight to the Lord for *forgiveness*. And he got it! He got up from his prayer (you can read it in Psalm 51) a clean man inside. The Lord put away his sin and never held it against him again. David went back to being king, and a religious leader, and the writer of psalms, and the model for the Messiah, without the Lord hesitating a moment about it. (You can be sure he went back changed; the Lord doesn't allow us to sin again — he *saves from sin*.) Many sinners with guilt-ridden consciences wish they could get such a complete deliverance like that! David was a rare believer who understood the value of the Lord's name.

The prophets, who came later in Israel's history, preached against Israel's many sins. Before the Exile their sins were mainly idolatry, and after the Exile their sins were mainly being lax about restoring the true worship in the Temple. But the message of the prophets was always the same:

> *Return to him you have so greatly revolted against, O Israelites.* (Isaiah 31:6)

> *I have swept away your offenses like a cloud, your sins like the morning mist. Return to me, for I have redeemed you.* (Isaiah 44:22)

*Seek the L*ORD *while he may be found; call on him while he is near.* (Isaiah 55:6)

*"Return, faithless people; I will cure you of backsliding." "Yes, we will come to you, for you are the L*ORD *our God."* (Jeremiah 3:22)

*Declare a holy fast; call a sacred assembly. Summon the elders and all who live in the land to the house of the L*ORD *your God, and cry out to the L*ORD. (Joel 1:14)

*This third I will bring into the fire; I will refine them like silver and test them like gold. They will call on my name and I will answer them; I will say, 'They are my people,' and they will say, 'The L*ORD *is our God.'* (Zechariah 13:9)

We could quote many more passages, but the point was always the same: they were to return to the Lord. He didn't expect them to make themselves holy first and *then* return to him, but return to him *as sinners* seeking his righteousness, and let *him* solve their problem of sin. They should have known that this is what the Lord wanted them to do because they knew his Name: the compassionate and gracious God, slow to anger and abounding in love. He will save them from their sin if only they will *come.*

The wicked, however, had no hope. They refused to turn to the Lord, so they had to do without his mercy and drink the cup of death instead.

This is what the Sovereign LORD, the Holy One of Israel, says: "In repentance and rest is your salvation, in quietness and trust is your strength, but you would have none of it." (Isaiah 30:15)

So he gave them over to destruction; read the following verses in Isaiah 30 for what God did to them. And yet he ends even this section with an announcement of the Gospel, the name of the LORD, the compassionate God ready to forgive sinners who will come to him!

Yet the LORD longs to be gracious to you; he rises to show you compassion. For the LORD is a God of justice. Blessed are all who wait for him! (Isaiah 30:18)

One more example of the name Yahweh in Scripture. When Jesus came to earth, his main job was this: "He will save his people from their sins." (Matthew 1:21) He didn't come to smash sinners, or destroy them, as his disciples wanted him to do. (Luke 9:52-55) He came to *forgive* them. "It is not the healthy who need a doctor, but the sick. I have not come to call the righteous, but sinners to repentance." (Luke 5:31-32) We will discuss this more in the last chapter, "The Master Key," but we want to see here that the whole point of Jesus' ministry was to reveal the forgiving Father who will gladly welcome and completely forgive any sinner who comes to him in repentance and faith. You can't miss the point when God himself comes down to show you the way! In other words, Jesus showed us the meaning of the name Yahweh in a new and powerful way that laid the foundation for the Church, where God lives with his forgiven people.

Did Christ show us the other side of the name, the part about what he thinks of the wicked? Yes; at one point he was venting his frustration with the Jews who, typically, knew all about what the Law *said* but nothing about what it *meant*. They had the answer right in front of them; the whole book pointed to the mercy of God, who is really Jesus Christ. "Yet you refuse to come to me to have life." (John 5:39) *That* was their worst sin. And for that they would not live to see the mercy of God.

O Jerusalem, Jerusalem, you who kill the prophets and stone those sent to you, how often I have longed to gather your children together, as a hen gathers her chicks under her wings, but you were not willing! Look, your house is left to you desolate. I tell you, you will not see me again until you say, "Blessed is he who comes *in the name of the Lord.*" (Luke 13:34-35)

Praise him by name

Calling on God by his name when we pray is only half the story. Remember that God is most interested in getting glory; he bends all things in this world to achieve this important goal. If you don't understand why he would be so keen on getting glory, go back to the chapter on Glory and think about why he so much deserves glory — and why he isn't getting it from us. Sin and death have denied the Lord what he fully deserves, and the primary function of the Church is to give the Lord the glory he deserves for a change.

Praising his Name will most glorify him, I believe, once we understand why he needs glory. His names glorify him in a way that few other things do. We can testify to what the Lord has done for us, and that will glorify him. But his own names say it better than our childish explanations of what we think the Lord did in this circumstance and in that event. When we are at a loss for words, in other words, all we have to do is pull out some of his names and they will do the talking for us.

The Bible tells us that praising his name is a powerful way to glorify God:

> *O LORD, our Lord, how majestic is your name in all the earth! You have set your glory above the heavens.* (Psalm 8:1)

> *Ascribe to the LORD the glory due his name; worship the LORD in the splendor of his holiness.* (Psalm 29:2)

> *Sing the glory of his name; make his praise glorious!* (Psalm 66:2)

> *Praise be to his glorious name forever; may the whole earth be filled with his glory. Amen and Amen.* (Psalm 72:19)

> *Ascribe to the LORD the glory due his name; bring an offering and come into his courts.* (Psalm 96:8)

There are many other passages that teach about the glory of God's name, and the importance of bringing people's attention to what his names mean. You will find them if you are paying attention during your reading. Remember that glory means *who gets the credit* — God claims to be what he is by giving *himself* that name, and nobody else can truly claim that same name. Only God is the Provider, only he is the Savior, only he is the Light and Life.

There are two main reasons for glorifying God through his names: *first*, the news needs to get out that our God is like this. People don't know! Or because of their sin they don't want to know God; they want to keep wallowing in their sin and dying without hope. But they need to hear that there is a Judge of all men, a Righteous Judge who knows their hearts and their sin against him. They need to know that God is the Creator of the Heavens and the earth, that the earth isn't running on its own but according to the plans of the Maker. It depends on him for everything — because he is the Provider for every living creature. They need to hear that Christ is the only Way, Truth, and Light; otherwise they will look in other directions for purpose and meaning to their lives and turn their backs on his wise counsel. That isn't very smart when he is such a Wonderful Counselor! The world needs to see that the Lord is the God of Abraham, Isaac and Jacob, the forefathers of the covenant of the faithful, so that they will feel the need to get into the covenant community themselves and get the same blessings that he gave those men.

Many people are used to saying "Praise the Lord" and "Hallelujah" without giving much thought to what they are saying. In the first place, you may not have known that the word "Hallelujah" is a Hebrew word that means, when translated, "Praise the LORD." (The "jah" at the end is the shortened form of Yahweh.) Second, what are you praising him for? Just to say "Praise the Lord" isn't saying anything about him. Praise means to give him glory, to give credit to him for being a certain way or for doing something in particular. You have to say something about him if you want to praise him. You will find that the Bible writers knew what to say when they wanted to praise him; they often turned to one of his names for something to say about him. For one of many examples, study Psalm 103.

I hope you realize that to glorify God in this way, you need to *know* his names. And that knowledge will only come by studying the Word that describes his names. We keep coming back to that, don't we?

Second, the Lord gets glory through his names when we come back from the field, so to speak, full of wonder at what we have just experienced in his name. When the disciples went out to preach the Gospel, they found a new power in what they said and did in Jesus' name — and came back excited about it. "The seventy-two returned with joy and said, 'Lord, even the demons submit to us in your name.' " (Luke 10:17) Notice too what the writers of the Psalms are full of: amazement at the power, the wisdom, the riches of his name. His name works! The things that his names describe really are our salvation. When we call on his name and he lifts us up out of the dark world into a world of light and life and joy, we naturally praise him. What better way is there to say thanks than to give credit to him for being what he said he is? If he proves to be a fortress for us, he would like to hear back from us when our enemies run away and we are feeling free again. It would be a poor thing to get such a rich treasure and not even say thanks! The most natural thing to thank him for is what he gave us: the name that enriched us. The best *way* to thank him is to tell how true his name is. That brings him glory.

An Example

There's a fascinating example in the Bible of people who knew how to use God's names in prayer. In Acts 4 we are told that the new believers were persecuted for their faith in Christ; even Peter and John were arrested and interrogated. When the church got together to discuss the problem, they prayed for a solution. Here is their prayer.

> "Sovereign Lord," they said, "you made the heaven and the earth and the sea, and everything in them. You spoke by the Holy Spirit through the mouth of your servant, our father David: 'Why do the nations rage and the peoples plot in vain? The kings of the earth take their stand and the rulers gather together against the Lord and against his Anointed One.' Indeed Herod and Pontius Pilate met together with the Gentiles and the people of Israel in this city to conspire against your holy servant Jesus, whom you anointed. They did what your power and will had decided beforehand should happen. Now, Lord, consider their threats and enable your servants to speak your word with great boldness.

Stretch out your hand to heal and perform miraculous signs and wonders through the name of your holy servant Jesus." (Acts 4:24-30)

These believers proved, in the way they prayed, that they knew how to take advantage of the name of the Lord. **First,** notice whom they called on right away: *Sovereign Lord.* In the face of the opposition they were getting from sinful men — especially wicked men in power and authority in the community — this is the God they needed to go to for help.

The term "sovereign" of course refers to the one who is really in charge, the one who is the king over all other kings on the earth. The Greek name they use is *despota,* from which we get our word "despot" or absolute ruler, someone who has the power of life and death over his subjects. What a powerful name to start out their prayer with! They are quoting from Psalm 2 which is the "coronation ceremony" of the King of kings. In this psalm we learn several important things about how God is sovereign over all men on earth: *first,* he laughs at men's rebellion against him because he knows it won't amount to anything; he will do with them as he pleases and they can't do a thing about it. *Second,* he has already chosen a king to rule over the earth, without consulting any of us about it. *Third,* that king rules with an iron rod: he will not play games with us, but expects us to obey him and submit to him in all things. *Fourth,* for those who refuse to bend their knee to him, he will destroy them; and he isn't inclined to give them any second chances to get it right — "Kiss the Son, lest he be angry and you be destroyed in your way." (Psalm 2:12). This is the kind of king we have to deal with.

So when the believers want someone to help them, someone who can take care of these troublemakers, they go to *the only one who can!* You see, the name of God that is so well described in Psalm 2 attracted them and taught them what they can ask for and expect from him. They did *not* go to any man, be he king or prophet or counselor, for help to deal with wicked men in power.

Second, they call on the name of Christ: "your holy servant Jesus." (Acts 4:27) In fact they mention this name twice in their prayer. There is so much meaning in that name! First, the name Jesus itself means "Yahweh is salvation", showing the kind of ministry Christ would have among us. ("Jesus" is the Greek form of the original Hebrew name "Yehoshua" or "Joshua".) But the believers also home in on the fact that Jesus was God's *servant*. Jesus was careful to do everything that his Heavenly Father required of him; he himself mentioned several times that he did nothing apart from his Father's will. (John 6:38-39; 14:24) The Jews always did wonder what he meant by this. A servant represents the one who sent him; whoever resists the servant is really resisting his master. So when wicked men resisted him and put him to death, they were actually fighting God: even while they thought they were doing God a favor, they were really digging a grave for themselves.

Now the Lord has sent his apostles and other believers out to do his will. They carry his authority upon them; their work is his work, and whoever resists the spreading of the Gospel is fighting God. That's not safe. The enemies of God should fear for their souls when believers go to the Lord about being persecuted; it's only a matter of time till the Lord himself will visit them with fierce judgment.

What the believers are asking for, then, is for the Lord to clear the field of the opposition. To make the preaching go smoother, the Lord must come down and clear the way for them so that they can go about their duty again without being bothered. This is, after all, Christ's Gospel, the same news of the kingdom of God that the Lord himself preached while on earth. They weren't doing anything new but only carrying on *his* work. They were identifying themselves with "the holy servant" and claiming the same kind of power and protection and success that he had.

One more thing to notice. In our day it is fashionable to add the words "In Jesus' name, Amen" at the end of all our prayers. We wouldn't think to leave it off; somehow it wraps things up nicely and makes us feel that God will hear us if we do. But notice that these believers, who first heard the Lord's command to ask for things in his name ("I tell the truth, my Father will give you whatever you ask in my name" — John 16:23) did *not* end their prayer the way that we do. Yet they surely were sensitive to what the Lord commanded! They knew that the Father would only hear them if they *did* ask in Jesus' name. You can see from this prayer, however, that they homed in on Jesus' name (two of them, in fact) as the *main point* of the prayer, not just as a ceremonial afterthought. They started the prayer in his name, not ended it that way. They focused on the name of Christ throughout the prayer; they didn't wait till the end, as we do, and suddenly remember that they forgot to mention Christ's name — and hurriedly insert it so that God would accept their prayer. In other words, they understood how to use the name of Christ in prayer, whereas we seem to understand very little about it.

Notice however that *their* way worked. The building shook as the Holy Spirit came down on them in power. This was the Lord's way of answering them, and showing his intentions to make the way clear for them. When someone honors the name of the Lord as they did, the Lord answers with power and the treasures of Heaven. His names are literally keys to the throne room and they unlock treasure chests full of answers for life's problems. He loves for his people to call on his name.

Questions to ask

When you read the Bible, keep an eye open for the names of God. There are more than you might think! They are there for a reason; they are like gems lying on the ground waiting for you to pick up and use. But like any other key in the Bible, the names of God will require some thought if you want to get the most out of them.

- *What is the name?* Does God give a definition for it? Is there another passage in the Bible that will help you understand this name? Is this the only place the name is used, or is it used in other Scriptures? Sometimes you may have to go to a Bible dictionary to get the meaning of Hebrew or Greek names.

- *Why did the Lord reveal this name here?* Who needed it? Since his names glorify him, what was it about God that the people in the story needed to learn? Why does the name glorify him better than any other way? Did people get the point, or did they refuse to learn and trust in the new name? Does it help to make the story clearer? Does it explain his actions — the reasons he did what he did?

- *Why is no other god named this?* Why do other "gods" (whatever they might be, modern or ancient) fail to live up to this name? What will we get from the world if we don't go to God for what this name teaches us? What does the world want us to think about this name? Usually they have some way of denying that such a thing about God is true; does God have evidence that his name is accurate, that he really is what his name says he is?

- *Was the timing important?* If you watch the story line through the Bible you will see that the Lord carefully revealed certain things first, then other things next, and so on. He never dumped the entire revelation of himself on men but spread it over history. Where were the people in the story, as far as spiritual progress? Why was this name what they needed at that particular stage? What names are still to be seen? What is there in the future that will further reveal his names to us?

- *Is there another name of God that closely resembles this one?* Sometimes it takes some thought to find the difference between his names — for example, a *fortress* and a *refuge*. Don't assume that you know, at first glance, what his names mean. You may have to search for examples of how this name gets worked out in someone's experience to fully understand all its intricacies.

- *Is this a name that you thought you understood already?* We are hasty people; we like to do Bible study fast since we have many other things to do too. But the knowledge of God comes over time, through much effort, when we meditate on his Word. Chances are that you haven't seen *all* the places where this name is used, or found *all* the people who tried this name out to solve their problems, or even understood *all* the reasons the Lord used this particular name in one passage of Scripture. If you understand the name so well that you praise God for what it means, and you are in awe over how it opens up precious visions of the true God before you, then you are beginning to see him in his glory. Until then you don't know it as well as you thought. His names are his glory, and when you see his glory, you will certainly praise him.

Discussion Questions for Name

- The Bible says that God is jealous of his name. What does that mean?

- Do some of the names of God interrelate with each other? In other words, in some passages you will find two or more of his names together; is this significant?

- Can God's names help you when you witness to someone else?

- How can the names of God be used during a church service?

- What specific ways do people break the Third Commandment?

- Some gods, powers, and even humans claim to have the same name as the Bible's God has. Give some examples and whether they live up to their claim.

- Analyze the Lord's Prayer (Matthew 6:9-13) and show how God's name is used in it.

- Jesus said in John 17 that he revealed the name of God to people. How did he do that, and what did he reveal?

- Find some examples of people in the Bible who used the names of God to their spiritual profit.

- If the Temple was the place where God's Name dwelt, what happened to his Name when the Temple was destroyed by the Babylonians?

- In Revelation 14:1 it says that believers in Heaven will have the Lamb's and the Father's name written on their foreheads. What does that mean?

Key Eight: Prophecy

Key Eight: Prophecy

Prophecy is a subject that fascinates both believers and unbelievers. I have seen people who have no interest in God, and no concern for holiness, read books on prophecy with fascination and argue about how the world will end. All you have to do is browse the bookstores to see how interested people are in the subject of predicting the future. There seems to be something in human nature that wants to know the future, and is willing to believe even a fake who claims to have that secret knowledge.

The Bible itself is full of prophecy. But it is a different kind of prophecy than the variety we have in books today. In fact, the Bible's type of prophecy is so unique that it is easy to see the difference between Biblical prophets and modern soothsayers. It is also much more dependable: the prophets of the Lord gave us clear, unerring pictures of things to come that will affect every person on earth, and time will show that they were right.

The message of the prophets is startling, to say the least; it spells the doom of all the kingdoms of earth and the end of all wickedness. This isn't what unbelievers are going to want to hear! It gives hope to the children of God, however, because there will finally be a day when the Lord rules over all in holiness and justice and everything will glorify him. The prophets were the heralds of the coming of the kingdom of God.

We want to look at just the essentials of Biblical prophecy here. There is so much to study in this subject, and students have their favorite subjects and passages dealing with prophecy, that we just can't get into all of it here — nor would we want to. The idea is to lay down a foundation of the basics of prophecy first, then build upon that foundation in your own further study. But we can't continue to ignore the prophets — their messages extend from the first book of the Bible to the last book. Once we understand what prophecy really is, so much more of the Bible will become clearer to us.

What is Biblical prophecy?

The first thing we have to do is find out exactly what prophecy is *not*; we have to separate the truth from error. There is so much that goes under the name of "prophecy" nowadays that we need a clear definition of it if we hope to understand what the Bible is talking about.

First, prophecy deals with the Word of God. A Biblical prophet always repeated God's words, never his own words. These are things that the Lord showed him, and his job was to take those very words to the people. He wasn't allowed to add to or take away from the prophecy: "I warn everyone who hears the words of the prophecy of this book: If anyone adds anything to them, God will add to him the plagues described in this book. And if anyone takes words away from this book of prophecy, God will take away from him his share in the tree of life and in the holy city, which are described in this book." (Revelation 22:18-19) That's why they always added the words "... says the LORD" to their prophecies. So anybody who claims to be a prophet must prove that what he is saying is what the Lord says; that's a test that modern "prophets" can't pass. "To the law and to the testimony! If they do not speak according to this word, they have no light of dawn." (Isaiah 8:20)

Second, prophecy is *not* just predicting the future. This is a common misconception that many people have about it. Of course we all want to know what the future holds for us. For example, the stock market would love to know the future so that it can make a sure profit! If we knew what was coming in the near future, we could make plans to be ready for it and take advantage of the circumstances. We would know how to prepare when others don't know (which would give *us* an edge in the competition) and we can avoid the dangers that others don't see coming at them.

But just knowing what is going to happen isn't going to do us any spiritual good. People who eagerly listen to "prophets" that foretell coming events are hoping to get themselves ready for what they think will happen, but they are committing a fatal spiritual error. It's not the *physical* events coming that we need to know, but the *spiritual* events. It's not what this world will do to us that is important, but what God intends to do to us with a *new* world. Jesus taught this when he warned us not to store up treasures on earth (and that's exactly what we will do if we panic at the news of coming physical disasters!) but instead store up treasures in Heaven. (Matthew 6:19-21) "Therefore I tell you, do not worry about your life, what you will eat or drink; or about your body, what you will wear. Is not life more important than food, and the body more important than clothes?" (Matthew 6:25) The predictions of modern "prophets", you will find, always cause us to fear the loss of these material comforts, not spiritual treasures.

If prophecy were just a matter of predicting the future, then many strange things would qualify as prophets! Woolly worms would be prophets, according to farmers, because the color of their coats supposedly predict the type of winter to come. The sky would be a prophet; the old saying goes like this: "Red sky in the morning, sailors take warning; red sky at night, sailor's delight." There are other things that would have to be called "prophets" if prophecy were simply predicting the future. But obviously the Biblical prophets are more than weather indicators; they were dealing in spiritual themes, things that affect the soul — the "wind" of the Spirit, not of the atmosphere.

The prophecies recorded in the Bible do predict future events, but never in such a way as to help someone get rich by it. There is another motive, another reason why they tell us what will happen in days to come. The Lord isn't interested in telling us how to become more secure and safe in *this* world, but how to prepare for the *spiritual* world of God's coming kingdom.

Third, prophecy is *not* just confronting man with the Word of God. There are some people who define prophecy like this, and by doing so they make it seem as if prophecy goes on in the Church today all the time during preaching and teaching. The prophets of the Bible *did* confront people with the Word of God; in fact, they received the Word directly from God, stopped people in the streets, and waved it in their faces, so to speak, so that there was no mistake that God was speaking directly to them through the prophets.

But a prophet was more than this. When he spoke to the people, he was telling them things that were dead-on-target. For example, what he said about their hearts, good or bad, was true and accurate; it was as if he could see into their souls and he knew what God had to say to them. Of course he got this insight from the Spirit of God, who alone knows the hearts of men. But his message to them was the *truth* and nothing but the truth, in such a way that they were obligated to listen to him. God was opening their hearts up to the eyes of the prophet and he spoke to what he saw there.

Modern preaching can't claim this kind of direct inspiration. We hope to speak to the heart, but no man knows the heart of another. We are called upon to preach the Word "in season and out of season" (2 Timothy 4:2) in every circumstance that the Lord gives us the opportunity. But at no time do we know, for certain, that the word found its mark. Only the Spirit of God knows whether the hearer needs to hear this word and how he needs to apply it. Our duty is to proclaim the Gospel, but it is the Spirit's job to convict. We sow, but we don't know how the seed grows because only God makes it grow. (Mark 4:26-29)

So the Biblical prophet stood in a unique position. He could see into the hearts of the people, and he stood in the courts of the Lord to hear the very words of God. His job was to convey what he heard in Heaven to the situation that he saw in Israel. It was more than just wagging his finger in their faces, as modern preachers and teachers do. We *hope* that we are saying something that will fit the circumstances and need, but the prophet *knew* that he was.

There is something more that made the prophecies of the Bible so unique, something that separates them from all other kinds of predictions and prophets. If you study the prophets of Israel and listen to what they are saying, one theme stands out that describes what they were all about:

Prophecy reveals the coming kingdom of God.

You will find this theme in all the prophets in the Bible. They weren't content to foretell what the future was, nor did they just preach the Word of God to the Israelites. Their message focused on the kind of world that God intended to set up on earth. They challenged all the kingdoms of men that stood in opposition to God's kingdom and predicted their downfall. They foretold the day when God would come in power and set up his kingdom in their place. They described the kind of kingdom that it would be, and who would be citizens in it. They predicted what would happen to anybody who opposed the coming of his kingdom. They told what life would be like in God's kingdom, and how his kingdom relates to our world. In fact, there is little left to the imagination: do a complete study of the prophets and their message, and you will have a deep understanding of all the fundamental truths of God's coming kingdom. Even the New Testament has little more to add to the picture that the Old Testament prophets gave us.

Every prophet dealt with the issue of the kingdom of God. For example, let's look at some of the major prophets and their messages:

• **Isaiah** predicted who would rule over this kingdom, and described the kinds of work he would do in it:

> For to us a child is born, to us a son is given, and the government will be on his shoulders. And he will be called Wonderful Counselor, Mighty God, Everlasting Father, Prince of Peace. Of the increase of his government and peace there will be no end. He will reign on David's throne and over his kingdom, establishing and upholding it with justice and righteousness from that time on and forever. The zeal of the LORD Almighty will accomplish this. (Isaiah 9:6-7)

• **Ezekiel** predicted the sort of people who would be citizens in this kingdom, and the way they would be made acceptable to the king:

> I will give you a new heart and put a new Spirit in you; I will remove from you your heart of stone and give you a heart of flesh. And I will put my Spirit in you and move you to follow my decrees and be careful to keep my laws. (Ezekiel 36:26)

- **Daniel** predicted what the King would do to the kingdoms of this world, to make way for the coming kingdom of God:

> While you were watching, a rock was cut out, but not by human hands. It struck the statue on its feet of iron and clay and smashed them. Then the iron, the clay, the bronze, the silver and the gold were broken to pieces at the same time and became like chaff on a threshing floor in the summer. The wind swept them away without leaving a trace. But the rock that struck the statue became a huge mountain and filled the whole earth. (Daniel 2:34-35)

Enoch predicted the day when the Lord would come in wrath and destroy his enemies. (Jude 14) Jeremiah called the Israelites to return to God, repent of their sins, and prophesied that the Lord would rule among them in peace. (Jeremiah 3:11-18) Hosea warned the Israelites that the King would come against them in anger and judge them in righteousness. (Hosea 5) Joel prophesied about the Day of the Lord, when the Spirit would come upon God's people and the Lord would save those who call on him from the coming disaster. (Joel 2:28-32) Amos foretold of the day when wicked Israel would be restored and the Lord's kingdom would be rebuilt. (Amos 9:11-14) We could go through every prophet like this. Their message was always the same: what would it be like when the Lord came in person and set up the kingdom that he was longing to see on this earth, among men?

The kingdom of God

We modern readers of the Bible don't understand much about kings and kingdoms. There is a richness in this idea that we would do well to stop and think about.

A good king had some responsibilities toward his kingdom that he took seriously. Bad kings fill our history books; they lived off the wealth of their subjects and seemed to have no other purpose in life but to enjoy themselves. But good kings were in a position to *help* their subjects. They had the resources and the authority to make sure that life went smoothly all through the kingdom. For instance, the king was the protection of his people. If some enemy showed up on the border with an army, the king would muster his own army and meet the threat. His people depended on him to protect them. Another thing that the king did was to make laws that would create order and justice in the land: he would make sure, through his sheriffs, that those laws were obeyed. He coined money and encouraged business so that the people could work and support themselves and live in prosperity. The king, in other words, was the center of the kingdom, the one reason why everything in the land was successful. He had much responsibility on his shoulders.

The Lord is this kind of king over his people. The things he wants to do for his people are things that can be done only by him — we rely on him as much (or more!) as we would an earthly king. For example, he intends to feed us, to protect us, to give us the treasures of Heaven, to govern us with just laws, to punish the wrongdoers, to forgive those who come to him for mercy, and so on. It really is a *kingdom* that he intends to set up among us.

The reason this is so important is that right now we are suffering under the kingdoms of the world; we can't get free to live in God's kingdom yet. The king of the dark kingdom — Satan — rules not as a good king but as a ruthless and merciless tyrant over ignorant souls who are ready to follow him into death and Hell.

> As for you, you were dead in your transgressions and sins, in which you used to live when you followed the ways of this world and of the ruler of the kingdom of the air, the spirit who is now at work in those who are disobedient. All of us also lived among them at one time, gratifying the cravings of our sinful nature and following its desires and thoughts. Like the rest, we were by nature objects of wrath. (Ephesians 2:1-3)

Satan is the epitome of a bad king: he saps the strength and resources of his subjects to achieve his own selfish ends, and then leaves them to die in misery and spiritual poverty. The wages of the enemy, paid out at the end of life, will make many a soul regret ever having been born. The kingdom that we live in now has these characteristics:

• ***Rebellion***. Hardly anybody takes God seriously, and nobody follows all his commands in a way that would please him. We are sinners from birth, determined to turn our backs on anything that even resembles outside control. "They are all hardened rebels, going about to slander. They are bronze and iron; they all act corruptly." (Jeremiah 6:28) We don't have to be particularly bad to qualify as rebels; there are some very nice people in this world who have no intention of doing what God said to do in his Word. We are all infected with this rebellion in our hearts. If we don't know how bad we are, all we have to do is read the Law of God and we will soon be finding all sorts of things that we don't like about this God who wants to rule and control every little thing in our lives.

• ***Self rule***. If we don't want to obey God in all things, then whom will we obey? Ourselves! We make the rules, we form our own opinions on what is right and wrong, we set the standards that we want to live by. We have put ourselves in God's place and we want to do things our way. "'Let us break their chains,' they say, 'and throw off their fetters.' " (Psalm 2:2) Remember what Eve did in the Garden? She used her feelings and her reason to judge whether eating the fruit would be right. (Genesis 3:6)

• ***Ignorance***. When you rebel against God's rule over you, and you rely on your own opinions to guide you in life, you are headed off into the darkness. God is the only light in God's universe; we are fools to think that we can live in God's world, use God's physical blessings, breath God's air, and get away with ignoring God in how we live. "For although they knew God, they neither glorified him as God nor gave thanks to him, but their thinking became futile and their foolish hearts were darkened. Although they claimed to be wise, they became fools." (Romans 1:21-22) People do stupid things in this world, all the way from the kings and presidents to the lowest ranks of society. We hurt each other and ourselves for no good reason, we fight like children, we labor to accumulate wealth that does us no good at all, we parade around in our "glory" without having anything to be proud of — man is a foolish creature for all the brains that the Almighty has supposedly given him! And this comes from turning our backs on the One who has all wisdom.

• _**Devastation**_. The previous points lead to this one: when everything is in such hopeless confusion, and man in his ignorance "rules" over it all using the same old ways that don't work and never will work, the house is eventually going to collapse. We have seen this happen over and over again in history. The history books ought to be re-written with this in mind. The grand schemes of men and nations have always failed because they will not bend their knee to their Creator. There have always been death and destruction, failure and misery, sickness and injury, poverty and shame, because of _man's sin_. God didn't _make_ the world this way! It's about time we took credit for what we have done to this world: it's our fault that things are in such a hopeless state. God made the world _good_ (Genesis 1:31); we have ruined it for no good reason.

• _**No purpose**_. People need a reason to live. If they keep running into failure, if success and happiness and peace never happen, they become discouraged. For a while we can talk ourselves into thinking that our work means something, that our efforts are not in vain. But more often than not we are faced with hard reality when our work unravels, our efforts go unnoticed, the world passes us by as if we had never lived, and all the results of our work are gone by the time the next generation takes over. "What does a man get for all the toil and anxious striving with which he labors under the sun? All his days his work is pain and grief; even at night his mind does not rest. This too is meaningless." (Ecclesiastes 2:22-23) This is what makes people commit suicide, this ultimate emptiness to life. It's not a pleasant thing to face at the end of life, when we struggle to the finish and then have to look over a meaningless past when we lay down to die.

As you can see, something needs to be done. Man has never been able to solve his problems; we are just getting deeper into trouble from generation to generation. And since it seems that we are intent to keep on living the old way, without God, things never will improve in this earth. Also, since the devil is really behind the confusion and destruction and only uses man as a dupe for his ends, the picture looks pretty grim. No matter what the politicians and economists and educators say, we will never achieve a perfect society.

But when a person becomes a believer he enters a new world — a place where God rules, not man or sin or the world or the devil. The change is immediate and noticeable. Here God makes the decisions, and things go the way the Lord wants them to go. He intends to change everything that we are used to, because it all needs changing! The Prophets tell us reasons that God wants to set up his new kingdom:

- ***To lay the Law down.*** When the Israelites came out of Egypt and were headed for their new home in Canaan, they first had to stop at Mt. Sinai to learn the rules — they were in God's kingdom now, and they had to live in a way that would please him from now on. The Lord always does that; our former way of living is unacceptable to him, and he won't rest until he teaches us to obey him.

     As the Israelites moved into Canaan, however, they forgot the rules — or they didn't care to remember them. They broke God's commands over and over, and then went back to him in their troubles (and we always end up in trouble when we live our own way!) and wanted him to save them. Well, he did; he is a God of mercy who forgives the wicked and gives them another chance. But he expected them to *turn* from their wickedness and walk in holiness again if they wanted him to keep on blessing them. Living in God's kingdom means learning *and doing* what God commands.

When things got so bad in Israel that almost nobody was obeying the Law of God, the prophets hammered at them repeatedly. Someday, they promised, the Lord will come and set up his kingdom among them once more — only this time he will *make sure* they obey his commands.

> I will give you a new heart and put a new spirit in you; I will remove from you your heart of stone and give you a heart of flesh. And I will put my Spirit in you and *move you to follow my decrees and be careful to keep my laws.* (Ezekiel 36:26-27)

For once the Lord is going to have a place where everyone does what *he* says, not what *they* want. The first message of the prophets was obedience to the King.

• **_To undo the damage._** We can't conceive of the damage that our sin has done, not only to the world but to ourselves as well. We like to think that we can do something to heal the hurts, and when we become a Christian the Spirit of God *will* start the process of healing in our lives. But the full healing and restoration won't happen until God sets up his kingdom in full force. Then there will be such massive changes that it will be obvious how little of the first, damaged world the Lord could use — and how much new material had to take its place.

The prophets promised an entirely new world to replace this one: "Behold, I will create new heavens and a new earth. The former things will not be remembered, nor will they come to mind." (Isaiah 65:17) In this new world, there would be no crying or dying young, labor that brings no fruit, or warfare. (Isaiah 65:19-25) Even the damage that sin has already caused in the past will be taken away, and what we lost will be given back to us: "I will repay you for the years the locusts have eaten." (Joel 2:25)

We have all learned more of the world's wicked ways than is good for us. We have sat at the feet of the devil, our first master, and become skilled at rebellion and sin. It comes naturally to us. But when the Lord destroys the devil's kingdom and sets his up — and *if* you become a citizen in that kingdom — you must be re-made, from the heart out, so that your first inclination won't be sin anymore. "Therefore, if anyone is in Christ, he is a new creation; the old has gone, the new has come!" (2 Corinthians 5:17) He can't have rebellion spoiling his new world! That's why the prophets encouraged us with the change that would come over us when we step into this kingdom: "Forget the former things; do not dwell on the past. See, I am doing a new thing! Now it springs up; do you not perceive it? I am making a way in the desert and streams in the wasteland." (Isaiah 43:18-19) In this new world there won't be any more hurt or damage, because all those who live there will be holy and upright like God is.

• ***To get rid of sin.*** The last point is related to this one, just as the effect comes from the cause. Sin is what has damaged the world — sin brought suffering and death. Root out the cause and you no longer have the damage; take away sin and you no longer have any reason to die.

To God, sin is the worst thing in the universe. "Sin is lawlessness." (1 John 3:4) If he is the King, then *there must not be a trace of sin in his kingdom.* He just can't abide it. Sin is our way of telling him that he doesn't know what he is doing, he can't take care of his creatures the way they need, he doesn't have our best interests at heart, he won't let us do what we want, and a host of other insults that make the angels themselves shudder to hear. If we could just see the wrath that rises in God's eyes when an insolent little creature rebels against him, we just might think twice about defying God Almighty.

All the prophets talked about what God thinks of sin, and they all warned the people what God promised to do about sin. In his kingdom, sin is the worst thing you could possibly do against the Lord, and you can't expect to get along with him in any way as long as you still have sin in your heart. He promises to *destroy* the wicked: "You are destroyed, O Israel, because you are against me, against your helper." (Hosea 13:9) "I will bring you into the desert of the nations and there, face to face, I will execute judgment upon you." (Ezekiel 20:35) "Your warriors, O Teman, will be terrified, and everyone in Esau's mountains will be cut down in the slaughter." (Obadiah 9) There are hundreds of passages like these; the message is that he intends to get rid of the wicked once for all — there will no longer be any wicked in his kingdom.

He also intends to do something about the sin in his children's hearts. Sin is a spiritual cancer; he must root it out completely, because the least little sin in Heaven would bring it all crashing down into ruin just as it has here on earth. "The remnant of Israel will do no wrong; they will speak no lies, nor will deceit be found in their mouths. They will eat and lie down and no one will make them afraid." (Zephaniah 3:13) There will finally be a day when everyone will be nice to each other, they will have others' best interest at heart, they will love each other and their God with all their hearts. If nothing else, Heaven will be so good because of this one thing!

• *To bring peace.* It seems as if war is part of the fabric of this world. There is always somebody fighting somebody somewhere! It's in man's heart to be jealous of others, to want what others have, to prove one's superiority over others, to rule over others in such a way as to grind one's subjects into the dust. Man is not a kind and compassionate ruler — he's not even a good neighbor most of the time!

Someday the Lord intends to put an end to all the fighting, bickering, backbiting, jealousies, quarrels, malicious slander, opposition and wars that so fill our lives. His kingdom is going to be a place of peace, where we will lay down the weapons of war because they will no longer be necessary. People will actually love each other for a change! "He will judge between the nations and will settle disputes for many peoples. They will beat their swords into plowshares and their spears into pruning hooks. Nation will not take up sword against nation, nor will they train for war anymore." (Isaiah 2:4)

Jesus is called the "Prince of Peace" (Isaiah 9:6) because he is going to bring together people who couldn't live with each other here in this world. People who are like lambs — weak and not at all aggressive — will live comfortably with those who have personalities like wolves and couldn't help but trample on other's feelings. "The wolf and the lamb will feed together, and the lion will eat straw like the ox, but dust will be the serpent's food. They will neither harm nor destroy on all my holy mountain, says the LORD." (Isaiah 65:25) The kingdom of God is where a person's character takes a change for the better: if we are going to live in peace with each other there, we *have* to become different from what we are now!

• ***To pour out the best things.*** One thing that a good king does is provide good things for his people. It's to his best interest to make sure they are taken care of. If they are all sick and starving, he's going to have more than his share of problems ruling them; but if he makes sure they are well-fed and prosperous, they'll gladly do whatever he says and follow him wherever he leads.

The Lord is no slouch in this area; he intends to do "immeasurably more than all we ask or imagine, according to his power that is at work within us." (Ephesians 3:20) The prophets described a world that only a fool wouldn't be interested in. "I will be like the dew to Israel; he will blossom like a lily. Like a cedar of Lebanon he will send down his roots; his young shoots will grow. His splendor will be like an olive tree, his fragrance like a cedar of Lebanon. Men will dwell again in his shade. He will flourish like the grain. He will blossom like a vine, and his fame will be like the wine from Lebanon." (Hosea 14:5-7)

God, of course, has at his disposal the treasures of Heaven — more riches and joys and pleasures than mortal man can imagine, let alone hope for. If we just got a glimpse of what it is like to live with God, we would gladly leave behind all the poor substitutes of this world that we call pleasures. "The seed will grow well, the vine will yield its fruit, the ground will produce its crops, and the heavens will drop their dew. I will give all these things as an inheritance to the remnant of this people." (Zechariah 8:12) He promises good things in his new kingdom primarily as incentives so that we will more willingly leave behind the "riches" of this world that don't really satisfy the heart.

• _**To make an eternal kingdom.**_ There is one fact about all the kingdoms of this world that nobody can deny: they all come to an end some time. If you can imagine it, there have been kings and kingdoms for thousands of years in this earth; the ancient civilizations of Babylon and the Sumerians, for example, flourished 3000 years before Christ was born! To put some perspective on how vast a time that has been, just think about what all has happened in history in the 2000 years since Christ. Where have all those kingdoms gone? Where is their glory now, their laws and armies and businesses and families and everything they thought was so important? The people have long been dead, and their works buried in the sand.

But that isn't going to happen to God's kingdom. He wants to set up a throne that will never fail, a king who will never die, a law and government that will never change or be repealed, even a people who will live forever. This is one kingdom that will be so full of the glory of God that it will not be allowed to fail; it must continue forever, if for no other reason than the fact that it will be a witness to the perfection of the One who rules over it. "Of the increase of his government and peace there will be no end. He will reign on David's throne and over his kingdom, establishing and upholding it with justice and righteousness from that time on and forever." (Isaiah 9:7) "Son of man, this is the place of my throne and the place for the soles of my feet. This is where I will live among the Israelites forever." (Ezekiel 43:7)

The kingdom of God will last forever for several reasons: *first*, it isn't made out of materials of earth, but spiritual materials that are designed to last forever. "His kingdom is an eternal kingdom; his dominion endures from generation to generation." (Daniel 4:3) *Second*, God will live there — and he is eternal; it takes on his characteristic. "The LORD, the LORD, is the Rock eternal." (Isaiah 26:4) *Third*, it exists solely to glorify God, and something that has this calling cannot fail. *Fourth*, he promised his saints a rest from the changeableness and emptiness of this world, and he will not go back on his word. "Because God wanted to make the unchanging nature of his purpose very clear to the heirs of what was promised, he confirmed it with an oath." (Hebrews 6:17)

• ***To bring about real justice.*** History has been such a disappointment for those looking for justice, for righteousness among men, that it would be a devastating blow to the people of God and the honor of God himself if this issue wasn't addressed at the end of time. In fact, this is one thing that God is looking forward to on Judgment day: when justice will finally be dealt out as each man, woman and child deserves.

Justice is giving to each person what they deserve. There has been very little of that in this world, for one reason or another. For one thing, human beings don't know the hearts of men well enough to give them what they deserve — neither good nor bad. "The LORD does not look at the things man looks at. Man looks at the outward appearance, but the LORD looks at the heart." (1 Samuel 16:7) For another thing, the Lord, who knows what we all deserve, hasn't given it to us yet. The wicked sin with gay abandon thinking that since nothing bad happens to them then God isn't as serious as everyone says he is about sin. (Ecclesiastes 8:11) The righteous lose hope when they see the wicked succeed and their own efforts fail. (Psalm 73:2-16) But this can't continue; the whole mess looks as if God isn't in control of things when he really is. There must be a day of reckoning when the confusion gets straightened out and God gets the credit he deserves.

"But let justice roll on like a river, righteousness like a never-failing stream!" (Amos 5:23) With this cry the Lord is going to set things to rights again. In his kingdom there will never again be wickedness. The righteous are going to live in peace, and be rewarded for their faithfulness. The wicked are going to be punished to the full extent of the Law, which is a terrifying prospect. "I will scatter them among nations that neither they nor their fathers have known, and I will pursue them with the sword until I have destroyed them." (Jeremiah 9:16)

He promises to destroy the wicked; they aren't going to get away with anything they have done in the past. "Listen! I am going to bring a disaster on this place that will make the ears of everyone who hears of it tingle. For they have forsaken me and made this a place of foreign gods; they have burned sacrifices in it to gods that neither they nor their fathers nor the kings of Judah ever knew, and they have filled this place with the blood of the innocent." (Jeremiah 19:3-4) But he also promises to bless the righteous; their faithfulness will not go unrewarded. "Instead of their shame my people will receive a double portion, and instead of disgrace they will rejoice in their inheritance; and so they will inherit a double portion in their land, and everlasting joy will be theirs. For I, the LORD, love justice; I hate robbery and iniquity. In my faithfulness I will reward them and make an everlasting covenant with them." (Isaiah 61:7-8)

• ***To get God glory.*** We have already seen in a former key that God intends to get glory someday, though he gets very little credit right now for what he does. Glory, we saw, means *who gets the credit*. And since man usually takes the credit for things that happen, everyone thinks that God has very little to do with the world as a whole. This is going to change someday when he sets up his kingdom and tears down the useless kingdoms of men that haven't done a thing that is worth keeping.

God cannot allow people to steal his glory: "How can I let myself be defamed? I will not yield my glory to another." (Isaiah 48:11) In God's kingdom, everyone will know how great God really is. There we will all see impressive proofs of his wisdom and strength, we will find out how much he was involved in the world's history, we will learn the depth of his love for his people and his wrath against the wicked, and many more things that are unknown and hidden right now. For those who love the Lord, that view of his glory will be the greatest sight in their lives. The Lord's people long for the day when God will finally get the credit for being who he is:

All the angels were standing around the throne
and around the elders and the four living
creatures. They fell down on their faces before
the throne and worshipped God, saying: "Amen!
Praise and glory and wisdom and thanks and
honor and power and strength be to our God for
ever and ever. Amen!" (Revelation 7:11-12)

The wicked are going to get straightened out
about the glory of God also: "I will display my glory
among the nations, and all the nations will see the
punishment I inflict and the hand I lay upon them. From
that day forward the house of Israel will know that I am
the LORD their God." (Ezekiel 39:21-22) There won't
be any mistake about who will punish the wicked for
their sins; they will know that the One they sinned
against has finally caught up with them and is giving
them what they deserve.

The two greatest prophets

Out of all the prophets mentioned in the Bible, there were two
men who were greater prophets than all the rest, and you might be
surprised at who they were! The first one was Moses:

Since then, no prophet has risen in Israel like Moses,
whom the LORD knew face to face, who did all those
miraculous signs and wonders the LORD sent him to do
in Egypt — to Pharaoh and to all his officials and to his
whole land. For no one has ever shown the mighty
power or performed the awesome deeds that Moses did
in the sight of all Israel. (Deuteronomy 34:10-12)

This is a high rating for a prophet! Moses had a position with
God that no other prophet in the Old Testament had, because the job
that he had to do was unique. In one of the stories recorded in the book
of Numbers we learn more about the kind of relationship that Moses
had with the Lord:

When a prophet of the LORD is among you, I reveal myself
to him in visions, I speak to him in dreams. But this is not
true of my servant Moses; he is faithful in all my house.
With him I speak face to face, clearly and not in riddles;
he sees the form of the LORD. (Numbers 12:6-8)

Why was Moses so privileged? It was because of what he had
to do, the job that the Lord gave him to perform — it was the most
important event in Israel's history. Think about the life of Moses. First
he led the Israelites out of Egypt and across the Red Sea. He then took
them to Mt. Sinai where they met the Lord and received his Law. Then
he led them through the desert to the Promised Land, fighting enemies
and doing miracles and teaching them the words of God. What was
happening here? It wasn't just an interesting history; he wasn't just a
handy person to have around. *The Lord was forming the nation of
Israel through the ministry of Moses*; everything that Moses did during
this period had consequences for thousands of years into the future.
Through Moses the Lord gave them the Law, formed the people into a
nation, governed them, led them from death to life, gave them the
Tabernacle and the system of sacrifices for forgiveness of sin, provided
for their every physical and spiritual need, told them the very words of
God — the Lord was literally using Moses to form the new Israelite
nation. The work of Moses was the foundation that all the future
Israelites, including kings and prophets, built upon. It's no wonder that
the Jews have always held Moses in such high honor!

You can see, then, why Moses was so important a character in
the Bible. But why was he called a prophet? Because he was the
messenger of the *kingdom of God*, the man through whom the Lord set
up his kingdom among the Israelites and ruled them. Moses' ministry
was entirely kingdom work, from first to last. In fact, he dealt with all
the aspects of God's kingdom — the rules of living, punishing the
guilty, forgiving sinners, and the duties of worship. This is the first
time that God set up a kingdom on earth; and, characteristically, he did
a complete job of it, leaving nothing to men's opinions or imagination.

Future prophets always referred back to the books of Moses;
they called people to remember and get back to the kingdom that
Moses set up at the beginning. They are often called "interpreters" of
the Mosaic Law because they applied the Law to particular problems.

They rebuked the people for straying away from the kingdom laws that God gave them through Moses; they proved that the people were guilty of breaking the Law; and they called them to turn back to God using the means that Moses had set up in the Tabernacle and sacrifices. They never preached a different kingdom, however — they always predicted the restoration, the renewing, of the kingdom of God, the one that Moses set up for them, and they foretold the time when the Lord would return and make things as they were in the old days. Once again, promised the prophets, the Lord would rule among his people as he did in the beginning, and the nation would return to the principles laid down in the Law of Moses.

This kingdom was physical, of course. The Tabernacle was a physical thing, the sacrifices were animals, the Promised Land was Canaan, the enemies were Philistines and Egyptians, and the Law of Moses dealt with issues like touching dead bodies and washing utensils before using them. But it was a kingdom nevertheless, the place where God ruled over his people and they obeyed his will completely — or were supposed to. Moses revealed to the people the ways that the Lord ruled over them. He opened their eyes to the fact that the Lord really did forgive their sins when they brought their sacrifices, that the Lord's strong arm was why they always won the battles against their enemies, that the Lord would miraculously provide for their needs, and so on. Moses showed them the spiritual God behind the physical events; he was revealing the *kingdom of God* at work in the world of men.

However, the Lord never intended this physical kingdom to be the last word. As it says in Hebrews, "it is impossible for the blood of bulls and goats to take away sins." (Hebrews 10:4) The kingdom that the Lord set up through the ministry of Moses was a shadow of the reality: "The Law is only a shadow of the good things that are coming — not the realities themselves. For this reason it can never, by the same sacrifices repeated endlessly year after year, make perfect those who draw near to worship." (Hebrews 10:1) The physical kingdom was a lesson in stone for the Israelites, but the Church of Christ needs more than stone to survive: it needs the Spirit of God. For this we need a new prophet, a man equal to Moses — or greater than Moses, considering the job to be done! — a man through whom the Lord would introduce a *spiritual* kingdom that would solve all the problems that the first kingdom couldn't touch.

That prophet was Jesus Christ. In fact, Moses himself predicted his coming:

> The LORD your God will raise up for you a prophet like me from among your own brothers. You must listen to him . . . I will raise up for them a prophet like you from among their brothers; I will put my words in his mouth, and he will tell them everything I command him. (Deuteronomy 18:15,18)

Peter, in his first public sermon after Pentecost, told us plainly that this prophet that Moses predicted is Jesus Christ — Acts 3:22-23.

Jesus had the *same kind* of job that Moses had, which puts the two men above all the other prophets in the Bible. They were actually working on the same project, the same house, two aspects of the same kingdom of God. We read that the work that Jesus had was "phase two" of the same job that Moses started:

> He was faithful to the one who appointed him, just as Moses was faithful in all God's house. Jesus has been found worthy of greater honor than Moses, just as the builder of a house has greater honor than the house itself. For every house is built by someone, but God is the builder of everything. Moses was faithful as a servant in all God's house, testifying to what would be said in the future. But Christ is faithful as a son over God's house. And we are his house, if we hold on to our courage and the hope of which we boast. (Hebrews 3:2-6)

Jesus came to make the shadows of the Mosaic kingdom a spiritual reality, not only among the Jews but among the Gentiles as well. He proclaimed the Law of the kingdom (see the Sermon on the Mount), he showed the power that would build the kingdom (through miracles and the Spirit), he identified the real enemies of the kingdom (the Pharisees who were dead spiritually), he demonstrated his intent to take care of his subjects (by providing for their needs, physically and spiritually), he even announced himself King (though of the spiritual kingdom, not one of *this* world). In the ministry of Christ we learn all the aspects of the *new kingdom* that God intends to set up all around the world, over peoples of many nations and cultures, across all time and into eternity. Again, there is nothing left to human opinion or imagination; Jesus covered it all and through his apostles continued to reveal the nature of the kingdom of God that Christians find themselves in.

Just as succeeding prophets clarified and enforced the first kingdom that the Lord set up through Moses, the apostles made the spiritual kingdom of Christ easier to understand and see. Take John for an example. In his book of the Revelation of Jesus Christ, he describes what Jesus is doing and will do in the churches and the world, and what the kingdom will finally look like when it is all done. At no point did he stray away from Jesus' original message; the prophecies outlined in Revelation are fuller statements of the original message that Jesus preached. And his point wasn't to entertain, or scare, or do anything other than describe the outworking of Psalm 2 — the King ascending to the throne of the universe!

Carried along by the Holy Spirit

One of the hallmarks of true prophecy is that the Spirit of God is behind it all. In Peter we have this doctrine taught plainly:

> Above all, you must understand that no prophecy of Scripture came about by the prophet's own interpretation. For prophecy never had its origin in the will of man, but men spoke from God as they were carried along by the Holy Spirit. (2 Peter 1:20-21)

In other words, the Spirit taught the prophet the right words to say and the right time to say them. This makes the words of the prophet the *Word of God*, and not just the words of men. This means that we have to take their message seriously — as Peter tells us:

> And we have the word of the prophets made more certain, and you will do well to pay attention to it, as to a light shining in a dark place, until the day dawns and the morning star rises in your hearts. (2 Peter 1:19)

The prophets themselves testify to the same thing.

> Here is my servant, whom I uphold, my chosen one in whom I delight; I will put my Spirit on him and he will bring justice to the nations. (Isaiah 42:1)

> Then the LORD came down in the cloud and spoke with him, and he took of the Spirit that was on him and put the Spirit on the seventy elders. When the Spirit rested on them, they prophesied, but they did not do so again. (Numbers 11:25)

> I have heard that the spirit of the gods is in you and that you have insight, intelligence and outstanding wisdom. (Daniel 5:14)

> On the Lord's Day I was in the Spirit, and I heard behind me a loud voice like a trumpet, which said: "Write on a scroll what you see and send it to the seven churches. (Revelation 1:10-11)

Why was it important that the Spirit be so involved in the prophecies of these people? Here are some reasons to think about:

- ***Dead-on accuracy.*** A prophet without the Spirit's help wouldn't know any more than you or I would. He couldn't see into a person's soul at all, and whatever he might think up to say to them wouldn't necessarily be accurate. At best he could only analyze the outward actions and judge from that. But "the LORD does not look at the things man looks at. Man looks at the outward appearance, but the LORD looks at the heart." (1 Samuel 16:7) When the Spirit confronts sinners, you can be sure that he knows exactly what is in their hearts and minds. So when the Spirit opened the eyes of the prophet to see the hearts of his hearers, that man spoke from certain knowledge — not just from guesses about them.

A good example of this is when Isaiah brought God's judgment to the Israelites. Remember that judgment starts with looking at the facts and deciding what is really going on; a judge in the courtroom has to do that because nobody is going to tell the truth about themselves! So the Lord also has to bring the truth to light, so that everyone can see that his justice is fair. Isaiah looked at the Israelites and the Lord showed him a rebellious people, in spite of the outward show of religion.

> The Lord says: "These people come near to me with their mouth and honor me with their lips, but their hearts are far from me. Their worship of me is made up only of rules taught by men." (Isaiah 29:13)

Isaiah, on his own, may have been fooled by them; but the Lord isn't fooled by man's show and pretense. We should realize that we are dealing with someone who can see into our souls, who knows our thoughts and feelings, who has watched us from the day we were born. We may fool other people but someday the Lord is going to call us to account for everything that we are. The prophets were only giving us a glimpse of the profound knowledge that God has of every one of us; that's why Peter recommended that we take their words seriously.

• *A spiritual kingdom.* The kingdom that God is going to set up among us isn't just another version of an earthly kingdom. There have been plenty of those and none of them can do what our souls really need. The Lord is going to set up a spiritual kingdom, something that will do us some real good for a change. Jesus told us that those who worship God must worship him in Spirit (John 4:24) — because that is the only way into his presence, the land of the Spirit. If we don't know how to get there or where this spiritual world is, then we had better find out; someday this physical world will disappear and only God's spiritual world will be left! Where will you be when that happens?

In Matthew 5 Jesus shows us the spiritual nature of God's new kingdom. He went over some of the old territory with the Jews, things that they knew by heart — at least they *thought* they understood these things. But they were surprised to see the old doctrines in a new light. They learned that murder starts in the heart. (Matthew 5:21-22) They learned that adultery wasn't just an outward act, it was a sin of the heart — and one could easily be guilty of adultery (and therefore under the curse of the Law) just by thinking unclean thoughts. (Matthew 5:27-28) The longer that Jesus taught them, the more they realized that the rules for this kingdom were spiritual, the punishment for sin was on spiritual level, the king examined their souls (not just their outward actions) for obedience to his laws, and the rewards were spiritual. Anybody who was listening that day ought to have seen that Jesus had no intention of setting up an earthly throne in Jerusalem. He was laying the groundwork for a kingdom that is *not* of this world — a place where the explanation for everything in it is the Spirit of God. In fact, he was already sitting on his throne, there on the mountainside, ruling over his subjects and laying the Law down — if people only had the eyes to see it.

• ***Correctly interpret events.*** There are always two sides to every question, and it's usually wise to get the story of what happened from several witnesses because the circumstances may be open to various interpretations. But in God's kingdom there isn't any room for anybody's opinions or interpretations except God's views. What he says is the truth; what he tells us is the *only* correct way to look at things. We don't need opinions from others (especially sinful and ignorant men, who don't have a chance of getting the truth right!) when God has spoken.

When the Israelites found themselves suffering again under the oppression of their enemies (this time it was the Babylonians) they probably looked at it as you or I would — it was a clear-cut case of a stronger bully beating up on a helpless little nation. If it were up before today's United Nations, there would be a stern warning against the Babylonians to stop their aggression.

But the prophet learned that there was an entirely different reason behind what was going on. Israel deserved this beating; in fact, God himself was punishing the Israelites for their sins by using the Babylonian army. "I am raising up the Babylonians, that ruthless and impetuous people, who sweep across the whole earth to seize dwelling places not their own ... O LORD, you have appointed them to execute judgment; O Rock, you have ordained them to punish." (Habakkuk 1:6,12) At first that astonished even the prophet himself (Habakkuk 1:13); so it was obvious that this idea wasn't his. It was a new and unexpected interpretation of the situation that showed the Israelites the truth about what was going on. If it weren't for the prophecy, they would have never gotten the point and would surely have reacted the wrong way to it.

This means that we ought to go back and re-write our history books. God has an entirely different viewpoint on everything that happens in this world. If we could see what he sees, we would know why things happen — and that knowledge would be far different from what we think we know now. That's exactly what the messages of the prophets are: the view from God's vantage point over all the earth, as he directs men and nations to work out his eternal purposes. In other words, we are going to get the *wrong idea* of what happens in life and why it happens until we turn to the prophets for the correct interpretation of the events.

• *__Reveal the mind of God.__* The last point leads into this one, but there is much more to learn than the explanation of the events of history. God thinks profound things, things that are far above the ability of man to comprehend unless someone reveals to us a little bit of the thoughts of God. That someone is the Spirit.

> For who among men knows the thoughts of a man except the man's spirit within him? In the same way no one knows the thoughts of God except the Spirit of God. (1 Corinthians 2:11)

What will the Spirit reveal to us about God's thoughts? *First*, how he feels about the wicked. His plans for the wicked are frightening; if they only knew what was going to happen to them, they would live their entire lives in terror. (Jeremiah 19:3) *Second*, how he feels about his people. His love for them is profound; he likens it to the love of a husband for his wife. Read especially the prophet Hosea for this idea. *Third*, the things that he thinks are important. We think that making a living and a name for ourselves is of primary importance; but to God these are small and insignificant things. "What is highly valued among men is detestable in God's sight." (Luke 16:15) To the Lord there are far more important things to do and get ready for: his glory, the coming of perfect justice, the glorious eternal kingdom, the new heavens and the new earth, and many more things that we give little thought to. These are the things that God is thinking about right now. You can read all about them in the prophets.

The Spirit reveals — *the kingdom of God*. He wants to open our eyes to what it is like there, the things we can expect to see and find there, the rules for living there, the people who will one day live there, and most of all the glorious King who rules over the whole realm and what he is like. The Spirit wants to teach us a great deal about this kingdom, and he decided to do it long before the New Testament was ever written: he started during the Old Testament prophets. It is there that we will learn much of what God's kingdom is like. Both Jews and

Christians must turn back to the prophets for this material, because there is much in the Old Testament that the New Testament doesn't bother to go over again. If we don't find some of this material in the New Testament books it isn't because it doesn't apply anymore (as some people believe) but that it was already covered in the Old Testament. It's like sending a math student back to the basics to learn what he should have learned already; the advanced texts aren't going to go over it again.

Let's take one prophet and find examples of what we can learn from him about the kingdom of God. Isaiah teaches us many of the basics:

• ***Sinners don't belong in the kingdom.*** "'Woe to me!' I cried. 'I am ruined! For I am a man of unclean lips, and I live among a people of unclean lips, and my eyes have seen the King, the LORD Almighty.'" (Isaiah 6:5) When Isaiah saw the Lord in his glory, he realized that the fatal flaw of every human being is *sin*; that alone will disqualify us from ever being a part of God's kingdom.

There are certain qualifications to be a citizen of a nation on earth, but none of them require that we are *holy* from the inside out. They can't do that because nobody can be that perfect! But God sets the standards in his kingdom. He is utterly holy, so holy that he can't stand to look upon sin. "Your eyes are too pure to look on evil; you cannot tolerate wrong." (Habakkuk 1:13) And he will never, ever tolerate a sinner in his kingdom — nor anybody who even might sin. This means that the wicked may as well give up the thought of being there unless something drastic happens — like a complete change of heart and life. But *this is* the hope of the righteous, who long for a place where there will no longer be the burden of sin, either their own or others'.

Don't miss the point about how one becomes a citizen! Notice in this passage that the Lord himself takes away our offensive sin, from the offering at the altar, by burning it out of us. All this is symbolic of the things that Jesus would do in his own sacrifice; but the point is that someone is made fit for living in God's kingdom by the actions of God alone. When God works on our hearts (through the Spirit, saving us from our sin), and he is satisfied that we are pure and upright (in the image of Christ, in other words) he will welcome us into the eternal dwelling.

• *__What kind of king will rule over it?__* "For to us a child is born, to us a son is given, and the government will be on his shoulders. And he will be called Wonderful Counselor, Mighty God, Everlasting Father, Prince of Peace. Of the increase of his government and peace there will be no end. He will reign on David's throne and over his kingdom, establishing and upholding it with justice and righteousness from that time on and forever." (Isaiah 9:6-7) He will be a king far above the kings of the earth, able to deal with matters of the heart.

Our nation's leaders have a tough time (when they are so inclined, that is!) coming up with laws that will be fair to everybody; judges try to figure out what will be just to both parties involved; teachers try to present their subjects in such a way that their students will learn the most; businessmen try to make a profit and yet keep their employees happy too. It is impossible to do any of this perfectly, however. Nobody is able to create a perfect society and therefore *nobody ever has*.

But Jesus is fully capable of running the kingdom of God — he has all wisdom, all power, and all insight into the hearts of men. He loves justice (being perfectly holy and righteous) and so he will judge all cases of conscience fairly and perfectly.

> The Spirit of the LORD will rest on him — the
> Spirit of wisdom and of understanding, the Spirit
> of counsel and of power, the Spirit of knowledge

and of the fear of the LORD — and he will delight in the fear of the LORD. He will not judge by what he sees with his eyes, or decide by what he hears with his ears; but with righteousness he will judge the needy, with justice he will give decisions for the poor of the earth. He will strike the earth with the rod of his mouth; with the breath of his lips he will slay the wicked. Righteousness will be his belt and faithfulness the sash around his waist. (Isaiah 11:2-5)

With qualifications like these, he will be well able to rule over and support the eternal kingdom of God and take care of all its special needs. When it is still running perfectly an eternity from now, that will be a testimony to his amazing powers and abilities as King.

• ***What will the people of this kingdom be like?*** "This is the one I esteem: he who is humble and contrite in spirit, and trembles at my word." (Isaiah 66:2) In earthly kingdoms the important people are the ones with power, money, and impressive reputations. If you don't have these things then you are a nobody. It seems that the young, the strong, the beautiful and the rich get everything they want in life.

But in God's kingdom everything goes to the humble, the repentant, and the "nobodies" of this world. "Whoever wants to become great among you must be your servant, and whoever wants to be first must be your slave — just as the Son of Man did not come to be served, but to serve, and to give his life as a ransom for many." (Matthew 20:26-28) This is how things are in God's kingdom: the first shall be last and the last shall be first, the ones who lay down their lives for the Gospel will be rewarded with eternal life, the meek shall inherit the earth. Paul reminded the Corinthians that they were chosen out of the low levels of society:

> Brothers, think of what you were when you were called. Not many of you were wise by human standards; not many were influential; not many were of noble birth. But God chose the foolish things of the world to shame the wise; God chose the weak things of the world to shame the strong. He chose the lowly things of this world and the despised things — and the things that are not — to nullify the things that are, so that no one may boast before him. (1 Corinthians 1:26-29)

It's going to be a real surprise when the great and mighty of the earth are shut out of the kingdom of God, and the lowly slaves of their earthly kingdoms are let into glory to assume positions of authority and power.

• ***Who will build the kingdom?*** "He saw that there was no one, he was appalled that there was no one to intervene; so his own arm worked salvation for him, and his own righteousness sustained him." (Isaiah 59:16) When a kingdom has to be built — a kingdom that must be eternal, perfect, and full of what God's children will need to serve him — there is only One who can do that adequately. They say that if you want a job done right, do it yourself. In this case the Lord does exactly that: he can't trust man to create a perfect and holy world, so he himself will do it.

In earthly societies things get done when men and women work hard and apply their skills to make it happen. But in God's kingdom, it is all *his* doing. "For from him and through him and to him are all things. To him be the glory forever! Amen." (Romans 11:36) God alone knows how to build the kingdom, he alone has the strength and time to build it, he has his own purposes for it, and he alone can judge whether it is meeting his expectations. He is the only one who can prevent sin and death from touching his pure kingdom — we are infected with these spiritual diseases, which means that the kingdom would definitely suffer at our hands.

Thank God that he is doing it all! We wouldn't have Heaven to look forward to if it were up to man in any way.

• ***What will happen to this physical world?*** "See, the LORD is going to lay waste the earth and devastate it; he will ruin its face and scatter its inhabitants ... The earth will be completely laid waste and totally plundered. The LORD has spoken this word." (Isaiah 24:1,3) If this is what he has planned for the earth, it would be wise for us to make plans for moving to God's kingdom and forget about setting our hearts on anything here. The things of earth aren't capable of bearing the weight of eternity; they can't show forth the full glory of God as the Lord wants to do in Heaven. Earth won't last forever, and it would be a mistake to make the kingdom of God out of earthly building blocks. It would be like the builders of Babel using "brick instead of stone, and tar for mortar." (Genesis 11:3)

Paul knew about these prophecies; that's why he counseled us to "set your hearts on things above, where Christ is seated at the right hand of God. Set your minds on things above, not on earthly things." (Colossians 3:1-2) And Jesus taught us to "store up for yourselves treasures in Heaven, where moth and rust do not destroy, and where thieves do not break in and steal." (Matthew 6:20) Peter, a student of the prophets who paid attention to what they taught (2 Peter 1:19) recalled the words of the prophets (2 Peter 3:2) and warned that the earth would someday be totally destroyed. (2 Peter 3:7-10) Finally, Hebrews tells us to find a kingdom to stand on that cannot be shaken — because someday this world is going to be shaken like snow off a tree limb, and only God's kingdom will remain. (Hebrews 12:26-28)

Remember, you just saw these ideas in the Old Testament prophets. If the New Testament also teaches such things, it's only because they got their information from the prophets too. The Spirit of

God revealed the kingdom of God so clearly in the prophets that there are many things we will not learn about it until we go back to their teachings and learn from them. Jesus said something once along this line:

> *They have Moses and the Prophets; let them listen to them.* (Luke 16:26)

I hope you catch the significance of his remark. Not only will we learn from the prophets about the kingdom, that is the *only* place to turn for much of the information about it. Furthermore, what they said is sufficient for even New Testament Christians!

Let's look at an example of this. When you think of all the passages in the Bible that talk about sanctification, which one naturally comes to mind? Is there a famous passage that teaches what happens inside us when we believe in the Lord? How about this one?

> For I will take you out of the nations; I will gather you from all the countries and bring you back into your own land. I will sprinkle clean water on you, and you will be clean; I will cleanse you from all your impurities and from all your idols. I will give you a *new heart* and put a *new spirit* in you; I will remove from you your heart of stone and give you a heart of flesh. And I will put *my Spirit* in you and move you to follow my decrees and be careful to keep my laws. You will live in the land I gave your forefathers; you will be my people, and I will be your God. I will *save* you from all your uncleanness. (Ezekiel 36:24-29)

I highlighted the words and phrases that some people think are only in the New Testament. As you can see, this is such a good explanation of what the Lord does that we can hardly think of a better one! There are many other crucial doctrines of the eternal kingdom that are taught and explained in the Old Testament prophets. This is why Jesus sent us back to them, if we want to learn the truth about what he came to do. Without this valuable information we wouldn't have a clue about what he did in the Gospels! This is probably why people get so confused about who Jesus really is: they don't know the Old Testament that describes him.

A message of war

There is another theme running through all the prophets that we would do well to notice. In the old days of kings and kingdoms, when one king decided to invade another kingdom, he would send out a messenger with a warning: surrender or be annihilated. The messenger would ride out alone between the two armies with a white flag and deliver the ultimatum, and return to his king with their answer. In the same way, the Old Testament prophets were like messengers of the Most High as he prepares to invade earth's dark forces.

This is not a game that God is playing with us. When we turned against him in rebellion in the Garden of Eden, we threw down a challenge to his right to reign over us. We ruined his earth, we defied his Law, we insulted his glory and majesty, we set about using his blessings that he provided for our own wicked purposes, and we accepted as our leader and new head the most despicable creature in God's sight: the devil. There's no mistake about it, we have put ourselves solidly in opposition to God. We are his sworn enemies.

There is only one thing to do to solve the problem: wage war. This rebellious kingdom that the devil leads must be destroyed; there must not be a single stone left standing on another. God will be the complete victor in this war between kingdoms:

> The LORD Almighty [*in Hebrew, the **LORD of Hosts***] is mustering an army for war. (Isaiah 13:4)

> Who handed Jacob over to become loot, and Israel to the plunderers? Was it not the LORD, against whom we have sinned? For they would not follow his ways; they did not obey his law. So he poured out on them his burning anger, the violence of war. It enveloped them in flames, yet they did not understand; it consumed them, but they did not take it to heart. (Isaiah 42:24-25)

I myself will fight against you with an outstretched hand and a mighty arm in anger and fury and great wrath. (Jeremiah 21:5)

We could quote many passages from the prophets like these. To God, our problem isn't just a matter of sin and death, destruction and misery, ignorance and materialism; it is much more serious than that. *We are attacking his kingdom.* So he approaches the problem as a general does: wary and ready to do damage to the enemy.

* ___The kingdom of God is under attack___. The nations and peoples of earth all have the same problem: they hate God and the way he wants to rule over them in all things. "Why do the nations conspire and the peoples plot in vain? The kings of the earth take their stand and the rulers gather together against the LORD and against his Anointed One. 'Let us break their chains,' they say, 'and throw off their fetters.'" (Psalm 2:1-3) When the Israelites demanded a king, the prophet Samuel realized (through the Spirit who showed him what was really in their hearts) that they were actually rebelling against *God's* rule over them. They wanted a man who was like them — a sinner — who wouldn't demand perfect obedience from the heart. "It is not you they have rejected, but they have rejected me as their king. As they have done from the day I brought them up out of Egypt until this day, forsaking me and serving other gods, so they are doing to you." (1 Samuel 8:7-8)

* ___Behind it all is the purpose of Satan___. This we discover from the New Testament prophets and apostles. The devil is "the ruler of the kingdom of the air, the spirit who is now at work in those who are disobedient." (Ephesians 2:2) His declared purpose is to oppose the coming of the kingdom, and he finds all sorts of devastating ways to do that. He's the one, remember, who in pride opposed the Almighty and was thrown out of Heaven as a result. He leads the armies of the wicked. "For our struggle is not against flesh and blood, but against the rulers, against the authorities, against the

powers of this dark world and against the spiritual forces of evil in the heavenly realms." (Ephesians 6:12) People often don't know that they are dupes in the devil's service, but what they end up doing is proof of it: they lie, they destroy, they maim, they steal God's glory, they do everything that God expressly said not to do — they are truly children of the devil. "You belong to your father, the devil, and you want to carry out your father's desire." (John 8:44) We read more of his struggles against Heaven in the book of Revelation, and the eventual victory that God will get over him.

• *War is the only way to solve it.* War is a bloody and brutal business; there is nothing pretty about it. But sometimes it is the only way to solve a problem. In the case of a rebellious human race standing firmly behind the devil, doing everything it can to stop and turn back the purposes of God, war is the only way to break the opposition and destroy the works of the evil kingdom. When Jesus came to earth, he realized that he was entering into battle: "He who does what is sinful is of the devil, because the devil has been sinning from the beginning. The reason the Son of God appeared was to destroy the devil's work." (1 John 3:8) So the prophets predicted the coming of the LORD of Hosts. The "hosts" that it is referring to are the angels that go with God into battle. It is a formidable sight, to see God surrounded by thousands of his angels, all armed and determined to destroy their objective. Once when the prophet Elisha was surrounded by enemy soldiers, he prayed that the Lord would reveal the true situation to his fearful servant. "Then the LORD opened the servant's eyes, and he looked and saw the hills full of horses and chariots of fire all around Elisha." (2 Kings 6:17)

What is so amazing about the Lord is the tactic that he uses with his enemy. He is so confident of victory that he actually tells us ahead of time what he is going to do and how he is going to do it. No general would ever give away secrets like that to the enemy! But the Lord does it for several reasons: *first*, to show us how futile it is to resist him.

There is no doubt about the outcome of this war; we are committing suicide to fight against the Lord in any way. He has never lost his cause yet and he never will. *Second*, to make us re-think what we are doing. If the outcome is so certain, what are we doing staying in the enemy ranks? It's time to switch sides and run to the throne of grace and plead for mercy before he destroys us along with the other rebels. "Kiss the Son, lest he be angry and you be destroyed in your way, for his wrath can flare up in a moment. Blessed are all who take refuge in him." (Psalm 2:12) *Third*, to get glory out of the situation. This war is going to go exactly according to the word of the prophecy. Every detail will happen just as it is written, because the Lord is in full control of the situation. There will be no surprises for him, only for us. When it is all done, he is going to taunt his enemies and please his people when he reminds us that it happened exactly as he said in the prophets. "Who foretold this long ago, who declared it from the distant past? Was it not I, the LORD?" (Isaiah 45:21)

What are the weapons that the Lord uses against his enemies? Not the weapons of this world; they are forged in Heaven, they have power to crush the enemy in ways that no earthly weapon could do. "The weapons we fight with are not the weapons of the world. On the contrary, they have divine power to demolish strongholds." (2 Corinthians 10:4) If two warring armies both have the same kinds of weapons and strategies, the battle will be a long and costly one because either side has a good chance of winning — and losing. But if one side has a weapon that the other doesn't have, the battle is over sooner because the new weapon gives superiority. The Lord's weapons are all new, and the world doesn't have or even understand any of them. I wish we could get into a full-scale study of the weapons of Heaven, but we don't have time or space here. There is one, however, that deserves mention: one of the prophets announced to the enemies of God that he would unleash a new weapon that would crush them, and bring in God's kingdom like a steamroller. "Not by might nor by power, but by my Spirit, says the LORD Almighty." (Zechariah 4:6) There is no way that a human being, no matter how determined, can stand up against the power of the Spirit. Therefore the Spirit would do much of the work of the kingdom of God — as we can see in the stories of the New Testament.

Is Heaven the kingdom of God?

When we talk about the kingdom of God as being spiritual, does this mean that Heaven itself is the kingdom? Is the kingdom somewhere other than on earth? Do we have to wait to be in the kingdom — till we die and our souls "fly upward" free into God's presence? In other words, *where* is the kingdom of God?

Jesus provides the answer to this puzzle. When he came preaching the good news of the kingdom, he said it this way: "The kingdom of God is *near*." (Mark 1:15)

> Once, having been asked by the Pharisees when the kingdom of God would come, Jesus replied, "The kingdom of God does not come with your careful observation, nor will people say, 'Here it is,' or 'There it is,' because the kingdom of God is *within you*." (Luke 17:20-21)

Since the kingdom is spiritual, it doesn't come down in a form that shoves aside other earthly kingdoms. It coexists in the same time and place: while presidents and kings and rulers run their kingdoms, the Lord is also here running a kingdom of his own. While Pilate judged Jesus and sent him to his death, Jesus judged Pilate and marked him for condemnation. While the Jews worked to put an end to the new Christian Church through persecution, Paul worked to build up that Church across the Roman Empire.

There is a sense, however, that the kingdom of God is rooted in Heaven. For one thing, Heaven is God's throne where he rules over the nations of the earth. There is where you will find him, if you want to see him in his glory. All the prophets who got a vision of the Lord on his throne saw him in Heaven. (Isaiah 6:1-3) Our souls will find rest in Heaven, with God, where Jesus himself sits in judgment over the nations right now. (Psalm 2, Colossians 3:1-2) A second reason is that Heaven is the destination of all God's people: in Revelation we see the Lord's plans to make Heaven the dwelling place both for himself and his people. We are going *there* for our reward, because it is in Heaven that our reward is waiting for us. All of God's treasures are stored there. (Matthew 6:20-21)

The Lord wants to invade the earth, however; he wants to start the war that will eventually lead to the destruction of all earthly kingdoms and powers that resist his will. So rather than wait for everyone to die and go to Heaven, he brings the kingdom here, on earth, as an advance into enemy territory and starts pulling people into it immediately. If we had eyes to see, we would see Heaven as the center of focus in God's great spiritual kingdom, but we would also see a frontal advance of that kingdom extending down to the earth in certain spots here and there all over the globe. It doesn't cover the entire earth and include every person, because most of the world still lies under the control of the evil one. (1 John 5:19) But the front line is pushing everywhere, winning converts and extending farther into the enemy's territory. More and more people are leaving the kingdom of darkness and coming into the kingdom of light as the Gospel spreads from generation to generation: "But whoever lives by the truth comes into the light." (John 3:19)

This means that the kingdom of God is here on earth now, and the rules of the kingdom apply to those who live inside its pale. Jesus, in his prayer to the Father, prayed for his followers because of the difficulty that they would face having to live in two kingdoms like this! "My prayer is not that you take them out of the world but that you protect them from the evil one. They are not of the world, even as I am not of it." (John 17:15-16) And as it says in Hebrews, we are aliens while in this world because our citizenship is in God's kingdom. We actually straddle two kingdoms: our bodies are in this world, but our hope is for the day when we will enter fully into God's eternal kingdom and quit our connection with all earthly kingdoms.

Another thing to consider: even though God's kingdom is spiritual, it has a profound and lasting effect on earth. Some Christians believe that the spiritual things of God are *spiritual* and therefore have nothing to do with the affairs of earth; faith is only good for what will happen to us in Heaven, after we die. But that's not what happened during the ministries of the prophets. When they prophesied to the people, they told them of things that would happen *here and now* when God came to straighten things out. The Lord intends to correct earth's problems, not ignore them. He is offended with what we have done with his creation and will not rest until he makes it right and exacts payment from the criminals responsible for the damage.

God will do it, and he will do it by his Spirit, using miracles of course, starting in the souls of men and addressing the spiritual problem of sin which is responsible for the disaster of earth. But the solution extends to the physical realm as well. People are going to start living in this world in a way that pleases God. They are going to obey him in their relationships with each other, they will offer their bodies as a "living sacrifices, holy and pleasing to God — this is your spiritual act of worship. Do not conform any longer to the pattern of this world, but be transformed by the renewing of your mind." (Romans 12:1-2)

This is why the prophets spend a lot of time describing the kind of life people would live when God's kingdom comes. There wouldn't be any more cheating or lying or murder; there would be justice in the land; people would live in peace with each other; and "every man will sit under his own vine and under his own fig tree, and no one will make them afraid." (Micah 4:4)

What people argue over the most when it comes to prophecy is what exactly this will look like: what is going to happen when God's kingdom comes? Will it be completely spiritual? Will the earth become a paradise while God rules from Heaven? Or is the kingdom never going to be more than a spiritual reality seen only by the eyes of faith as it quietly advances through the ages of the dark world? That, I believe, the Bible isn't so clear about (or perhaps I should say that *I'm* not so clear on it!). A lot of the language used to describe the kingdom is symbolic, a lot of prophecies haven't been fulfilled yet, the situation has changed in some important ways when the focus switched from the Old Testament Israelites to the New Testament Church, the way that some of the prophecies concerning Christ turned out were surprising, and the New Testament doctrine of Heaven is an advanced concept over what the Old Testament has to say about it. All these facts and more make prophecy a difficult subject to nail down to specifics. Perhaps we never will know the full truth until the Last Day when the kingdom of God is made plain for all to see.

At any rate we mustn't get lost in the details when there is so much to profit from in the basics. The prophets spoke of God's coming kingdom, and Jesus said that it is here — so let's follow the Lord's counsel and struggle to enter into it: "From the days of John the Baptist until now, the kingdom of heaven has been forcefully advancing, and forceful men lay hold of it." (Matthew 11:12) It would be a shame to argue over *how* it will come and then not enter into it!

An example

In 1 Kings 14 there is a classic example of a prophet and his ministry — a man whom you probably have heard very little about. It has all the essential elements of true, God-inspired prophecy that we have been looking at.

Here is the story. Jeroboam was the king of the northern kingdom, Israel. Though the Lord chose him for the job, he ended up leading the people into idolatry. His son came down with an illness so he sent his wife disguised to Ahijah the prophet to find out what would happen to the boy. Now Ahijah was old and blind, but when Jeroboam's wife came to him he immediately knew it was her. He told her that the boy would die, and also told her that the Lord was going to take Jeroboam out of the kingship and put someone in his place who would do right for a change. And according to his prophecy, their son died when she reached home.

This prophecy fits the pattern of true prophecy in several ways:

The Spirit of God guided Ahijah. Ahijah was old and blind, unable to see anything; furthermore Jeroboam's wife went disguised and should have been able to fool him easily. But the Spirit is the one who moves the prophets in what they say, and the Spirit gives them deep knowledge that the physical eye can't see. The prophet not only knew her, he immediately knew why she came and the real reason that the boy was ill. How did he know this? The Spirit of God told him! In the Spirit he could see the entire situation, even though he was physically blind. To him, Jeroboam's sin was like a glaring light that had to be addressed above all else.

Jeroboam, typically, was looking for the wrong thing.
As is usual with most people, he wanted a prediction of
the future — but not about God's kingdom. He was
afraid for his son's life, that's all; to him the prophet's
job was to tell him what would happen physically. But
it's vain to use the Lord's prophets like that. They
foretell the future, but not in the way that we are looking
for. They foretell what will happen when God comes
down and straightens out the *moral* mess that we've
created with our wickedness and rebellion.

God confronted the sin. To God, this was the main
issue. Jeroboam went to Ahijah for a prediction about
his son's life; God, however, got down to the more
important matter of Jeroboam's sin. And he doesn't
mince words about it. Don't miss the point that the
prophet was only the bearer of God's message; it was
really the Lord who confronted Jeroboam, not Ahijah.
A true prophet will be so bold with the message of
God's coming kingdom that he will stand up to kings
and presidents and anybody, no matter what their
authority and position on earth — because he has a
message from the King of all kings that they need to
hear. Sin is an affront to the King of all the earth, and
the Lord will respond in kind: a formal challenge, a
threat to tear their kingdoms out of their hands and give
them to others who *will* do as God says.

The King was going to do some cleaning up. It's
noteworthy that Jeroboam was put into his position of
authority by the Lord himself; God alone sets up kings
and tears them down, because he is the King of kings.
He arranges the nations as he chooses and they all must
serve his purposes or he will do away with them.
Jeroboam, although the Lord's choice at first, strayed
from the original plan. He was leading the Israelites
into idolatry. So God intended to put a brutal stop to
Jeroboam's wickedness (the dogs and birds would eat
the bodies of Jeroboam's remaining family!) and find
someone else who would do the job right. This is war,

and Jeroboam found himself on the wrong side of the battlefield facing Someone who was about to annihilate him.

Questions to ask

Be careful when you read the prophets. Many people get stuck on a certain idea in these books and go off in unprofitable directions. Remember, the point of Biblical prophecy isn't about what is going to happen in world events, but what is going to happen when God comes to build his kingdom. This will have results in the physical world, but the focus is on God and his spiritual kingdom as he rules over this world in victory. Above all, remember that the Holy Spirit is called the "Spirit of prophecy." If you want to understand the prophets, be sure to ask the Lord to reveal their message to you through the Spirit; you won't understand it otherwise.

Ask these kinds of questions as you read:

- *First get the context.* To whom is the prophet talking? What situation prompted his prophecy? When did the prophet live? What was his background? Did he understand his times — is there proof here that he saw the truth about his hearers' hearts? Did it say how he got it? Is there any clue that he got his message from God — that these are really God's words? Did the prophet claim credit for any of it?

- *What was the prophecy itself?* Does it focus on sin? Is it the warning of a coming King who intends to destroy his enemy? Did the prophet have to spend much time explaining why God was so angry with them? Why do you suppose that was? Did the prophecy predict anything? Was it going to be an immediate fulfillment or something far in the future? Was it for unbelievers or believers? What did God expect his hearers to do? Were they to repent, or was he not giving them time to repent? What was the language of the prophecy — was it symbolic, or literal? Some prophecies came in strange dress: as a parable, a miracle, a puzzle, and other ways.

Was it a wooing of a straying Israel back to the God who loved her? Or was it a terrifying pronouncement of doom? Does the prophet take the hearer back to Moses and the Law? What does he say about the Law and the kingdom that Moses instituted? Is there anything said about the new Kingdom — or the new King?

- ***What happened when the prophecy was given?*** Did the hearers accept the message and change? Or did they reject it, and if so why? What did they do to the prophet? Was the prophecy given several times or only once? How are people treating the prophecy today? Was it fulfilled then? Or is it yet to be fulfilled? Or perhaps it was for then and now and in the future?

- ***What does this prophecy say to the Church of Christ?*** The Word of God is profitable in some way to every one of God's children; all of it was given to us to read and meditate on. As Peter said, we would do well to think about what the prophets taught. What lessons are here for us? Is the prophecy still to be fulfilled in the future? Has it already taken place? Does it describe something that we don't have yet? In Hebrews 11 it tells about things that God held back from giving the Old Testament saints, so that "only together with us would they be made perfect." (Hebrews 11:40) Is that obvious in this prophecy?

Discussion Questions on Prophecy

- Most of the quotes in this chapter came from Old Testament prophets. Are there New Testament passages that confirm all the things that the prophets taught?

- How would you use the message of the prophets when talking to unbelievers?

- Knowing what is coming, how then should you live?

- How can you tell when a prophet has been sent by God and when one hasn't?

- How do you decide what part of a prophecy is literal and what is symbolic?

- Jesus said that prophets get harsh treatment (Matthew 13:57; Matthew 23:37); they always have. Why is that?

- Is there a difference between Old Testament prophets and New Testament prophets? If so, what is it?

- Jesus called John the Baptist the greatest of the prophets. Why was that?

- Are there modern prophets sent from God?

- Many of the prophecies predicted the coming of Christ, and the New Testament is careful to point them out to us. Why does the Lord want us to notice them?

Key Nine: Deliverance

Key Nine: Deliverance

Everyone who even believes in a God will call on him when they need help. People all around the world know that God is for getting them out of trouble. Sometimes life's problems become overwhelming and we are in deep trouble, with no way out, and there is nobody to turn to except the God we believe in. It's a basic human instinct in all of us; even those who claim they don't believe in God will, at disaster's door, cry out, "God help me!" just as quickly as anybody else.

I believe that God made us this way on purpose; deep down inside we all know that he is always there to "help us in our time of need." (Hebrews 4:16) But what happens if he doesn't answer us? There are many people who call on God to deliver them and they get no response, no help — they are left to struggle in their problem and often fail. If God is our deliverer, why doesn't he help us *every* time we need help? He promised to hear us when we call on him: "Everyone who calls on the name of the LORD will be saved." (Joel 2:32)

But as is typical of human nature, we believe only what we want in the Bible and ignore the rest. For example, in that same passage Joel goes on to say this: "for *on Mount Zion* and *in Jerusalem* there will be deliverance, as the LORD has said, among the survivors whom the LORD calls." (Joel 2:32) Not everyone who calls on God for help will find that help. The Bible doesn't teach that God will help *everybody* who needs it; only those who come to the *right place* looking for help will find it.

We mustn't misunderstand the free offer of the Gospel. Although God offers salvation to any who come to him, we can't expect him to be so willing to get a sinner out of his troubles only to watch him plunge back into sin! We show the same reluctance to help an incurable drunk: giving him money is the same as helping him get drunk again. The Lord is just as discriminating when it comes to handing out spiritual help. "Do not give dogs what is sacred; do not throw your pearls to pigs. If you do, they may trample them under their feet, and then turn and tear you to pieces." (Matthew 7:6)

God's love is free, and he always helps those who don't deserve his help. "He causes his sun to rise on the evil and the good, and sends rain on the righteous and the unrighteous." (Matthew 5:45) But many have found out that it is foolish to presume on God's goodness. For example, the story of the rich man and Lazarus shows us someone who enjoyed this life's blessings and yet ended up in Hell. He found out that all those good things were really a curse against him. He got no *deliverance* from God, however, which is what he really needed. (Luke 16:19-31)

As you can see, there is more to the subject of deliverance than just expecting God to get us out of our troubles. Since it deals with the fate of our souls — since we must be saved or we will be eternally lost — we must find out the truth about *whom* God will save, *when* he saves, and *how* he saves. Fortunately the Bible is full of stories of deliverance; it teaches about it from many different angles. God saved individuals and cities and nations from all kinds of troubles, and recorded the details for us so that we can learn what really went on and what we can expect in our day. And since salvation is man's greatest need, it is the Bible's greatest story.

We must pay more careful attention, therefore, to what we have heard, so that we do not drift away. For if the message spoken by angels was binding, and every violation and disobedience received its just punishment, how shall we escape if we ignore such a great salvation? This salvation, which was first announced by the Lord, was confirmed to us by those who heard him. God also testified to it by signs, wonders and various miracles, and gifts of the Holy Spirit distributed according to his will. (Hebrews 2:1-4)

What is deliverance?

The Bible uses two words interchangeably — "deliverance" and "salvation" — but they both mean the same thing; they both describe the same reality. When the Lord says that he is going to deliver someone, it means this:

Deliverance means getting someone out of the danger they are in and into a safe place.

At first glance this looks obvious; but let's see what the Bible says about deliverance:

> ***The danger is real.*** When we plead with God to get us out of the mess that we are in, we expect him to answer us immediately. It never occurs to us that he might *not* deliver us — but that's exactly what happens to most people! They turn to him for help because they are sure that the trouble they are in justifies getting God to deliver them; but nothing happens. People all around the world are still hungry, still oppressed, still struggling against odds that are beating them. And though they ask God to help them, he doesn't.
>
> This is why, by the way, people make up false gods. The God of the Bible doesn't give them what they want, so they make up a god that will. They want to sin — and since the Lord won't allow that, they invent Baal who gives his blessing on whatever sins they want to commit. It's a devious and clever way around the strict requirements that the Lord has, but it never works: those gods are only made of stone and wood and things of this world and can't help anybody, no matter how loudly we cry out to them.
>
>> Half of the wood he burns in the fire; over it he prepares his meal, he roasts his meat and eats his fill. He also warms himself and says, "Ah! I am warm; I see the fire." From the rest he makes a god, his idol; he bows down to it and worships.

He prays to it and says, "Save me; you are my god." They know nothing, they understand nothing; their eyes are plastered over so they cannot see, and their minds closed so they cannot understand. No one stops to think, no one has the knowledge or understanding to say, "Half of it I used for fuel; I even baked bread over its coals, I roasted meat and I ate. Shall I make a detestable thing from what is left? Shall I bow down to a block of wood?" (Isaiah 44:16-19)

The reason that God won't often save those who call on him is this: he has a different view of what danger is than we have. Many saints in the Bible found out that they can go without more things of this world than they thought and still be well off spiritually! Lazarus, for example, was poverty stricken: covered with sores, oppressed even by the dogs, he remained in that condition all his life until he died. (Luke 16:20-22) The Lord didn't see fit to rescue him from troubles that we would have thought were a just cause for deliverance.

Other people found the same thing: Abel was killed, not rescued, from his brother's murderous hand. (Genesis 4:8) Jeremiah was hauled off to Egypt, against his wishes, by the idolatrous Jews hoping to escape the Lord's wrath against them. (Jeremiah 43:6) Samson, though he was getting revenge on his enemies, died with them. (Judges 16:30) Peter and many of the rest of the apostles died for their faith. The Israelites who were threatened by the Babylonians were not rescued but rather beaten and hauled off into exile. (Jeremiah 52) These and many others found that, just when they needed help the most, the Lord refused to extend his hand and deliver them out of their troubles.

Others were tortured and refused to be released, so that they might gain a better resurrection. Some faced jeers and flogging, while still others were chained and put in prison. They were stoned; they were sawed in two; they were put to death by the sword. They went about in sheepskins and goatskins, destitute, persecuted and mistreated. (Hebrews 11:35-37)

Obviously the Lord won't always deliver his people from physical dangers and trials. We can do without *a lot* of this world's "essential" comforts. If this is all the danger we are in — losing our physical well-being — the Lord isn't necessarily ready to rescue us yet.

To him, "danger" means something far more serious than going without food or comforts of this life, or being oppressed by our enemies, or even death. We can experience all these things and *still not be in danger* as far as the Lord is concerned. What *he* thinks is real danger is —

• *To lose your soul.* "What good is it for a man to gain the whole world, yet forfeit his soul? Or what can a man give in exchange for his soul?" (Mark 8:36-37) The soul is the most precious part about us; it is our soul that needs to be saved, not so much our bodies. Our soul is under attack from the world, the flesh, and the devil — they are all trying to keep us out of Heaven. Lose your body, and you have only lost a few years of life; but lose your soul, and you have lost eternity.

• *When his honor and glory are at stake.* "How can I let myself be defamed? I will not yield my glory to another." (Isaiah 48:11) God's glory, as we have seen before, is more important to him than anything. He wants to be known as the God he is! He will not tolerate any misconception about him, any falsehood, any threats to his rights as Lord over all. He gets positively angry when people take away from his glory. Judgment Day is the time he set to get back all the glory he deserves and hasn't been getting in history.

- *A threat to the Church*. "For I am with you to rescue and save you, declares the LORD. I will save you from the hands of the wicked and redeem you from the grasp of the cruel." (Jeremiah 15:20-21) We see this in the Old Testament with the Israelites, and the New Testament with the Church. These are God's people, his nation, his flock, and he won't let them be destroyed. The Church is where he lives; it is the house of God. The Spirit works in the Church as he enables each person to help build others up in faith and grace and live together peaceably. Whatever disturbs the peace and work of the Church, and the well-being of the people of God, is of great concern to the Lord.

- *A challenge to his eternal purposes*. "My purpose will stand, and I will do all that I please ... What I have said, that will I bring about; what I have planned, that will I do." (Isaiah 46:10-11) Perhaps we don't understand how important it is to God that his will be done. He has plans for everything in the world: he wants to do certain things to the earth, to the wicked, to his people, in Heaven and the preparations there, to his enemies, to the Church, and many more things. He is the Project Scheduler, arranging all things throughout history exactly according to plan, getting it ready for the Last Day when the great work of God will be unveiled in all its glory. Anything that threatens to disturb his will about *anything* is something he considers a danger.

Now if any of *these* things happens, the Lord gets positively motivated to do something. Little else concerns him like these dangers do. We might think that our troubles are enough to get God moving and do something to help us, but we may be surprised when he shows little or no interest in rescuing us from our "troubles." They aren't threatening anything that he considers worth saving. But if our souls are in danger, or the Church, or his glory or purposes, he immediately comes to the rescue with massive firepower from Heaven. He can't afford to let dangers like these destroy his eternal work.

Physical dangers often have natural solutions. If you don't have enough to eat, it may be because you aren't working hard enough or at the right job. If you need money to pay your bills, it may be that you spent your money on things you didn't need. The Lord will often leave us to figure out our own answers (guided by sound principles in his Word, I might add!) for your problems. They don't require a miracle because there are good enough answers for them in the way the world naturally works. But when these spiritual dangers come upon you, there aren't any answers for them in the world — that's the whole point. Only an answer from God's world can satisfy the need and free us from the danger. A miracle is necessary because nobody but God can solve the problem. The problem affects eternal issues, and we need resources from Heaven to make sure that the tremendously important spiritual needs are met.

• ***We can't help ourselves***. The very idea of deliverance means that we need outside help. We are in a situation that we can't get out of; we may have tried everything we know, and done everything there is to do, and still have gotten no relief. Unless God helps us we are lost; we are helpless in the face of the danger, like "a sheep led to the slaughter."

All the Bible stories about deliverance take pains to make this point plain. Each person who cried out to the Lord to save them was in a corner, with nobody else to help them, and unless the Lord saved them they would have been lost. Take, for example, the story of the Israelites leaving Egypt. When they came to the Red Sea they were stuck: the sea was in front of them, and Pharaoh's army was right behind them. What were they to do? They were about to be annihilated or, at the very least, dragged back into slavery. They weren't soldiers, so they had no hope of beating the Egyptians; and they weren't able to cross the Red Sea with all their families and possessions. *They could do nothing at all.* Their *only* option was to call on the Lord to save them, and he did.

The stories of deliverance were designed to teach us this. You can tell when you are in the kind of danger that only God can rescue you from: there's absolutely nothing that you or anybody else can do to help. If someone else could help us, why would we need God? If we can figure a way out of our problem ourselves, why turn to the Lord for help? There are just some things that only he can do, and if he doesn't then we are in irreversible trouble. Our society doesn't understand this very well: it keeps coming up with "solutions" to problems that aren't really solutions. The world's solutions sound reasonable — a job will solve poverty, jails will solve crime, schools will solve ignorance, wars will solve social issues. But those ways of solving problems have no power to rescue us from our real trouble, which is *sin.* Only God's answers will strike at the root of the problem, and when he does then the ills of society disappear too.

• ***We've got to get out.*** The answers to our problems are never as simple as changing the circumstances so that we can get along better. The answer is to *get out* of the danger. We can't remain in it any longer; for various reasons, we have to get out of the danger before we can really say that we've been saved from it.

Again, the stories of deliverance in the Bible teach this very plainly. They were never left in the danger; the

Lord got them out of there. Lot had to *get out* of Sodom, not just find a better way to live with the wicked in that city. The Israelites had to *get out* of Egypt and slavery, not just get their conditions changed to something more comfortable. David had to *get away* from Saul, who was seeking his life. Paul had to *get out* of Damascus or he would have been killed.

One reason that the Lord must get us out of the danger is this: he intends not only to rescue us, but to lay waste to the area once we are out. After all, our enemies put us in the danger we got into; we fell into their hands, helpless, and they were about to destroy us. The Lord didn't miss that fact. Anybody who dares to touch his precious ones will find him to be a God of wrath. Like a father who rushes to rescue his little one, the Lord shows his great love in how he will move Heaven and earth to help us — and then turn in anger on those who endangered us. Once he gets us out of harm's way, he will come back and deal with his enemies harshly, by blasting them and the whole area until there is nothing left. "Our God is a consuming fire." (Hebrews 12:29) We don't want to be there when that happens.

Another reason he has to get us out is so that we are finally out of harm's way. It's no rescue if he *leaves* us in the danger we are in! That's no deliverance. He wants to see us free from the thing that was hurting us. When the Israelites left Egypt, they were no longer slaves, nor did they have to be. They were free to follow the Lord. Their past was just a bad memory; the Lord comforted and strengthened them with a new life without that danger. Anything that threatens the spiritual life and health of his people has to be stopped; he cannot allow them to continue in those conditions.

When the Lord rescued his people, he often did it in a hurry — that is, they took very little with them as they left the area. For example, the Israelites left Egypt with only what they could carry. They were in a hurry to get out, so much so that the Lord forbade them to put yeast in their bread because it would take too long to rise and they didn't have that time. But even if we have to leave behind all the things that are precious to us, it is more important to get out of harm's way than to preserve the things in this world that we love. Remember, the Lord thinks that the danger to our souls is far worse than having to go without the comforts of this life. The new life that God calls his children to will have more than enough to satisfy any losses incurred in this world: "And everyone who has left houses or brothers or sisters or father or mother or children or fields for my sake will receive a hundred times as much and will inherit eternal life." (Matthew 19:29)

Now turn to Matthew 1:21. When Jesus was born to Mary, he received a new name — a name that reflected the job he came to do. "She will give birth to a son, and you are to give him the name Jesus, *because he will save his people from their sins*." (Matthew 1:21) When people say that the Lord has saved them, and they still wallow in their sins as if nothing has changed, then that's a plain denial of the meaning of the word *deliverance*. Jesus came to *save* us from our sins, not leave us in them. Deliverance means *getting out* of danger, not remaining in it. We will all have sin in us for our entire lives, it's true, because we still have the old nature with us. But the process of saving us from that sin has started: the Lord is crucifying that sin through the Spirit, we are getting victory over the former oppressor, and we are looking more and more like him — holy and righteous in our daily walk. That is, if he really is saving us!

• *__Only God can deliver us__*. If we could really see the danger we are in, and the kinds of damage it could do to us, we wouldn't wonder at why we are so helpless. Our enemy is unseen, powerful, skillful, ruthless — he has been at this deadly game for a long time and we are only ignorant children compared to him. "For our struggle is not against flesh and blood, but against the rulers, against the authorities, against the powers of this dark world and against the spiritual forces of evil in the heavenly realms." (Ephesians 6:12) Who can fight against something like that? We don't even know where to start; it's like a child fighting a tank with a toy gun.

The Lord, however, is the Master of taking care of problems like that. He has weapons that we don't even know about; he has all wisdom and skill to guide him in what to do and when to do it. The Lord is also ruthless when it comes to his enemies. He will have *no mercy* on those who put his children into danger — their lives are forfeit. We couldn't have anybody better than our God to come to our aid.

It's a shame that we often turn to God *last* when we need help. For some reason we like to try all the other options first, and resort to prayer and faith only when everything else has proved futile. This just shows an abysmal ignorance of who God is. If we could see his strength, and his great wisdom, and know his undying love for all his people, we would go to him *first* with our problems!

Again, this is the purpose of the deliverance stories in the Bible — to show us our God at work, and to convince us that here is someone who really can help us in our time of need. There's nothing like hearing the testimony of someone who has experienced God's deliverance for convincing us to wait for the same thing. God can do the impossible. (Luke 1:37) When we see that, we will trust him to deliver us too from whatever spiritual problem we are in, knowing that he *can* and he *will*.

• **_The result is freedom._** This may seem obvious by now, but we have to say it because the application seems to escape us too often. When the people in the Bible times were delivered, they were free from the danger;

they were no longer under its influence, they were away from it and safe. The problem is *gone*. That's how the Lord delivers his people.

Remember what the Lord considers to be danger. When he saves the **soul**, he saves it from sin and death to the extent that we no longer come under the burden of either. He saves us to eternal life, free from sin and death, and no longer under their dominion. When the Lord saves his **honor and glory**, he gets eternal and satisfying glory, so much so that even his enemies are forced to admit his greatness and give him the credit he deserves. That's victory. When the Lord saves his **Church**, he removes all the things that threaten its life and peace and makes a place fit for a King to live in, a place of love and peace and obedient service. There will no longer be anybody or anything there to disturb his house. When the Lord saves his **plans and purposes**, he overrides the will of men and nations and forces them to conform to what *he* wants. *Every* knee will bow before the King.

The situation that he saves us *into* is a place of freedom, a place where the old dangers can't exist. He saves *from* fear *to* confidence, *from* hate *to* love, *from* sin *to* righteousness, *from* oppression *to* freedom, *from* lust *to* purity. Of course, many people don't want to leave those old conditions! That's why they hate the idea of being saved. But for those who have experienced the salvation of the Lord in Christ, this is a *new life* — a new creation that they would never trade for the old ways. "Therefore, if anyone is in Christ, he is a new creation; the old has gone, the new has come!" (2 Corinthians 5:17)

When the Israelites were saved from the Egyptians, they crossed the Red Sea and immediately became a new nation; they were free from slavery because their former masters were dead. It was impossible for them to go back, and it was impossible for Pharaoh to follow them to the Promised Land and enslave them again.

The Lord makes a new world for us, a place where we will never be in that danger again. For example, anybody who has called on the Lord Jesus Christ to save him from his sin has found a *freedom* from sin:

> For we know that our old self was crucified with him so that the body of sin might be done away with, that we should no longer be slaves to sin — because anyone who has died has been freed from sin. (Romans 6:6-7)

And when we are free in Christ, the old danger is gone; we will never be in danger from it again.

> For we know that since Christ was raised from the dead, he cannot die again; death no longer has mastery over him. (Romans 6:9)

If we didn't get this total freedom in him, it wouldn't be true deliverance — only a cruel joke. God doesn't do that to his people. He leads them into an open area, away from the burdens and troubles:

> The LORD is my shepherd, I shall not be in want. He makes me lie down in green pastures, he leads me beside quiet waters, he restores my soul. He guides me in paths of righteousness for his name's sake. (Psalm 23:1-3)

This is also, by the way, the surest test as to whether you really are saved. If you now have freedom from that old problem, then you can be assured that God saved you from it. If you are still fighting the problem and losing, then you aren't saved from it yet. I know this is obvious, but some people like to claim salvation when they don't really have a good reason to. They don't have to guess, however, whether God saved them or not

— the results of his work (unlike false gods, who are long on promises and short on results) are always very real. I can't find any place in the Bible where it says that God saved someone and yet they were *still in* their danger.

Famous rescues of the Bible

Now that we have discovered the principles of Biblical deliverance, let's look at some of the more famous examples of deliverance in the Bible and see these principles at work.

• **Noah** — The world was in such a state of wickedness that God had finally had enough; he was going to rise up in wrath and show sinners what he not only *could* do, but *would* do to them when they made him angry. It was to be such an awesome destruction that the human mind staggers at the thought: a worldwide flood, killing every living thing on the planet. "I will wipe mankind, whom I have created, from the face of the earth — men and animals, and creatures that move along the ground, and birds of the air — for I am grieved that I have made them." (Genesis 6:7)

Noah was the only person on earth who pleased God, and we know that he did that only by faith. (Hebrews 11:7) But this presented a few problems! If the Lord would have destroyed Noah too, then there would be no family for the coming Messiah; there would be no humans left at all to have mercy on and build a Church with. Furthermore, since Noah was truly righteous, it wouldn't have been right to destroy him along with the wicked. So something had to be done to keep Noah safe while the rest of the world perished — hence the ark in which Noah, his family, and representatives of all the animals of the world were saved from the Flood.

All the elements of Biblical deliverance are here: the danger was real and on its way (though Noah's neighbors laughed at the idea); Noah certainly couldn't save himself from the disaster; something had to be done, however, because the Flood was going to sweep everything away; God alone knew what to do and helped Noah get ready for it; and the result was freedom — true deliverance from the disaster. What God saved him into was a new world, clean of its former wickedness, and a new start on God's plans for humanity.

• **Lot** — Another instance of the Lord losing patience with the wicked was the time he destroyed Sodom and Gomorrah. (Genesis 19) Again, he planned a devastating attack that would totally wipe out the people living there; it was going to be quick and overwhelming, and they would have no chance of escape. But again, there was the problem about what to do with any righteous people who happened to be living there — he couldn't just wipe them out too! So a rescue was necessary.

Abraham was the one who prayed for Lot's safety. As the bearer of the covenant, and as Lot's uncle as well, he felt responsible to make sure his nephew would be saved. He prayed that the Lord would be true to his Name and not punish the righteous along with the guilty:

> Far be it from you to do such a thing — to kill the righteous with the wicked, treating the righteous and the wicked alike. Far be it from you! Will not the Judge of all the earth do right? (Genesis 18:25)

Abraham knew what to focus on — the glory and honor of the Lord. It would have been bad for Lot to be caught up in the general destruction; but it was unthinkable that the Lord would advertise to the entire world such a careless and unloving attitude toward his special people. Either he loves them or he doesn't! Either he can rescue them from danger or he can't. His honor was at stake here, so he had to get Lot out of there before the disaster struck.

He did it by sending in two angels who brought Lot and his family out before the Lord destroyed Sodom. Notice that the Lord wasn't content with simply improving Lot's circumstances. Peter tells us that Lot was "a righteous man, who was distressed by the filthy lives of lawless men (for that righteous man, living among them day after day, was tormented in his righteous soul by the lawless deeds he saw and heard.)" (2 Peter 2:7-8) The solution was not to make his neighbors easier to get along with! The solution was to get Lot *out of Sodom*; the Lord was going to lay waste to the entire area, and he couldn't — wouldn't — do it until Lot was out of the way. "But flee there quickly, because I cannot do anything until you reach it." (Genesis 19:22)

• **Israelites in Egypt** — Certainly the all-time classic deliverance in the Old Testament is when the Lord brought the Israelites out of Egypt. You can read the story in Exodus 7-15. But one thing to consider about this story is this: why did the Lord deliver them? Was it just to save their skins, to get them out of slavery? There have been many other peoples under the same conditions that the Lord did *not* deliver.

This is an example of what the Lord considers danger and what we consider danger — they are often not the same. In this case, the danger was that unless he brought them out of Egypt into their own land, and serving him alone as King, there would be no Temple, no sacrifice for sin, no nation of Israel, no Messiah, and ultimately no Church! The entire future of all of God's people hung in the balance. Now *that's* important to God! Such issues motivate him to rescue his people so that his plans and purposes for them and their children to follow will succeed. There was a lot more at stake here than their own discomfort or desires.

The story of their deliverance follows the classic line: the danger was real; they certainly couldn't help themselves (they were slaves, unfit to throw off Pharaoh's control and they owned no weapons with which to fight); they had to get *out of Egypt* (because they couldn't stay *there* and be God's people, for many reasons); only God could get them out (Egypt was the most powerful nation on earth at the time, and Pharaoh was determined to keep them); and finally, the Lord did bring them into freedom (they ended up on the other side of the Red Sea, with the Egyptians dead behind them and no danger of ever going back into bondage). Then off they went to the Promised Land!

• **The Judges** — When the Israelites moved into the Promised Land, their first job was to exterminate the pagans who lived there. It was harsh, but the reasoning was sound: unless they got rid of these people who lived in wickedness and worshipped false gods, they would also turn to those false gods and reject the Lord who gave them this land. But they didn't do what the Lord told them to do: they left some of the peoples there, which proved to be their undoing.

The succeeding generations who didn't know Moses or Joshua forgot the commands that the Lord gave the Israelites and pretty much did what they wanted instead of what the Lord wanted. Then the Lord, in anger, gave them over to their enemies to be oppressed. After a period of persecution the Israelites got tired of that and turned back to God, pleading with him to rescue them from their enemies. He did. This happened over and over again; they would return to their sin, he would let them get into trouble, then they would pray for deliverance and he would send a judge to rescue them. (Judges 2:10-19)

What was at stake here? Certainly not just human lives, nor even the welfare of a nation. The Lord showed what he thought of what we call "humanitarian issues" in the way he treated the Canaanites — he had them destroyed without mercy. What was at stake with the Israelites was *his kingdom*. If he would have let them fall under their enemies, he would have shown himself to be a poor King who couldn't take care of his people! Furthermore, his intention all along was to *save* them from their sins. He couldn't let them all die in their sins, because that would have brought great doubt on the Lord's ability to save people from sin. Therefore a rescue was necessary: he defeated their enemies so that they weren't oppressed anymore, and the land rested for some years until the next cycle of sin, repentance, and salvation.

• **David** — Early in David's life he was anointed to be the king of Israel, even though Saul was already the nation's king. David was obviously a better choice, and he had the Lord's favor as well as the favor of the prophet Samuel. So Saul grew extremely jealous of David and hunted him out in order to kill him. The Lord rescued David many times by keeping him just one step ahead of Saul at every turn.

Why was David rescued from trouble and others weren't? Why is it that the Lord pulled David out of harm's reach, when he often doesn't do that for others — perhaps even people we know? Consider who David was: he wasn't like Saul, as Samuel said when he accused Saul of treachery to the Lord: "But now your kingdom will not endure; the LORD has sought out *a man after his own heart* and appointed him leader of his people, because you have not kept the LORD's command." (1 Samuel 13:14) In David the Lord had someone who would make sure that his commands would be obeyed to the letter. David would be careful to honor the Lord, and lead Israel in the ways of the Lord. David was key to the success of the Lord's plans for Israel. Not only this, but David was also the model for the Messiah — his job and how he did it would be the pattern for the same work and ways that the Lord

Jesus would show later. David's work was extremely important, not just for himself but for the life of the entire Church. The Lord rescues people who are busy about his work.

• **Daniel** — When the Israelites were captives in Babylon (due to their sin, in fact, which brought the Lord's punishment down on their heads, and now they had to pay the price for their rebellion against him) there was a new generation of men and women who were careful to follow the Lord's commands. The purpose of the Exile wasn't lost on them. Someday the Lord would take their people back to Jerusalem and their homeland, and they would begin anew in obedience and humility. Daniel, one of the captives, was to train the privileged Jews, who would be allowed to return, in the ways of the Lord.

The Lord often tested Daniel's faith, along with others of his generation. For example, King Darius the Mede once passed a law requiring all who lived in the entire land to worship himself, as if he were a god — they weren't allowed to worship any other gods. Daniel, of course, who would only worship the Lord of Israel, refused. He was immediately brought into the king's presence, accused, found guilty, and thrown into a den of hungry lions. It seemed that this was the end of the line for Daniel.

But the Lord had other ideas. He sent angels who locked the lions' mouths shut; Darius and his administrators were amazed at the kind of God who could do this miracle. And there is the point of the story: God got glory that day, not Daniel. The king learned that there was a God in Heaven to reckon with, and only he deserved worship. If it was only Daniel's life at stake, then he may have been killed as so many other Christians have been throughout history. But in this instance the Lord decided that delivering Daniel would lead to something greater in the Kingdom of God. (Daniel 6)

• **The exiles return** — When the seventy years of punishment were up, the Lord allowed the exiles to leave Babylon and return to Jerusalem and rebuild their city and homes. But that return wasn't just a quiet, natural event that would have happened on its own. Typically when a nation was carried off into exile to a foreign land, it ceased to exist — their peoples intermarried with their captors and there was no nation to speak of any more. In the case of the Jews, however, they remained separate from their captors during their exile; this was the first step of the coming deliverance of the Lord.

The second step was the spiritual purging they went through. A couple of generations of God-fearing Jews grew up. They got the point of the exile, and when they went back to Jerusalem they weren't going to make the same mistake their forefathers had made. They learned that the Lord is the *only* God to worship; in fact, they made that point rather strongly with their Babylonian captors on several occasions! (Daniel 3-6)

The third step was the amazing concessions that their captors made at the end. Cyrus the Persian not only allowed them to go back, but he supported them with money and troops and threatened anybody who would not also lend the Jews a hand in rebuilding Jerusalem. Who was behind this change of heart of a pagan, seemingly someone who would have no interest at all in the things of the Lord?

> I will raise up Cyrus in my righteousness: I will make all his ways straight. He will rebuild my city and set my exiles free, but not for a price or reward, says the LORD Almighty. (Isaiah 45:13)

It was obvious that the Lord paved the way for them to return to Jerusalem. The string of miracles that let them leave Babylon, find help from their enemies, and rebuild the Temple and their homes was an impressive example of the Lord's ability to deliver his people from their oppression. The end result? They were free to serve him again in the holy city and in the Temple.

• **Jesus as an infant** — You might have forgotten that even Jesus was rescued! While he was still an infant, Herod (the king of Palestine at the time) sent troops to kill all the male children two years old and under, which would virtually insure that this new challenger to his throne would be put to death. At this point Jesus, though he was the Son of God and had all the attributes of God, was helpless in the face of this danger. He could do nothing at all to save himself. What was at stake? The future of the entire Church! Though it's unthinkable, what would have happened if Herod had killed Jesus? There would be no sacrifice for our sins, there would be no life from the dead, the devil would have remained our master, and God would have had no option but to destroy the world again as he did in Noah's day. Obviously this rescue was necessary for many reasons.

And notice that God was behind the deliverance, though Jesus' parents were the ones who carried it out. God sent them a dream warning them of Herod's intentions; he told them where to go and when to go; he then told them when it was safe to come back. (Matthew 2:13-23) The One who knows all men's hearts was making sure that the wicked wouldn't do anything that would endanger his plans.

• **Paul** — The apostle Paul was delivered many times from all kinds of dangers. His own words say it best:

I have worked much harder, been in prison more frequently, been flogged more severely, and been

exposed to death again and again. Five times I
received from the Jews the forty lashes minus
one. Three times I was beaten with rods, once I
was stoned, three times I was shipwrecked, I
spent a night and a day in the open sea, I have
been constantly on the move. I have been in
danger from rivers, in danger from bandits, in
danger from my own countrymen, in danger
from Gentiles; in danger in the city, in danger in
the country, in danger at sea; and in danger from
false brothers. I have labored and toiled and
have often gone without sleep; I have known
hunger and thirst and have often gone without
food; I have been cold and naked. (2 Corinthians
11:23-27)

If it were only Paul's personal safety at risk, he would
have gladly left this world and gone to be with the Lord.
(Philippians 1:23) But the Lord's work was at stake:
the believers needed his ministry, Gentiles all around the
Roman empire needed to hear the Gospel, there were
new churches to start. He had to stay alive and able to
keep ministering to people's needs. "But it is more
necessary for you that I remain in the body."
(Philippians 1:24) It was also obvious, as you read
about some of the rescues he experienced, that the Lord
was rescuing him from all those dangers; neither he nor
anybody else could have done those miracles.

This is only a small sampling of the rescues recorded in the
Bible. There are so many, in fact, that when you think about it, it
seems as if this is a subject that the Lord wants us to learn all about.
There are more details to deliverance than you might realize; the ways
he does it, the reasons for doing it, when he does it, to whom he does it
— it requires many examples and much study to fully explore the
subject.

But in all of these rescues you will see the same basic themes,
and there is a reason for this: the Bible is showing you what is *really*
involved in a deliverance that comes from the God of the Bible, as

opposed to a "deliverance" from another god or from our own hands. To summarize, if you are looking for deliverance from the Lord, you should expect to see this kind of deliverance: *first*, you are in a danger that God thinks you need rescuing from; *second*, there's nothing you can do to help yourself — that's why you need to turn to God to do it all for you; *third*, you have to get out, you have to be completely free from the problem — anything else short of that is not a deliverance; *fourth*, God alone has what it takes to rescue you — which is a miracle (since he builds up his kingdom on miracles); and *fifth*, the Lord will get you out of the problem and put you in a place where you will be free to enjoy him and follow him.

Why does the Lord deliver?

In a certain sense we will never know why the Lord delivers people from their problems. None of us deserve deliverance; if he gave us what we really deserved, we would all be destroyed. If you don't know the devastating effect that human sin has had on the world and on ourselves, you need to study that first before you study about the Lord's amazing forgiveness of sin. It's a miracle that he had mercy on any of us.

But in another sense we know exactly why he delivers us: for the sake of his glory. We already studied what his glory means — when he gets the credit for being what he is and doing what he does. He is so jealous of his glory, he is so intent on getting credit for being the only God and the only Savior of men, that in everything he does he draws attention to himself to make us aware of who he is and depend on him more. He glorifies himself in all his works. Not because he is proud (like we would do) but because the whole world needs to know the truth about him and come to him for life and light.

So he delivers people to get glory. A rescue shows off a great deal about God. Here are some things that stand out about him in the Bible's stories of deliverance:

• ***He shows us his amazing mercy.*** We don't deserve for the Lord to take such a close interest in our welfare. Our danger, after all, is often due to the sin we ourselves have committed; why should he hold back on the punishment he warned us about? Why, when he told us repeatedly that we would get into trouble if we rebelled against him, would he forgive us and forget our sin and get us out of the mess we got ourselves into? It's because we have a God who is "a compassionate and gracious God, slow to anger, abounding in love and faithfulness, maintaining love to thousands, and forgiving wickedness, rebellion and sin." (Exodus 34:6-7)

The Israelites were a good example of this. They richly deserved destruction many times over; after having received the Lord's Law, and been made his special people (a privilege that no other nation on earth could claim) they still turned their backs on him and worshipped false gods, over and over. He had no good reason to save them from their enemies, and they had no reason to expect him to. But he did — many times, even after they had committed some unbelievable sins. If there is one thing that stands out in the stories of their deliverance, it is this fact that he will save even the worst sinner if they will only turn to him in repentance. Paul himself was a trophy of the Lord's amazing mercy:

> Here is a trustworthy saying that deserves full acceptance: Christ Jesus came into the world to save sinners — of whom I am the worst. But for that very reason I was shown mercy so that in me, the worst of sinners, Christ Jesus might display his unlimited patience as an example for those who would believe on him and receive eternal life. (1 Timothy 1:15-16)

Sometimes the Lord saved someone that we would think was a righteous man, someone who deserved to be saved. But when you look closer you will see that even the best of men have failed the Lord in unbelievable ways: Abraham, the man of faith, sometimes turned away from faith and schemed his own solutions; David, a man after God's own heart, committed murder and adultery; Paul was a former persecutor of God's Church. None of us really deserve God's mercy, and it would be just and right if the Lord just left us in our troubles to die, considering what we've done against him. So in every story of deliverance you will see the Lord putting aside the memory of the person's sins and rescuing him *anyway*.

• **_He shows us his powers_.** A deliverance was a special occasion for the Lord to show off his overwhelming power. Nothing on earth can stand in his way when he rescues his people. His power breaks chains, shakes mountains, floods the entire earth, burns cities to ashes, calms raging storms, and devastates armies. He wants us to be impressed with the kinds of things that he did back then; he wants to convince us, as a matter of fact, that he can do *anything he wants to do*.

God's power is something that we don't understand very well. He doesn't use the kinds of force that we are familiar with. He uses his Spirit, which proves to be much stronger than any power on earth. "Not by might nor by power, but by my Spirit, says the LORD Almighty." (Zechariah 4:6) His Spirit split apart the Red Sea for his people and brought it crashing back on the Egyptians. His Spirit held Peter up on top of the waves. His Spirit doesn't need to use the powers of this world like we have to. While we rely on science to unleash new powers to make our lives more comfortable and efficient, the Lord bypasses science and creation and *with his finger* does what we can only dream of doing. And he was never at a loss for what to do, or how to do it: whatever he wanted to do he did immediately with no problem. There was never a question whether he *could* do something, only if he *would* do it.

• **_He defeats his enemies_.** When God rescues his people we see the wrath of God unleashed against our enemies. He not only forces them to let go of us, but when we are safely out of the way he proceeds to destroy them completely.

The Lord is our Father; he considers his people to be *his children*, not just puny creatures that he could easily do without. And any father worth his salt will react immediately when his child is in danger. He will, in fact, be ready to give his life to protect his little ones. This is how the Lord reacts to the wicked who oppress his people. He rises up in wrath, smoke and lightning surrounding his angry countenance; and he throws aside Heaven and earth to reach his children in distress. Then after he lifts them up to a safe place, he turns all that awesome and inconceivable power towards the poor fools who dared to touch his little ones. Read Psalm 18 for a wonderful picture of God rescuing his child from the enemy. The poetry there is meant to show you the feelings that go through God's heart when we are in that kind of trouble.

Another picture that the Bible uses to show us God's unfathomable love for us is the relationship between a husband and wife. Let someone dare to touch his wife and a husband will react in violent anger. "Jealousy arouses a husband's fury, and he will show no mercy when he takes revenge. He will not accept any compensation; he will refuse the bribe, however great it is." (Proverbs 6:34-35) If someone dares to harm the bride of Christ in any way, he will pay for it with his life. When Paul saw that the Galatian church was accepting some false doctrines, he lashed out in fury at the criminals who were leading them into error: "If anybody is preaching to you a gospel other than what you accepted, let him be eternally condemned!" (Galatians 1:9) You can be sure he was revealing the mind of God towards people who do that, which means that someday the Church of Christ will be delivered of such heretics — the Lord himself will destroy them.

• *He accomplishes his purposes.* Usually when his people needed rescuing, more was at stake than their personal safety or comfort. It looked as if he was rescuing the Israelites from physical disasters; but actually there were spiritual issues involved whenever he felt the need to deliver them from their troubles. Their failure meant failure to the cause, to the glory of God, to the very meaning of what it means to be the people of God. Remember that the Lord was doing much more with the Israelites than he did with any other nation on earth — including any nation today.

For instance, if he would not have rescued the Israelites from Egypt, there would have been no nation of Israel, no Law, no Temple and sacrificial system, no Promised Land, and ultimately no Christ. He couldn't let them stay in slavery to Pharaoh and still accomplish his purposes in divine history. So he rescued them. He doesn't do the same for other nations, because he isn't building a kingdom through them as he did with the Israelites!

When God wants to do something, he steamrolls his way through all opposition. Nothing holds him back from his plans. There is too much at stake to let man overrule God's will! Not only does he have exacting plans for all of history and every human being, but it all has to be done to perfection and it has to be done on time. It is all due to be completed on Judgment Day; on that day he will reveal all his works to show how strong and wise and loving and holy and righteous he is. He cannot and will not allow any creature to ruin that day for him.

His unchangeable will is often why people are rescued. In case the Israelites thought that they were better than the other nations — and that's why the Lord did so much for them — he cleared up that mistake in a hurry!

> Understand, then, that it is not because of your
> righteousness that the LORD your God is giving

you this good land to possess, for you are a stiff-necked people. Remember this and never forget how you provoked the LORD your God to anger in the desert. From the day you left Egypt until you arrived here, you have been rebellious against the LORD. (Deuteronomy 9:6-7)

He only helped them through their troubles because he had his own objectives to accomplish. This didn't do anything for their pride! But it helps to see that the Lord's will is much more important than our own, and we shouldn't be surprised to see him putting aside our wants and wishes and doing what he wants instead.

If we understand what moves God to do what he does, we will take advantage of that knowledge — especially if he encouraged us to do that! Jesus once complained that the unbelievers are more canny about their business than God's people are. "For the people of this world are more shrewd in dealing with their own kind than are the people of the light." (Luke 16:8) If God delivers in order to get glory, then *use* that argument when you ask him for deliverance. For example, Moses knew how to approach God when he needed a rescue. When the Israelites heard about the enemies living in the Promised Land, they refused to go in and take the land, even though the Lord commanded them to. He grew extremely angry with them and threatened to destroy the entire nation, and to make Moses and his family into a new nation. Moses immediately sensed trouble — to God's glory.

Then the Egyptians will hear about it! By your power you brought these people up from among them. And they will tell the inhabitants of this land about it. They have already heard that you, O LORD, are with these people and that you, O LORD, have been seen face to face, that your cloud stays over them, and that you go before them in a pillar of cloud by day and a pillar of fire by night. If you put these people to death all at one time, the nations who have heard this report about you will say, 'The LORD was not able to bring these people into the land he promised them on oath; so he slaughtered them in the desert.' Now may the Lord's strength be displayed, just as you have declared: 'The LORD is slow to anger, abounding in love and forgiving sin and rebellion. Yet he does not leave the guilty unpunished; he punishes the children for the sin of the fathers to the third and fourth generation.' In accordance with your great love, forgive the sin of these people, just as you have pardoned them from the time they left Egypt until now. (Numbers 14:13-19)

Moses knew how to approach God for deliverance. He aimed at what is precious to God; he didn't waste his time with secondary issues, no matter how troublesome they were. There are certain things that God cannot allow to happen or be threatened, and *that's* why he will deliver us from our troubles. We would do well to learn what those issues are and start pleading for them instead of what he isn't so concerned about, if we expect to get answers to our prayers.

What he delivers from

We saw already that the Lord decides first whether we are in real danger before he agrees to rescue us. We think that danger comes in physical ways: poverty, hunger, disease, no spare time to enjoy ourselves, nasty neighbors and poor neighborhoods, crooked politicians, wars and earthquakes, and all the ills that have worried men and nations for ages and driven them to seek help from their gods. But these things don't always worry our God. He has left his people to suffer under all these ills and more without doing anything to rescue them. This sounds pretty bad, but perhaps the explanation is found in Ecclesiastes:

When times are good, be happy; but when times are bad, consider: God has made the one as well as the other. Therefore, a man cannot discover anything about his future. (Ecclesiastes 7:14)

As Jesus pointed out once, "He causes his sun to rise on the evil and the good, and sends rain on the righteous and the unrighteous." (Matthew 5:45) We can't expect to escape the ups and downs of living in this world; we are all a part of the way life works. The Lord never promised to deliver us from this world's problems: "In this world you *will* have trouble." (John 16:33)

What he *did* promise to deliver us from, however, are the following:

- **_Sin_** — Sin is our biggest problem. We don't think so, but then that's typical of human nature: we can be in the most terrible danger imaginable and never care about it or even be aware of it. Sin is opening its jaws of destruction around us like a lion; every step we take in its direction is another step closer to eternal damnation. We have to get free of our sin or we will die.

  When Cain was angry with God for not accepting his sacrifice, the Lord pointed out how close he was to disaster: "But if you do not do what is right, sin is crouching at your door; it desires to have you, but you must master it." (Genesis 4:7) Cain ignored the Lord's advice and walked straight into disaster; he lived to regret his foolishness.

  The complex and often confusing system of sacrifices that the Lord set up in the Tabernacle through Moses was for one single reason: to rescue the Israelites from their sin. There were often physical symbols in the Old Testament times that represented spiritual things; but their sins that made the sacrifices necessary were not symbolic, they were real. Anybody who failed to take advantage of all those sacrifices and instructions would immediately lose his life by God's command.

  Sin is the deadliest enemy we have. Sometimes it's hard to think about; we make a mistake when we think of sin as something concrete, as if we can just shoot it and be done with it. Sin is the *attitude* we have toward whatever God says to us: whether it's some truth he wants us to believe or some command he wants us to obey. The sinful heart doesn't want to hear it; that's the root idea of sin. We would rather do anything else than listen meekly to God and do what he says.

Jesus came primarily to cure us of that attitude. "You shall call his name Jesus, for he shall save his people from their sins." (Matthew 1:21) When he delivers his people from their sins, they will *want* to obey God with all their hearts, in everything he tells them. They will believe only what *he* says is true, not what the world or even their own fallen reason tells them. But it's not going to be easy to change people from sinful rebels to believing, humble saints: "I told you that you would die in your sins; if you do not believe that I am the one I claim to be, you will indeed die in your sins." (John 8:24) It's going to take a rescue from Heaven, using the Spirit of God, doing things that no human law or good intention has ever been able to do.

• **_Death_** — Death is the result of sin. "You must not eat from the tree of the knowledge of good and evil, for when you eat of it you will surely die." (Genesis 2:17) Modern experts are deceiving people when they say that death is a normal part of life. We die because of our sin against God; it is a fearful judgment against us because of all the ways we have brought dishonor on the Lord and ruined ourselves and the rest of creation. If it weren't for our sin, none of us would have to die.

Death is the last enemy in this world that we have to face, but it is often the most terrible. Some people are terrified to die because they don't know what lies on the other side of the grave. We are most afraid of what we don't understand — and none of us fully understand death. It's such a brutal end to all our dreams and works and hopes and comforts. It tears families apart, ruins plans, tears down the works of men, and puts the plans and works of others in danger. Sin reduces proud kings to the level of the slaves they oppressed. But it's often the relief of the righteous: "When the wicked perish, there are shouts of joy." (Proverbs 11:10)

Although the wicked deserve death, the righteous are hoping for a rescue. Not that they don't deserve the same judgment! We are all sinners and none of us deserve anything good from the Lord. But because of his unfailing mercy, the Lord has in mind to rescue some people from the destruction that would otherwise come upon them. He will see to it that they will not die — they will instead live forever. Death is not the last word for them. David understood this: "You will not abandon me to the grave, nor will you let your Holy One see decay. You have made known to me the path of life; you will fill me with joy in your presence, with eternal pleasures at your right hand." (Psalm 16:10-11) There *will* be a resurrection for God's people.

There are two kinds of death: physical death, which all of us must experience; and spiritual death, which God's special people won't have to endure. We all must die physically because we are children of Adam — the man whom God cursed with death in the first place: "Therefore, just as sin entered the world through one man, and death through sin, and in this way death came to all men, because all sinned ..." (Romans 5:12) There can only be one fate for sinful flesh — to be put to death. God determined at the beginning that sinners must not be allowed to eat of the Tree of Life and live forever in their sin. (Genesis 3:22)

But those who have been made alive in Christ will, at the Last Day, have their dead bodies raised and re-made — not in sin but in righteousness — to live forever. Furthermore, they will escape the *second* death, which will come on unrepentant sinners at the end of time. This is by far a worse danger than the first death: "They will throw them into the fiery furnace, where there will be weeping and gnashing of teeth." (Matthew 13:42) "He who overcomes will not be hurt at all by the second death." (Revelation 2:11) "Blessed and holy are those who have part in the first resurrection. The second death has no power over them, but they will be priests of God and of Christ and will reign with him for a thousand years." (Revelation 20:6)

• **_Our enemies_** — If we counted anybody who doesn't like us as our enemy, probably everyone we know would qualify somehow. Even our best friends and our closest relatives have a few problems with us. So we can't call down fire on whoever we think is the enemy; for all we know, the Lord has plans for that person's salvation in the future. Remember that *we* were once on the wrong side of Judgment too! We were enemies of God ourselves at one time.

God considers an enemy to be this: someone who *will not* bend their knee to him. Notice it isn't what the person thinks of *us* that makes them an enemy, but what they think of the Lord. If they hate God then they will hate you also, as long as you are following the Lord and trying to please him. They will do anything they can to stop you in your obedience and faith. That's an enemy that God thinks you need deliverance from.

When the Philistines persecuted the Israelites, the Lord rescued his people from the enemy. But remember that the Israelites were God's holy people, and Israel was the nation of God where he ruled as King, and the Tabernacle was the source of their special knowledge of the only true God (versus the false gods of their enemies). The Philistines weren't just attacking the Israelites, they were challenging God — and that meant war from Heaven. David understood this when he told Goliath, "You come against me with sword and spear and javelin, but I come against you in the name of the LORD Almighty, the God of the armies of Israel, whom you have defied." (1 Samuel 17:45) Whoever attacks God's people attacks God himself.

Never underestimate what the enemies of God are really trying to do. Sinners may give good reasons for their actions — the courts nowadays are full of people fighting for their "rights," for example, and it seems as if nobody is wrong and everyone has the right to live as they please — but we are only seeing a small part of the picture. To see the whole story, turn to the book of Revelation and see the true nature of the powers of earth and their inhabitants. They blaspheme God, they slander his glory, they make war against the saints, they force everyone on earth to worship them and their false gods, and they believe the lies of the devil who is the arch-enemy of God. (Revelation 13) The whole earth is in rebellion against God: "We know that we are children of God, and that the whole world is under the control of the evil one." (1 John 5:19) That's the true nature of this world and those who have not been converted. That's why Paul thanked God for Jesus "who gave himself for our sins to rescue us from the present evil age." (Galatians 1:3)

• ***The world*** — We have to be careful about how we understand this word; it's used in two senses in the Bible. First, it means the earth and everything that God created. There is nothing wrong with this world; in fact, God himself declared that it was "very good." (Genesis 1:31)

Second, the "world" also means the *world system* that is against God, his works, and his truth. It's a vast network of evil that stretches around all of God's created earth. It drives men everywhere to rebel against God and ruin all of God's works. Satan was there at the beginning, making sure that what God wanted to happen would *never* happen in this world: "He said to the woman, 'Did God really say, You must not eat from any tree in the garden?' " (Genesis 3:1) During all of history he and the dark forces that rule this world system actually control history and its events (or so they think). It's *that* world that we Christians are fighting against.

For our struggle is not against flesh and blood, but against the rulers, against the authorities, against the powers of this dark world and against the spiritual forces of evil in the heavenly realms. (Ephesians 6:12)

John warned us about being friends with the world: "Do not love the world or anything in the world. If anyone loves the world, the love of the Father is not in him." (1 John 2:15) Paul told us that we have to *come out* of the world; the Lord is going to deliver us from the world, not leave us here to die with the rest of the rebels. "Therefore come out from them and be separate, says the Lord. Touch no unclean thing, and I will receive you." (2 Corinthians 6:17) To God, the world is full of darkness and dangers and enemies, and he positively will *not* leave his people in it. He intends to rescue them out of this world.

• ***The wrath to come*** — The last danger to face mankind is one that comes from God himself. If we think that we have done well in this world by escaping the ills that most people have to suffer under, and death is gentle to us, we still have to face God on the day of Judgment. That is going to be an eye-opener for most people.

Some of the people in the Old Testament got a chance to see God in his glory, on his throne in Heaven. When Isaiah saw him, he was terrified and despaired of his life. "'Woe to me!' I cried. 'I am ruined! For I am a man of unclean lips, and I live among a people of unclean lips, and my eyes have seen the King, the LORD Almighty.'" (Isaiah 6:5) Even in the New Testament the sight of God — even Jesus himself — is awesome. John was staggered at what he saw in Christ; "When I saw him, I fell at his feet as though dead." (Revelation 1:17)

The reason that God is so fearful to behold is that he is so holy; when we see that, we know that we are in immediate trouble. A sinner in the hands of an angry God! What will we do if he is displeased with us? "Our God is a consuming fire." (Hebrews 12:29) God will not put up with sinners forever; someday he will bring history to an end, destroy the world, and bring all souls before him in judgment. "For we must all appear before the judgment seat of Christ, that each one may receive what is due him for the things done while in the body, whether good or bad." (2 Corinthians 5:10) Nobody will escape, and we will all get an education on just how holy and demanding God really is.

The only ones who will survive this ordeal will be the ones who have already found refuge and safety in the Lord Jesus, who is the only salvation given to men in preparation for this event. This is what is meant by "being saved." Any who are not found in the Lamb's book of life will be thrown into Hell. (Revelation 20:15) Does this worry you? If not, you are in for a rude awakening when God proves his point to you in a terribly harsh way. He doesn't show any mercy to those who are stubborn to the end. There is nothing loving about eternal punishment. "For the great day of their wrath has come, and who can stand?" (Revelation 6:17) But if you believe in Jesus, and what he came to do — to save sinners from death and Hell — then you are going to find God to be a welcoming Father on that day. His people are going to escape the wrath to come. "Jesus, who rescues us from the coming wrath." (1 Thessalonians 1:10)

These are the things that God wants to rescue us from. For many people, they weren't problems in the first place! If this is all that the Lord will do for them, they don't want it; they don't want anything to do with the salvation that the Bible talks about. So they turn to other gods who will save them from the kinds of problems that *they* want solved. In the meantime, however, their souls starve for the bread of Heaven and they get no answers to life's most serious problems. On the day of Judgment, they will have no one to save them when finally even God turns on them.

One more point.   What looks like a rescue from a physical danger on the surface actually hides a spiritual rescue underneath. Let's take another example: Lot was rescued from the disaster that came on Sodom. But was it just his life that God saved? Peter gives us a clue on this:

> ... and if he rescued Lot, a righteous man, who was distressed by the filthy lives of lawless men (for that righteous man, living among them day after day, was tormented in his righteous soul by the lawless deeds he saw and heard) ... (2 Peter 2:7-8)

Obviously he did escape with his life. But according to this passage, he was oppressed by the spiritual wickedness that was going on all around him. It seems obvious to me that when the Lord brought Lot out of Sodom he also brought him out of *spiritual oppression*. He wouldn't have to live his days in "distress" and "torment" any more. This is true of many more rescues in the Bible than you might think. That should make us think twice about asking for a deliverance from something that isn't necessarily a spiritual danger; the Lord may not give you what you ask for.

How he delivers

There is one very important fact about the way that the Lord delivers his people: you can never predict how he will do it. Try as you might, across all the stories in the Bible you can't come up with just a single method that he used to pull off his rescues; he used many different techniques to do it. Here are a few:

- *He saved Noah by means of an **ark**.*

- *He saved Lot by sending **angels** to bring him out of Sodom before the city was destroyed.*

- *He saved Joseph through well-timed **circumstances** — unbelievers often call it "chance."*

- *He saved the infant Moses by means of a **basket** in the reeds, and through **Pharaoh's daughter**.*

- *He saved the Israelites from slavery through **ten plagues**, through the **leading of Moses**, and by **splitting apart the Red Sea**.*

- *He saved the Israelites in the Promised Land from their enemies through the **Judges**.*

- *He saved David from Saul through **Jonathan's** intervention, and the vast regions of the **desert**.*

- *He saved Hezekiah and Jerusalem from destruction by **killing** the enemy soldiers **while they slept**.*

- *He saved Daniel from the lions by sending **angels** to shut their mouths.*

- *He saved the three children of Israel from the fiery furnace through one who looked like "**a son of the gods**."*

- *He saved the exiles by moving **Cyrus'** heart in their behalf.*

- *He saved the infant Jesus through **dreams** to his parents.*

- *He saved Paul and Silas in prison by sending an **earthquake**.*

You see, in each situation the problem was unique and so the answer was unique. They could never predict how the Lord would solve their problem; they could only wait on him and see what he would do. This means that there is no single way he uses to deliver us from our problems. We can't say, in a neat formula, that the Lord delivers by means of **_(fill in the blank!)_** Why is this true?

First, he has different things to accomplish in each rescue. There are many circumstances to take care of: not only is the danger always different, but the needs of the person involved are different. Noah not only had need of his personal safety, but he needed his family to be saved from the Flood too if there were going to be enough people to repopulate the earth; he couldn't do it alone! And the animals had to be saved to restore order to the world. So the ark was especially fitting to the needs at hand. In contrast, Lot got out of Sodom with only his two daughters and his wife — and even she was lost. He had nothing to start over with; he left it all behind in the burning city. But then the Lord didn't want him to bring away anything from Sodom — so God used the angels to hurry him out, in a matter of a few hours, because that's what was necessary at the time.

Second, we can't predict what he will do because the Lord uses miracles to solve our problems. Miracles are by nature unfathomable; they are answers from Heaven that turn the world upside down. For example, the Lord saved Naaman from leprosy by having him dip himself in the Jordan River seven times. Now Naaman would never have been able to predict that the Lord would use such a "cure"; in fact, he was offended at the thought —

> But Naaman went away angry and said, "I thought that he would surely come out to me and stand and call on the name of the LORD his God, wave his hand over the spot and cure me of my leprosy. Are not Abana and Pharpar, the rivers of Damascus, better than any of the waters of Israel? Couldn't I wash in them and be cleansed?" So he turned and went off in a rage. (2 Kings 5:11-12)

So when we presume to tell the Lord how to save us, he isn't impressed. He is going to do it *his* way, which means that his solution is always a surprise to us, especially when it works!

Third, our unbelief sells him short. We can't predict how he will rescue us because basically we think *he can't.* We limit him to our failures, to our ignorance; we think he labors under the same difficulties that we ourselves have. So he gets no glory from us when it comes time for a deliverance! He won't allow that, however; he intends to deliver us in a way that will astonish and surprise us. He will prove to us that he is indeed a God who does the impossible.

For example, when the Israelites were wandering in the desert, they came face to face with a sobering problem: there was no water out there. Millions of people were in daily need of water and they were in the wrong place to find it. So they complained against Moses for leading them out there in the first place, and against God for not having enough sense to lead them in the direction of lots of water. This, of course, was a personal insult against the Lord who can do "immeasurably more than all we ask or imagine." (Ephesians 3:20) So he did the impossible: he had water come out of a rock, a place where there previously was no water. (Exodus 17:1-7) They should have been ashamed of their unbelief when he ended up giving them exactly what they needed.

If we can't predict how the Lord will save us, then there's an important practical point about all this. When it comes time to ask the Lord for your deliverance, *don't tell him how to do it.* He knows better than you do how to get you out of your troubles. Too often we tell him not only how to deliver us, but when to do it! As if the Almighty needs our advice on the matter! We don't even understand the extent of the problems that we face. Since our souls are at stake, and the Lord's honor, and the welfare of the Church itself, we hardly know what to say or how to pray — only that something is wrong and that we need help. It is foolishness to expect the Lord to conform to our understanding and give us what we want; we are better off accepting whatever he gives us.

Besides, he intends to answer our prayers with the treasures and powers of Heaven; who understands such things? It is going to be surprising to us when it comes — they are better than we could have imagined, and not at all what we would have predicted, since our experience is severely limited to the things of this world. So the only thing you can do is "present your requests to God." (Philippians 4:6) He will answer you with something that is beyond your ability to predict: "And the peace of God, which *transcends all understanding*, will guard your hearts and your minds in Christ Jesus." (Philippians 4:7) You will be glad you didn't require from him any particular way of rescuing you when he gives you something better than you could ask for.

Perhaps the most unpredictable and astonishing of God's rescues recorded in the Bible is the deliverance he provided for his people in Jesus. What makes it even more amazing is that he spelled it all out beforehand! The prophecies were all there; repeatedly he told the Israelites how he would rescue them from sin and death. The Messianic prophecies fill the Old Testament; anybody who wanted could have studied them and been ready for the coming of the great Deliverer. Yet were any of them ready? Did they recognize it when it came?

> He was in the world, and though the world was made
> through him, the world did not recognize him. He came
> to that which was his own, but his own did not receive
> him. (John 1:10-11)

They should have known; Jesus rebuked them for not knowing. They had ample warning for hundreds of years that he was coming. "You diligently study the Scriptures because you think that by them you possess eternal life. These are the Scriptures that testify about me, yet you refuse to come to me to have life." (John 5:39-40) But they missed it entirely! They never guessed that the Lord would send a Deliverer in the form of a servant, a man like them, one abused and finally crucified. They even taunted him with insults to that effect, that he couldn't even save himself: "Come down from the cross and save yourself!" (Mark 15:30)

Yet this was the true deliverance sent from Heaven for all who believe. The blood of their bulls and goats weren't able to save them from their sins; the blood of Jesus, however, will save any sinner from all his sins, forever. (Hebrews 9:13-14) The unexpected cross unleashed a power that threw the devil back in defeat and laid an eternal foundation for the Church; life came from it, not death. So you can see that even when God explains to us how he intends to deliver us, we still won't understand it nor will we know what to expect until he actually comes and delivers us; his ways are far above our ways.

When will the Lord deliver?

The Lord is not our personal bellboy. He doesn't bow down at our feet and wait for our every wish, and jump when we snap our fingers. Even though his promises to deliver us are sure and certain, there are certain conditions to be met. He will only deliver us when those conditions exist, not before.

> • ***When we call on him.*** This is the beginning point; you must start here if you want God to help you. "Seek the LORD while he may be found; call on him while he is near." (Isaiah 55:6) It seems obvious that if we want the Lord to save us then we must call on him; but many people refuse to do that — for many reasons. But until they do, they will get no help from him.
>
> The reason that this is so important is that we are finally admitting that only God can help us. We have given up on other solutions, we admit that we need a miracle from God, we believe the testimony about God in the Bible that he is the only solution for our problems — so the Lord gets glory when we turn to him and give him credit for being what he is. We have seen these ideas in former keys — they come together when we believe in the Lord and come to him for what only he can do.
>
> You can see now why many people will not turn to him. They don't want the God of the Bible; they want some other god who will deliver them from physical disasters and leave them alone in their sin. Everyone on earth is in spiritual trouble, but only a few are going to cry out to the true God to save them from *that*. As for the rest, the Lord will despise them because they would not come to him to have life:

> Pour out your wrath on the nations that do not acknowledge you, on the kingdoms that do not call on your name. (Psalm 79:6)

This verse reminds us of another important key — the name of God. Be sure, when you call on him to save you, that you call on the name of the Savior that the Bible talks about. Identify the God that you want by name. The God of Israel, the Father of our Lord Jesus Christ, saves from *sin*: "You are to give him the name Jesus, because he will save his people from their sins." (Matthew 1:21) He is pleased when you call him by his proper name. That way he knows that you want him and not a false god.

• ***When we repent.*** Whenever someone wanted something from the Lord, they had to turn their backs on their sins first. God refuses to save us on *our* condition that we be allowed to continue living in our sin. When the Israelites cried out to God to deliver them from their enemies, he wanted to hear their confession and repentance first before he would lift a finger to help them. For example, when the Israelites complained against Moses and the Lord for bringing them out into the desert and harsh conditions, the Lord responded by punishing them with poisonous snakes set loose in the camp. Only when they realized what they had done would the Lord consent to deliver them from the snakes. "We sinned when we spoke against the LORD and against you. Pray that the LORD will take the snakes away from us." (Numbers 21:7)

Why does he insist that we repent? Because it was our sin that got us into the mess we are in, that's why. He won't give booze to a drunk; he won't throw his pearls to swine who will only despise his gifts. He wants to deliver us into life, into righteousness, into holiness. He will not allow sinners to live with him in Heaven! They have to agree to turn their backs on their former way of living before he will agree to save them from their troubles.

If this sounds hard, remember that he considers the danger to your soul to be much greater than the danger to your body. Actually you can afford to lose everything you have in life; it isn't so important to him that you save your neck, but that you come out of sin and into holiness. For this reason there are many people who cry out to the Lord to save them from their troubles and he pays no attention to them at all; they insist on keeping their sin, and therefore he won't touch them.

Notice however that confession and repentance are all that he is after. If God held back deliverance until he was sure we would never sin again, *none* of us would be saved. He is merciful; he doesn't require that we become perfect, just repentant. He *wants* us to be perfect (Matthew 5:48), but he doesn't make that a condition for our salvation. *He* will do the making perfect, not us! He saved the Israelites again and again because of their heartfelt confession; he was surely grieved when they went back to their sin, but he never withheld his salvation when they came back to him. The Lord is like that; he forgives "not seven times, but seventy-seven times." (Matthew 18:22) Of course he knows whether someone confesses from the heart; nobody can fool him. But it does encourage us to see that he will keep helping us while we struggle with sins that seem too difficult to overcome. He will never turn away anybody who really repents even if it's the same old sin that they are struggling with. As long as they want salvation from sin, he will give it to them.

What about those who need deliverance and it wasn't their sin that got them into trouble? There were holy men, like Noah and David, who needed a rescue and had no glaring sin to confess. In their case the need is still to turn to the Lord and *turn away* from the world, which is the same thing as turning away from one's sin. They rejected the world's answers, the world's hollow promises, the world's way of doing things and waited on the Lord alone for what they needed. Anybody, sinner or saint, has to reject the world and throw themselves at God's feet and wait on him if they expect to get anything from him.

• ***When he sees the danger.*** As we mentioned before, the Lord will move when he thinks it's time to move — and not until then. When *he* becomes concerned about how things are turning out then he will start doing something about it. We can't force the Lord into action just because we are starting to panic; we are afraid of losing our comforts, our earthly wealth, our reputation, our friends and family, our health, even our lives, when really there may be no danger to our souls or to God's glory. In fact, in losing what is most precious to us in this world we may be in the best position to glorify God the most.

God can see things much better from his position than we can from ours. Like an individual soldier in the battlefield, we lose our sense of direction and purpose in the heat of battle, and we are doing well to just keep swinging our weapon at the enemy directly in front of us. The Lord, however, from his position as general, can see the whole sweep of the battle as it progresses, and he is quite capable of directing his forces where he needs them. If he decides that the group of soldiers that we are a part of must make a desperate charge at the enemy, then it's time we did our job for the cause, whatever it may cost us. There is much more at stake here than our own personal interests.

When the Israelites were defeated again by their hated enemies the Philistines, during the time when Eli was the high priest over the Tabernacle, they must have thought that the Lord either didn't know what he was doing or just didn't care about them. How could he let those pagans defeat his special people? And when Eli himself died, along with his sons, and the *ark of the covenant itself* fell into the Philistine hands, there was just no good explanation for that. But time showed that the Lord never lost control; he wanted them to suffer defeat at the hands of the enemy to purge the evil out of Israel. He finally did do something, however, when his ark was in danger; through a series of miraculous events he brought the ark back to safety. (1 Samuel 4-5) So we have to learn what the Lord considers danger and what he isn't so worried about preserving.

• ***Past the last hope.*** It's rare that the Lord will immediately rescue his people. There were times when someone called to him for help and he delivered them right away; but more often than not he waited for a while — in fact, he often waited until all hope was gone. Then, when they thought he had forgotten them, he rescued them.

One of the ***Ways*** of the Lord, as we have seen, is that he works through time. There are many reasons for this (you can refer back to that key for more information) but one important reason is so that we will lose all hope of anything in this world to help us. When we are trapped by danger, and it seems that we are about to be destroyed because all hope and even the possibility of a rescue is impossible, *then* he will deliver us with an impossible rescue. He is setting this up for the greatest effect, of course; we need a good lesson on how amazing a Savior he is. He already knows he is the only hope, but we need more convincing of that.

Again, the Israelites at the Red Sea are a good example of how long the Lord will wait until deliverance arrives. There was no hope, they were trapped, and it seemed as if the Lord had handed them over to the enemy to die. And the three Israelites who defied Nebuchadnezzar's order to worship his idol: they didn't get their deliverance until *after* they were thrown into the fiery furnace! Talk about waiting until the last minute! But the Lord will not share his glory with another, and he doesn't want us to call on him for help and then, when time gets short, give up on him and try another god. He will often wait until the bitter end to try our faith and see if we really do believe he is our only hope.

- ***When he gets the most glory.*** A deliverance is the Lord's chance to show the world what he is capable of doing. Of course he is going to set it up for the maximum effect: when people hear of what he did for someone who didn't deserve it or was in such impossible trouble, he's going to get glory out of it and more people will come to him for the same thing.

While the Israelites were wondering why in the world he chose the way he did to deliver them from Egypt, the Lord was getting glory out of it. By the time they reached Canaan, the pagans had heard all about the story of the plagues on Egypt and the parting of the Red Sea; they had heard about the manna and water in the desert; they had heard about the Lord's victories over the enemies who fought against Israel. If the Israelites had wondered about the wisdom of how he chose to lead them in the past, they didn't wonder any more when they arrived at Jericho for the biggest job yet:

> I know that the LORD has given this land to you and that a great fear of you has fallen on us, so that all who live in this country are melting in fear because of you. We have heard how the LORD dried up the water of the Red Sea for you when you came out of Egypt, and what you did to Sihon and Og, the two kings of the Amorites east of the Jordan, whom you completely destroyed. When we heard of it, our hearts melted and everyone's courage failed because of you, for the LORD your God is God in heaven above and on the earth below. (Joshua 2:9-11)

You may think that it is high time for the Lord to do something about your troubles; but he may think that the time has not yet come — it may be that he will get more glory, and in the process help you the most, if he waits a while for events to unfold more.

You see, deliverance doesn't happen just because we want it to. If these are the conditions for deliverance, we can be certain of one thing: *not many are saved*. For one reason or another, people don't want to meet these conditions to be rescued — they would rather live in their sins. They don't want to repent and turn their back on their former way of living. They don't want to wait on God while they see their chances slipping by them. They aren't interested in God's glory, especially if they have to do without what they need in order to bring him more glory; and they hate to let God decide whether they really are in danger. Jesus said once that "wide is the gate and broad is the road that leads to destruction, and many enter through it. But small is the gate and narrow the road that leads to life, and only a few find it." (Matthew 7:13-14) Many people would love to be saved from their troubles, but few are willing to meet God's conditions for deliverance.

If you want to see someone who understood the conditions and submitted to them willingly and wholeheartedly, read about the woman who anointed Christ. She knew that she *must* be delivered from her sin; she wept at Jesus' feet and humbled her soul before him in the hope that he would have mercy on her. She put herself completely in his hands, like a little child in the hands of her father, willing to accept anything that he might do for her. She had no answers of her own, and dared not suggest what the Lord should do for her. All she knew was that she was in trouble and he was the only one who could save her. This simple, humble faith so impressed Jesus that he compared her actions to what the Pharisees did: she understood more about the true nature of God's deliverance than the so-called experts understood. Therefore she was delivered from her sins, and they weren't. (Luke 7:36-50)

An example

The story of Jonah is about a double rescue. To summarize, the Lord called the prophet Jonah to go to the Ninevites and preach to them, telling them that unless they repented of their wickedness he was going to destroy the city. Jonah, however, hated the Ninevites — they were the sworn enemies of Israel! He refused to do any such thing and headed off in the opposite direction. When he took a ship to Tarshish, the Lord raised a storm that terrified the sailors. Once they discovered that they had a trouble-maker on board, they threw him overboard — and a huge fish swallowed him whole.

Jonah had time to think in there, and he turned to the Lord for help. The Lord heard his cry and caused the fish to spit him out onto dry land, and Jonah went on to Nineveh to preach his message. Remarkably they believed him and repented in dust and ashes, and the Lord spared the city from destruction.

> • ***What was the danger?*** The mission was in danger. Jonah was supposed to go preach to the Ninevites so that they would be saved from the destruction coming; if they didn't hear about it and repent, they would be destroyed. But how could they hear if Jonah went in the wrong direction?
>
> The Lord rescued Jonah from the fish, but he did it for a better reason than delivering him from death: he changed the prophet's mind about his job. As we see later in the story, Jonah knew full well that the Lord is merciful to his enemies and ready to forgive them when they repent. (Jonah 4:2) Jonah himself wasn't so forgiving toward them, however. The deliverance that Jonah experienced was *in his heart*; it was the Lord softening up a judgmental and hard heart toward those whom God wishes to save. When Jonah repented of his attitude, then the Lord rescued him and sent him on his way again.
>
> And the Ninevites were in great danger too, but it wasn't just the physical danger that God threatened them with.

Their wickedness put them in this dangerous position; the Lord, by sending a threat to them ahead of time, was really giving them a chance to turn from their wickedness and seek salvation from their *sins*. That is the greater danger.

• ***Could they help themselves?*** Neither Jonah nor the Ninevites could do a thing to avoid the danger they were in. Jonah was helpless in the storm as well as in the fish; the Ninevites were an open target to God who sweeps nations away with his hand.

• ***Did they have to get out of danger?*** Obviously! Jonah couldn't stay in the belly of the fish for long. And he couldn't remain hard of heart for long or he wouldn't have gotten to the Ninevites in time to warn them of the disaster that was coming. The Ninevites themselves had to get out of their sin fast, while there was still time. There was no time for fooling around, no half-way measures allowed. They did do something right away that showed how quickly they left their wicked ways: the king himself proclaimed a fast and a time of extreme humility before Jonah's God. "Let man and beast be covered with sackcloth. Let everyone call urgently on God. Let them give up their evil ways and their violence." (Jonah 3:8) Anybody who was found still in their sins when the destroying angel came would be destroyed.

• ***Who saved them?*** The Lord himself saved each of them. It says that "the LORD commanded the fish, and it vomited Jonah onto dry land." (Jonah 2:10) And when the Ninevites repented — when they satisfied the conditions for deliverance — the Lord relented and held back the disaster he had threatened. "When God saw what they did and how they turned from their evil ways, he had compassion and did not bring upon them the destruction he had threatened." (Jonah 3:10) He called back the bombers, so to speak, and stopped the raid from going through with its orders.

- *__What was the result?__* The result in Jonah's case was a mixed bag. He was free again, and he used his freedom to go to Nineveh and do the job that the Lord gave him to do. That's good as far as it goes, because the Lord's plans got back on track again. But there was still this hatred in Jonah's heart for his old enemies. When he saw them repent and escape the destruction, he got angry again and refused to rejoice in their salvation. God had to work on his heart some more to teach him what divine love is all about.

As far as the Ninevites were concerned, they were no doubt greatly relieved when the promised disaster didn't come. They were free, they were alive, they were still in one piece — but not to continue in their sins. The Lord set them free, through repentance, to serve and obey him for a change. We don't know how long this lasted, but at least some of them got the point.

Questions to ask

It's fascinating to read about the deliverance stories in the Bible, but don't miss the main point. They are specially designed to teach you the kind of deliverance that God will do for his people: the conditions that have to be met, the dangers he rescues from, the spiritual state that the people themselves are in, and so on. All of these stories are for the purpose of teaching you so that you can be saved. "All Scripture is God-breathed and is useful for teaching, rebuking, correcting and training in righteousness." (2 Timothy 3:16) To get more out of the story, ask these questions of it:

- *__What was the danger?__* Was it a physical danger or a spiritual one? Was it the person involved who was in danger, or was it the purposes of God, or was it God's glory? Who or what was the danger itself — inanimate objects, men, nations, demons, powers of darkness, angels? What would have happened if the person wouldn't have been rescued? Was it an immediate danger, or was it something that would unfold over a long period of time?

- *Who was being rescued?* Was it an unbeliever or a believer? Did they want to be rescued? Did they deserve to be rescued? Did they call on God to help them first? What did they ask for? Did they repent first before asking for deliverance? Or if they were holy men under danger from enemies, what did they appeal to when they cried out for help — their own righteousness or the Lord's mercy? Was it a single individual or a group of people or an entire nation? What name did they use to call on God?

- *How did the Lord deliver them?* Did he use anything in the world as a "medium" through which he brought about the rescue? Did he do it quickly or over a length of time? Did he use sinners to rescue a saint? If he used people to rescue other people, did the rescuers necessarily know what was going on — did they know that they were being used by God to rescue this party?

- *Did it work?* Did it bring the person out of danger — completely out? How did it do that — by removing them from the scene physically, or by other means? How do we know it worked — were there signs that the Lord had indeed rescued them? Did they go back into trouble and need deliverance again? If so, how many times did the Lord rescue them from their troubles? Was there any rescue in the Bible (that God did!) that *didn't* work? What was the response of the person that was saved?

- *What do you learn about God and his ways from this story?* You should be able to see what God hates, what God loves, what events in history he is keeping his eyes on, what he takes little notice of, how he loves his people, how he deals with the wicked, his reasons for delivering, his purposes in history, and many more things about him. We learn what our God is like when we see him in action; his works reveal his character.

• ***Did this problem happen more than once in the Bible?*** Was there another place and time when this same kind of problem showed up? Did God use different means to deliver them in each situation? Do the New Testament situations differ in any way from the Old Testament rescues, as far as method and goals? Why or why not?

Discussion Questions For Deliverance

- Will the Lord deliver someone because of another person's faith?

- It seems we are living in an age and culture that is rapidly looking like Sodom in its wickedness. Should we pray that the Lord will deliver us out of the place we live in, as he did for Lot?

- What does John 17:15 teach about deliverance?

- If we pray for deliverance, and it doesn't come right away, how can we know whether the Lord will eventually answer our prayer or whether he doesn't feel that it's necessary to deliver us from our problem?

- If the righteous are rescued, what will happen to the wicked?

- What are the steps of salvation from sin?

- When you are witnessing to an unbeliever, what must you tell them about deliverance? Be specific.

- What does it mean to be delivered from demon possession? How does it happen? Does it happen in our day, or was it just something that happened in Bible times?

- How can you tell if someone is really "saved"?

- What can we say about someone who was delivered physically but not spiritually? Use the story of the ten lepers (Luke 17:12-19) as an example.

- Can you lose your salvation? If so, what does that say about God's deliverance? Give Scriptures to support your argument.

Key Ten: Covenant

Key Ten: Covenant

The idea of *covenant* is much more important in the Bible than you might imagine.   It spans the entire book, from Genesis to Revelation.   It not only has to do with the covenant people Israel but with the covenant people of the Church — as the following passages will show you:

> *On that day the LORD made a covenant with Abram and said, "To your descendants I give this land, from the river of Egypt to the great river, the Euphrates."* (Genesis 15:18) The Lord made a special covenant, or agreement, with Abraham that would be passed down through his descendants like an inheritance.   It gave them certain "legal" rights to the promises of God.   It forms the basis of the covenant that God has with his special people in all ages and in every nation around the world — the people of the Church itself.

> *"See, I will send my messenger, who will prepare the way before me. Then suddenly the Lord you are seeking will come to his temple; the messenger of the covenant, whom you desire, will come," says the LORD Almighty.* (Malachi 3:1) This is a prediction of the coming of John the Baptist and of Jesus himself, who would usher in the covenant that God wants to make with his people.   The ministry of Jesus, in other words, is about this covenant between God and man.

> *In the same way, after the supper he took the cup, saying, "This cup is the new covenant in my blood, which is poured out for you."* (Luke 22:20) Christ here takes a special Jewish ceremony (the Passover) and makes it one of the foundation ceremonies of the Christian Church — and calls it the new covenant

between God and his people. The Church, therefore, instead of getting rid of the idea of covenant, gains an even deeper insight into it and value from it.

Then God's temple in Heaven was opened, and within his temple was seen the ark of his covenant. (Revelation 11:19) If anybody thought that the covenants between God and man were only temporary and for earthly use, this passage shows this to be untrue. In Heaven, right now, the Lord keeps his covenant with his people and intends to keep it for all time. It is an *eternal* covenant.

As you can see, the covenant is not only a running theme throughout the Bible, it is the only reason that anybody, Jewish or Gentile, gets anything at all from the Lord. Most people hope that the Lord will do something good for them; but only those who are "heir to the covenant" have the legal rights to the good things of God. "Therefore, the promise comes by faith, so that it may be by grace and may be guaranteed to all Abraham's offspring — not only to those who are of the law but also to those who are of the faith of Abraham. He is the father of us all." (Romans 4:16)

What is a covenant?

In our day we use contracts and lawyers and courts to make agreements with each other, and we have all sorts of ways to make the other party keep their side of the bargain. But in the days of Abraham they had none of these things; so they had to use a different system for keeping agreements with each other.

The word "covenant" was simply a legally binding agreement between two people. In it they agreed to do certain things for each other. But the Hebrew word for "covenant" is *berith* (pronounce, buh-REETH) which is usually used with the word "to cut." There is an amazing reason for this. When two people wanted to make this kind of agreement, they would get some animals and, with a sword, cut them into halves and lay the halves out on the ground, making a path down between them. Then one person would walk down the path between the animal halves and declare what he agreed to do for the other person. The idea was that if he failed to do as he agreed, the offended party would have the legal right to take a sword and do to him what was done to the animals! Then when he was finished making his promise, the other person would do the same. As you can imagine, people didn't enter into an agreement like this unless they were serious about it!

Now turn to Genesis 15 for an example of how a covenant was done. In it the Lord instructs Abraham to cut a heifer, a goat and a ram into halves and lay them out on the ground in two rows. Then when Abraham was put into a deep sleep (so that he could see the Lord come down in a vision), the Lord himself walked down through the animal halves and declared his agreement with Abraham.

> When the sun had set and darkness had fallen, a smoking firepot with a blazing torch appeared and passed between the pieces. On that day the LORD made a covenant with Abram and said, "To your descendants I give this land, from the river of Egypt to the great river, the Euphrates — the land of the Kenites, Kenizzites, Kadmonites, Hittites, Perizzites, Rephaites, Amorites, Canaanites, Girgashites and Jebusites." (Genesis 15:17)

What is truly amazing is that the Lord was submitting himself to the hands of Abraham in this agreement; he (the Author of life!) was putting his life on the line. He would keep the terms of this agreement or willingly forfeit his life. This should show you how seriously he took the covenant with Abraham. There was absolutely no question that the Lord was going to do what he promised.

The second amazing thing about this story is that God did *not* require Abraham to walk down between the animal halves. Normally they would both do it; but in this case the Lord knew that Abraham and his descendants would surely put the covenant in jeopardy if it depended on them in any way. So God took upon himself to keep both sides of the bargain. Not that he was allowing Abraham to get away with sin in the future. But he knew that Abraham *would* sin — and since the covenant was tremendously important to the Lord, he was acting now to protect it from any future threats to its fulfillment.

The Covenant with Abraham

What was this covenant that the Lord made with Abraham? There *was* a covenant made before this time with Noah; but Abraham was the first important step in the process of salvation. For a long time the Lord was preparing an answer to the sin and death that man had introduced into his perfect creation. Now, in Abraham, he was ready to start unfolding it into human history. The covenant with Abraham is the beginning of the answer that we have all been looking for.

The Lord promised to do four things for Abraham and his descendants:

> **To give him a son:** Abraham and Sarah had no children when they moved to Canaan in obedience to the Lord's command. They were advanced in years at the time, and had basically given up hope that they ever would have a natural-born son. But the Lord promised them that they would, in fact, have their own son — clearly an impossible thing.

>> But Abram said, "O Sovereign LORD, what can you give me since I remain childless and the one who will inherit my estate is Eliezer of Damascus?" And Abram said, "You have given me no children; so a servant in my household will be my heir." Then the word of the LORD came to him: "This man will not be your heir, but a son coming from your own body will be your heir." (Genesis 15:2-4)

> He was too old to have a son, and his wife was long past the child-bearing age for women. God was promising them the impossible — a miracle, which happens to be the very method he uses to build his kingdom. At one point they both laughed at the idea of having a son in their old age; when the boy was born, then, they named him "Isaac" which means "he laughs" (perhaps because the Lord had the last laugh in this!).

The promise was fulfilled in Genesis 21:

> Now the LORD was gracious to Sarah as he had said, and the LORD did for Sarah what he had promised. Sarah became pregnant and bore a son to Abraham in his old age, at the very time God had promised him. (Genesis 21:1-2)

To give him the land: When the Lord brought Abraham to Canaan, it wasn't just for a sight-seeing tour! He had Abraham look around at this new place and promised him that one day, both he and his descendants would own this land.

> Lift up your eyes from where you are and look north and south, east and west. All the land that you see I will give to you and your offspring forever. (Genesis 13:14)

The problem was that this would have to be as much of a miracle as the first promise! The Canaanites who already lived there wouldn't take kindly to an alien with strange ways and accents settling down among them, taking their valuable pasture and resources — they especially wouldn't appreciate his notions of owning the whole place someday! So they no doubt kept their eye on him at all times and encouraged him to move on, not settle down. (You can see this very thing happen in the story of Isaac — Genesis 26:12-31.)

The fulfillment of this promise came about in a strange way, certainly not in the way that Abraham would have wanted. Sarah his wife eventually died, and after Abraham mourned over her he looked around for a place to bury her. Since he had no land of his own, he went to the Hittites (a Canaanite tribe living near Hebron) and asked to buy from them a field with a cave in it so that he could bury her. They agreed on a price and the deed was made out in Abraham's name; he became the legal owner of a piece of Canaanite property for the first time.

> So Ephron's field in Machpelah near Mamre — both the field and the cave in it, and all the trees within the borders of the field — was deeded to Abraham as his property in the presence of all the Hittites who had come to the gate of the city . . . So the field and the cave in it were deeded to Abraham by the Hittites as a burial site. (Genesis 23:17-18, 20)

The remarkable thing about this transaction was that it was the beginning of the fulfillment of the second promise that God made with Abraham. He was to become owner of the entire land, in spite of the Canaanites already living there. This was the first step to that ownership. It happened in the midst of trial; certainly Abraham didn't want his wife to die. Nevertheless that trial was the means that the Lord used to bring about what otherwise would have never happened. He had the deed in hand.

To make a great nation from him: The Lord promised Abraham that not only would he get a son, but his descendants would become so numerous that they would be a great nation that nobody could count.

> I will make you into a great nation. (Genesis 12:2)

> He took him outside and said, "Look up at the heavens and count the stars — if indeed you can count them." Then he said to him, "So shall your offspring be." (Genesis 15:5)

Now Abraham couldn't become a nation all by himself. And his son couldn't become a nation without getting married. So they had a problem on their hands: where to find a wife for Isaac? Abraham absolutely refused to get one of the local Canaanite girls for Isaac's wife; they were pagans, worshippers of idols and would lead his son into wickedness and away from the Lord. So Abraham had his servant go back home to Haran where his extended family still lived and find a wife there.

Most people use this story as an example of how to find a suitable marriage partner. But we miss the main point of the story if we limit ourselves to just that. Genesis 24 is really showing us the beginning of the fulfillment of the third promise — the making of a nation. He provided a wife (Rebekah) to be the mother of Jacob, who was the father of twelve sons, who were the fathers of the twelve tribes of Israel. The promise had begun to unfold!

> And they blessed Rebekah and said to her, "Our sister, may you increase to thousands upon thousands; may your offspring possess the gates of their enemies." (Genesis 24:60)

To bless the nations through him: When man first sinned in the Garden of Eden, he brought upon himself and the entire world a tremendous curse of misery and death. As far as God was concerned, this was the worst thing that could have happened to his beautiful creation. He didn't curse us because he liked to, but because he had to. He had to confront sin with the severity of the Law because justice is important to him.

But the Lord never did like that answer for the entire world. From the very beginning he set about putting together a new answer for the problem of sin and death. He hinted at what it might be in Genesis 3:15, but he didn't really say yet what he had in mind.

Now in Abraham's life he was ready to start putting the plan into action. The first step was to promise Abraham that he would be a blessing to the nations:

> And all peoples on earth will be blessed through you. (Genesis 12:3)

> And through your offspring all nations on earth will be blessed. (Genesis 22:18)

This blessing would overturn the original curse that fell on mankind. But what would it look like? Again, Abraham got a "foretaste", a glimpse of what that would look like, in his own experience. The Lord told him one time to take his only son Isaac and sacrifice him to the Lord "on one of the mountains I will tell you about." (Genesis 22:2) So Abraham took Isaac there and started to draw the sacrificial knife across his son's throat. Immediately the Lord stopped him and commended him for his faith.

What went through Abraham's mind during this crisis? He was about to lose his only hope! Upon Isaac rested the future of the entire covenant; it didn't make sense to put him to death, even if it *was* in obedience to the Lord. But the Lord showed Abraham a truth there that strengthened him to go on with the act:

> Abraham reasoned that God could raise the dead, and figuratively speaking, he did receive Isaac back from death. (Hebrews 11:19)

Abraham learned about resurrection that day; he got the first sample himself when the Lord gave Isaac back to him. This was in fulfillment of the fourth promise — the blessing that God had in mind, eventually, for people all around the world: life from the dead, eternal life.

So in Abraham's own lifetime he saw the beginning of all four of the promises that God had made to him in the covenant. They weren't complete fulfillments; his descendants would see much more as God kept these promises of the covenant. But they were foretastes, glimpses, the first experiences of the reality that God had for him and his children.

What Abraham hoped for

We must move on, however. The Lord had much bigger things in mind for Abraham and his children. Not only was the first taste of the promises insufficient, but all that came after that for many centuries failed to exhaust what God had in mind for Abraham's family. "These were all commended for their faith, yet *none* of them received what had been promised. God had planned something better for us so that only together with us would they be made perfect." (Hebrews 11:39-40)

Imagine a huge mansion, and the front door leads into a small room. From there you can go on into the rest of the mansion and see the richness and vastness of the place, or you can stay there in the little front room and miss out on the rest. Abraham's taste of what God had in mind in the covenant was like that little first room. The covenant was actually referring to the huge spiritual realities that lay beyond the limitations of time and space; it speaks of the Kingdom of God, Heaven, the vast treasuries that lay in God's eternal vaults. The front room is part of the mansion, but it hardly begins to show us what lies beyond its doors.

Abraham himself knew that he was only tasting the first fruits of the Kingdom of God. We have proof of this from the inspired writers of the Bible, who knew for certain (through the Spirit who knows the thoughts and hearts of all men) what went through Abraham's mind during his life. In fact, without this testimony we would never know for sure what Abraham knew! But we *can* know with confidence what Abraham really believed about these things.

Let's go through each of the four promises in the covenant and see what Abraham knew then about it or would eventually come to know:

The promise of the son: Abraham knew that his son Isaac wasn't the full promise that God had in mind, when the Lord promised to give him a son. We have proof of this from Jesus himself:

> Your father Abraham rejoiced at the thought of seeing *my day*; he saw it and was glad. (John 8:56)

There were several things about the birth of Isaac that taught Abraham what Jesus himself would be like. *First*, Isaac was a miracle baby — his birth was biologically impossible. Sarah was long past her age of bearing children. So was Jesus a miracle baby: he was born with no earthly father, by the action of the Holy Spirit on his mother Mary. *Second*, the covenant that the Lord gave Abraham was to be passed on to Isaac, not to the other son Ishmael (who was born of the slave woman). Isaac was the rightful heir of all that Abraham owned, including the special promises of the Lord. In the same way, Jesus is the rightful heir of all the promises of God, since he is the only natural Son of God. *Third*, as we shall see in a minute, Isaac's life was all but lost by God's decree, and yet Abraham received him "back from the dead." Jesus actually went through that death (a sacrifice, by the way, like Isaac was supposed to be) and still came back from the dead.

So Abraham knew, in several important ways, what God had in mind for the Son who was to come in the future. How much more he knew about Jesus, we don't know; but we do know, on the testimony of Jesus himself, that he understood the basics of the Christ child.

The promise of the land: Abraham also knew that the dusty piece of real estate called Canaan wasn't all that God had in mind when he promised him and his seed the land. Again, we don't have to guess what was in his mind; we have testimony from someone who was certain about how much Abraham knew about this matter:

By faith he made his home in the promised land like a stranger in a foreign country; he lived in tents, as did Isaac and Jacob, who were heirs with him of the same promise. For he was looking forward to the city with foundations, whose architect and builder is God. (Hebrews 11:9-10)

This is another amazing statement, something that we couldn't be sure of unless we had this testimony. Abraham was glad enough to see that his immediate posterity would have a place to live, but the Lord showed him that Canaan itself wasn't good enough for *all* the people of God who would end up coming into the Kingdom. In fact, he himself looked forward to a far better place to live than Palestine, as these verses assure us.

The city that this refers to is the New Jerusalem that the New Testament describes, especially in the book of Revelation. (See Revelation 21-22) Christians don't lay claim to the old Jerusalem like the Jews do; we know that God's Temple is in Heaven, that he lives among his people — the Church — and we are to set our eyes on things above, where Jesus is now, not on things below. (Colossians 3:1-3) This world will one day disappear in judgment, and all of God's faithful servants, including Abraham himself, will live with God in Heaven forever.

In fact, Abraham got there ahead of us! Jesus himself assures us that Abraham has gone to his reward — not to the land of Canaan that his earthly descendants inherited from him, but the land of glory that God originally planned to give him. You can see this testimony in the story about Lazarus and the rich man. (Luke 16:19-31)

The promise of the nation: Abraham saw the beginning of the promise of a great nation when he got his son Isaac a wife and they started their family. Whether he knew at the time what would come of this marriage, we don't know; we do know that Abraham knows *now* what came of it! Obviously, as we see in the story of Lazarus (Luke 16), after Abraham died he evidently went into the presence of God. Shortly after arriving, he started receiving visitors — his own "children", in fact! As each new generation of Jews came and went in Canaan, some of them at least went on to glory to join Abraham there in Heaven. But don't miss the significance of who these people are: they are heirs of the promise of Heaven, just as Abraham was, because they are *children* of Abraham.

We don't know how many people there are in Heaven now, but we do know that the number is growing. Lazarus obviously is one of them. But look again at the testimony of Jesus, who came from Heaven and is an eyewitness of what is going on there right now:

> I say to you that many will come from the east and the west, and will take their places at the feast with Abraham, Isaac and Jacob in the kingdom of Heaven. (Matthew 8:11)

The family of Abraham is getting larger, and they are gathering in Heaven for the great feast that God has planned for them. Perhaps Abraham was surprised to see *so many* Gentiles there, and *so few* of the Jews there! "But the subjects of the kingdom will be thrown outside, into the darkness, where there will be weeping and gnashing of teeth." (Matthew 8:12) At any rate he knows now exactly what God had in mind when he promised that he would become the father of a great nation.

The nation, of course, is the Church of God — the body of Christ, which consists of all believers whether they are Jew or Gentile. There used to be strict regulations about letting Gentiles around holy things, especially the Temple. But in Christ the barrier was broken down and the two parties were made one body, one believing Church. (Ephesians 2:11-22) Not everyone who was born a Jew became part of the Church, which shows that God never had only the physical family of Abraham in mind when he made that promise at the beginning. Only those who had the faith of Abraham would be a part of the family of God.

The promise of the blessing: When Abraham came so close to sacrificing his son Isaac, he thought that death was certain. But he also knew that God wouldn't leave it that way. We already saw the testimony of Hebrews about this:

> Abraham reasoned that God could raise the dead, and figuratively speaking, he did receive Isaac back from death. (Hebrews 11:19)

In other words, he learned something about God and his ways: the Lord intends to raise his promised children from the dead. Death will not be the end of us; we will live again, never to die again, to serve the Lord forever.

How much Abraham really knew about the resurrection that God has in mind for the Church of Christ, we don't know. Perhaps he didn't know the many details that we have now in the Scriptures — like the teachings of Thessalonians and 1 Corinthians 15. But he did understand the concept, and he knew the mind of the Lord about the matter. As far as God is concerned, death is *not* the last word over us: Abraham knew this for certain about his own son. There was just too much hanging in the balance, too much to happen in the coming kingdom, to let death be the end.

The resurrection is the great hope of the Church, and it's a hope that the unbelievers don't have. Nobody but Abraham and his children have the right to expect that God will raise them out of the grave into newness of life and give them eternity in Heaven. It's a special promise to the family of Abraham; it is going to overturn everything that sin and death has done to ruin us. The resurrection will be much more than just a physical reversal, however; it will be a new kind of life — as Paul carefully explains in 1 Corinthians 15. This life will defeat death forever; it will be a life to God, never to sin or darkness.

Now these promises are things that every Christian knows about and hopes for. What we may not have known, however, is that they were originally given to Abraham long ago! They aren't our property but his property. We have them only by inheritance; he had them given to him directly by God. Abraham has the signed covenant in his hand, so to speak; that's his hope. We, however, have to prove that we are actually his children if we want to share in his property.

Let's look at this another way. What could you possibly be hoping to get from God except these four things? Isn't **Christ** the very one you love the most, your only Friend and Savior, your "all in all?" Isn't **Heaven** your hope, the place that Jesus went to prepare for your coming, your only home? Isn't the **Church** the place where God meets with you through others and their ministry and good works for you, your real family when your earthly family is long gone? Isn't the **resurrection** going to be the end of all that is bad in this world and the start of an eternity of bliss and joy and holiness? What more could you want but these things? What else did you hear about in the Gospel and put your hope in?

My point is that *this is* your faith; there isn't anything else important that you could want from God but these promises. So if these are what you want and expect because of your faith, you are wanting the *covenant promises* that the Lord gave Abraham long ago! These spiritual realities, as fully as you know them now, were what Abraham received from God's hand. This is the Gospel. And if you want Abraham's property, you must prove your relationship to him in order to legally get it. Only Abraham's heirs will get the promises of God.

The importance of genealogy

The Jews have always been extremely careful about their family histories. They kept strict records of their fathers, and their fathers' fathers, and so on — as far back as the beginning of the nation itself. There was a good reason for this, however: it proved their legal claim to the promises of God.

If one of our ancestors died and left a large estate for the heirs, we would have to be able to prove in court that we are one of the legal descendants if we want to receive part of the inheritance. Without that proof, we would have no legal claim to the estate. People all around the world, in all sorts of cultures, deal with this same problem, and so they have various ways of keeping track of what their family line is.

But the Jews' family genealogies extended further back than most other people bother to keep records for. Every one of them could trace their family back to Abraham himself! For instance, let's look at Moses' family record:

> These were the names of the sons of **Levi** according to their records: Gershon, **Kohath** and Merari. Levi lived 137 years. The sons of Gershon, by clans, were Libni and Shimei. The sons of Kohath were **Amram**, Izhar, Hebron and Uzziel. Kohath lived 133 years. The sons of Merari were Mahli and Mushi. These were the clans of Levi according to their records. **Amram** married his father's sister Jochebed, who bore him Aaron and **Moses**. Amram lived 137 years. (Exodus 6:16-20)

Levi was the son of Jacob, who was the son of Isaac, who was the promised son of Abraham — and so Moses had proof that he was directly descended from the heir of the covenant. Without this proof he would have no right to the promises of God.

The Law itself forbade anybody but a descendent of Aaron to act as a priest in the Temple. "This was to remind the Israelites that no one except a descendant of Aaron should come to burn incense before the LORD, or he would become like Korah and his followers." (Numbers 16:40) In order to serve the Lord in the Temple, a man had to prove that he was in the family line of Aaron. Some people who claimed to be in that family couldn't prove it! For example, when Ezra and the exiles returned from captivity in Babylon to Jerusalem, their job was to rebuild the city and the Temple and restore the worship of God as it had been before the exile. One of the first orders of business, therefore, was to find enough priests to begin the sacrifices in the Temple. Some of them, though, couldn't prove their ancestry:

> The following came up from the towns of Tel Melah, Tel Harsha, Kerub, Addon and Immer, but they could not show that their families were descended from Israel: The descendants of Delaiah, Tobiah and Nekoda 652. And from among the priests: The descendants of Hobaiah, Hakkoz and Barzillai (a man who had married a daughter of Barzillai the Gileadite and was called by that name). These searched for their family records, but they could not find them and so were excluded from the priesthood as unclean. The governor ordered them not to eat any of the most sacred food until there was a priest ministering with the Urim and Thummim. (Ezra 2:59-63)

Earlier, when the Israelites came out of Egypt and swept into the Promised Land, they divided up Canaan by tribes: each person belonged to a particular tribe, named after one of the original sons (or grandsons) of Jacob, and all the people in that tribe would live in the part of Canaan assigned to them. For example, the descendants of Judah lived in the area where Jerusalem is, and the descendants of Dan lived in the northernmost reaches of Palestine. It was obvious why a strict record of a person's family tree was important: they got part of the promised land if they could show that they were part of the family. In fact, there was one family who had only daughters — no sons — who nevertheless claimed part of the inheritance:

> Now Zelophehad son of Hepher, the son of Gilead, the son of Makir, the son of Manasseh, had no sons but only

daughters, whose names were Mahlah, Noah, Hoglah, Milcah and Tirzah. They went to Eleazar the priest, Joshua son of Nun, and the leaders and said, "The LORD commanded Moses to give us an inheritance among our brothers." So Joshua gave them an inheritance along with the brothers of their father, according to the LORD's command. (Joshua 17:3-4)

We still see this practice of keeping strict family records in the life of Christ himself. At the beginning of the gospels of Matthew and Luke, we find the family tree of Jesus:

A record of the genealogy of Jesus Christ the son of David, the son of Abraham. (Matthew 1:1)

He was the son ... of Abraham ... the son of God. (Luke 3:23, 34, 38)

In all these records, you will notice, the Jew was careful to show his direct line of descent from Abraham. The promises were given directly to *Abraham* — never directly to anybody else. The only way that someone could lay claim to those promises was to prove that they were children of Abraham. Everybody in Israel knew this, and that's why they kept such strict records of their families.

The promises

We know that the Israelites had a long history that the Old Testament records for us, but many Bible students often don't realize that Israel's history was really the fulfillment of the covenant that God made with Abraham. The Lord gave them what he *promised* them, and the Old Testament is a full account of that.

- **The land:** The land, obviously, was Canaan itself, a narrow strip between the desert of Trans-Jordan on the east and the Mediterranean on the west, Syria on the north and Egypt and Arabia on the south. Though it was small, it was the choicest piece of the entire area. It was, in those days,

... a land flowing with milk and honey. The land you are entering to take over is not like the land of Egypt, from which you have come, where you planted your seed and irrigated it by foot as in a vegetable garden. But the land you are crossing the Jordan to take possession of is a land of mountains and valleys that drinks rain from heaven. It is a land the LORD your God cares for; the eyes of the LORD your God are continually on it from the beginning of the year to its end. (Deuteronomy 11:9-12)

The Israelites loved it. This was their new home, prepared by God himself, and they defended it against all enemies who tried to take it away from them. They passed the land on to their children, who passed it on to theirs. The land was so important to them that they wept when they lost it. "By the rivers of Babylon we sat and wept when we remembered Zion." (Psalm 137:1)

It was their idolatry that brought about the loss of the land. They just wouldn't listen to the Lord's warnings and turn away from the false gods they were worshipping. When it came time to punish the Israelites for their unbelievable wickedness against the Lord, he took them out of their beloved land and sent them into exile to Babylon. For seventy years, as the Lord put it (2 Chronicles 36:21), the land "rested" from the sins of the people while they languished in captivity, with plenty of time to think about their wicked ways. But when the time was up, the Lord brought them back to the land — not because they deserved it, but because it was part of the unbreakable covenant he made with their father Abraham:

When seventy years are completed for Babylon, I will come to you and fulfill my gracious promise to bring you back to this place. For I know the plans I have for you, declares the LORD, plans to prosper you and not to harm you, plans to give you hope and a future. (Jeremiah 29:10-22)

The books of Ezra and Nehemiah record the return of the exiles to their land and the rebuilding they did. It was a great day to remember when they got their land back.

• **The nation:** Every nation had a king, and the Israelites were no exception. Their king was much different from other kings, however! The Lord himself ruled over the Israelites, as he promised to do for Abraham and his descendants:

> I will establish my covenant as an everlasting covenant between me and you and your descendants after you for the generations to come, to *be your God* and the God of your descendants after you. (Genesis 17:7)

The Lord gave them, at the very beginning, the Law that would be the government over them. He made them into a nation and brought them into their own land. He protected them from their enemies, through judges and kings. He blessed them with rain (what other king could do such a thing?) and caused their fields to yield rich stores of food. He punished lawbreakers and kept the peace in the nation. He did everything that a good king is supposed to do — even more, since he could do the impossible that no earthly king could have done for them.

The Israelites knew that they had a good king. They enjoyed privileges that no other nation on earth could claim:

> What other nation is so great as to have their gods near them the way the LORD our God is near us whenever we pray to him? And what other nation is so great as to have such righteous

decrees and laws as this body of laws I am setting before you today? (Deuteronomy 4:7-8)

Though other nations have claimed to have God as their king (as ours does today, since we consider ourselves to be a "Christian nation"), Israel was the only *nation* for which this was really true. All other instances are only *individuals* who belong to God and are a blessing to the nation in which they live.

• **The blessing:** The Lord promised to bless Abraham, his descendants, and all nations through his descendants. Since the curse upon mankind was real, the blessing therefore was real as well. When the Lord brought together the people of the covenant he also started the process of reversing the curse that all nations on earth are burdened with.

The answer was a complex one and took a long time to work out. But the initial stage was the complete system of Temple worship and animal sacrifices that the Law prescribes. The Law itself, as a matter of fact, was also part of the answer. What it all amounted to was this: the Lord gave the Israelites the answer to man's fundamental problem of sin in these ceremonial requirements.

First, the Law was a description of sin — which is the critical first step in the process of salvation. Other nations had no idea what sin was, or even that God was angry with them in any way. Judgment Day is going to be quite a surprise for them! It's far better to *know* what angers God so that we can find out how to avoid or fix the problem. The Israelites realized the tremendous privilege that they had over other nations in this regard: " He has revealed his word to Jacob, his laws and decrees to Israel. He has done this for no other nation; they do not know his laws. Praise the LORD!" (Psalm 147:19-20)

Second, the Lord gave them the solution for the problem of sin: the Temple and its ceremonies. To know what sin is, this is inside knowledge that any wise man would love to have. But to be *forgiven* of that sin — this is beyond what we could reasonably expect! Our offenses against God deserve death, not forgiveness; a just judge would pass no other sentence on sinners like us. Here was the mercy and grace of God at work, carefully teaching the Israelites what they needed to do to in order to get forgiveness for their offenses against him — sins that they knowingly committed as well as unknowingly. The sacrifices themselves taught the people that their sins deserved death. But they also taught them that God accepts the death of another in their place, as long as the sacrifice is acceptable to the strict requirements that the Lord has. No other nation on earth experienced the love and mercy of God in this way. Their entire history was a cycle of sinning against God, going to him in repentance, and finding him ready to forgive everything they had done. We learn from them the depths of human sin, and the unfathomable grace of God to sinners.

Third, the Lord gave them access to himself. The Temple was where his throne was, and the Israelites came there to meet with him. Men all over the world have wished they could meet God face to face, if for no other reason than they wanted to know what he was like. But only the Israelites had the privilege of meeting with God. This means that they heard him speak his truth to them, they could present their requests to him, they would get answers to their prayers, they could worship him in his glory and majesty, he could lead them in his ways, and all the other advantages that come with knowing God personally.

• **The son:** This promise came about in the history of Israel in a different way than the Israelites would have expected. They were the descendants of Abraham and, because of that fact, had the legal right to claim all that the Lord had promised their father Abraham. Right from the beginning the legal descendants of the line of Abraham had to be distinguished from the ones who had no legal claim: Ishmael, though a son of Abraham, was not the son of Sarah and therefore had no right to the inheritance. The Lord himself decided the issue: "But my covenant I will establish with Isaac." (Genesis 17:21) So Ishmael had to find himself another place to live; he couldn't stay in Abraham's camp any longer.

Isaac had two sons also, and the Lord decided that only one of them would be the heir to Abraham's inheritance — the one that nobody would have expected. Although Esau was the older son and should have received the inheritance, Jacob was the one whom God picked as the heir.

> "Was not Esau Jacob's brother?" the LORD says.
> "Yet I have loved Jacob, but Esau I have hated,
> and I have turned his mountains into a wasteland
> and left his inheritance to the desert jackals."
> (Malachi 1:2-3)

That sounds pretty severe, but the Lord chooses whom he wants and nobody can say anything about it. Paul assures us that this is the Lord's prerogative:

> Just as it is written: "Jacob I loved, but Esau I hated." What then shall we say? Is God unjust? Not at all! For he says to Moses, "I will have mercy on whom I have mercy, and I will have compassion on whom I have compassion." It does not, therefore, depend on man's desire or effort, but on God's mercy. (Romans 9:13-16)

The rest of the history of Israel reflects these early choices on God's part: all the descendants of Jacob went to the Promised Land and enjoyed the blessings of the covenant made to their father Abraham. But they shouldn't have been so arrogant at times, as they were when they looked across the borders at their unbelieving neighbors. Like Jonah, who hated the Ninevites so much that he thought it was unjust of God to offer them mercy, the Jews generally looked down on the "goyim" (as they called anybody who wasn't Jewish). They thought that God only loved Jews; they thought that someday *they* would be the master race who would rule the world under the Messiah.

The reason that they shouldn't have felt this way about themselves is that the Lord told them specifically that he had plans to include some Gentiles into the family of Abraham. That promise was all through the Old Testament. For example, look up these references: Genesis 49:10; Psalm 2:8; Psalm 22:31; Psalm 46:4,10; Psalm 72:8-19; Isaiah 9:2-7; Isaiah 24:16; Isaiah 65:1; Ezekiel 47:3-5; Daniel 7:13-14; Zechariah 8:20-23 (these are just a few of the passages). Let's look at one here: the prophet Hosea spoke of a people who would become his chosen people.

> I will plant her for myself in the land; I will show my love to the one I called 'Not my loved one.' I will say to those called 'Not my people,' 'You are my people'; and they will say, 'You are my God.' (Hosea 2:23)

Even in the promise given to Abraham, the Lord hinted that there would be non-Jews who would enjoy the covenant blessings: "And all peoples on earth will be blessed through you." (Genesis 12:3) Not until we read what happened in the New Testament, though, do we find out exactly what the Lord had in mind for the Gentiles. So the question was, who is really the promised son?

So the Israelites enjoyed the fulfillment of the covenant that God made with Abraham — on the physical level. They were the physical descendants of Abraham, and so they had the right to the terms of the promises that dealt with physical fulfillments: Canaan, the

Temple, the animal sacrifices for sin, the Law, the kings, protection from the Philistines, and so on.

You must keep in mind, however, as you read the Old Testament and what happened then, that everything that happened to the Israelites was because of the covenant with Abraham. They were like no other nation on earth. The Lord dealt with other nations on the basis of his being their Creator: he made them, they failed in their job to show forth his glory in their lives, and they had only his wrath to look forward to. But the Israelites were God's chosen people, the ones who knew the Law and what sin was, who knew the way of salvation from sin, who could approach God for mercy and forgiveness. Theirs was the *way of life*. "You Samaritans worship what you do not know; we worship what we do know, for salvation is from the Jews." (John 4:22) This special relationship was due solely to the agreement that was first made between the Lord and Abraham, and everything in their history reflected this relationship. They were *the people of the covenant*; that's why they had the life they had.

Who are the heirs?

When it comes time to divide up an inheritance, the big question is this: who are the rightful heirs? Whoever wants to put in his claim to the property has to demonstrate, with legal proof, that he is an heir of the person who left the property. He has to have something that the court recognizes that proves his claim.

When the Lord first made his covenant with Abraham, he gave him a sign to pass on to all his descendants — the proof of being in the family and therefore rightful heirs.

> This is my covenant with you and your descendants after you, the covenant you are to keep: Every male among you shall be circumcised. You are to undergo circumcision, and it will be the sign of the covenant between me and you. (Genesis 17:10-11)

Anybody who was not circumcised was to be thrown out of the camp; he had no right to the privileges and blessings of Abraham's inheritance. "Any uncircumcised male, who has not been circumcised in the flesh, will be cut off from his people; he has broken my covenant." (Genesis 17:14)

The Jews held on to this custom for their entire history; they still do to this day. It is a sign that they are the covenant people of God, and they wouldn't give it up for anything. The problem is, however, that they misunderstood the true depth of the covenant promises (unlike their father Abraham, who understood it very well) and the real meaning of circumcision itself.

When John the Baptist announced the coming of Christ, he challenged the Pharisees and Sadducees who came to him for baptism. He knew they were hiding behind outward physical forms, claiming to be heirs of the covenant solely by their physical descent from Abraham.

> And do not think you can say to yourselves, "We have Abraham as our father." I tell you that out of these stones God can raise up children for Abraham. (Matthew 3:9)

Here was the first hint of the coming upset, the fall of the Jews and the kingdom of God being given to the Gentiles instead. Jesus makes it even plainer in his teaching. When he told the Jews that they needed to believe what he was teaching them and turn their backs on what they had learned from their father (he meant the devil!), they answered him in this way:

> "Abraham is our father," they answered. "If you were Abraham's children," said Jesus, "then you would do the things Abraham did." (John 8:39)

In other words, in Jesus' opinion these Jews were *not* the children of Abraham! Evidently it requires *more* than being of physical descent to claim the covenant promises. The reason is this: the Lord promised much more than physical blessings to Abraham, which, as we've seen already, Abraham knew full well. The covenant has a rich deepness that physical fulfillments can't fully satisfy.

Let's follow Paul's argument about this. He tells us that he would even give up his own salvation for the sake of his Jewish brethren:

> For I could wish that I myself were cursed and cut off from Christ for the sake of my brothers, those of my own race, the people of Israel. Theirs is the adoption as sons; theirs the divine glory, the covenants, the receiving of the law, the temple worship and the promises. Theirs are the patriarchs, and from them is traced the human ancestry of Christ, who is God over all, forever praised! Amen. (Romans 9:3-5)

He's referring to the covenant blessings, of course, that the Jews enjoyed all through the Old Testament history. The problem is that they didn't do what God required! They ended up in abject failure not because there was anything wrong in God's covenant, but because of their sin. Then Paul tells us the truth about who are children of Abraham and who aren't:

> It is not as though God's word had failed. For not all who are descended from Israel are Israel. Nor because they are his descendants are they all Abraham's children. On the contrary, "It is through Isaac that your offspring will be reckoned." In other words, it is not the *natural* children who are God's children, but it is the *children of the promise* who are regarded as Abraham's offspring. (Romans 9:6-8)

Then in Galatians he says, point blank, who are the true children:

> If you belong to Christ, then *you* are Abraham's seed, and heirs according to the promise. (Galatians 3:29)

There is now no question who are the true heirs of Abraham. Though the Jews claim the inheritance through physical descent, they only got the physical fulfillment of that covenant as long as they weren't also of the *faith* of Abraham. That faith is what lifts someone up into the spiritual level of the covenant and makes them heirs of the true depth of the covenant. That faith, we find out, is given to the

Gentile as well as to the Jew, a truth that escaped legalistic Jews and surprised even the apostles when the Spirit led them to preach the gospel to the Gentiles. See the story about Cornelius for an example of their surprise and God's gift. (Acts 10)

But what about the sign of circumcision, the mark that proved legal descent from Abraham and gave the right to the inheritance? Even that had two levels: the legalistic Jews still circumcise their males and claim the covenant promises (the physical level, by the way — they want nothing of the spiritual reality in Christ!). Gentiles, however, whether they are physically circumcised or not, also *must* have the sign on them to prove their legal claim to the promises. And *they do!*

> In him you were also circumcised, in the putting off of
> the sinful nature, not with a circumcision done by the
> hands of men but with the circumcision done by Christ.
> (Colossians 2:11)

Theirs is the spiritual inheritance, and so the circumcision is also spiritual, of the heart, doing what the physical symbol couldn't do but still pointed to. The point of circumcision, which Abraham also knew, wasn't just a mark on the flesh but a spiritual reality: it showed that this person was spiritually ready, spiritually fit, for the things of Heaven, for the spiritual inheritance in Christ. It's God's own mark on a man for something he sees in the man's heart.

> A man is not a Jew if he is only one outwardly, nor is
> circumcision merely outward and physical. No, a man
> is a Jew if he is one inwardly; and circumcision is
> circumcision of the heart, by the Spirit, not by the
> written code. Such a man's praise is not from men, but
> from God. (Romans 2:28-29)

The only thing left to look at now is this question: were there, in the Old Testament, people who qualified to be heirs on *both* levels of the covenant? Certainly, starting with Abraham himself. John 8:56 and Hebrews 11:10 both testify to the fact that Abraham was an heir of the spiritual kingdom that the covenant talks about. So such a thing was not only possible in the Old Testament, it was necessary if they wanted to claim part of that inheritance. There were others who, as we see in Hebrews 11, understood the real issue at stake in the covenant. So there are some Old Testament Jews in Heaven now, though not all of them are. There were many, unfortunately, who inherited the physical promises of the covenant but were strangers to the spiritual inheritance in Christ, as Paul told us in Romans 2.

To summarize, who then were the true heirs of the covenant? Only those who could show legal descent. The heirs of the physical promises were the Jews, who carried on their bodies the mark of circumcision. But there was much more to inherit than the physical promises! There were certain ones of Abraham's children who bore in their *hearts* the marks of circumcision, by God's hand, which proved their descent from Abraham. "The LORD your God will circumcise your hearts and the hearts of your descendants, so that you may love him with all your heart and with all your soul, and live." (Deuteronomy 30:6) There were also some Gentiles with the same proof of descent, who also laid claim to the promises of the covenant. This was no surprise to those who knew what God had in mind all along, but it was a surprise to those who thought that only Jews would be children of Abraham.

Fine-tuning the Covenant

There were a couple of times when the Lord added a new dimension to the covenant. The **first** was the covenant statement he made with the Israelites after their rescue from Egypt, at the foot of Mt. Sinai in the desert.

When the Israelites were still in Egypt, they were the slaves of Pharaoh and suffering terribly under oppression. That in itself wasn't reason enough for the Lord to rescue them, however! Many peoples have been slaves and oppressed, and the Lord didn't see fit to rescue them. But the Israelites were different: their father was Abraham, and the Lord had made a special agreement with Abraham and *all his children.*

God heard their groaning and he remembered his covenant with Abraham, with Isaac and with Jacob. So

God looked on the Israelites and was concerned about them. (Exodus 2:24-25)

We must keep in mind that all the events that were to follow were the result of the covenant with Abraham, not because of feelings that the Lord necessarily had for the Israelites themselves. That covenant was the driving force behind everything that the Lord did with the Israelites. He brought them out of Egypt according to the covenant promises. The next step was also in keeping with the covenant: he took them to Sinai where he gave them his Law, the Ten Commandments and all the explanatory laws that went along with them.

The Law itself is described as a "covenant", as the following passage shows:

> And he wrote on the tablets the words of the covenant — the Ten Commandments. (Exodus 34:28)

It's an agreement between the Lord and his people, just as any covenant is. The agreement was this:

> Be careful to follow every command I am giving you today, so that you may live and increase and may enter and possess the land that the LORD promised on oath to your forefathers. (Deuteronomy 8:1)

> Take to heart all the words I have solemnly declared to you this day, so that you may command your children to obey carefully all the words of this law. They are not just idle words for you — they are your life. By them you will live long in the land you are crossing the Jordan to possess. (Deuteronomy 32:46-47)

At first glance it looks as if the Law had replaced the covenant with Abraham — as if getting the blessings of God depended on obedience now, not faith. But that's not true. Without getting into a full-scale discussion of the Law (which can be very complex — the greatest minds in the Church have grappled with this issue!) we can say at least a few important things about it. *First*, the initial relationship between God and the Israelites was grace, not obedience. The Lord rescued them *first*, according to the covenant to Abraham, *then* he gave them the Law. Paul tells us that —

> The Law, introduced 430 years later, does not set aside the covenant previously established by God and thus do away with the promise. For if the inheritance depends on the Law, then it no longer depends on a promise; but God in his grace gave it to Abraham through a promise. (Galatians 3:17-18)

Second, the Law only described what God expected his covenant people to act like. He doesn't want sinners in his kingdom but righteous servants. The circumcision symbolizes a circumcised heart: a heart that has the sin, the old man, cut away from it. He wants a holy people; the Law not only described what holiness is, it prescribed the remedies for sin and a way to get back to holiness when the people strayed from their terms of the covenant.

So the Law was only supporting, not replacing, the original covenant that God made with the descendants of Abraham. It's actually a fuller statement of what the meaning of circumcision is. There *is* an additional element to the Law — the fact that they had to keep the Law to stay in God's favor — but we will look at that aspect below under the heading "Old Covenant — New Covenant."

The **second** refinement to the Abrahamic covenant was the promise that the Lord gave to King David, the man after God's own heart. David played a critically important role in the Kingdom of God: he was the model for the Messiah who was going to come and sit on David's throne someday. David's character, his job as king, and his spiritual activities taught the Israelites what the Christ would be like.

The Lord made this promise to David and his descendants:

> The LORD declares to you that the LORD himself will establish a house for you: "When your days are over and you rest with your fathers, I will raise up your offspring to succeed you, who will come from your own

body, and I will establish his kingdom. He is the one who will build a house for my Name, and I will establish the throne of his kingdom forever. I will be his father, and he will be my son. When he does wrong, I will punish him with the rod of men, with floggings inflicted by men. But my love will never be taken away from him, as I took it away from Saul, whom I removed from before you. Your house and your kingdom will endure forever before me; your throne will be established forever." (2 Samuel 7:11-16)

Later David refers to this agreement as a "covenant" —

Is not my house right with God? Has he not made with me an everlasting covenant, arranged and secured in every part? Will he not bring to fruition my salvation and grant me my every desire? (2 Samuel 23:5)

But unless the Lord calls it a covenant as well, we can hardly include it into the overall covenant that he made with Abraham. But the Lord *does* call it a covenant:

As for you, if you walk before me as David your father did, and do all I command, and observe my decrees and laws, I will establish your royal throne, as I *covenanted* with David your father when I said, "You shall never fail to have a man to rule over Israel." (2 Chronicles 7:17-18)

Again, this wasn't a new covenant but just an expansion of the original covenant made with Abraham. The new idea was the *Messiah*, the Anointed One, the King yet to come that David symbolized. Just as David was the king of the covenant people, who drew all the people together into one nation and made them invincible against their enemies, the Messiah would do the same for *all* of God's people, Jew and Gentile.

David provided a new model for the people of God, one that you will appreciate more if you read the story of the Israelites as they struggled for hundreds of years under the period of the Judges. Until David came, the people had no centralized leadership, no "head of state" that would make them into one nation. They didn't have a very good system for worship either, for that matter, as you can see in the story of Eli and him losing the ark to the Philistines. (1 Samuel 4-5) But with David the whole nation is pulled together under one head, one government, and one purpose. David makes plans for the Temple and starts collecting materials for his son Solomon to build it. David finally settles the problems with their enemies, especially the Philistines. It was literally because of David that Israel became rich and prosperous, safe, honoring to God, and with a definite purpose in the world.

In other words, David was the *facilitator* of the covenant, the one who made it work. Through him the promises in the covenant came to be; without him, the outcome was still in question. It was that aspect that was so new to the covenant (not that it was new to God — he had this in mind from the very beginning!) yet was so necessary to its fulfillment. And it's easy to see how this applies to Christ, the son of David. In Christ is the government of God's people, their protection, their worship, their treasures from Heaven, their food and drink, their purpose for living. "For no matter how many promises God has made, they are 'Yes' in Christ." (2 Corinthians 1:20) Christ is so central to the success of the covenant that Paul makes him the real object of the promise to Abraham in the first place:

> The promises were spoken to Abraham and to his seed. The Scripture does not say "and to seeds," meaning many people, but "and to your seed," meaning one person, who is Christ. (Galatians 3:16)

Whoever is in Christ will experience the full depth of the covenant promises. But more on this later in the chapter "The Master Key."

So the covenant needed a couple of further refinements, some fine-tuning, to be fully understood. As it was given to Abraham, there were some questions about how the Lord intended to fulfill those promises. The Law and the covenant to David add the necessary framework to better understand what was in God's mind. They also prepared the way for the coming of the Christ who would build upon the Old Testament foundation and finally fulfill the covenant to Abraham and his children.

The faith of Abraham

We already looked at faith in a former key, but I want to go back and look at *why* faith is so important in relation to the covenant. We find the best explanation of this relationship in Romans 4 where Paul tells us what the spiritual link is between Christians and Abraham.

Abraham demonstrated all the necessary steps for true faith, a faith that pleases God. This is more important than it might appear. Abraham was a model for all Christians: we all must be like father Abraham if we hope to get anything at all from God. Paul makes this point in Romans when he says this:

> What then shall we say that Abraham, our forefather, discovered in this matter? If, in fact, Abraham was justified by works, he had something to boast about — but not before God. What does the Scripture say? "Abraham believed God, and it was credited to him as righteousness." Now when a man works, his wages are not credited to him as a gift, but as an obligation. However, to the man who does not work but trusts God who justifies the wicked, his faith is credited as righteousness. (Romans 4:1-5)

In other words, righteousness — the very thing that all sinners need, the thing that will keep us safe on Judgment Day — comes through *faith*, not by any good works on our part. In case anybody was confused about the role of the Law (and many people are — they think that the Lord will be pleased with them and give them the promises of the covenant if they obey the Law) Paul tells us that Abraham's faith was *before* the coming of the Law, not after. God's gifts are based on the covenant with Abraham, not the Law. (Romans 4:9-15)

Why is faith so critical for the covenant? Remember the main point about faith: faith lives in the light of the Kingdom of God. It takes as real what the physical eye can't see. Faith — in the case of the covenant — sees the blessings promised to Abraham's children that are stored up in Heaven for them, and lives here on earth as if those things are real and on their way. In other words, faith believes God when he says that these promises made to Abraham *really are* the blessing in life that you've been looking for. The richness of the covenant is the answer to all your problems and life from the dead. Nobody will see that without faith.

The Jews who relied on their circumcision and their own obedience to the Law didn't have the faith of Abraham — and so missed the fact entirely that the covenant is spiritual, not physical. They missed the fact that Jesus is the fulfillment of the covenant made to Abraham. They didn't see the Heavenly Jerusalem that God was promising Abraham, though Abraham did see it through faith. (Hebrews 11:10) Instead of living in the light of Heaven, of the spiritual reality of the covenant, they lived "by sight" (2 Corinthians 5:7) and so missed out on the covenant.

The kinds of promises that God made to Abraham require faith; without it we will never see what God has in mind for his children. But with faith we can see far more than the eyes of flesh can see — more even than the physical descendants of Abraham saw. This means, of course, that even Gentiles who aren't of physical descent from Abraham can claim him as their father.

> Therefore, the promise comes by faith, so that it may be by grace and may be guaranteed to all Abraham's offspring — not only to those who are of the law but also to those who are of the faith of Abraham. *He is the father of us all.* As it is written: "I have made you a father of many nations." He is our father in the sight of God, in whom he believed — the God who gives life to the dead and calls things that are not as though they were. (Romans 4:16-17)

This explains why the physical children of Abraham didn't understand what Jesus was doing at all, yet those who were not Jews could easily see the point. The Jews didn't have faith, and the Gentiles did. The unbelieving Jews obviously were not children of the covenant, and the believing Gentiles were obviously children of Abraham!

Old Covenant — New Covenant

The Bible is divided into two major sections: the Old Testament and the New Testament. The word "testament" is really another name for "covenant" — and that points out an important truth about the covenant that we need to notice.

The fact that there is an "old" covenant and a "new" covenant has been a source of great confusion to many Bible students. The book of Hebrews especially makes a point about the difference between the covenants; the old is gone, useless to us now, and the new covenant is what we live by. But too many Christians take it a step further and say that nothing in the Old Testament is worthy of a Christian's attention — because it all belongs to the "old" covenant! It's unfortunate that the entire Old Testament comes under the heading "old."

But before we charge off in the wrong direction, we need to sort out what Hebrews is talking about. In one sense the old is gone, yet in another sense it is still in force. The covenant made with Abraham is the *eternal* covenant made with all Abraham's children, fulfilled in Christ himself. If we turn our backs on *that* covenant, we are rejecting the entire ministry of Christ just as the Jews in his day rejected him. I hope we aren't that foolish!

What Hebrews is referring to when it talks about the "old" covenant is the idea in the Law that we noticed before: that the Jews had to keep the commands of the Law if they wanted to live in the land. *They* had to keep the Law, if they wanted to please God. That's the fatal flaw in the system, however. Nobody can keep the Law perfectly to God's satisfaction. He knew that ahead of time, however; it was no surprise to him that sinners couldn't live in perfect righteousness! He wanted to prove that point to us so that we would look to another source than ourselves for righteousness. "What, then, was the purpose of the Law? It was added *because of transgressions* until the Seed to whom the promise referred had come." (Galatians 3:19)

Here is the passage in Hebrews:

But the ministry Jesus has received is as superior to theirs as the covenant of which he is mediator is superior to the old one, and it is founded on better promises. For if there had been nothing wrong with that first covenant, no place would have been sought for another. But God found fault with the people and said: "The time is coming, declares the Lord, when I will make a new covenant with the house of Israel and with the house of Judah. *It will not be like the covenant I made with their forefathers when I took them by the hand to lead them out of Egypt*, because they did not remain faithful to my covenant, and I turned away from them, declares the Lord. This is the covenant I will make with the house of Israel after that time, declares the Lord. *I will put my laws in their minds and write them on their hearts*. I will be their God, and they will be my people. No longer will a man teach his neighbor, or a man his brother, saying, 'Know the Lord,' because they will all know me, from the least of them to the greatest. For I will forgive their wickedness and will remember their sins no more." By calling this covenant "new," he has made the first one obsolete; and what is obsolete and aging will soon disappear. (Hebrews 8:6-13)

Notice two things about this passage: *first*, the "old" covenant that he refers to here is the one he made with Israel when they came out of Egypt. Now the only agreement that he made with the Israelites at that time was the one he made at Mt. Sinai — the Law, in other words. This is *not* referring to the Abrahamic covenant! As Paul assures us elsewhere, the Law never set aside the eternal covenant that the Lord made with Abraham. "The Law, introduced 430 years later, does not set aside the covenant previously established by God and thus do away with the promise." (Galatians 3:17)

Second, the problem here is obvious: the people weren't keeping the Lord's commands. The problem wasn't the Law itself, but the hearts of sinners. So the solution *wasn't* to get rid of the Law. The solution was to write the Law in their hearts in such a way that they would *have* to obey it, in spite of themselves. And this wasn't a problem that only the New Testament picked up on. The Old Testament also complains about the waywardness of God's people because of this very flaw in the system — that no sinner on his own can keep the righteous Law. In fact, the same solution that Hebrews gives for this problem also appears in the Old Testament:

> I will give you a new heart and put a new spirit in you; I will remove from you your heart of stone and give you a heart of flesh. And I will put my Spirit in you and *move you to follow my decrees and be careful to keep my laws*. (Ezekiel 36:26-27)

As you can see, the solution was never to destroy the covenant with Abraham, nor was it even to do away with the righteous requirements of the Law. The solution was to put the burden of doing the Law on the Lord's shoulders and take it off ours. Paul affirms this solution in Romans: "... in order that the righteous requirements of the law might be *fully met in us*, who do not live according to the sinful nature but according to the Spirit." (Romans 8:4) Christ fulfills the Law for us, and through the Spirit makes us holy with *his* righteousness. Then the Law will be satisfied with us.

So the idea of the "old" refers to the *way* that the Israelites were to achieve righteousness, not the righteous standards themselves. The Law wasn't done away with, nor (Heaven forbid!) was the covenant with Abraham done away with. What God did throw out was the idea in the Mt. Sinai agreement that the people had to keep the Law themselves in order to please him.

Does this agree with the rest of Hebrews? Most certainly! Hebrews talks about the sacrifices that *they* had to provide, the Temple that *they* had to build, the blood of animals, the priests who worked in the Temple — all the works of men. God commanded it, and man did it. That's how the entire Sinai system worked. But in Christ we have a work done entirely by God, not by man: Jesus is the priest, Jesus is the sacrifice, the sacrifice is given in the Heavenly Temple, the blood is the blood of the Son of God — none of it is by man's hand. This is for a good reason: God wants this thing to work, not fail. So he does it himself (remember the original covenant with Abraham where only the Lord walks down through the halves of the animals?) so that he will be certain that he will get salvation for his people.

If anything, this new arrangement makes the covenant with Abraham even more certain. God is going to *keep* his bargain with Abraham and his descendants; there is absolutely no question as to the outcome. Man can do nothing to mess it up.

An example

There's a powerful example of the covenant and the legal requirements for claiming its blessings in an incident in Christ's ministry. When Jesus was done preaching in a certain area of Galilee, he left there and went to non-Jewish territory — the area of Tyre and Sidon. While there, a Canaanite woman (non-Jewish, in other words) came to him and pleaded with him to heal her demon-possessed daughter. Jesus refused to talk to her.

This is so out of character for him that it surprises us at first. Why didn't the one who loved sinners respond to her? The man who rescued the woman caught in adultery, who ate at the houses of tax collectors and sinners, who offered the water of life to a sinful Samaritan woman, wouldn't even talk to this Canaanite woman. Why not?

The woman wouldn't give up, however; she evidently made a pest of herself to the point that his disciples pleaded with him to at least send her away. His response was even harsher than his silence:

> I was sent only to the lost sheep of Israel.
> (Matthew 15:24)

Finally the woman came to him and knelt before him, pleading with him for help. Then he says the most startling thing of all — an outright insult!

> It is not right to take the children's bread and toss it to
> their dogs. (Matthew 15:26)

Where is the famous love of Christ?! To unravel this mystery, we have to go back to the terms of the covenant that Abraham received from God. We have to keep in mind this one important fact: everything that Jesus is, everything he came to do, was *in fulfillment of the covenant to Abraham*. God had the gospel in mind, in other words, when he made those promises to Abraham. The promises weren't limited to physical fulfillments but all the spiritual richness that is in Jesus Christ.

Second, remember that the covenant was given to Abraham and his *legal descendants* — nobody else had any right to them. God bound himself with an oath, with the threat of death, to keep this covenant with Abraham's family.

So when this woman asked for something from Jesus, *he had to refuse her* on the basis of the legality of the thing. She was asking for one of the blessings in the covenant, something that she had no rights to, and he had no right to give her. If he had just given her what she wanted, he would have broken the terms of the covenant and every Jew in Palestine could have justly cried out for God's blood! But the covenant was a precious thing to God, and Jesus was not about to compromise any of God's promises. His refusal was no less than him giving honor to the promise that God made to Abraham and his seed.

And there's where the story starts to break open. *Who* are Abraham's heirs? Notice what the woman says next:

"Yes, Lord," she said, "but even the dogs eat the crumbs
that fall from the master's table." (Matthew 15:27)

That statement was like a brilliant spotlight out of Heaven that revealed the true nature of this woman's heart. Here was the *same faith* that moved Abraham to believe in the promises of God. Jesus recognized it immediately: "Woman, you have great faith! Your request is granted." (Matthew 15:28) In other words, it turned out that here was one of the children of Abraham, not born by physical descent but by spiritual descent from her spiritual father. Because she had *the faith of her father Abraham*, she was an heir of all the promises of the covenant and could rightfully lay claim to any of them — which is exactly what she was doing here.

Jesus granted her request on that basis — legally she had the right to claim something from the Son of God, and legally he had the duty to give it to her. He could not deny her. Until she proved her claim, he was under no obligation to do anything for her; but once she provided proof of her family relationship, he willingly gave her what rightfully belongs only to the children of Abraham.

Questions to ask

You have to get a good understanding of the covenant first before you can start using it to decipher passages in the Bible. We can look at it like this: the first eleven chapters of the Bible, Genesis 1-11, are basically an introduction to the rest of the book. This introduction tells us the problem that all mankind has, and why God isn't happy with us. It also describes one solution to the problem — judgment and wholesale destruction on the entire earth.

Genesis 12 is the first chapter of the *new* solution to man's sin: the way of grace, forgiveness, sacrifice, the family of God. Significantly it begins with the story of Abraham, the first man who experienced this new way of dealing with sinners. His experience is the model for all the rest of God's people. The agreement that God made with him is the *same one* that he makes with *all* of his people; the faith that Abraham had is the kind of faith that we *all* must have. This is why Abraham is so important for the entire Church.

Once you understand what God did there with Abraham, you can begin looking for the covenant — and God's fulfillment of it — in the rest of the Bible. It is everywhere, if you just have the eyes to see it. Everything that God did for the people of Israel was because of the covenant with Abraham. And I hope that you have also seen that the covenant is for the Church of Christ — which means that the covenant really comes alive in the New Testament. Jesus came to fulfill that covenant in ways that the Jews hardly predicted, in ways that surprised even the most devout of them. The Gentiles finally tasted the blessings in the covenant in Christ. The end of time will be the final fulfillment of all the things that God had in mind from the beginning — and Abraham's family will then be complete.

When you read the text, therefore, look at it in terms of the covenant given to Abraham. Ask what the Lord is giving someone in this story, to whom is he giving it, what was the reason they were getting it, who didn't get it, and why it is a fulfillment of the covenant.

If you keep the covenant in mind as you read, a lot more of the events in the Bible are going to make sense to you, and you will also feel much more a part of what is going on — since the same things are promised to you as well.

Discussion Questions For Covenant

• The Jews were the original heirs of the covenant. Do they still have any claims to it? Why or why not? What do they have to hope for?

• Are the physical things promised in the covenant still things for God's people to hope for?

• What does Acts 15:5-21 teach us about the current terms of the covenant?

• What were the main points for the early Christians to learn in the story about Cornelius, a Gentile, becoming a Christian?

• What was the basis of Paul's hope in the covenant? (Remember, he was a Jew.) Does Philippians 3:2-11 say anything about this?

• How does the covenant relate to sharing the Gospel with unbelievers?

• There are threats against covenant breakers listed in Deuteronomy 28. Which covenant does this refer to? How do you know?

• Does the death of Christ have anything to do with the scene in Genesis 15?

• Look through the New Testament and see if you can find the basis for the precious promises of the Gospel in the covenant terms given to Abraham.

The Master Key:
Jesus Christ

The Master Key: Jesus Christ

Jesus Christ is the object of a Christian's faith; we believe that we need nothing else but Jesus to be saved. As Paul put it, "For I resolved to know nothing while I was with you except Jesus Christ and him crucified." (1 Corinthians 2:2) A person's faith doesn't have to be complex, or bound up in bewildering doctrine, or take years to figure out. If we have Jesus, we have everything we need.

On the other hand, Jesus is a profound reality; saying "all we need is Jesus" is like saying "all we need is the universe!" Too many people think that it's enough to say "I believe in Jesus" and that will save them. *What is it* about him that they believe? Why do they think that Jesus is all that they need? Have they looked "beneath the cover" yet and seen "how wide and long and high and deep is the love of Christ, and to know this love that surpasses knowledge?" (Ephesians 3:18-19) Do they realize that Jesus is as mysterious and as complex as the God of the Bible — that he is "the radiance of God's glory and the exact representation of his being?" (Hebrews 1:3) Do they know *how much* God has put in Christ for us? "For no matter how many promises God has made, they are 'Yes' in Christ." (1 Corinthians 1:20) They say that we must have a simple faith in Jesus, but can they say (as Paul did), "I *know* whom I have believed, and am convinced that he is able to guard what I have entrusted to him for that day?" (2 Timothy 1:12) Did they know that Jesus is the righteousness of God, the work of God, the ways of God, the names of God, the Prophet, Priest and King, and many more offices and functions?

Our "faith" needs to be more than just saying, "I believe in Jesus." We need to know who he is, and what he does. We need to know why believing in Jesus is the key to our faith. In fact, the more we know about him the more we will believe in him — faith and knowledge *must* go together when it comes to believing in Jesus. Paul said that our goal is that "we all reach unity in the faith *and* in the knowledge of the Son of God and become mature, attaining to the *whole measure* of the fullness of Christ." (Ephesians 4:13) What we need is a well-rounded, filled-out picture of who Jesus is — then our faith will be based on what we *know* about him. Then we will trust him for things that are true about him, not for things that we have made up.

Knowing Jesus — whether you mean knowing him personally or knowing facts about him — will save you and spiritually enrich you, if you use that knowledge in the way that God intended. The Gospels primarily, and of course the rest of the Bible as well, show us what is in Jesus that we can lay claim to and use. It's like buying a tool at the hardware store: it usually comes with instructions on how to use it, so that you don't have to figure it out yourself. The Scriptures teach us what is in Jesus that we can use to grow spiritually and grow closer to God. This isn't just a frill, something that we could use *if* we want to; it's the whole point of the revelation of Christ in the Word. Unless we learn the whole truth about him, and how to have faith in him, we will never get any benefit from knowing him.

That knowledge comes, of course, from studying God's Word — the Bible. In fact, this is the only purpose of the Bible — to teach us about Jesus. The whole book is about him, from first to last. This may surprise you; it certainly surprised the Jews when Jesus told them! "You diligently study the Scriptures because you think that by them you possess eternal life. These are the Scriptures that testify about me, yet you refuse to come to me to have life." (John 5:39-40) The covenant with Abraham is sealed in Christ's work, the Law talks about Christ as King and his government, the prophets announced the coming of Christ's kingdom, Joseph and David were types and examples of Christ — everything in the Old Testament teaches us something we need to know about Jesus. And of course the New Testament continues the story and teaches us much more about him that we need to know, so that our faith will be based on knowledge and not just guesses and feelings. The little pieces in the Old Testament that the saints of those days learned were actually previews or snapshots of the whole truth that is in Jesus; in the New Testament we see the entire picture brought together.

We have spent a lot of time in the Old Testament while studying the Keys, and there's a reason for this: the Old Testament is our schoolmaster that teaches us the fundamental truths about Jesus.

"So the Law was put in charge *to lead us to Christ* that we might be justified by faith." (Galatians 3:24) Now that we are in Christ, we are no longer "under the supervision of the Law," but hopefully we haven't forgotten its lessons! Paul tells Timothy that the Old Testament is "the holy Scriptures, which are able to make you *wise for salvation through faith in Christ Jesus.*" (2 Timothy 3:15) That's a remarkable statement — something that today's Christians need to take seriously, especially when they refuse to even look in the Old Testament for anything!

Why do we look at Jesus now, after studying the Ten Keys? Because everything that we have studied in the keys will find its fulfillment and clearest expression in Christ. He is "Immanuel" — "God with us." The Keys showed us in detail what our God is like and what he does; I hope you didn't miss that point. Now in Jesus our God comes to us, in person, and we should be able to see those same truths in him clearly. In fact, it's been a little difficult saving some of these points till the last chapter! There were many times when the best example of a key was to be found in the person and ministry of Christ. It helped to see the Old Testament examples of each key, but now we will see it unfold completely in Jesus.

There are two ways to look at this relationship between Christ and the Keys. The *first way* is to consider the Keys a primer to Christ — if you want a solid course on who Jesus is and the work that he does, study the Keys first, one by one. Master them, and you will understand him. Go back through the Old Testament and study each key, understand what it means and how to use it when studying a Biblical passage. Then when you get to Jesus, you will stand a better chance of understanding why he did what he did.

The *second way* that the Keys and Jesus relate is that you can see each of the Keys *in Jesus* — in everything he did and said. These Keys describe how God works, so we ought to see them in the Son of God too, in every part of the Gospels, and recognize them again in the New Testament Epistles. For instance, when a museum wants to show an exhibit that has peculiar properties that can't be seen in ordinary light, they will put it under ultraviolet light — then people can see its unique characteristics. That's what the Keys do when we look at Jesus in their light: they show us things that otherwise we would have missed about him.

If we have learned our lessons well in the Old Testament then we won't miss the point when we come to study the life of Christ. He **revealed** the Father to us, he did the same **works** that God did in the Old Testament, he did them the same **way**, people had to have **faith** in him, he did his works to get **glory**, he revealed God's **name** to the people through his ministry, he built his kingdom through **miracles**, he **prophesied** about his kingdom and set up laws to govern his people, he came to **deliver** his people, and he was the fulfillment of the **covenant** to Abraham.

So to sum up, first go to the Keys and learn *them* if you want to know more about Jesus; then when you look at Jesus, make sure you do it in light of the Keys so you don't miss anything important.

Why is it that Christ is such a rich example of all the Keys? Because he is the full expression of the works and ways of God. Hebrews says it best:

> In the past God spoke to our forefathers through the prophets at many times and in various ways, but in these last days he has spoken to us by his Son. (Hebrews 1:1)

God revealed each key in many ways in the Old Testament, but always in a "snapshot" that enticed us with the truth without showing all the truth. This means that if we aren't careful to balance everything that we read in the Old Testament, we are liable to get things wrong about God. But Jesus is the *fullness* of God; he is the balanced presentation of the facts of God. In him all these ways and works of God come together into one person. In the span of one lifetime we see all the works of God, and the ways of God, and miracles, and revelation, and the glory of God. He so perfectly displayed the Father that we do not need to look any farther for a better description of who God is. And where God is, all the Keys will be found, especially when God comes close enough to us that we can see him and touch him — then everything about him becomes plain to see.

As we study the work of Christ, there are two things that the Keys are going to do for us: **first**, they are going to explain what we see in him. When you understand the Keys well, you will begin to better understand Christ himself. The Keys explain why he did things the way he did, and what he was trying to do, and how he did them. So many people either have a superficial understanding of Christ or they don't understand him at all, because they don't know the Keys. Unless you know what the Keys of the Bible are, you can hardly expect to get the point about Jesus! He is the light that fully illustrates the meaning and importance of these Keys; if you don't know that, you will be as much in the dark about him as the Jews were who saw him and still didn't believe. (We already saw a beautiful example of this in the story of the Canaanite woman, in the *Covenant* key.)

Second, the Keys will show us the connection between Jesus and the rest of the Bible. Many Christians separate Jesus from the Old Testament, thinking that he came to start a new thing that had nothing to do with the old ways. That is *not* true. You will find in Jesus the same truths, the same God, the same ways that you read about in the Old Testament. This becomes clearer as you understand the Keys better. You will also see that Jesus was determined to do things the *same way* that God did them in the Old Testament, for some very good reasons (one being that he wanted to prove to us that he is the Son of God!). The Keys show the invisible, spiritual lines that connect all of God's truth.

Once you start understanding the Keys in the rest of the Bible — especially in the Old Testament where so much of our faith is explained and described — the story of Jesus suddenly becomes a brilliant light that shines back through that history. You will realize that he was the point all along. From the very beginning, God had in mind the reality of Christ as he shaped and formed the Israelites through all their experiences. The Jews should have realized this about Jesus when he finally came. Here was the one that their entire Bible points to! Even Gentiles can see this if they study the Old Testament carefully. When we see Jesus in the Old Testament — in other words, we see that the theme of the entire Bible is Jesus Christ and what God wants to do for all his people in his Son — that makes the Bible appear as a single book, with a single purpose.

So studying Christ in light of the Keys is going to put some substance to our faith. Instead of just "believing in Christ" in a shallow way, we will "be prepared to give an answer to everyone who asks you to give the *reason* for the hope that you have." (1 Peter 3:15)

An entire book could be written about how each key relates to Jesus Christ! There's just so much to study in this area that we can't hope to cover it all here. So, all we can do now is outline the bare essentials, the important highlights of Jesus and the Keys. You can explore the subject further on your own.

Revelation

The Gospels, of course, is the story about Jesus Christ. What we often miss, however, is that this is God that we are seeing in action, not just man.

Remember the point about revelation: *the Bible is the revelation of* **God**. Ironically this can be too simple an idea to grasp when one reads the Gospels! These books reveal *God* to us, just as much as any other book in the Bible. In this case, however, they are revealing the Son of God, who in turn is revealing his Father in Heaven.

If Jesus came only to teach us how to be more pleasing to God — in other words, if he only showed us what a good man must do — then the Gospels aren't any different (or better!) than sacred literature of other religions. Hinduism and Buddhism, for example, show us examples of "holy" men that we should imitate. But Jesus came to do something much more important than that! He revealed God to us in his own work and words; we should be able (if we have the Spirit of God, that is) to see our God in action when we look at Jesus. Only God could do these things. That's what irked the Jews so much — Jesus didn't claim to be just a holy man, but the Son of God who has come down from Heaven. "I am the living bread that came down from Heaven." (John 6:51) "You are from below; I am from above. You are of this world; I am not of this world." (John 8:23)

His claim to be divine makes his ministry special and different from other "holy" men; it also is what requires the most faith from us.

- **Jesus Christ reveals God.** Even though the Lord had revealed himself in many ways in the Old Testament — and it should have been sufficient for the

Jews to understand and believe — it remained for Jesus to come close and show us a loving God who reaches down and saves his people personally. The Old Testament information about God was good as far as it went; but it's hard to put all that together and form a picture of what God is really like. There are so many stories, and so many lessons, that it's difficult to understand God in his many roles.

Jesus solved the problem when he came and, in the span of a single lifetime, showed us the full nature of God and the kinds of things he does. You could say that he was a "summary" of the Old Testament doctrine of God. He did and said the things that the Lord has always done and said throughout history. He so clearly revealed the God of the Old Testament that the Jews should have recognized their God when they saw Jesus! He did the same works, he issued the same Law, he came to set up the same promises found in the Old Testament, his purposes were none other than those that the Lord had been predicting for thousands of years. Jesus did absolutely nothing that wasn't already revealed, promised, accomplished, symbolized or prophesied in the Old Testament! The reason for this is, of course, that he is the same God working on the same plan of salvation promised since "before the creation of the world." (Ephesians 1:4)

This is why the Gentiles who know so little about the Old Testament can know so much about the true God after studying the life of Christ. He is the Israelite God whom the Jews rejected and now he has now gone to the Gentiles with the promised salvation. It was offered to the Jews first, because this was their inheritance. Since they rejected it, the Lord now offers the same salvation to those who weren't natural children of Abraham but nevertheless are of the same faith. You must see that we have the same God — now in Christ — that the Jews had all through their history.

Jesus revealed God in the flesh — which means that he came here, within our reach, where we can see and touch him and know for sure that such a God exists.

> That which was from the beginning, which we have heard, which we have seen with our eyes, which we have looked at and our hands have touched — this we proclaim concerning the Word of life. The life appeared; we have seen it and testify to it, and we proclaim to you the eternal life, which was with the Father and has appeared to us. We proclaim to you what we have seen and heard, so that you also may have fellowship with us. And our fellowship is with the Father and with his Son, Jesus Christ. (1 John 1:1-3)

We don't need to wonder whether the Israelite God really exists. He has come to us and shown himself to us.

When he came, he did *the work of God*. " 'My food,' said Jesus, 'is to do the will of him who sent me and to finish his work.' " (John 4:34) "For the very work that the Father has given me to finish, and which I am doing, testifies that the Father has sent me." (John 5:36) Nobody else could do the kinds of things that Jesus did — for a very good reason! Only God can do such things. "No one ever spoke the way this man does." (John 7:46) He did miracles with his own finger, he set up the kingdom of God, he answered prayers, he forgave sins (see the fascinating example of this in Mark 2:1-12 where even the Pharisees admit that — "Why does this fellow talk like that? He's blaspheming! Who can forgive sins but God alone?"), he knew the minds and hearts of men and women, and many more things that only God can do.

The Jews were wrong about their God in many ways — Jesus corrected those false notions. For example, they had an unhealthy view of the Law of God. They felt that if they kept the outward requirements of the Law then God would be pleased with them. During Jesus' entire ministry he made it plain that he and his Father were *not* pleased with such a superficial understanding of the Law.

> Woe to you, teachers of the Law and Pharisees, you hypocrites! You are like whitewashed tombs, which look beautiful on the outside but on the inside are full of dead men's bones and everything unclean. In the same way, on the outside you appear to people as righteous but on the inside you are full of hypocrisy and wickedness. (Matthew 23:27-28)

There were many more false notions of theirs that he corrected. Keep in mind, however, that his wasn't the opinion of only one man; *God* was here among them, straightening out their thinking. If they really wanted to please God, then they had to listen to Jesus and do what he said.

One more thing that Jesus revealed that shocked those who saw it was the love of God. The Old Testament talked about God's love — in strong terms, too, like that of a husband for his wife. But in Jesus we see the true nature of God's love for his people. After Jesus lived and died and rose into Heaven, when the apostles gathered their wits and looked back at the event of Jesus' life and ministry, they were shocked to see God's amazing love — it staggered the imagination. Here was enough material to write books forever!

> But God demonstrates his own love for us in this: While we were still sinners, Christ died for us. (Romans 5:8)

> For I am convinced that neither death nor life, neither angels nor demons, neither the present nor the future, nor any powers, neither height nor

depth, nor anything else in all creation, will be able to separate us from the love of God that is in Christ Jesus our Lord. (Romans 8:38-39)

And I pray that you, being rooted and established in love, may have power, together with all the saints, to grasp how wide and long and high and deep is the love of Christ, and to know this love that surpasses knowledge — that you may be filled to the measure of all the fullness of God. (Ephesians 3:17-19)

Jesus showed us how far God will go to save his people. We had no idea that the Creator, the Judge of all men, the Holy One, would stoop to being one of us, call us brothers, forgive us, lift us up out of death into life, and promise us a place at his right hand as his children! It's beyond comprehension, and nobody would have expected such a deep and convincing display of love — but there it is in Jesus.

• **Jesus Christ is the perfect revelation.** In the Old Testament there were symbols, types, prophecies, mysteries, and pieces of revelations of Christ. But in the New Testament, the light shone in its full brilliance; there was no longer any mystery to our salvation. What was difficult for the Jews to piece together before was now proclaimed plainly in Jesus. What the Old Testament saints struggled to understand, the New Testament saints can understand easily because of Christ in the New Testament.

Perhaps the best example of this is the Old Testament doctrines of the Messiah and the Suffering Servant. The prophets spoke of the coming Anointed One, who would sit in David's throne and rule over the earth. But they also spoke of the Servant who would be rejected and persecuted. How can you put both of these pictures into one person? We don't know for sure, but it's likely that even the most devout of the Old Testament saints never understood this. We, of course, can understand it very well — Jesus is the King of kings, and he lived as a man and died on the cross for the sins of his people. In other words, his life reveals the truth.

Another Old Testament symbol sheds its mystery in Christ — the Passover Lamb. Since the beginning of the Jewish race the Passover has been celebrated in Jewish homes in commemoration of the Exodus from Egypt. But nobody knew that this was a type of the greater deliverance from sin and death that God would give his people in the death of Christ — a far more important salvation than bringing the Israelites out of physical slavery! It's easy to see now, however, since the true object of the Passover ceremony has come and done *his* work of deliverance.

The Old Testament dealt with issues on a physical level. Canaan was the Promised Land, the Temple was where salvation could be found, the blood of bulls and goats bought forgiveness for sinners, and so on. But now Jesus has come to reveal the spiritual depth of what the Lord had in mind for his people. "God is Spirit, and his worshipers must worship in Spirit and in truth." (John 4:24) So we now see Heaven as the Promised Land, the Heavenly Temple, and the body and blood of Christ as our sacrifice from sin and death. We also see the true spiritual depth of the Law (see Jesus' comments on this in the Sermon on the Mount — Matthew 5-7) — to the degree that, without Christ working his righteousness in us, we can never satisfy the Law's infinite demands. We need these new insights in Christ so that we won't make the same mistake that the Jews did.

• **Jesus reveals salvation.** Another thing that Jesus revealed was the process of true salvation. Though the Old Testament described what one must do to please God, we have to remember that much of this was on a physical level and it wasn't something that God intended his eternal Church to rely on. He would never expect the Gentiles, for instance, to reinstate Temple worship and live in Canaan! The physical realities were symbols of the spiritual truth, not replacements for them.

This matter was high on the list of priorities for Jesus' ministry. The first recorded act of Jesus straightening out someone's thinking about *how to be saved* is recorded in the story about the woman at the well:

> You Samaritans worship what you do not know; we worship what we do know, for salvation is from the Jews. Yet a time is coming and has now come when the true worshipers will worship the Father in Spirit and truth, for *they* are the kind of worshipers the Father seeks. (John 4:22-23)

Another thing that he revealed is this: the true danger to our souls is *sin* — which is found deep in the heart of every human being:

> "Don't you see that nothing that enters a man from the outside can make him 'unclean'? For it doesn't go into his heart but into his stomach, and then out of his body." (In saying this, Jesus declared all foods "clean.") He went on: "What comes out of a man is what makes him 'unclean.' For from within, out of men's hearts, come evil thoughts, sexual immorality, theft, murder, adultery, greed, malice, deceit, lewdness, envy, slander, arrogance and folly. All these evils come from inside and make a man 'unclean.' " (Mark 7:18-23)

He also revealed who our true father is: "You belong to your father, the devil, and you want to carry out your father's desire." (John 8:44) He knew what people really thought of him: "Why are you trying to kill me?" (John 7:19) He told us what we must do to be saved: "Come to me, all you who are weary and burdened, and I will give you rest. Take my yoke upon you and learn from me, for I am gentle and humble in heart, and you will find rest for your souls. For my yoke is easy and my burden is light." (Matthew 11:28-30) If we will only listen to Jesus and come to him to be saved, his way, we will find what our souls need.

Jesus is revelation; who could have known these things except God? Men have searched out the truth since the beginning of history, yet they haven't found any answers that can improve the state of our souls, let alone how we can get along with each other. Yet Jesus, in the short span of three years, revealed the wisdom and mind of God! What he said is counsel that brings life and light: "The words I have spoken to you are spirit and they are life." (John 6:63) This is truth that changes the heart and sets us in new directions.

Don't miss the fact that *Jesus is the revelation of God*, which means he is unique — we are not like him. So many people turn the stories of Jesus into moralisms — lessons on good things to do and bad things not to do — as if we could be like Jesus if we tried hard enough! Jesus was the *only* man who could live in perfection; if anything, his good life shows the rest of us what we are not! What we ought to learn from his perfect life is that we need his righteousness, not our own, if we hope to be pleasing to God. Jesus is the only one with God's complete approval: "This is my Son, whom I love; with him I am well pleased." (Matthew 3:17) If we want that same approval, we must go to Jesus and have *him* save us from our sins.

Lastly, the apostles in their letters understood very well the purpose of the coming of Christ. Some modern writers accuse the apostles of creating a new doctrine, truths that Jesus never preached, in order to make the Church a powerful dynamic that would overturn the Roman Empire — which, they say, wouldn't have happened if people only had the little bit of truth that Jesus himself provided. Not only is that a slander against the apostles, who only passed on faithfully what they learned from Jesus their Master (2 Peter 1:16-21; 1 John 1:1), but it shows an abysmal ignorance of the true nature of Christ. These "experts" must have clean missed the point when they read the Gospels! The apostles saw God in Christ; that's why they say such fantastic things about him. That's also why they see the same things in the Old Testament; they quote the Old Testament prophecies and types to better explain the person and work of Christ. They knew that here was their God, and their job was to make that plain to God's people.

Miracle

There were two things that Jesus did throughout his entire ministry:

> Jesus went through all the towns and villages,
> teaching in their synagogues, preaching the good
> news of the kingdom and healing every disease
> and sickness. (Matthew 9:35)

The teaching showed the wisdom of God; he revealed the truth about God's kingdom and how to enter into it. The healings, however, had to do with miracles, and that's what made his claim of being the Son of God so convincing. The miracles that Jesus did could only have been done by God himself. He expected people to believe the things he preached because of the miracles that he performed — the miracles should have convinced people that they were dealing with God here.

> Go back and report to John what you hear and see: The
> blind receive sight, the lame walk, those who have
> leprosy are cured, the deaf hear, the dead are raised, and
> the good news is preached to the poor. (Matthew 11:4-5)

Jesus expected people to *believe in him*, as one would with God, because of the miracles that they saw him perform:

> But if I do it, even though you do not believe me,
> believe the miracles, that you may know and understand
> that the Father is in me, and I in the Father. (John 10:38)

The writers of the epistles recognized the importance of miracles in Jesus' ministry.

> This salvation, which was first announced by the Lord,
> was confirmed to us by those who heard him. God also
> testified to it by signs, wonders and various miracles,

and gifts of the Holy Spirit distributed according to his
will. (Hebrews 2:3-4)

I hope you don't miss the point of all this. Remember what the
definition of a miracle is: **A miracle is what God does for us
directly, apart from natural means.** Jesus did the impossible; he
bypassed the laws of nature and did whatever he wanted to do. The
miracles were proof that Jesus was no ordinary man, nor even a
prophet, that simply went around Palestine doing good. His name was
true: *Immanuel* — "God with us" — was here doing things his way,
doing the impossible, doing what people needed and what the world
couldn't do for them.

Everything about Jesus was a miracle! His birth was a miracle,
signaling the arrival of someone from Heaven. The doctrine of the
Virgin Birth is the foundation stone of the entire life and work of
Christ, who came to build the entire kingdom of God through miracles.
It should have been a signal to everyone that his wouldn't be an
ordinary life, nor would his ministry be ordinary.

There was just no accounting for the things that Jesus did and
said, except through miracle. He "grew in wisdom and stature, and in
favor with God and man." (Luke 2:52) Where did this boy get the
wisdom to amaze the scribes and experts of the Law?

> Isn't this the carpenter's son? Isn't his mother's name
> Mary, and aren't his brothers James, Joseph, Simon and
> Judas? Aren't all his sisters with us? Where then did
> this man get all these things? (Matthew 13:55-56)

When the Spirit of God came down on him in power, he started
his public ministry by immediately doing miracles. He changed water
into wine, he walked on water, he stilled the storm with a command, he
raised the dead, he healed the blind and lame and demon-possessed, fed
thousands with a few loaves of bread, he found money in a fish's
mouth, he spoke and forced back a company of soldiers — the types of
things that he could do would impress even the hardest skeptic. No
other person in the entire Bible was the means of so many miracles in
such a short span of time.

Miracles, you will remember, are the necessary building blocks of God's kingdom. We can see from the life of Christ that the Lord performed miracles constantly; so we may conclude that he considered them to be indispensable means of building his kingdom. God's people are in desperate need of answers to their problems and the world just can't help them. As the woman with the hemorrhage discovered, after she went to many doctors and found no help, only Jesus can do what she needed. (Luke 8:43-48)

We are to learn two things about Christ through the miracles that he performed. *First*, as we've seen above, the miracles prove that he was more than man — he was the Son of God who alone can do such things. *Second*, he intends to build his entire kingdom through miracles. He didn't do those things only for the people he met during those three years! His vision, his promise, was to found the *eternal Church* on miracle work — because we need the finger of God if we want to be forgiven and live forever.

> Believe me when I say that I am in the Father and the Father is in me; or at least believe on the evidence of the miracles themselves. I tell you the truth, anyone who has faith in me *will do what I have been doing*. He will do even greater things than these, because I am going to the Father. *And I will do whatever you ask in my name*, so that the Son may bring glory to the Father. You may ask me for anything in my name, and I will do it. (John 14:11-14)

There's the promise for more miracles, and it's right in line with the work he started during his earthly ministry.

The four essentials of a miracle are clear to see in the work of Christ. **_First_**, a miracle is something that only God can do. There is no question that what Jesus did was the hand of God. "But if I drive out demons by the finger of God, then the kingdom of God has come to you." (Luke 11:20) As we saw before, this proves that Jesus is the Son of God. It also shows *who* has to solve our problems! If the kinds of problems that people had could only be solved by Jesus, then anybody (including us) who wants help must turn to Jesus for a miracle —

nothing short of that will do. Our problems require divine answers, the impossible — not the answers of the world.

Second, man can't do these things. When Jesus came there were lepers, blind men, dead people, hungry people, sinners, "lost sheep of Israel" — because nobody had been able to help these people overcome their problems yet. None of the sufferers had ever found help for their problems from the religious experts. There is no help in man; men are long on promises but short on results. The people flocked to Jesus because he had what nobody else had been able to do for them.

Third, people desperately need the miracle. When Jesus looked at the people he saw how much they needed the hand of God in their lives. "When he saw the crowds, he had compassion on them, because they were harassed and helpless, like sheep without a shepherd." (Matthew 9:36) They were dying without him; without the miraculous hand of God, they were helpless and hopeless. Jesus came to do for them what no man could do — he stood in the gap, and it was up to him to save them. "It is not the healthy who need a doctor, but the sick." (Matthew 9:12)

Fourth, it works. There were no half-way measures, no disappointing results, no failures; what Jesus did was surprising and successful. His work was so powerful that it startled people. Those who were blind could see now, as if they had never been blind. The dead came back to life. The storm was calmed. The Pharisees were dumbfounded; how could they fight against a man who did such staggering miracles and never failed at them? For example, they once hoped to catch Jesus in violation of the Law. The Law forbade anybody to work on the Sabbath; Jesus, they knew, was fond of doing his miracles on the Sabbath. But when Jesus healed a particular man his own way, immediately, in front of everyone, and made a sermon out it to boot, the Pharisees lost again! All they could do was sulk and plan how they might get rid of him in some other way; his miracles were just too powerful to fight.

> Another time he went into the synagogue, and a man
> with a shriveled hand was there. Some of them were
> looking for a reason to accuse Jesus, so they watched

him closely to see if he would heal him on the Sabbath. Jesus said to the man with the shriveled hand, "Stand up in front of everyone." Then Jesus asked them, "Which is lawful on the Sabbath: to do good or to do evil, to save life or to kill?" But they remained silent. He looked around at them in anger and, deeply distressed at their stubborn hearts, said to the man, "Stretch out your hand." He stretched it out, and his hand was completely restored. Then the Pharisees went out and began to plot with the Herodians how they might kill Jesus. (Mark 3:1-6)

If the Pharisees could keep the problem limited to arguing with Jesus about doctrine, they might win (or so they thought). But when he did these amazing miracles in front of everyone, there was no way to fight the facts.

What kinds of miracles did Jesus do? He mainly did physical miracles. There were several reasons for this: *first*, the Jews were still at the physical level as far as their understanding of God's kingdom. God had been working with them in the past through the Temple, through animal sacrifice, through the land of Canaan — and doing physical miracles among them was in line with that. It proved that God was keeping his promises concerning the physical kingdom that they had lived in all this time.

Second, they were easier to see than spiritual miracles. Jesus could have done (and still does!) many miracles among them dealing with people's sins and their souls; but who would have seen and believed except the ones he did them to? One time when Jesus actually did turn to someone's spiritual problem first, the Pharisees objected that such a thing was God's work, not man's. They were right, but they weren't giving Jesus credit for being the Son of God. Nevertheless, so that they wouldn't think that he couldn't do such a thing, he healed the man of his paralysis as well as his spiritual illness. So the physical miracle demonstrated his right and ability to do any spiritual miracle he chose to do.

"Which is easier: to say to the paralytic, 'Your sins are forgiven,' or to say, 'Get up, take your mat and walk'?

But that you may know that the Son of Man has authority on earth to forgive sins...." He said to the paralytic, "I tell you, get up, take your mat and go home." (Mark 2:9-11)

Now, however, the kingdom of God has stepped up into a spiritual level with the Gentiles being admitted to the Church. His kingdom is not *of* this world (John 18:36) although it is partially *in* this world. We don't need to build the spiritual, eternal kingdom of God with physical miracles but with spiritual miracles. Jesus made provision for this too, before he left this world —

I tell you the truth, anyone who has faith in me will do what I have been doing. *He will do even greater things than these*, because I am going to the Father. (John 14:12)

Notice that Jesus isn't doing away with miracles, but instead planning for greater miracles than the ones he did while on earth. The kingdom of God depends on miracles.

One more point about the miracles of Christ. They are a testimony to the Lord, and encouragement to us to go to him for whatever miracle he wants to do for us. We have just as many problems as the people in his day had! Whom do we turn to for help? After reading the stories of the things that Jesus did, who else *would* we turn to for help except him? Can you think of anyone better? Do you know of anybody who could do greater things than these? Isn't this a convincing demonstration of who your Savior is? If you see that, then God accomplished his purpose for recording the miracles of Christ in the Gospels.

Ways

We saw that the ways of the Lord reflect his personality; he prefers to do things a certain way, and that makes him different from other gods. And we can best get to know his ways when we live with him: the closer we get to someone, the more time we spend with them, the better we will know them and their characteristic ways of doing things.

We will never see the ways of the Lord so clearly as we do in Jesus. In the Old Testament the Israelites had to go to God through physical symbols in order to know him. But even then they couldn't get very close to him because of his utter holiness. Now in Christ God has come to us — "The Word became flesh and made his dwelling among us." (John 1:14) Now we can live *with* him, one on one, and we can see his ways plainly as we have never seen them before. "That which was from the beginning, which we have heard, which we have seen with our eyes, which we have looked at and our hands have touched — this we proclaim concerning the Word of life." (1 John 1:1)

But in getting to know him better, we will run up against things that we definitely don't like about him! It's like that with anybody: if we just have a casual acquaintance with someone, we get along fine. But if we spend much time with them, little things that they do start to get on our nerves. As time goes on, if we haven't learned to deal with their ways, we develop serious problems with them. The same is true with our relationship with the Lord — his ways will offend us. As was true of the God of the Old Testament, the God of the New Testament has ways that are *not* our ways; they are higher than our ways. (Isaiah 55:8-9) We aren't going to like the way he does things. But his ways are our *salvation*, they are our *life* — they are the only way to do things if we hope to be saved. We just have to change our ways and get in step with him.

Christ's ways always work. He used some completely unexpected methods to achieve his ends, and even though people thought he was crazy, he always achieved his ends. He knows what he is doing. Over and over people found out that his way is the best way, his way leads to life and the knowledge of God. Any other way of solving one's problems will inevitably fail.

> Therefore everyone who hears these words of mine and puts them into practice is like a wise man who built his house on the rock. The rain came down, the streams rose, and the winds blew and beat against that house; yet it did not fall, because it had its foundation on the rock. But everyone who hears these words of mine and does not put them into practice is like a foolish man who built

his house on sand. The rain came down, the streams rose, and the winds blew and beat against that house, and it fell with a great crash. (Matthew 7:24-27)

Jesus knew that he was offending people with the way he went about doing things; but he never apologized about it — he expected them to *change their ways* and follow him. He wanted them to live, not die.

Since Jesus is the Son of God, we should expect to see in him the same ways that the Lord had in the Old Testament. Let's look at his life and watch him in action:

- ***He works through his people:*** You would think that if Jesus had critical work to do in the Kingdom of God, he would do it himself. After all, can he really depend on sinners to help build a kingdom of righteousness? Can he depend on people who are ignorant of the truth of God to know the right things to do and how to do them? But he chooses to call servants from among men and women, "co-laborers" who would help him build his kingdom. He is the Master Administrator. You probably know people who can't let those under them do a simple job; they have to do it themselves before they are happy with it. Jesus, however, assigns important work to his people and *expects* them to do it well. The outcome is never in question — he gives them his Spirit, so that they know *what* to do and they *can* do it to his satisfaction — but they at least have to get busy doing it. He isn't going to do everything.

On several occasions in the Gospels we see Jesus working through others to accomplish his purposes. For example, he sent the seventy two disciples out to preach in the villages — being only one man, he himself couldn't cover all the territory necessary in such a short time. He empowered them, however, before they went out. They knew what to say, how to say it, how to act, and what to do if people rejected the message. What happened when they came back to report to him? "The seventy-two returned with joy and said, 'Lord, even the demons submit to us in your name.' " (Luke 10:17) Perhaps they didn't realize the power that they were using — their ministry worked because Jesus worked through them, through the Spirit of God.

The most unexpected and thought-provoking example of this principle is what happened at Pentecost. Jesus had by this time left earth and returned to his Father in Heaven. The disciples couldn't imagine what would happen next; they wondered why Jesus didn't "restore the kingdom to Israel." (Acts 1:6) Why did he go away and leave them alone? They didn't understand his ways of doing things, however. *They* were the ones who would carry the Gospel "in Jerusalem, and in all Judea and Samaria, and to the ends of the earth!" (Acts 1:8) Of course they couldn't do this on their own; the Lord filled them with the Spirit (Acts 2:1-4) and showed them the way to carry out their mission. But the Lord wasn't going to do it for them! If the world is ever going to hear about the grace of God in Christ Jesus, it must be through God's people — empowered and led by the Spirit, of course, but nevertheless through them.

This was something that the disciples should have expected; it was the last command of Christ while on earth.

> Therefore go and make disciples of all nations, baptizing them in the name of the Father and of the Son and of the Holy Spirit, and teaching them to obey everything I have commanded you. And surely I am with you always, to the very end of the age. (Matthew 28:19-20)

• *He works through time:* It's always amazed me that the Lord chose the way he did to bring salvation to men on earth. He could have just reached down and plucked up sinners here and there, cleansed their hearts, lifted them up to Heaven, and be done with it. But he chose instead to come personally as a human being and spend thirty three years working out the process of salvation, and then spend the next 2000 years nurturing and growing the Church.

The first thirty years of his life were strictly for preparation. If someone from our own century could have gone back in time and visited Jesus in his home town, working alongside his father Joseph in the carpenter shop, eating meals with the family — that person probably would have become extremely impatient with Jesus! Why was he so content to wait? Why didn't he announce his royal intentions at the beginning? There are several answers to this: *first*, he was growing "in wisdom and stature, and in favor with God and men." (Luke 2:52) Even though he was the Son of God, he was also the Son of Man — and "he learned obedience from what he suffered." (Hebrews 5:8) *Second*, if he would have begun his ministry in his youth, people would have considered him a child prodigy and praised him for the wrong reasons. Faith is genuine when we believe that a man *like us in every way but sin* is really the Son of God — not because a child can do amazing things.

When he finally did start his public ministry, he chose the slow route to train his followers. He took about three years to do it, teaching by word and example, step by step. They got impatient at times and wondered when he was going to make his political move; but he never gave in to their impatience. Once his own brothers urged him to go public with his views; but Jesus knew that neither the time nor the motive was right:

> The right time for me has not yet come; for you any time is right. The world cannot hate you, but it hates me because I testify that what it does is evil. You go to the Feast. I am not yet going up

to this Feast, because for me the right time has not yet come. (John 7:6-8)

When the end came, when Jesus hung on the cross dying and his disciples scattered through fear, it seemed that Jesus had waited too long and now the enemy had won. But finally at Pentecost we see the tremendous wisdom behind the Lord waiting, waiting, waiting for all these years. Now he unleashed what he had been patiently working on and hoping in — and it burst like a bombshell on the Jewish and Roman world, eventually toppling empires because of the Lord's wise planning and overwhelming power. At the end we can see the wisdom of his timing, though those with him at the time couldn't see the sense in his waiting.

• ***He wins by losing:*** We have no better example in all of Scripture of this principle than in Jesus Christ. He knew that success, ultimately, would only come at the end of a long road of seeming failure. It seems like upside-down logic, I know, but remember that his ways always work. This strategy sure did work in the history of Christ.

The prophets predicted his strategy, though nobody understood *why* someone would do things like this:

> He had no beauty or majesty to attract us to him, nothing in his appearance that we should desire him. He was despised and rejected by men, a man of sorrows, and familiar with suffering. Like one from whom men hide their faces he was despised, and we esteemed him not. (Isaiah 53:2-3)

He was born in a stable, to poor parents, with the stigma of an illegitimate birth to his name (untrue, of course, because God was his real Father). He grew up in obscurity, with no wealth or education or great reputation in his favor. When he began his ministry he preached and did miracles; he never did a thing to overthrow the government or take the reins of power from the authorities. For this he was despised and rejected even by his own disciples. Though he was the Son of God, and deserved honor and glory from every living creature on earth, he was spat on by those who didn't deserve to tie his sandals.

The crowning injustice to the person of Christ was the crucifixion, when wicked men laid hold on the Holy One and put him to death on false charges. There he was, in all his shame, apparently defeated for good. Even his disciples left him in shame and fear. And while the human spectators mocked him, the devil, we can be sure, laughed in glee at the easy victory he had just won over his eternal enemy.

They shouldn't have been so confident in their success over him. The shame and crucifixion of Christ was a heavy blow that many souls will pay for dearly in eternity; there was nothing imaginary or shallow about that bloody loss. But in that very defeat was his complete victory over his enemies. It was in the *cross* that sinners find forgiveness, by God's decree; in that *blood* we are washed clean of our sins. By *dying* he set the stage for the resurrection, which is our hope. In his *death*, we live.

And as for the devil and his works, the death of Christ was like an atomic blast right in his face! Completely unexpected, Jesus destroyed the works of the devil in his crucifixion by opening the gates of death and Hades and letting the captives go free. The kingdom of darkness sustained a mortal blow on that day from which it will never recover. It was the beginning blast of a series of attacks carried on by the Church of Christ that will one day completely destroy the works of the devil.

It doesn't make sense to us that someone can win by losing, but we can't argue with something that works. "I tell you the truth, unless a kernel of wheat falls to the ground and dies, it remains only a single seed. But if it dies, it produces many seeds." (John 12:24) We can only look amazed at what Jesus accomplished by his life of suffering and death, and thank God that he knows what he is doing. And we should expect to follow him in that same way, since it works so well: "Anyone who does not take his cross and follow me is not worthy of me." (Matthew 10:38)

• ***He works through his Spirit:*** When Jesus began his ministry, the first thing he did was receive the power of the Spirit of God. "And as he was praying, Heaven was opened and the Holy Spirit descended on him in bodily form like a dove." (Luke 3:21-22) The type of work he was to do, we would do well to notice, was to be done *in the Spirit*.

Remember that the Spirit does two things: *first*, he reveals the things of God so that we can see them. Physical eyes can't see the world of God, but the eyes of the soul can if the Spirit gives life and opens its eyes. *Second*, the Spirit empowers — he makes it possible for a person to live and walk in the presence of God and do things that please God.

Jesus did both these things in his ministry: he revealed the Father and his spiritual world to those who had "eyes to see and ears to hear", and he empowered people to live and obey. That's what the miracles were all about. He also never used the weapons of this world to achieve his ends or fight off the enemy; he knew that would be useless. The weapons of the Spirit are far more powerful than the weapons that this world can muster in defense. For example, he spoke the *Word of God* (which is elsewhere in the Scriptures called the "sword of the Spirit" — Ephesians 6:17, see also Hebrews 4:12) and enemies cringed in fear and followers rejoiced. He was careful to do things in such a way as to ensure success; therefore he relied on the Spirit on all occasions.

He also promised his followers that he would pour out that same Spirit on them so that they would continue his work, in the way he prefers that it be done. It first happened at Pentecost (Acts 2:1-4) — that's what makes that day so special in the history of the Church. They will be filled with the Spirit, empowered by the Spirit, taught by the Spirit, led and counseled by the Spirit — every blessing that is promised us in Christ comes by way of the Spirit of God. And our own work must also depend completely on the Spirit of God. If it is, it will be Jesus working through us (since he works through the Spirit) instead of our own works which are unable to achieve anything that would please our Father in Heaven.

There is one thing that we should keep in mind about Jesus' ways. Since he was so close to us, close enough that we can easily learn how he likes to do things, this should help us see those same ways in the things that God did in the Old Testament. He is the best and clearest revelation of the ways of the Lord. Use that which is the easiest to see and understand to help you get the meaning of other passages of Scripture that aren't as easy to get hold of. You will see these same ways in the Old Testament stories of God, since Jesus is the Son of God and does all things the same way as his Father does.

Works

If we accept the fact that Jesus is the Son of God, we should expect to see him doing the works of God. If he does, that would be the greatest proof of who he is and where he came from that we could possibly ask for.

Remember that the point of the works of God is this: they are things that only God can do. No man, no matter how powerful or wise or influential he may be, can hope to do the things that God does. Man has his own works to do, but there are many things that we must not do or even try to do, because they are the sole domain of God. We would be stealing his glory and pretending to be God if we dare to attempt them.

The Jews, of course, knew this was true — they were very jealous of God's honor and they gave him alone the glory of being who he is. But in their zeal for the uniqueness of their God, they closed their ears to the testimony of Jesus Christ when he appeared among them. He claimed right from the beginning to do the works of God. " 'My food,' said Jesus, 'is to do the will of him who sent me and to finish his work.' " (John 4:34) "I have testimony weightier than that of John. For the very work that the Father has given me to finish, and which I am doing, testifies that the Father has sent me." (John 5:36) The Jews knew immediately what he was claiming in these statements — he was claiming to be the Son of God, because he did the works of God. That's why they were so offended with him, not because he was doing good for those in need. "For this reason the Jews tried all the harder to kill him; not only was he breaking the Sabbath, but he was even calling God his own Father, making himself equal with God." (John 5:18)

But Jesus used this fact constantly as proof of his claim. "But if I drive out demons by the Spirit of God, then the kingdom of God has come upon you." (Matthew 12:28) And when John the Baptist wondered if Jesus was the promised Messiah, Jesus sent this proof back to him:

> Go back and report to John what you hear and see: The blind receive sight, the lame walk, those who have leprosy are cured, the deaf hear, the dead are raised, and the good news is preached to the poor. Blessed is the man who does not fall away on account of me. (Matthew 11:4-6)

Notice that last comment: he knows that many people will look at him *as a man*, even though he has done all these miracles, and refuse to give him the glory he deserves as the Son of God.

It's not hard to see that the things that Jesus did are different from any works that other men have done. Nobody has given us the true meaning of the Law as Jesus did. (Matthew 5-7) Nobody has raised people from the dead by speaking. Nobody has ever stilled a storm with a command. Nobody has ever spoken and opened the eyes of the blind. The works of Jesus are unique among all the works of all men in all history; none of the rest of us have been able to even begin to do the things that he did. It amazes me to hear modern liberals teach that the only thing to learn about Jesus is that he is our example of how to live. Not only are we unable to be perfect as he was, we also can't do the works that he did — *because he is God*, and we aren't.

What were the works of Christ? The same things that we saw in the Key of the works of the Lord. Here are those seven groups again:

- **Creation and Providence:** Jesus created things from nothing — he usually used a base to start from, but the starting point certainly had nothing to do with the result! He made wine from water, and he made bread for thousands of people from a few loaves. He also took care of his people, which is what we mean by Providence. For example, he told Peter where to find a coin to pay his taxes with (in a fish's mouth!), he gave food to the hungry, he healed sickness, he took care of all kinds of needs that people had. These were things that only God could do for his creatures.

  Does he still do these works for us? Absolutely! He creates a new heart in us, makes us into a "new creation" — turns a sinner into a saint and a rebel into a servant. He continues to provide for our needs, so much so that Paul could say that "I can do everything through him who gives me strength." (Philippians 4:13) In Christ is everything we need for faith and holiness. Read the New Testament Epistles for a complete description of Christ's continuing work of Creation and Providence in the Church and in individuals' lives.

- **The making of Israel:** When Jesus began his ministry, he started picking out people to be in his new Kingdom. He called out certain men to be his disciples. He went to "sinners and tax collectors" and gave them the Good News. He went to the sick, the dead, the helpless, the poor, the humble — and with them formed a new Church with himself as the Head. There were many who were not part of this new Kingdom, the Pharisees and teachers of the Law for example, and the Romans (with a few notable exceptions!). But the family of God grew larger as Christ called more and more out of darkness and into light. He made them children of the light, with rights to the inheritance of Heaven. This is Israel, as God sees it; Jesus was making a new nation out of the Israelites, a faithful "remnant."

The New Testament Epistles make this plainer, in case we can't understand what Jesus was doing in the Gospels. Paul said that in Christ the two warring factions — the Jews and the Gentiles — come together in one body, making one family. (Ephesians 2:11-22) Now we see what God had in mind when he first promised to make himself a people: they are from every nation and tribe, and they are all one in the Lord Jesus Christ.

• **Judgment:** Jesus often demonstrated his insight into men's hearts. Only God can see the heart as it really is; the rest of us have to go on appearances and actions. But Jesus, being the Son of God, doesn't have our limitations. He could tell when someone was lying, or saying things behind his back. He caught the Pharisees doing this all the time. When the rich young ruler came to him about eternal life — and confidently claimed to have done all the Law — Jesus knew that this man's heart was in poor spiritual condition. Just a little test was all it took to expose the man's true condition to all who were watching. (Matthew 19:16-22)

Jesus still judges men's souls. John wrote that Jesus' "eyes were like blazing fire." (Revelation 1:14) He also examines the Churches (Revelation 2-3) and tells them what they are doing right and what they are doing wrong. Only God can judge the heart like that.

• <u>**The coming of Christ:**</u> Of course the plans for Christ's first coming were all laid out before he arrived. We're not told exactly how the Father and the Son worked together on this project during the times of the Old Testament; we know that the Son of God had a lot to do with the preparations for the Incarnation because the New Testament tells us so. But when Christ stepped onto the stage of history prepared for him, he never hesitated a single instant — he knew exactly what to do at all times. He knew, for example, the prophecies about his person and work and did all things to make sure those prophecies were fulfilled. He knew the mind of the Father, he knew the works that the Father had prepared for him, and he never let a man or circumstance get in the way of doing all that he came to do. Even when Peter tried to get him to turn away from certain death in Jerusalem, Jesus' words showed his amazing insight, purpose and determination: "Get behind me, Satan! You are a stumbling block to me; you do not have in mind the things of God, but the things of men." (Matthew 16:23)

Nothing was accidental to Christ, nothing was a surprise. Everything went according to plan. It was so well done that his last words were, "It is finished!" So he was just as much a participant in his great work as the Father. But then did he leave all this behind and go off for a vacation? No — all that work also included the laying of the foundation for the Church, work that we still benefit from today. He is still working out the details for his spiritual kingdom: fitting the Church together so that it will be a fit house for God to live in, and the Second Coming when he plans to wrap everything up.

• <u>**Building the Kingdom:**</u> The first sermon that Jesus preached after he started his official ministry was this: " 'The time has come,' he said. '*The kingdom of God is near*. Repent and believe the good news!' " (Mark 1:15)

The reason he started out like this is because he was the King, coming to assume the government. The prophet Isaiah predicted what he would come to do:

> For to us a child is born, to us a son is given, and *the government will be on his shoulders*. And he will be called Wonderful Counselor, Mighty God, Everlasting Father, Prince of Peace. Of the increase of his government and peace there will be no end. He will reign on David's throne and over his kingdom, establishing and upholding it with justice and righteousness from that time on and forever. (Isaiah 9:6-7)

He went right to work. He laid the Law down in the Sermon on the Mount. He protected his people by fighting off the enemy. He fed and cared for his people, as any good king would do. He picked and trained workers to proclaim his Word and decrees. He judged men's hearts. He did all the things that a king would be expected to do when he comes to assume the throne.

He still rules — over the Church, of course, as its Head and Lord. We are to do *his* will, not ours, and he tells us his will through his Word and Spirit. He still takes care of us as our King, and we are to trust in and depend on him for real grace, real help in time of need, instead of other rulers who promise much but deliver little.

• **The Last Day:** Jesus talked a good deal about the Last Day. Not only did he tell us what would happen then, he plans to be there heading up the whole thing! He promised to give rewards to those who faithfully served him; and I hope you realize that only God can rightfully promise someone the treasures of God. He warned people that they would face him on Judgment Day; therefore be careful of their words and actions. Paul tells us that Jesus is there, now, at the right hand of the throne of God, putting his enemies under his feet.

And in Revelation we see the Lamb on the Throne of God, receiving glory and honor and holding in *his* hand the judgment of all men and all the earth. Paul said that "we must all appear before the judgment seat of Christ, that each one may receive what is due him for the things done while in the body, whether good or bad." (2 Corinthians 5:10) On that day, people will finally realize that Jesus was no ordinary man: he was God in the flesh, and they should have taken him more seriously.

• **Scripture:** Obviously the words of Christ became Scripture — the Gospels that we now have — and what he said was no accident but on purpose, for the benefit of the entire Church. What we may not realize at first, however, is that these were the words of God himself — not just of a man. Though modern unbelievers don't give Jesus credit for being more than a man, and having the wisdom of men, the Bible claims otherwise. Jesus himself is the "Word of God"; anything he says is directly from the mouth of God. This is true even in a mystical sense, in that the *person* of Christ and all his *works* are the Word of God too — God said that such and such will be done, and Jesus did it. He himself said that his words are *life* — a statement that no man could possibly make. Too often we read the words of Christ as if they were just counsel that we can take or leave at our discretion. They aren't: this is *God* talking to you. You must hear and obey, trust and follow. The words of Christ, and by definition the words he gave his disciples in the letters that they wrote, are God's sole message to the Church.

If these are the things that Jesus did, then surely God was here doing his work!

There are two points to keep in mind about the works of Christ. *First*, there were many things that he did while he was on earth, that are recorded in the Gospels. Those are his finished works for the sake of the entire Church. That work built the foundation of God's eternal kingdom and laid the first course of stones to form the walls, so to speak. The rest of us depend on what he did then — not that he will do it again, or that he still does it among us, but they made possible the faith that we now have. But there are also many things that he does *now*, through the ages of the Church, beginning with the time of the apostles and finally ending at Judgment Day. For example, he lives to intercede for his people before the Throne of Grace. (Hebrews 7:25) If he didn't do that, God wouldn't show us any mercy. He also rules his Church, he is destroying the works of the devil, he is putting his enemies under his feet, he is preparing a place for us in Heaven, and many more things that we learn from the Epistles of the New Testament. In other words, his work is not done! We also hope and depend on that work.

Second, the Lord showed us all, in the works recorded in the Gospels, what he can and will do for his people everywhere and through all time. We tend to forget that he is the Lord of us all; he didn't do these things only for the people in his day but for all of us. The feeding of the thousands from a few loaves of bread is a good example. It's obvious that he met *their* immediate needs, but how does that help us now? Well, he said in another place that he himself is the bread from Heaven that will be available to all of God's children — and if we want to live, we must "eat the flesh of the Son of Man and drink his blood." (John 6:53) He also set up a mechanism in that story that perhaps you may have missed. When the disciples protested that the people were too far away from town to get food easily, Jesus answered them with a challenge: "They do not need to go away. *You* give them something to eat." (Matthew 14:16) That of course puzzled them. Then Jesus blessed the bread and "gave them to the disciples, and the disciples gave them to the people." (Matthew 14:19) There's the mechanism: he gives to the disciples, and they give to us. Is this still the way things work? Yes! Our food is the Word of God, the testimony that the apostles got from the Lord and carefully recorded for our sake. Every time we read the story of Jesus, we are eating at the disciples' hands who got it straight from the Lord. Faith sees that.

Glory

We learned about glory that it is a matter of giving credit where credit is due. And in God's case, it is also his overwhelming presence, that thing about him that makes us fear him and feel as nothing compared to him.

But we also learned that God gets very little glory from man. Though he fully deserves credit for doing everything for us, we don't recognize his importance in our world — we attribute circumstances and the flow of history to chance, luck, the weather, our own wisdom and skill — anything but God.

Jesus is, again, the best example of the Key in every way. There is more to Jesus Christ than the human mind can possibly conceive; he is the Son of God, and he deserves credit for being everything that this world and the Church have ever needed and ever will need. But the story of the glory of Christ as it appeared among men became the biggest letdown in all history! Incredibly, yet predictably and true to form, men refused to give him glory.

It says in Hebrews that Jesus is the perfect statement of the glory of God. "The Son is the radiance of God's glory and the exact representation of his being." (Hebrews 1:3) In other words, though we learn much about God in the Old Testament, we will see it best in the person and work of Christ.

There are two ways to see glory in Jesus Christ. ***First***, Christ himself was glorious. Everything he did demonstrated his perfect knowledge, his awesome power, his unerring judgment, his amazing love, his fierce wrath and irresistible power against his enemies — here was a force and presence to be reckoned with. Everywhere he went, people were amazed at what he did and said.

No one ever spoke the way this man does. (John 7:46)

Where did this man get this wisdom and these miraculous powers? (Matthew 13:54)

The people were amazed at his teaching, because he taught them as one who had authority, not as the teachers of the law. (Mark 1:22)

There is a prophecy in Isaiah that everyone knows — we hear it every Christmas season, though few people realize the significance of what it's saying. The prophet told of the time when Jesus would come to claim the throne, and shoulder the government of God's people. When he comes, the prophet said, he will prove to be more than anybody expected:

> And he will be called Wonderful Counselor, Mighty
> God, Everlasting Father, Prince of Peace. (Isaiah 9:6)

These names reflect the kinds of things that Jesus can do and what he is like. Do you see anything here that a normal man, even though he has every advantage in this world he could hope for, could possibly do? These claims are beyond our abilities! Yet Isaiah didn't hesitate to attach these names to Jesus Christ, who alone can do what these names declare. He is the *Wonderful Counselor* — when he counseled someone, they heard the mind and wisdom of God, and there was life in listening to him and obeying his every instruction. When he performed miracles, he showed how *mighty* he is to save his people and defeat his enemies. In him the Jews saw the Old Testament God that they said they believed in; the *Everlasting Father* revealed himself in the work that Christ did on earth. Finally, the Lord set up a spiritual kingdom, complete with redeemed saints chosen to inherit eternal life, which would last forever — thus proving his name the *Prince of Peace*.

Now Jesus always did say that he didn't come to glorify himself. "If I glorify myself, my glory means nothing. My Father, whom you claim as your God, is the one who glorifies me." (John 8:54) If he would have given himself the credit for everything he did, he would have ruined the whole purpose of his coming: to reveal the God of the Old Testament to the Jews who claimed to believe in him. He didn't get glory by drawing attention to himself, but by doing the works of God the Father who sent him. In that act of submission to the Father, he got the credit for being *from* God and the *Son* of God. Nobody else could glorify the Father in the way that he did.

<u>Second</u>, the Lord Jesus Christ also glorified the Father as well as himself. If we only had the Old Testament, we would know a great deal about God and be better off for it. But that wasn't enough to enter Heaven with. The spiritual descendants of Abraham need more than the Old Testament types and shadows, the symbols and promises. They need to see this God who had been hiding himself in parables and stories and mysteries and promises.

When Jesus came and showed them the Father, they didn't just hear news about God — they were in the very presence of the LORD of Israel. They were awed by his authority; he taught "as one who had authority." (Mark 1:22) He skillfully manipulated the religious leaders who could do nothing to stop him. He commanded demons, and they (in fear) obeyed him immediately. When soldiers came to arrest him, they fell back on the ground, helpless in *his* hands, when he said "I am he." There was something about Jesus that changed the atmosphere wherever he went; he was no ordinary man. This is the glory of God's presence.

Jesus also glorified God by the things he taught and did. He was careful to give God glory for the things that he deserves glory for. "No one is good — except God alone." (Luke 18:19) "Be perfect, therefore, as your Heavenly Father is perfect." (Matthew 5:48) "For I did not speak of my own accord, but the Father who sent me commanded me what to say and how to say it." (John 12:49) "If you, then, though you are evil, know how to give good gifts to your children, how much more will your Father in Heaven give good gifts to those who ask him!" (Matthew 7:11) We can't begin to list all the things that Jesus gave God credit for.

Christ's works, too, showed the glory of God. "I have brought you glory on earth by completing the work you gave me to do." (John 17:4) His wisdom reveals just how much God knows about us and what we must do to be saved. His miracles demonstrate the method that God prefers to use to build his kingdom. His love shows the heart of God, and what he will do for his people. We have to get rid of whatever preconceived notions we might have about what God is really like, and listen as Jesus straightens out the story for us. Finally, in the person and work of Christ, God is going to get the glory — the credit — that he deserves. If the Old Testament confused anybody about what God is like, they can learn the truth in Christ.

Now for the incredible letdown. Though Jesus deserved all glory for being from Heaven, for being the Son of God, for coming to do the work of God, he got little credit for any of that. Though he revealed the Father in profound ways, so that anybody who wishes will find the Father in him and find salvation from sin and death, hardly anybody came to him for that. They would rather die than come to him to have life. They ignored his words and held onto their false notions about God. Jesus was rejected wholesale by almost everyone he came in contact with. The Jews — God's very own people whom he called out of Egypt and prepared for this day of the Messiah — rejected Jesus. The disciples left him in his hour of suffering. The Romans mocked him and crucified him. Pilate looked straight at him and didn't see the truth of God that he was looking for. He died on the cross, shamed, forsaken even by his Father, and mocked by the devil as well.

That's not all! After his death, though the disciples testified to his resurrection, stories were circulated that Jesus' body was actually stolen and the disciples really made the resurrection thing up — a falsehood that the Jews still believe. Speaking of the Jews, they still call him "the Bastard" (that's their word, capitalized and all, not mine!) because they think he was born out of wedlock — not as the Gospel stories claim. Men and nations all around the world, all through history, have heard about Jesus and laughed at his "naive" ideas about a kingdom. People still reject his counsel, refuse to follow his ways, they mock and persecute his followers, they even use his name as a curse word! It's incredible how much glory Jesus deserves and how little he actually gets. He has always been, and will always be (as long as this world goes on), the most misunderstood and most despised man that ever lived. In him the glory of God shines the brightest, yet almost nobody sees it; they only see something worthless instead.

He knew this would happen, though. We don't have to feel sorry for him; it's not as if he tried and failed, and now he is in Heaven licking his wounds. Remember that he wins by losing — he was crucified "from the foundation of the world", and was well-prepared for the poor reception that he got. He often made reference to this unfortunate but expected situation: "Only in his hometown and in his own house is a prophet without honor." (Matthew 13:57) "The Son of Man will go just as it is written about him." (Matthew 26:24) "If the world hates you, keep in mind that it hated me first." (John 15:18)

He was willing to set aside his glory to save souls. Once when the disciples reported that a certain town refused to let him in to preach, they asked him to pray down fire from Heaven and destroy that town. Actually that fits in with God's glory: anybody who refuses to glorify God is going to be destroyed, someday; they deserve it for such an insult. But Jesus' answer was typical of his "later, not now" approach.

> When the disciples James and John saw this, they asked, "Lord, do you want us to call fire down from Heaven to destroy them?" But Jesus turned and rebuked them, and they went to another village. (Luke 9:54-56)

Now is the day of salvation, not judgment. Thank God that he is willing to put off getting glory, or credit, for everything that he is. If he was impatient about getting glory, he would have destroyed the earth long ago and made things right. But "he is patient with you, not wanting anyone to perish, but everyone to come to repentance." (2 Peter 3:9) That is the *only* reason he hasn't insisted on getting all the credit due him *now*.

Someday, though, the situation will change. We mustn't underestimate God's passionate longing for glory. He does everything to that end, and whatever credit he didn't get along the way he *will* get at the end of time. He has been waiting for a long time for the Last Day! On that day he will get everlasting glory — and Jesus will be at the center of it all. "Look, he is coming with the clouds, and every eye will see him, even those who pierced him; and all the peoples of the earth will mourn because of him." (Revelation 1:7) On that day, people will realize that Jesus was God's Word to mankind, and they should have taken him seriously. They don't serve him now, but they will all serve him then — either in eternal misery or in eternal bliss.

> Therefore God exalted him to the highest place and gave him the name that is above every name, that at the name of Jesus every knee should bow, in Heaven and on earth and under the earth, and every tongue confess that Jesus Christ is Lord, to the glory of God the Father. (Philippians 2:9-11)

In other words, God will finally be satisfied that everything is finished when Jesus gets the glory he deserves.

Faith

Many, if not all, who read about Jesus feel that his story is uncomplicated and easy to understand. After all, isn't it all there in the Bible where anybody can read it? The life of Jesus is clearly laid out in the Gospels for all to see. The prophets predicted exactly what he would do when he came; there was plenty of forewarning. The New Testament Epistles discuss every angle about Jesus, so that by the time we get to the end of the Bible we could consider ourselves experts on the subject of Christ.

Yet in spite of the overwhelming material about him, even though his entire person and work have been carefully explained in the Bible, we can still not see the point about him. Take the Pharisees for an example. They knew what the prophets had to say about the Messiah; they were experts in the Law (they certainly knew more about it than we do!), and they didn't need anybody to tell them what it said. They also saw Jesus work and teach for three years, first-hand. They were eyewitnesses of Christ. Yet they never saw who Jesus really was, nor did they put their faith in him. That's the problem right there: though they saw with their eyes, they couldn't see him in faith.

Faith is living in the light of God's world. It is being able to see, with spiritual eyesight, the things of God as they really are. Remember that it isn't just believing that certain doctrines are true, that the Bible says things that we hold as fact. The devil believes those same facts! When we have faith, our souls are made alive to the things of God — we know for certain that God exists, that he rewards those who seek him with the treasures of Heaven. (Hebrews 11:6) When the Lord shines his spiritual spotlight on our world, we see its true nature and turn away from it; we learn to trust him instead of putting our hope in anything or anybody in this world.

Seeing Jesus for who he really is requires a faith that is beyond the ability of man. It was hard enough for the Israelites to live by faith in the Old Testament — especially when many of the promises were on a physical level where anybody could see and touch them. But everything about Jesus on the physical level was misleading; nobody who saw him would have guessed that this was the Son of God with treasures from Heaven, able to save the soul. As we have already seen, he laid aside his glory and for a while appeared in the flesh, as a man, humble and obedient to his Father's will, walking the way of suffering and shame all the way to the cross. Anybody who looked at Jesus through a purely physical viewpoint could only see an aspiring prophet who failed in the end, because he refused to use reasonable ways to achieve his ends. And that's exactly what *almost everyone* saw in him.

But along the way there were a few who saw beyond the physical appearances — they saw the Son of God methodically, surely, wisely, skillfully reaching his goal in spite of the odds. The first ones who saw through the "veil of flesh" to the true meaning of his life were the wise men who came to worship him at his birth. The next incident was the time his parents took him to the Temple, where Simeon and Anna blessed God for having seen and touched — the Messiah.

> Sovereign Lord, as you have promised, you now dismiss your servant in peace. For my eyes have seen your salvation, which you have prepared in the sight of all people, a light for revelation to the Gentiles and for glory to your people Israel. (Luke 2:29-32)

It says that Jesus' parents marveled at what Simeon said about him, because they certainly didn't see that in their baby boy. It's because Simeon's eyes were opened to see the spiritual reality in Jesus, and what was going to happen because of him.

Very few people really saw the true nature of Christ; those instances stand out clearly when they did happen. For example, the Roman centurion surprised Jesus with his faith: he could see Jesus was the Master, able to command sickness in authority. Jesus responded that he had never met such great faith as his. (Matthew 8:10) And another time when Jesus asked his disciples who they thought he was, Peter answered *in faith*:

You are the Christ, the Son of the living God. (Matthew 16:16)

Jesus knew that Peter didn't see this on his own; rather his eyes were opened to the spiritual realities of God's world:

> Blessed are you, Simon son of Jonah, for this was not revealed to you by man, but by my Father in Heaven. (Matthew 16:17)

But these instances were rare, just as they are in our own day. People still don't see the truth about Jesus. Even many who claim to be his followers don't really see him in faith; they continue to follow their own will (even though he is King), they judge things by their own standards (even though he is the Wisdom of God), they struggle with their sins alone and try to reform themselves (even though he is the Savior), and so on.

Everything that Jesus did and said requires faith. Without faith he makes no sense at all, and we aren't inclined to rely on him for anything. But with faith he becomes our everything, the answer for every problem, the supply for every need, the truth that we've been looking for. If someone believes in Jesus, they need nothing else — because he is everything to them. Only faith is going to get a hold of the spiritual treasure in Jesus like that.

We can trace the steps of faith (as our father Abraham discovered them — see Romans 4) in our relationship with Christ. Those steps are the following:

- **God speaks his Word to us:** Jesus *is* the Word of God — "In the beginning was the Word, and the Word was with God, and the Word was God." (John 1:1) This is what God has to say to men all over the world, in every culture and time. He is the last word from God, the complete Word of God — we need look no farther than Jesus if we want to know what God has to say to us. This means that we have to pay close attention to whatever Jesus said, because God isn't going to say it twice. And what a message! He brought news from Heaven; he revealed the heart of God; he brought the Kingdom of God and set up its government; he calls people to change sides and leave the world of darkness and enter into the world of light — God's light. There is more to Jesus than just the words he spoke. We have to meditate on all his works, his becoming a man, his claims to divinity, how he fulfilled prophecy, and the promises he made for the future.

• **We want what he promises us:** Incredibly, most people aren't at all interested in what Jesus has to say, nor in what he offers those who follow him. The glitter and shallow promises of the world are just too strong a temptation for them, especially when they can't see the things that Jesus is talking about. But that's the whole point about true faith: someone who has faith has seen the reality of the glory of God in Christ, and that's what he wants. They don't see the carpenter's son anymore, but the King of kings, the glorious Lord who has all power and wisdom, opening up the treasuries of Heaven itself to those who will lay claim to them. When we see the preciousness of the things of God in Christ, the empty glitter of this world becomes like trash to us. We willingly follow him, even carrying a cross, if we can have what we see in him.

• **We face the impossibility of it:** Not that we become dreamers! Faith isn't a matter of dreaming or hoping for gold mountains that don't exist. Many people think that Christians make up all of this stuff about Jesus and being saved. But someone who has seen the Lord in his glory knows that it isn't myth or fancy or imagination; it is real enough to base one's life upon. Faith sees something real — it is there, in God's world, and now we know that it exists. Faith knows that there is much more to Jesus than meets the eye. He is the King, he is light, he is bread, he is the Wisdom of God — though ordinary sight can't sense any of that.

What most people do see, however, is that there is nothing in Jesus that would interest us. He isn't here on earth now but away somewhere in Heaven (if we even acknowledge that he still lives!) where he isn't involved with us anymore. His promises don't work, they aren't realistic, his ways are foolish, we make enemies when we follow him, he told us to do things that put our comforts and materialism at risk — nothing about Jesus makes any sense to the eye of flesh. Not only that, how can we believe that a man who lived 2000 years ago can be *our* savior? Believing in him now is like heading into a dead end with your life. The options in our modern world look much more realistic.

Faith knows that these things are true from the world's point of view. There's no sense ignoring the problems. In fact, there is great wisdom in seeing these impossibilities, because otherwise we wouldn't get a true picture of what Jesus really is. When we see that *there is nothing about Jesus from a physical point of view that can help us*, we are in a better position to focus on the way we have to approach Jesus — *spiritually*, through the Spirit, apart from the way we normally do things. "So from now on we regard no one from a worldly point of view. Though we once regarded Christ in this way, we do so no longer." (2 Corinthians 5:16) When you see what he *isn't*, then you can start taking advantage of what he *is*.

• **We wait:** Everything about Jesus and his ministry taught us the important lesson of waiting. He waited for all kinds of things: he patiently put up with people who didn't give him glory, or believe his words, knowing that the day would come when those things would happen. He followed his Father's instructions without running ahead and doing his own thing to speed the process up. He also taught us to wait on him — our reward for following him is going to come in the future, but not now. Even answers to our prayers might not come right away but only after we keep asking for them. The reason he was so willing to wait for things, and why he wants us to wait too, is because the reward that God has for his people is not of this world. (Hebrews 12:2) It is a spiritual reward; it will come in its full glory when there is a new heavens and new earth, when the saints are made completely righteous, when justice is finished and the wicked dealt with forever. Then Jesus plans to lead his people into the joy of the reward that has been waiting on them for ages.

• **We won't try it ourselves:** The work that Christ did ought to convince us of one thing: he is certainly capable of doing what we can't do. We have tried all our lives to solve our problems, to ease our consciences, to avoid sin — and gotten nowhere after all our efforts. If we had done anything at all that God would be pleased with, he wouldn't have felt it necessary to send someone to save us! But most people don't see that, and they keep trying anyway.

Some, however, give up — and let Jesus do it for them. If we are willing to wait for the reward that Jesus promises us, then we aren't going to try to do things that only God can do. That's easy to do once we see how completely successful Jesus is in changing the heart and leading us in the way of life. He has answers from Heaven that this world can't match. This world can't do the will of God, nor can it satisfy the needs of our souls. Nor can we do anything to help ourselves with our deepest spiritual needs. When we see that, we will wait on Jesus to give us what we need.

This is what it means to live by faith in the Son of God. It doesn't mean what many think it means — to just believe that he lived once, that he was a good man, that he said some wise things, or even to expect Jesus to give us a few blessings when we want them. Faith looks for and *finds* the Son of God, and will not let go of him until he blesses us with the treasures of Heaven. Anything short of that isn't true faith.

Jesus is so beyond the understanding of sinful men that it's never a question whether someone has faith in him. Faith is startling and unexpected when it happens, and it changes one's life completely. Many Christians who are honest consider faith to be a work of God, because we would never see the glory of Christ otherwise. People are either for him or against him; they are either in the light or in the darkness. When a person has faith, he sees a spiritual reality — and what he sees changes his life forever. It's not a matter of doctrines or feelings or hopes or guesses; he knows the truth because he sees it. How can you doubt what you have seen? But what we see requires a complete change of lifestyle, a change of friends and work and interests and emotions. We won't look the same as we did before we had faith. That's why Jesus said that it's simple to see if someone has faith — it's a matter of checking what kind of fruit comes from their lives. A fruit tree will yield the fruit peculiar to its kind; believers live in a way that pleases God, and they demonstrate by their lives that they know that the Kingdom of God is real and they must prepare for its coming. Paul said it like this: "The righteous will live by faith." (Romans 1:17)

Paul also discusses what this faith in Christ will bring us: righteousness. Being righteous means that God approves of us and allows us into his presence. Without righteousness — in other words, if we are still in our sin — we not only aren't allowed into his presence (and that means that prayer is impossible, and so is getting anything good from him) but he will hunt us down as an enemy! But with righteousness we can come to him without fear and he will give us what we ask. How in the world will a sinner and rebel get this kind of standing with the Holy God? The answer is in the precious righteousness of Christ. As we believe in him — which means we see his glory, we come to him as he has commanded, we lay down our arms against him, we plead for his mercy, we cling to his offer of free grace, and we do his will — God lays the perfect righteousness of Christ upon us (though we don't deserve it, this is what Jesus bought for us on the cross — the gift of his righteousness for all those who believe in him) and we become righteous in God's sight. "This righteousness from God comes through faith in Jesus Christ to all who believe." (Romans 3:22) There is much in this transaction that we don't have time to explore here in this short space; it would be a good study for you to see the importance of faith in our relationship to Christ. Romans is a good book to start with.

Christ also showed us how to live by faith by the way he lived. Remember that he set aside his glory, left the Father's side in Heaven, and came to earth where everything works on a physical level. To do what he had to do required an unfailing vision of Heaven, of the Father's will, of the "hope held out before him." (Hebrews 12:2) He had to see God's world clearly, at all times, so that this world wouldn't trip him up or confuse him. Faith — seeing God's world as real, and seeing this world in its true colors — accounts for everything that he did and the way he did it. For example, he had a knack for getting himself into trouble with the religious leaders! He kept saying and doing things that made them want to kill him. But he saw their hearts: he had to speak out against them, because they were "filled with dead men's bones" and leading others away from God too. To keep silent about them would have been criminal. Second, he had no doubt in the coming kingdom that would sweep away the works and kingdoms of these leaders. That's why he spoke so certainly of the coming kingdom. Through faith he saw all of this, and that's why he dealt with them as he did.

One more point about faith and Christ. Since he is the Word of God to the world, the message of salvation that we all must hear and believe, we can assume that the Old Testament saints needed him too. There aren't two ways of salvation in God's kingdom! We don't have time to get into all of that here, but we can notice that whatever good thing that God gave the Israelites was *through Christ*, who is the love of God to the people of God. He was slain from the foundation of the world, so all the mercy that God shows any of his people is because of the sacrifice of Christ. All the Old Testament saints had to wait for their reward — they didn't receive the final, spiritual end of their faith — until we came along (after the death and resurrection of Christ) and filled out the entire family of God. (Hebrews 11:39-40) So when you read about the Old Testament saints and what God wanted them to believe, keep in mind that they too had to see Jesus, in some way, in order to have true faith. They had to see the Gospel in the types and shadows and symbols in order to get true spiritual good out of them. Hebrews 11 will tell you some of those people who saw this.

Name

We already saw (in the chapter about the *Name* Key) that Jesus came specifically to reveal the name of God to men.

I have revealed your name to those whom you gave me
out of the world. I have made your name known to
them, and will continue to make you known in order that
the love you have for me may be in them and that I
myself may be in them. (John 17:6,26)

His purpose was to make the God of the Jews real to them.
They had by now gone through a long history with the Lord, and
learned many things about him.   But when Jesus came, he found a
people hardened to the person of God — they were more interested in
the Law and keeping themselves "holy" by their own definitions. God
was only a principle to them, a name they repeated in ceremony but
never called on. He was an idea to believe in, but never a person to
meet. So the Lord appeared to them in person to let them meet him
face to face:

That which was from the beginning, which we have
heard, which we have seen with our eyes, which we
have looked at and our hands have touched — this we
proclaim concerning the Word of life.   The life
appeared; we have seen it and testify to it, and we
proclaim to you the eternal life, which was with the
Father and has appeared to us. We proclaim to you what
we have seen and heard, so that you also may have
fellowship with us. And our fellowship is with the
Father and with his Son, Jesus Christ. (1 John 1:1-3)

Now they didn't have to rely on what they heard about God —
they could meet him personally and learn from him. They could take
his gifts right from his hands. They could experience first-hand his
love and care for them, as well as his anger against sinners. This is the
explanation of the name **Immanuel** — which means "God with us."

Jesus also gave them more than they expected to see. They
knew that God was love, but they had never seen love like this! The
words of Christ and his actions on behalf of undeserving sinners spoke
volumes about the love of God that the Jews needed to see and believe
in.   So they got a deeper appreciation for the **LORD** who is a
"compassionate and gracious God, slow to anger, abounding in love

and faithfulness, maintaining love to thousands, and forgiving wickedness, rebellion and sin." (Exodus 34:6-7)

He made the God of the Old Testament stories come alive — the old histories that spoke of what God did in the past for their forefathers, but what they never thought would happen to them. They saw their God come out of the pages of Scripture and touch them with the same power he used with Moses and Samson; they heard the same wisdom that taught Solomon almost a thousand years before; he performed the same miracles for them that he did for the ancient Israelites. That's why Jesus called him the **Living God** — the **God of Abraham, Isaac and Jacob** — who does the same things now that he did in the past.

Jesus not only revealed deeper meaning to the names of God from the Old Testament, he himself had many names that teach us what he is really like. For example, Philip Henry (the father of Matthew Henry, the famous Bible commentator), once preached a series of sermons on the names of Christ. Here is the list of names that he gives in that series:

> Foundation, Food, Root, Clothing, Head, Hope, Refuge, Righteousness, Light, Life, Peace, Passover, Portion, Propitiation, Freedom, Fountain, Wisdom, Way, Banner, Example, Door, Dew, Sun, Shield, Strength, Song, Horn, Honor, Sanctification, Supply, Resurrection, Redemption, Lesson, Ladder, Truth, Treasure, Temple, Ark, Altar, Our All, Husband, Father, Brother, Friend, Master, Teacher, King, Captain, Physician, Advocate, Shepherd, Elder, Inhabitant, Keeper

That's quite a list of names! Each of them describes something about who Jesus is or what he does for us. The point is that, unless we had these names of his, we wouldn't have known that he was that way — and we would have missed out on what he can do for us. But since we know what they are, we can study them and take advantage of what he is showing us. Like different dishes in a smorgasbord meal that are laid out and labeled, Christ is laid out in the Bible by name so that we can look each thing over and see what it is that we need in him.

He not only told us what his names are, he demonstrated each one of them for us so that we can see its depth and how it works. For example, he is the Bread from Heaven that the Father sends down to feed his people. The Jews didn't understand how he could be bread, and even less did they understand how in the world we are to eat him! (John 6:25-59) But we saw a few things about this already. For one thing, he is something that we get from the disciples — they take from Jesus' hands, and distribute it to the rest of us. (Matthew 15:32-38) So the Scriptures about him are something that we feed on and live on — the Bread of Life. Second, he showed us in the Last Supper that the bread in that ceremony symbolized his flesh, and the wine his blood. The Jews ate the Passover and were thus protected from the destroying angel; Christians, as they eat the body and blood of Christ in faith, are protected from the wrath of God. So our faith in his work of atonement and sacrifice for our sins is eating the spiritual bread of Christ too. You have to put all these things together to get the whole picture and something that is meaningful to your faith.

The name "Jesus" is his most important name, however. It is based on the old Hebrew name Yahweh that the Lord revealed to Moses in Exodus 34. **Jesus** is the Greek way of saying **Joshua** (you pronounce it as "Yehoshua"), which in Hebrew means "the LORD is salvation." There is the connection between *Jesus* of the New Testament and the LORD of the Old Testament — that same name reveals the same God at work. It's no wonder then that Jesus was such a perfect example of the God who is "compassionate and gracious, slow to anger, abounding in love and faithfulness!"

Remember what Peter said about the name of Christ? "Salvation is found in no one else, for there is no other name under Heaven given to men by which we must be saved." (Acts 4:12) When he said that to Jews, they should have flinched — they knew the utter holiness of The Name, and they were jealous for its glory. Here was Peter claiming the same glory for Jesus' name! He was calling up visions of the God of the Old Testament, the one to whom the Israelites called for help in their time of need. He was claiming that Jesus would save us just as the Lord did in the Old Testament, because we are dealing with the same God. The only difference now is that we can see our God, and touch him, and hear him clearly as he speaks to us. His power and ability to save his people remain the same, however.

Speaking of calling on the name of God, remember the verse that told the Israelites to do that? "And everyone who calls on the name of the LORD will be saved." (Joel 2:32) Some of the Israelites understood this and they called on him when they needed help. Most, however, turned to other gods and refused to call on him. "No one calls on your name or strives to lay hold of you." (Isaiah 64:7) Well, both of these truths are also in the New Testament. In order to find salvation from our sins, we have to call on the name of Jesus Christ. Only he can save us; only he can rescue us from sin and death. There is nobody else who can do that for us. But we *have* to call on him or he won't do it!

He told us many times the importance of coming to him:

> Come to me, all you who are weary and burdened, and I will give you rest. (Matthew 11:28)

> All that the Father gives me will come to me, and whoever comes to me I will never drive away. (John 6:37)

> If anyone is thirsty, let him come to me and drink. (John 7:37)

If we will just come to him and call him by name, he will respond immediately. The stories about the many people who came to him with their diseases are designed to show us this about him — his willingness when people will come.

But most *won't* come to him. After three years of ministry, he looked over Jerusalem and the hard-hearted Jews who refused to listen to his message of mercy:

> As he approached Jerusalem and saw the city, he wept over it and said, "If you, even you, had only known on this day what would bring you peace — but now it is hidden from your eyes. The days will come upon you when your enemies will build an embankment against you and encircle you and hem you in on every side.

They will dash you to the ground, you and the children within your walls. They will not leave one stone on another, because you did not recognize the time of God's coming to you." (John 19:41-42)

The LORD had come to them, and they still refused to call on him for help. So now they were going to experience some other realities of the names of God — the God of Justice, the LORD of Hosts, the jealous God.

Jesus' names are so important to understand and start using that he once complained that the disciples weren't taking advantage of them.

Until now you have not asked for anything in my name. Ask and you will receive, and your joy will be complete. (John 16:24)

Most twentieth century Christians think that this means attaching the phrase "In Jesus' name, Amen" at the end of their prayers. Although I wouldn't want to upset anybody's faith in the Lord who answers prayer, I might point out that none of the disciples used that phrase at the end of their prayers — not even *after* he encouraged them to use his name! You won't find that phrase anywhere in the New Testament. What you will find, however, are examples of the disciples using Jesus' name *throughout* the prayer, starting at the beginning. We saw an excellent example of how to do this in Acts 4. To them, his name wasn't a ceremonial afterthought to close things up nicely. *His name revealed something that they wanted.* They called on the Light, the Shepherd, the Lord of lords, the Resurrection, because they needed these things that were in his name. I like to think that this is what Jesus meant when he told them to use his name in prayer: pray *for what is in* his name. Then you won't be using his name to no purpose (which is forbidden in the Third Commandment), but instead for the purpose that he intended when he revealed it to us.

There is one more thing about Jesus' name that we should look at. His names reveal the truth about him — we've seen this already. That truth, however, will often surprise us; it doesn't always match our preconceived notions of who he is. When God announced the birth of

Christ through the angels, he told Mary and Joseph what to name the child:

> She will give birth to a son, and you are to give him the name **Jesus**, because he will save his people from their sins. (Matthew 1:21)

That name reveals why he came — to save us from our sins. Not our bills, or our neighbors, or our lack of free time, or whatever else may be bothering us. God looks at us and sees our sin like a glaring light in his eyes; he can't think of anything else. *We* can, though — we would rather think of anything else but our sins; but to him it is the first order of business. We have to have something done with our sin before he can do anything else for us. So when you call on the name of *Jesus*, remember what he is waiting for you to ask him.

Prophecy

Everyone knows that Jesus and prophecy go together. The Old Testament prophets made all sorts of predictions about Jesus: the circumstances of his birth and life, the kind of ministry he would have, the persecution he would go through, and so on.

For example, here are some of the Old Testament prophecies that told the Israelites what to expect when the Messiah would come:

Prophecy	Fulfillment	Prophecy	Fulfillment
Genesis 3:15	*Galatians 4:4*	Psalm 68:18	*Luke 24:50-51*
Genesis 22:18	*Ephesians 2:13*	Psalm 69:4	*John 15:23-25*
Genesis 49:10	*Luke 3:33*	Psalm 69:21	*John 19:29*
Numbers 24:17	*Luke 3:34*	Psalm 109:4	*Luke 23:34*
Deut. 18:15	*John 6:14*	Psalm 109:7-8	*Acts 1:21*
Psalm 2:6-9	*Ephesians 1:20-22*	Psalm 110:4	*Hebrews 6:20*
Psalm 2:12	*Philippians 2:10*	Psalm 132:11	*Ephesians 1:20*
Psalm 16:10	*Luke 24:6*	Isaiah 7:14	*Matthew 1:18*
Psalm 22:6-8	*Matthew 27:43*	Isaiah 9:1-2	*Matthew 4:12*
Psalm 22:16	*John 19:18*	Isaiah 9:6-7	*John 18:37*
Psalm 22:18	*Mark 15:24*	Isaiah 11:1-2	*John 1:32*
Psalm 27:12	*Matthew 26:60-61*	Isaiah 42:1	*Matthew 3:16*
Psalm 34:20	*John 19:33*	Isaiah 50:6	*Mark 14:65*
Psalm 41:9	*Mark 14:10*	Isaiah 53:3-5	*Matthew 8:16-17*

Isaiah 53:7	*Matthew 26:62-63*	Haggai 2:7	*Matthew 12:6*
Isaiah 53:9	*Matthew 27:57-60*	Zechariah 9:9	*John 12:13-14*
Isaiah 53:12	*Matthew 27:38*	Zech. 11:12-13	*Matthew 26:15;*
Isaiah 61:1	*Matthew 11:4*		*Matthew 27:6-7*
Jeremiah 23:5	*Revelation 11:15*	Zech. 12:10	*John 19:18*
Jeremiah 31:15	*Matthew 2:16*	Zechariah 13:7	*Mark 14:50*
Hosea 11:1	*Matthew 2:14*	Malachi 3:1	*John 1:29*
Micah 5:2	*Matthew 2:1*		

Though the facts about Christ are pretty clear to see when *we* read the Old Testament prophecies, they weren't always so obvious to the Israelites who first heard them! In fact, even the disciples didn't understand their meaning until the Lord explained it to them:

> They still did not understand from Scripture that Jesus had to rise from the dead. (John 20:9)

> "How foolish you are, and how slow of heart to believe all that the prophets have spoken! Did not the Christ have to suffer these things and then enter his glory?" And beginning with Moses and all the Prophets, he explained to them what was said in all the Scriptures concerning himself. (Luke 24:25-27)

Though it's good to know these prophecies, there's a reason that they are so important to the story of Christ. *They prove that we have here the Christ that God had been promising all along.* They serve to identify him; nobody else can claim to have fulfilled all these prophecies, so nobody else can claim the title of the Messiah that the prophets predicted. They were saying, in effect, "here is how you will know him when he comes — he will do this, and look like this, and say this, and so on." The Jews made a terrible mistake when they overlooked all the prophecies coming true before them in the person and work of Christ. As a matter of fact, they *were* careful to identify the true Messiah — remember that the Pharisees knew the Messianic prophecies too: "Look into it, and you will find that a prophet does not come out of Galilee." (John 7:52) If they cared to explore the matter further, however (which they didn't), they would have found out the truth of Jesus' birth and seen that it *was* a fulfillment of prophecy.

What most people often don't realize, however, is what the prophets were *really* saying about Christ. They weren't just predicting that he would come; if that was all that they were doing, they could have predicted the coming of Caesar and created as much excitement. Jesus is the King of kings, however — they prophesied the coming of the King from Heaven who would lay waste the kingdoms of this world and set up his own in their place.

> I have installed my King on Zion, my holy hill. I will proclaim the decree of the LORD: He said to me, "You are my Son; today I have become your Father. Ask of me, and I will make the nations your inheritance, the ends of the earth your possession. You will rule them with an iron scepter; you will dash them to pieces like pottery." Therefore, you kings, be wise; be warned, you rulers of the earth. Serve the LORD with fear and rejoice with trembling. Kiss the Son, lest he be angry and you be destroyed in your way, for his wrath can flare up in a moment. Blessed are all who take refuge in him. (Psalm 2:6-12)

> For to us a child is born, to us a son is given, and the government will be on his shoulders. And he will be called Wonderful Counselor, Mighty God, Everlasting Father, Prince of Peace. Of the increase of his government and peace there will be no end. He will reign on David's throne and over his kingdom, establishing and upholding it with justice and righteousness from that time on and forever. The zeal of the LORD Almighty will accomplish this. (Isaiah 9:6-7)

When the prophets brought their message of doom to the wicked kings and people of Israel, they threatened extinction to all the rebels. They told the people that the Lord was coming, and he would destroy the works of the wicked. They were warned. Now the King *has* come — Jesus stepped out on the battlefield ready to wage war against all those who would not repent of their sins and bend their knee to the Lord Almighty, just as the prophets had warned.

Do not suppose that I have come to bring peace to the earth. I did not come to bring peace, but a sword. (Matthew 10:34)

His first visit to earth wouldn't be his last; he will save the final judgment for the second visit. Now, however, was the time for laying the groundwork for a new kingdom, the kingdom that would finally grow until it would overwhelm the enemy's work and destroy all those things that are not of God. He worked carefully, methodically, skillfully; he selected the right people for each job; he avoided conflict for now. The foundation he laid was a spiritual one, of course, because the kingdoms of this world depend on physical wealth, power and weapons whereas the Kingdom of God depends on the power and wealth of the Spirit of God. When he was done laying the foundation, he said "It is finished" and left this world for the time being.

What is he doing right now? "A man of noble birth went to a distant country to have himself appointed king and then to return." (Luke 19:12) If you read farther in this story, you will see what he intends to do on the second visit: it is then that he will destroy this world, judge the wicked and throw them into Hell with the devil, and reward the righteous with eternal life. Then there will be a kingdom of peace, where there will be no more sin or rebellion or misery or death.

I saw the Holy City, the new Jerusalem, coming down out of Heaven from God, prepared as a bride beautifully dressed for her husband. And I heard a loud voice from the throne saying, "Now the dwelling of God is with men, and he will live with them. They will be his people, and God himself will be with them and be their God. He will wipe every tear from their eyes. There will be no more death or mourning or crying or pain, for the old order of things has passed away." (Revelation 21:2-4)

It's typical of the way that Jesus does things that he worked quietly, not lashing out now with Phase Two but only warning the people of what was to come in the future. They of course, not having faith to see the reality of what he was talking about, ignored him. They still do — Peter describes many people today like this:

They will say, "Where is this 'coming' he promised? Ever since our fathers died, everything goes on as it has since the beginning of creation." (2 Peter 3:4)

They are foolish to think this. His first time on earth was to get ready for the war to come; his second visit will be sudden and decisive:

But the day of the Lord will come like a thief. The heavens will disappear with a roar; the elements will be destroyed by fire, and the earth and everything in it will be laid bare. (2 Peter 3:10)

If you want to see the war that Jesus will wage against his enemies, read the book of Revelation. John, the last prophet of the Bible, shows us a vision of the King of kings coming to earth to destroy the wicked and all their kingdoms. He shows us how he will do it too — which may not be what you would have expected. For instance, his most powerful weapon against the enemy isn't bombs or money or politics or education (as we usually rely on when we try to fight the forces of evil) but the sword of the Spirit:

And out of his mouth came a sharp double-edged sword. (Revelation 1:16)

These are the words of him who has the sharp, double-edged sword. (Revelation 2:12)

Out of his mouth comes a sharp sword with which to strike down the nations. (Revelation 19:15)

The rest of them were killed with the sword that came out of the mouth of the rider on the horse. (Revelation 19:21)

You ought to know what that sword is — it is the Word of God.

For the word of God is living and active. Sharper than any double-edged sword, it penetrates even to dividing soul and spirit, joints and marrow; it judges the thoughts and attitudes of the heart. Nothing in all creation is hidden from God's sight. Everything is uncovered and laid bare before the eyes of him to whom we must give account. (Hebrews 4:12-13)

We also mustn't miss what Jesus did while he was here: he began building the Kingdom of God that would eventually replace the kingdoms of this world. His first recorded sermon was about the coming of this kingdom:

"The time has come," he said. "The kingdom of God is near. Repent and believe the good news!" (Mark 1:15)

This is exactly what the prophets had talked about. Jesus immediately made known the way his kingdom would operate: the wicked would not be allowed to live in it; the righteous must live in it by faith; it would be based on miracles; the works of the Lord would be its foundation. He set up the laws that he would use to govern the kingdom (see the Sermon on the Mount, Matthew 5-7). They weren't the Old Testament Law as the Jews liked to interpret it, because they thought that the superficial meanings of the Law were the point. No, the laws of this spiritual kingdom were to be spiritual and therefore of infinite depth — nobody but Jesus himself could hope to keep these laws! This means, of course, that he was also laying down the basis of how someone would be counted righteous in his kingdom — not by keeping the Law (only he could do that) but by believing on Jesus to save him from sin and the condemnation of the Law. So through faith in Christ, "the righteous requirements of the law might be fully met in us, who do not live according to the sinful nature but according to the Spirit." (Romans 8:4)

Remember the work of Moses, as the Lord worked through him to set up the new nation of Israel? They had just come out of Egypt and were an unruly, directionless mob. But at Mt. Sinai the Lord formed them into a nation, a kingdom, and pronounced himself as their God. He gave them the rules to live by (the Law) and told them what he expected of them and what he would do for them as their King. Jesus, if you can see it through faith, did that same thing in *his* ministry. The disciples had a feeling that he was doing this, but they misunderstood the prophecies and expected him to set up a physical kingdom. But he was nevertheless creating a people, a nation, and proclaiming himself as their King. This is why the writer of Hebrews teaches us that the work of Moses and Jesus are so similar — they both worked at setting up a new kingdom. The difference is that Moses was working for someone else; Jesus, himself the King, worked to build his own kingdom. Everything he said and did pointed to that end.

Deliverance

Every Christian knows that *Jesus saves*. The good news of the Gospel is that Jesus will save anybody who comes to him and repents of their sin. Experiencing this is called "being saved" — and that makes someone different from others who aren't saved. The Church is the group of people who have been saved by Jesus. Whether others like that or not (they accuse us of arrogance when we talk like this) we hold our salvation in Jesus to be a precious thing, something that we would never trade for the old life.

But it's strange how people stop at the gate, so to speak. We use Jesus for the sole purpose of getting us into the Church — then we forget about him. We go on in Christian life without giving him much more thought. We become more "mature", our interests widen out, we get busy with all sorts of "important" matters — yet what Christ said about the Ephesian church becomes true of too many of us: "You have forsaken your first love." (Revelation 2:4) Before long, life gets so complicated, relationships become strained, prayer is a chore, and there are more problems than answers. The old feeling that we had when we first met Christ is long gone, though not forgotten. It seems that we can't do anything to bring back that simple zeal and excitement that we had at first when we stepped from darkness into light.

The reason that people fizzle out over time is this: they don't understand the depth of the salvation that Jesus has for his people. They misunderstand him completely when they think he was just good for getting them into Christianity. He calls us to a *continual* salvation, not just an initial experience. He calls us to follow him daily, not just step through the gate he opened at the beginning and then wander around on our own. He leads the way in life; he didn't send us off with a blessing and a hope that we will make it okay without him.

Salvation isn't a superficial "it happened one night at a revival meeting" kind of thing; it is deep, powerful, life-changing, drastic, and completely effective. It may have started at the revival, but unless it continues and gets deeper and wider like a river, there is good reason to doubt that you found the Savior in the first place. There is nothing superficial about the Savior, or the work he wants to do to you.

The whole problem can be avoided by taking careful note of the name that the Father gave him at his birth:

> You are to give him the name Jesus, because he will
> *save* his people from their sins. (Matthew 1:21)

Remember what we learned about deliverance? God saves us from what he thinks is danger, not what we think is danger. We want God to save us from economic disaster, sickness and death, ruined reputations, too much work, and many other things that even pagans are interested in. He isn't as interested in saving us from these things as we are, however, because they don't put our souls in danger nor do they jeopardize the glory of God or the welfare of the Church.

What is killing us, however, is our sin. Typically, we don't see any danger in that. We go from day to day hardly giving our sins a thought; we consider ourselves to be pretty good people on the whole. You can tell what someone thinks about this when you listen to a person praying — or analyze your own prayers, for that matter. Where is the subject of your sin on the agenda of your prayers? Far from being a morbid topic and just "navel gazing", sin is a spiritual cancer that is eating your soul and life away and hurting other people too. When you come before the throne of God, it doesn't matter that you have already been "saved" — that helps, because you supposedly have discovered the way to salvation, which is by faith in Christ. Nevertheless, the Lord wants to discuss this matter of your sin with you, before you talk about anything else. Being saved doesn't mean that you're perfect now; it means that now you are going to work on what is hurting you and overcome it through Christ.

The reason that Jesus got the name he did is because sin is the thing he wants to deliver us from. It is a huge problem, much bigger than you can imagine, and he spent thousands of years developing effective answers to the problem. He is eager to get started. The solution will take the rest of your life, and he will use many ways of delivering you from sin in all kinds of circumstances. If you thought that "getting saved" was a one-time affair, you seriously underestimate what the Lord wants to do with you!

What will happen if you aren't delivered from your sin? Certain death:

> I told you that you would die in your sins; if you do not believe that I am the one I claim to be, you will indeed die in your sins. (John 8:24)

But if you go to Jesus to save you, this is what will happen:

> I am the resurrection and the life. He who believes in me will live, even though he dies; and whoever lives and believes in me will never die. (John 11:25-26)

Jesus intends to save his people from these kinds of things:

• **<u>Sin</u>** — As we saw, our most important problem is our sin. What exactly is sin? "Everyone who sins breaks the law; in fact, sin is lawlessness." (1 John 3:4) Sin is our rebellious attitude against everything that God says to us. We don't want to know his truth, we don't want to follow his commands, we don't want to do things his way, we don't value what he values, we love what he hates — everything that God stands for, we are contrary to. To see the extent of our sins, all we have to do is read in his Word and we will soon start running into all sorts of things that we don't like.

Jesus is going to change all that. First he tells us what sin is — because unless we get that straight we will never know why God is so displeased with us. He spent a lot of time in the Gospels telling us what sin is; for example, read the Sermon on the Mount. Second, he tells us what we must do to be saved — and it's not what we would have expected! Since salvation depends on what he does, not on what we do, he counsels us to come to him for salvation. He promised us that he will eagerly give it to us when we ask.

Then he took care of the Law's argument against us by dying on the cross in our place, so that we might be free from the condemnation of the Law. Next he ascended to Heaven to take his place as the first-born among many brethren in God's family — and therefore heir to the salvation that God had always had in mind for his children. Then he sent the Holy Spirit to indwell us, cleanse us, and guide us into righteousness. Finally he will call us Heavenward when the times shall end and we will be fully saved, not only from the power of sin but from its presence as well.

There is much more to the process of salvation than you may have thought! He did these things and many more so that we might eventually be fully saved; we can't make the mistake of believing that the first time we met him is the *only* time we will meet with him over this issue.

• **Death** — When Adam and Eve first sinned in the Garden of Eden, God pronounced a sentence of death upon them, and upon all their children. "Therefore, just as sin entered the world through one man, and death through sin, and in this way death came to all men, because all sinned ... " (Romans 5:12) It's inescapable, and it's not just a normal process of life. It's a terrible punishment for the way we have acted toward God.

Physical death, however, isn't the only thing waiting for us. There is a second death, far worse than the body dying, that we are headed for. "The lake of fire is the second death." (Revelation 20:14) It's that everlasting destruction that God has planned for all the wicked who wouldn't submit to his will, or plead for his mercy. And it's not just a momentary annihilation, that many people nowadays believe; *they hope* that it's momentary! But Jesus solemnly declared that —

> It is better for you to enter the kingdom of God with one eye than to have two eyes and be thrown into hell, where "their worm does not die, and the fire is not quenched." (Mark 9:47-48)

He ought to know; he came from Heaven where he had a good view of the end of the wicked. This is counsel from him so that we might do all that we can possibly do to avoid the second death.

There is only safety in him, however. Whoever throws their soul upon Jesus the Savior will find him a safe place when the Day of Judgment dawns. Millions outside of Christ will be thrown into Hell, because to God they are worse than useless to him — they are twisted and perverted in sin and they refuse to have anything to do with God. But just as David found, those in Christ will be safe while this terrible scene unfolds before them:

> A thousand may fall at your side, ten thousand at your right hand, but it will not come near you. You will only observe with your eyes and see the punishment of the wicked. If you make the Most High your dwelling — even the LORD, who is my refuge — then no harm will befall you, no disaster will come near your tent. (Psalm 91:7-10)

Jesus promised that on the Last Day, those who have their names in the Book of Life will escape the second death: "He who overcomes will not be hurt at all by the second death." (Revelation 2:11)

• **The wrath of God** — We often mistake the love of God as if he were only love, as if he would never punish or get angry with someone no matter how badly they have sinned. This is a fatal error that too many people make, and they are going to regret it if they don't get their information about the Lord straightened out before Judgment Day. God is holy before he is anything else; "Holy, holy, holy is the LORD Almighty." (Isaiah 6:3) He hates sin; his love shows itself by *saving* us from our sin, not tolerating us while we wallow in it unrepentant.

Jesus' entire ministry reflected this attitude — he worked diligently and skillfully to lay the groundwork of our salvation. He knows what is out there at the end of time! He knows what God thinks of sin, because he is the Son of God and he has the same feelings toward it. Jesus knew, because he came from Heaven at God's right hand, what God thinks of sinners:

> But I will show you whom you should fear: Fear him who, after the killing of the body, has power to throw you into hell. Yes, I tell you, fear him. (Luke 12:5)

Doesn't this make you think a minute about your personal safety? Jesus is in earnest: he knows the wrath of God against sinners; it is no laughing matter, nor should we discount it as an Old Testament myth that we moderns don't have to take seriously. Yes, we saw an angry God punish the wicked like Sodom and Gomorrah, and Korah, and the Philistines. And yes, we see almost none of that kind of thing in the New Testament. But Jesus assured us, many times, that this side of God hasn't gone away. He spoke of Hell — the wrath of God against sinners — more times than he spoke of any other single subject!

It's a fact that someday we will stand before God and give an account of ourselves. "Man is destined to die once, and after that to face judgment." (Hebrews 9:27) It's also a fact that we have to pass a stringent test, and it won't be what many people think it is. Most people will hear things like this:

> I never knew you. Away from me, you evildoers!
> (Matthew 7:23)

> And throw that worthless servant outside,
> into the darkness, where there will be weeping
> and gnashing of teeth. (Matthew 25:30)

> Depart from me, you who are cursed, into the
> eternal fire prepared for the devil and his angels.
> (Matthew 25:41)

But who will hear the good news, who will be welcomed into eternal dwellings? Those for whom Christ died, those who will escape the wrath of God because of what Jesus did for them. "For God did not appoint us to suffer wrath but to receive salvation through our Lord Jesus Christ." (1 Thessalonians 5:9)

There are several more points that we want to consider when studying the deliverance we have in Christ; they will remind us of the basic elements of deliverance that we have already seen.

• **The love of God**. There is no other story in the Bible that shows us so clearly how much God loves his people. What Jesus did is beyond the comprehension of man: why would he set aside his glory as the Son of God, take on the form of man, humble himself under the Law and sinners and suffering, die on the cross (the author of Life!), and do all this for guilty sinners who didn't deserve a bit of it? There's just no answer that a human being can understand. This is the love of God shining brightly and purely, in a way that we have never seen before. Jesus did all this for us so that we might be saved from sin and death and the wrath of God. How can we behold such a love and despise the salvation that he came to give us? "How shall we escape if we ignore such a great salvation?" (Hebrews 2:3) "This is how we know what love is: Jesus Christ laid down his life for us." (1 John 3:16)

- **The only Savior**. Only Jesus is the savior of men. There have been many "saviors" who promised us all sorts of things that we want, but none of them have really helped us with what we *need*. It doesn't help to win millions of dollars if our souls are lost. "What good is it for a man to gain the whole world, and yet lose or forfeit his very self?" (Luke 9:25) But Jesus can save from sin; he knows what it has done to us, he knows how to get us free from it, he knows what to ask from God to overcome our sin. He has the power to destroy sin's hold over us. "Salvation is found in no one else, for there is no other name under Heaven given to men by which we must be saved." (Acts 4:12) This isn't a boast, nor an arrogant attempt to elevate one's own religion over others, but a simple statement of fact. He *is* the only one who can save you.

- **Saved to be free**. Remember that deliverance doesn't mean anything if we end up back in trouble again. Jesus isn't such a careless or heartless (or powerless, as some make him out to be!) Savior that he will let us slide back into sin and death. Once he has us in his grasp, we are safe.

> I give them eternal life, and they shall never perish; no one can snatch them out of my hand. My Father, who has given them to me, is greater than all; no one can snatch them out of my Father's hand. (John 10:28-29)

What he saves us into is eternal life, where there will be no more sin or death. It will be pure joy, pure love, pure light — we will live directly from the hand of God himself, we will no longer need created things to live. There are many promises in the New Testament for what Jesus has in mind for his children; you can read some of them in the last chapter of Revelation, for example.

• **How and when**. You can learn a lot about how and when Jesus saves his people by reading the examples in the Gospels. Typically, he doesn't do it the same way every time, nor does he always do it just when we cry out to him the first time. For instance, the Canaanite woman had to prove her faith before he healed her daughter. The woman caught in adultery wasn't saved until she got in danger of her life; then Jesus commanded her to "go and sin no more" (a command, by the way, that had power in it — the Word of God creates willingness where there wasn't any before). Jesus counseled us to keep praying, even when God doesn't immediately answer, just as the woman who banged on the judge's door all night until he finally got out of bed and gave her what she wanted.

There is so much about deliverance and Jesus that we can't possibly go over even the basics here. I hope that you pursue the subject further on your own. Keep in mind what we saw in the Key about deliverance while you study the ministry of Christ, and you will discover more than you thought there was to know about this supposedly familiar subject.

Covenant

You can be sure that Jesus and the Father work together very closely on everything they do. What the Father wills, Jesus also wills. And they aren't careless or haphazard about what they do; they are the ultimate project planners. They worked on this thing about salvation from the beginning, mapped it all out ahead of time, planned every detail, laid the foundation for it all to make sure it would work, and followed the steps of the project as planned. They know that it will succeed in the end, and things will be right where they want them to be when time is no more and all come to the Judgment Seat of Christ for the final sentence.

When God first made the covenant with Abraham, therefore, you can be sure that Jesus was there too as part of the Godhead, making that covenant with the Father. We don't see the two of them separately at that point; but from some clues that we find in the New Testament

(which we will look at in a minute) we know that the covenant with
Abraham and his descendants was as much Jesus' business as it was the
Father's.

If this is true, it throws a whole new light on the ministry of
Christ recorded in the Gospels. We tend to view what he did as an
aberration of history, just something that he decided to do once. As if
he just showed up, taught and did miracles, and then left — with no
rhyme or reason for why he came! But if we look at his ministry as the
fulfillment of the covenant to Abraham then tremendous spiritual truths
open up before us. It gives meaning to the things he said and did, and
brings the story of the covenant to a finished polish.

Remember that in the covenant with Abraham, the Lord
promised that he would do four things for him and his descendants. He
sealed that promise with blood: if he would fail to do these things that
he promised, Abraham (or his descendants) would have the right to
split him in two just as the animals were. Ever since then we have been
anxiously waiting to see if God really would keep his promises.

Now in the person of Christ we see that God has come back to
keep his Word. He isn't going to break his promise to Abraham! Jesus
came to fulfill those four things that the children of Abraham were
heirs to. We have already seen much of how Jesus fits into the
covenant with Abraham, because we just can't talk of one without the
other. But we need to focus on Christ in particular so that we don't
miss the point.

- **The promised Seed:** In Galatians, Paul refers to the
covenant made with Abraham. The problem that the
Galatians were grappling with was that they thought the
Law was all-important; they thought they had to obey
the Law if they wanted to please God. But Paul took
them back to the covenant and showed them the thing
that God was really interested in:

    The promises were spoken to Abraham and to
    his seed. The Scripture does not say 'and to
    seeds,' meaning many people, but 'and to your
    seed,' meaning one person, who is Christ. What

I mean is this: The law, introduced 430 years later, does not set aside the covenant previously established by God and thus do away with the promise. (Galatians 3:16-17)

The *only* thing that we can do that will please God is believe *what* he has given us (the spiritual object of the covenant, in other words) — and *where* we must look for those promises. In the Israelites' day, the spiritual dimension of the covenant was not so clear to see (though Abraham saw it – with *faith* — "Your father Abraham rejoiced at the thought of seeing my day; he saw it and was glad." John 8:56). Now, however, we have heard the plain Gospel which says — *look to Jesus and you will be saved.* "For no matter how many promises God has made, they are 'Yes' in Christ." (2 Corinthians 1:20) He is the promised Child, the one through whom we will get our inheritance.

Paul refers to the way that Isaac was born — by miracle — as opposed to the natural means of Ishmael's birth. This has two fulfillments in Christ: first, his own birth was a miracle and therefore the work of God. Second, those who believe in him are also miracle babies:

> I tell you the truth, no one can see the kingdom of God unless he is born again . . . I tell you the truth, no one can enter the kingdom of God unless he is born of water and the Spirit. Flesh gives birth to flesh, but the Spirit gives birth to spirit. You should not be surprised at my saying, 'You must be born again.' (John 3:3-7)

We are born into Christ, into life, by the Spirit of God — a completely unaccountable thing, but real nevertheless. Once we were dead to God, now we are alive to him and fully aware of him. Once we were rebels with hearts of stone; now we have hearts of flesh and love to serve him.

Anybody who has been born again, who is one with Christ, is now heir of the covenant with Abraham. "If you belong to Christ, then you are Abraham's seed, and heirs according to the promise." (Galatians 3:29) You can see from this how crucial Jesus is to the fulfillment of that covenant. You can also see, hopefully, how important it is to be one with Christ. Outside of him there is no blessing, no inheritance, no life — only death with others who aren't of the Seed of Abraham.

• **The Land:** Again in Christ we have the answer to the perplexing question of what the people of God will inherit. The Jews looked forward to ruling themselves, living in Palestine without any outside interference — especially from the Romans. But Jesus never promised that to them; in fact, when prompted even by his own disciples to restore the land to the Jews, he changed the subject and spoke of more important things. (Acts 1:6-8)

What does God have in mind, then? Jesus told us what he was going to do when his work on earth was done: not to set up a throne and claim Palestine back from the enemy, but go *somewhere else* to prepare the Land that God had promised his people:

> In my Father's house are many rooms; if it were not so, I would have told you. I am going there to prepare a place for you. And if I go and prepare a place for you, I will come back and take you to be with me that you also may be where I am. You know the way to the place where I am going. (John 14:2-4)

Jesus said once that "my kingdom is not of this world. If it were, my servants would fight to prevent my arrest by the Jews. But now my kingdom is from another place." (John 18:36) He was interested in a new kingdom, a land where there would be no more sin or death. This world that we live in now will never qualify; it has been ruined by man and must be remade. Besides, the things that Jesus has in mind for his new world must last forever, without giving way to time or strain — and there isn't anything in this world that can build a kingdom like that.

Jesus has in mind to give his people a place where they won't need created things to survive, but they will live directly from the hand of God himself. Instead of treasures that rot or rust or can be stolen, he counseled his followers to look forward to treasures that last forever. (Matthew 6:19-21) We don't understand much of what Heaven is like, but we can know that the Lord made it in such a way as to satisfy our souls — truly "a land flowing with milk and honey", if it is anything like the Lord Jesus.

• **The Nation:** In Jesus there is a new nation, a new people of God. This is the mysticism of the Church. We can't understand how a collection of individuals, scattered all over the world and across thousands of years, can be one unified body of people. And we certainly can't understand how people can be one when they argue over every single thing in the Bible! It seems to the observer that this is a bunch of lonely individuals instead of one group.

But in Christ all believers are brought together to share one life. Just as Israel was one nation over against the rest of the nations of the world, Christians are one nation too — "There is *one body* and one Spirit — just as you were called to one hope when you were called." (Ephesians 4:3) And the Lord didn't just ditch the old system and do a new thing with the Gentiles. He *fulfilled* the old system by updating it, lifting it up to the level he intended for it. Then he brought the spiritual remnant of the Israelites together with the Gentiles (who had no rights to the original covenant, physically) and made them one people, calling the whole thing *Israel*.

For he himself is our peace, who has made the two one and has destroyed the barrier, the dividing wall of hostility, by abolishing in his flesh the law with its commandments and regulations. His purpose was to create in himself one new man out of the two, thus making peace, and in this one body to reconcile both of them to God through the cross, by which he put to death their hostility. He came and preached peace to you who were far away and peace to those who were near. For through him we both have access to the Father by one Spirit. Consequently, you are no longer foreigners and aliens, but fellow citizens with God's people and members of God's household. (Galatians 2:14-19)

Now he is the Head of the new body: he leads, he counsels, he decides, he directs, he feeds and cares for, he gets all the glory from, and he expects the services of the rest of the body. "And he is the head of the body, the church; he is the beginning and the firstborn from among the dead, so that in everything he might have the supremacy." (Colossians 1:18) "Now you are the body of Christ, and each one of you is a part of it." (1 Corinthians 12:27)

• **The Blessing:** We saw that, through the covenant, the Lord intended to overturn the effect of sin — which is death. After all, sin is what got us into the mess we are in, and unless God reverses the effects of death, we can't say that we have much going for us — even if we do call ourselves Christians! "If only for this life we have hope in Christ, we are to be pitied more than all men." (1 Corinthians 15:19)

The resurrection of Christ from the dead was the staggering news that the apostles had for the world. They could talk about "God with us", the teachings of the Messiah, the miracles, and the crucifixion — but the listening world would be no more impressed with that than with other wonders that have happened in history. But when Jesus rose from the dead, that gets the attention of everyone. When Paul preached to Festus about the Gospel, the Roman was interested but unimpressed; when he got to the point of the resurrection, however, he got an immediate reaction:

> "But I have had God's help to this very day, and so I stand here and testify to small and great alike. I am saying nothing beyond what the prophets and Moses said would happen — that the Christ would suffer and, as *the first to rise from the dead*, would proclaim light to his own people and to the Gentiles." At this point Festus interrupted Paul's defense. "You are out of your mind, Paul!" he shouted. "Your great learning is driving you insane." (Acts 26:22-24)

You see, if the resurrection is true, then that means that eternal life is true. It means that there is a judgment, there is righteousness, there is holiness, there is another world than this one — and there is a God who justifies sinners.

Jesus rose from the dead a *new man* — not physical, but spiritual. You can study the exact nature of the resurrection body in 1 Corinthians 15, the great chapter on the subject of the resurrection. What he rose *to* is eternal life at the right hand of God, "far above all rule and authority, power and dominion, and every title that can be given, not only in the present age but also in the one to come." (Ephesians 1:21) The resurrection of Christ opens up all kinds of new realities that are not in this world — they are the new kingdom, the new life and world that God has planned for his people.

Whoever is one with Christ is also one with his resurrection, and *there* is the fulfillment of the covenant for Abraham's descendants. "If we have been united with him like this in his death, we will certainly also be united with him in his resurrection . . . Now if we died with Christ, we believe that we will also live with him." (Romans 6:5,8) Whoever is one with him has no fear of death: "Blessed and holy are those who have part in the first resurrection. The second death has no power over them." (Revelation 20:6)

This aspect of our salvation was barely hinted at in the Old Testament, and it's an astonishing revelation of what God has in store for his people. It certainly makes sense for us to see if we are in Christ if we want to be justified and live forever.

There is an important "therefore" to all this. If Jesus is the fulfillment of the covenant with Abraham, if God put what he promised in Jesus and called us to come to Christ to get what we need — then *there is no other place that you can find blessings from God.* You can't expect God to save you or even do you *any* spiritual good unless you become one with Christ. You won't get what God promised Abraham by being children of believers, you won't get it just because you are a Jew, you won't get it by leading a good life, you won't get it by being religious or being baptized. The only way you can lay claim to the treasures of Heaven is if you have become united to Christ, through faith.

For you did not receive a spirit that makes you a slave again to fear, but *you received the Spirit of sonship.* And by him we cry, "Abba, Father." The Spirit himself testifies with our spirit that we are God's children. Now if we are children, *then we are heirs* — heirs of God and co-heirs with Christ, if indeed we share in his sufferings in order that we may also share in his glory. (Romans 8:15-17)

Anyone who is in Christ is heir to the covenant; anybody who isn't in Christ is outside the covenant. And you can be sure that, since the Lord made an oath in that covenant, he *will* stick to the terms of the covenant. We won't be able to talk him out of it.

The reason that the covenant is a Key to the Bible is this: it explains why we get *anything* from God. The Lord made the covenant at the very beginning of the Bible, and it directed all his actions toward the covenant people in the rest of the Old Testament. It finds its fullest and final expression in Christ — he came to seal the covenant and give it its true spiritual meaning. The Lord blesses the Church because of the covenant, and anyone who is in Christ is an heir to the covenant. At the Last Day, the heirs will assume their rightful places at the right hand of God and enjoy the promises of God forever, and those who refused to believe in the Lord Jesus will find themselves thrown out of the kingdom and denied the blessings of the covenant. The entire story of the Bible is really the unfolding of the story of the covenant to Abraham, and in Jesus we see what God intended to give his children all along.

These are the Keys as they relate to Jesus Christ. As you can see, they aren't accidental incidents in his life and ministry; they are the very purpose and work he came to do. Take the Keys out of Christ, and you don't have anything meaningful to believe in anymore. I'm afraid that too many people today, including church members, have only a superficial understanding of who Jesus really is. This has two results, of course: *first*, they can't mean much when they say that "they believe in Jesus." One can't make up what to believe in Jesus, nor can one be satisfied with believing a few superficial facts about Jesus' life. That isn't enough knowledge of Christ to save us. *Second*, they can't have much of an understanding of the rest of the Bible, especially the Old Testament, since the same themes in Christ's ministry can be found in the entire Bible. If you don't see it in Jesus, you probably missed it in the Old Testament too.

But once you learn what the Keys are, and can see them powerfully working in the New Testament stories and doctrine of Christ, you can say that you are finally getting the idea of the Bible and what God wants men to know about him.

Discussion Questions For The Master Key

Following are some questions about Jesus Christ that the material in the Master Key will perhaps help you answer:

- **Does Jesus rule now? Over what?**

- **What does Jesus do in the Church?**

- **Was Jesus in the Old Testament — when and where?**

- **How does Jesus relate to history?**

- **How much of our help does Jesus need?**

- **What part will Jesus have in the last days?**

- **Do we pray to Jesus or not? Why?**

- **Must every sermon be about Jesus? Why or why not?**

- **How do Jesus and the Spirit relate to each other?**

- **Is Jesus different in any way from the Father? If so, how?**

- **When Jesus and a sinner meet, who does what in the process of salvation?**

- **What will Jesus do after Judgment Day is all over?**

- **What will be our relationship to Jesus in eternity?**

Conclusion

Summary of Keys

Conclusion

Hopefully this study on the Keys has gotten you started in a fruitful study in the Bible. We didn't get into every issue and topic that the Bible discusses, because there are many other books that deal with those issues in ways that surpass what we can do here. What we have done, hopefully, is seen the important things that God wants *every* believer to know from his Word. Other issues are interesting and helpful, but these truths that the Keys deal with are our *salvation.* This is what we must learn and trust in if we hope to please God.

And the Keys hang together; they depend on each other, they help explain each other, and they are intertwined all through Scripture. It's encouraging to know that you are on the right track, that you are understanding the Word of God, when the pieces of his Revelation start falling into place and the whole thing starts making sense. At first you won't experience this much as you begin to study the Bible seriously; but if you make the Keys your primary focus, both they and the rest of the Bible will eventually get clearer to you and, therefore, become more precious and necessary for your life of faith in God.

You will notice from the discussion questions that there is much more to study in these areas. They were deliberately chosen in such a way as to get you thinking and studying on your own. The chapters themselves don't give you the answers (I wonder myself if there *are* answers to some of them!), though they do lay the foundation (which you should have picked up!) to help you at least grapple with the questions in a Scriptural way. Many of the questions are popular ones in current Christian discussion; hopefully, the Key will give you a new approach to the question so that you can find better answers.

When I was studying this material for myself, I suddenly discovered a passage in Psalms that caught my eye. Here it is:

Give thanks to the LORD, call on *his name*; make known among the nations *what he has done.* Sing to him, sing praise to him; tell of all his *wonderful acts. Glory* in his *holy name*; let the hearts of those who seek the LORD rejoice. Look to the LORD and *his strength*; seek his face always. Remember the *wonders he has done*, his *miracles*, and the *judgments he pronounced*, O *descendants of Abraham* his servant, O sons of Jacob, his chosen ones. He is the LORD our God; his *judgments* are in all the earth. He remembers his *covenant* forever, the word he commanded, for a thousand generations, *the covenant he made with Abraham*, the oath he swore to Isaac. He confirmed it to Jacob as a decree, to Israel as an *everlasting covenant*: "To you I will give the land of Canaan as the portion you will inherit." (Psalm 105: 1-11)

It struck me that this passage is telling us what are the *important* things to know about God. Too often we get caught up in what our society tells us is important, or what current issues are, or what misguided church members and leaders tell us we ought to know. This passage says that we need to know his *names*, his *miracles*, his *works*, his *covenant* with his people, his *judgments* (as King), his *Word* (revelation) — in other words, the very Keys that we have been studying! God wants us to dwell on these issues, to meditate on this knowledge that he thinks is profitable for us. Other things are interesting, some other things are a waste of our time — but *this* is our salvation and our spiritual well-being in God's kingdom. I believe that it's time we sit at God's feet and learn from him for a change.

Summary of Keys

What are the Keys?

- The Keys are principles that unlock the meaning of the Bible.
- Learn the Keys well, if you want to be able to use them successfully.
- Every passage in the Bible has one or more of these keys.

Revelation

- A revelation is the uncovering of what was hidden.
- The purpose of the Bible is to reveal God.
- Look for something about God in every passage that you study.

Miracle

- A miracle is something that God does for us directly, apart from natural means.
- Nobody else can do them, but we desperately need them.
- The Kingdom of God is founded on and built up by miracles.

Ways

- The Lord has certain ways of doing things.
- Our ways don't work, and his ways always work.
- We have to learn his ways and work with him, not against him.

Works

- There are certain things that only God can do.
- We need to know his works so that we can tell them apart from man's works.
- We need to go to God and ask him for his special works.

Glory

- Glory means who gets the credit.
- Though he deserves glory, he gets almost no glory for what he does.
- God wants glory so that people will hear about him and come for help.

Faith

- Faith is living in the light of God's spiritual world.
- The more we are convinced of the realities of God's world, the less we will be bothered by problems and temptations of this world.
- To please God, we must have the same kind of faith that Abraham had.

Name

- God's names tell us who he is and what he does.
- Ask him for what you want by calling on one of his particular names.
- God's special name — Yahweh — is the foundation of the Church's life.

Prophecy

- Prophecy is the announcement of the coming of the Kingdom of God.
- God will destroy the kingdoms of this world and set up his in their place.
- The Spirit of God told the prophets what to say, which means that their message is accurate and for the entire Church.

Deliverance

- Deliverance is getting someone out of what God considers to be danger.
- The Lord delivers us because of his glory: ask for it with that in mind.

- He delivers us in his own ways, and when certain conditions are met.

Covenant

- The Lord gives blessings to his people because of his covenant with Abraham.
- Abraham inherited both the physical and spiritual levels of the covenant.
- Abraham's heirs are those who have his faith and his circumcision.

The Master Key

- The best example of each of the Keys is Jesus himself.
- The Keys help us better understand Jesus and his work.
- The Keys show us the connection between Jesus and the rest of the Bible more clearly.